#

Story and Art by
Rumiko Takahashi

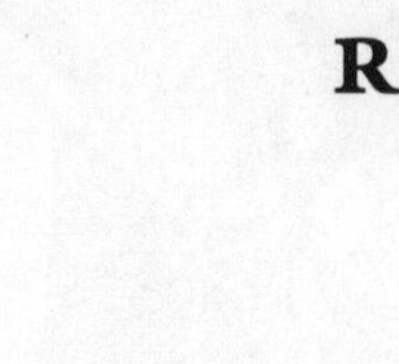

Characters

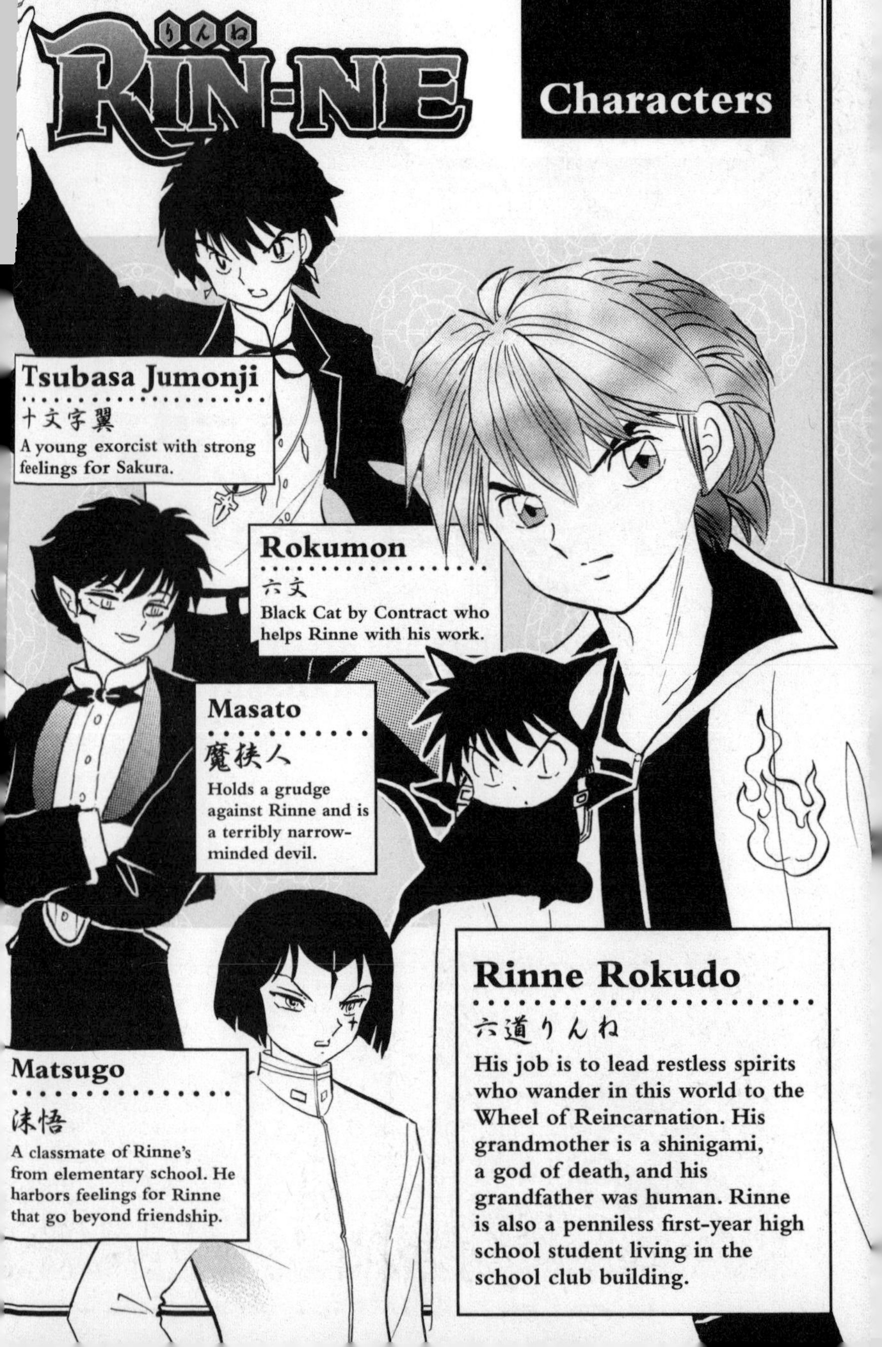

Rinne Rokudo

六道りんね

His job is to lead restless spirits who wander in this world to the Wheel of Reincarnation. His grandmother is a shinigami, a god of death, and his grandfather was human. Rinne is also a penniless first-year high school student living in the school club building.

Tsubasa Jumonji

十文字翼

A young exorcist with strong feelings for Sakura.

Rokumon

六文

Black Cat by Contract who helps Rinne with his work.

Masato

魔狭人

Holds a grudge against Rinne and is a terribly narrow-minded devil.

Matsugo

沫悟

A classmate of Rinne's from elementary school. He harbors feelings for Rinne that go beyond friendship.

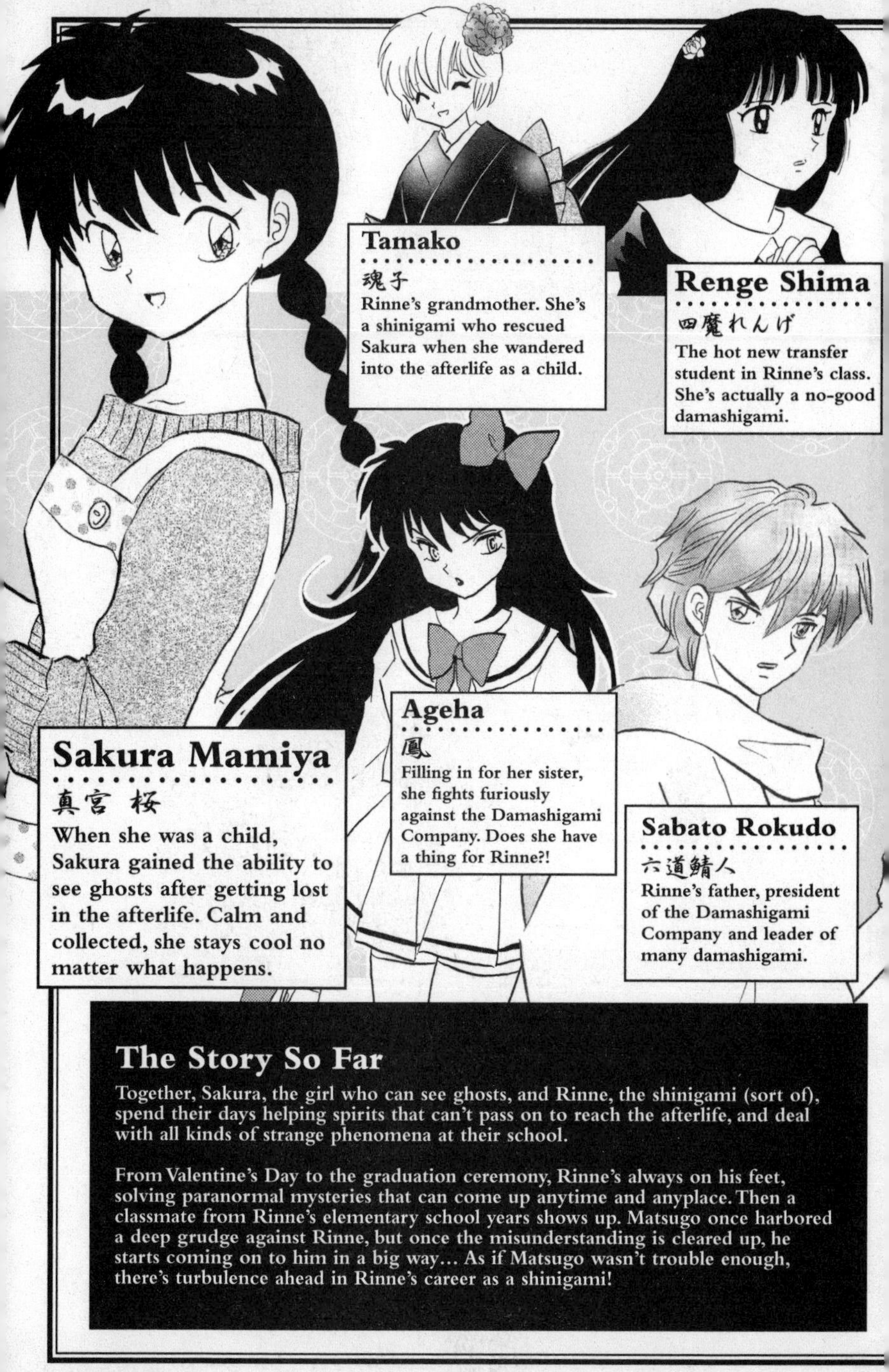
Tamako
魂子
Rinne's grandmother. She's a shinigami who rescued Sakura when she wandered into the afterlife as a child.
Renge Shima
四魔れんげ
The hot new transfer student in Rinne's class. She's actually a no-good damashigami.
Sakura Mamiya
真宮 桜
When she was a child, Sakura gained the ability to see ghosts after getting lost in the afterlife. Calm and collected, she stays cool no matter what happens.
Ageha
鳳
Filling in for her sister, she fights furiously against the Damashigami Company. Does she have a thing for Rinne?!
Sabato Rokudo
六道鯖人
Rinne's father, president of the Damashigami Company and leader of many damashigami.

The Story So Far

Together, Sakura, the girl who can see ghosts, and Rinne, the shinigami (sort of), spend their days helping spirits that can't pass on to reach the afterlife, and deal with all kinds of strange phenomena at their school.

From Valentine's Day to the graduation ceremony, Rinne's always on his feet, solving paranormal mysteries that can come up anytime and anyplace. Then a classmate from Rinne's elementary school years shows up. Matsugo once harbored a deep grudge against Rinne, but once the misunderstanding is cleared up, he starts coming on to him in a big way… As if Matsugo wasn't trouble enough, there's turbulence ahead in Rinne's career as a shinigami!

RIN-NE

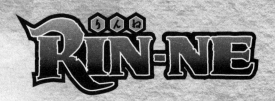

Contents

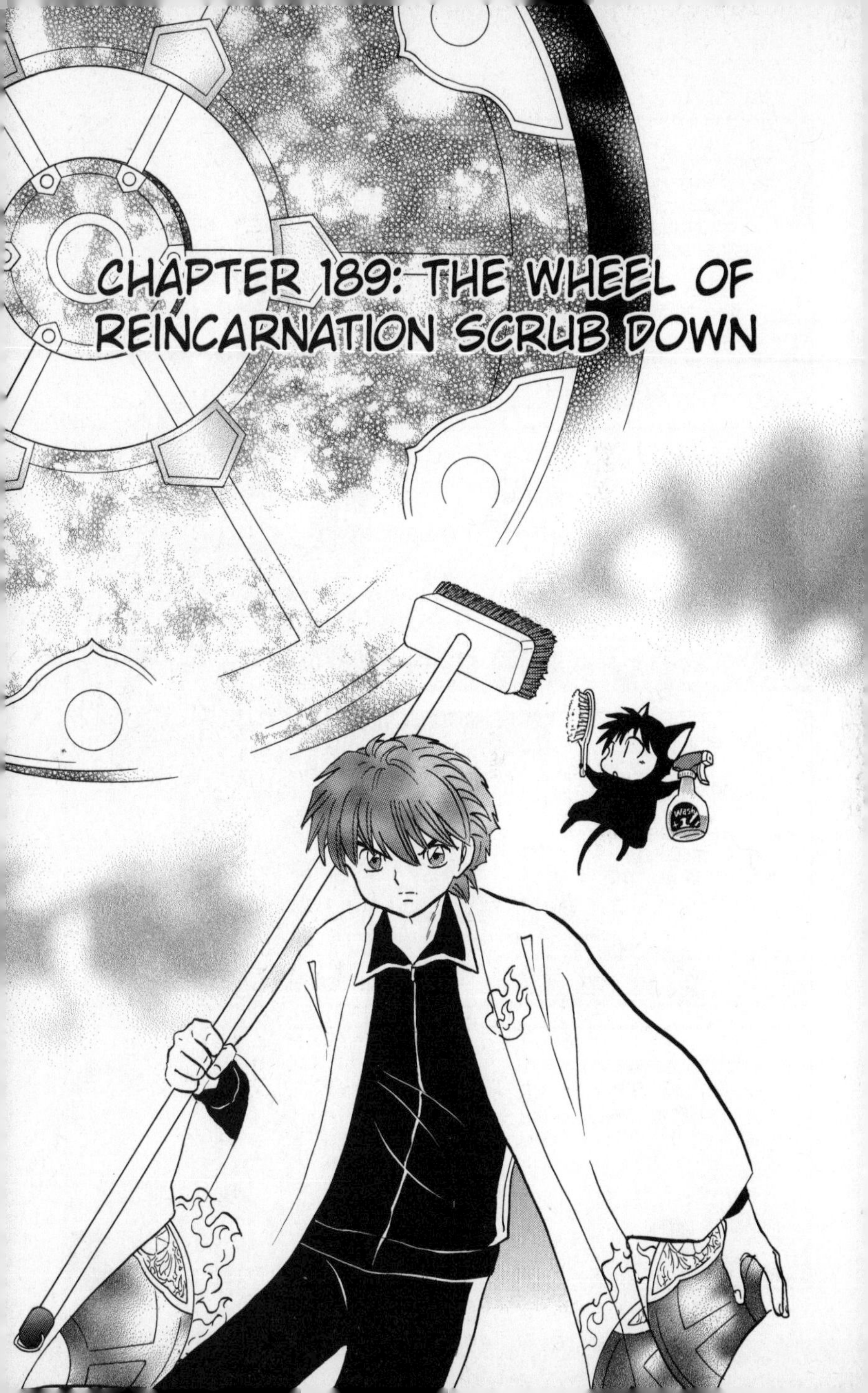
CHAPTER 189: THE WHEEL OF REINCARNATION SCRUB DOWN

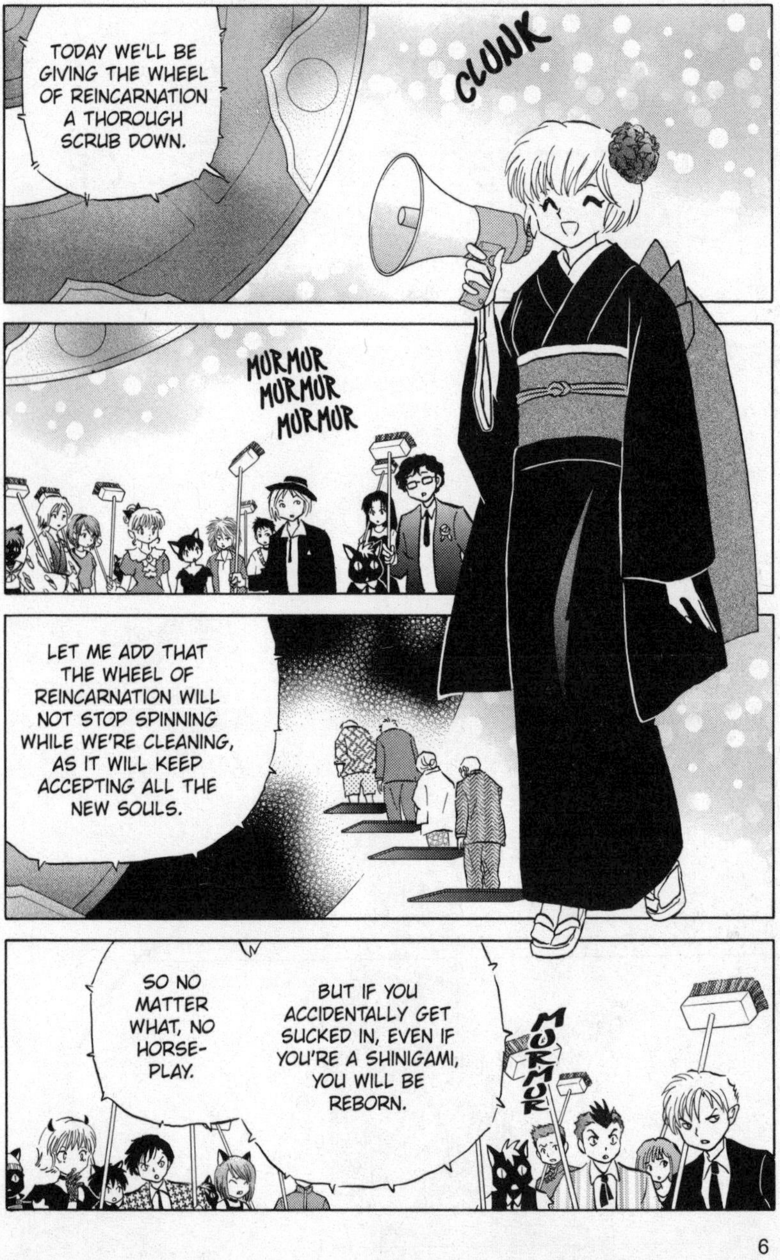
CLUNK
TODAY WE'LL BE GIVING THE WHEEL OF REINCARNATION A THOROUGH SCRUB DOWN.
MURMUR MURMUR MURMUR
LET ME ADD THAT THE WHEEL OF REINCARNATION WILL NOT STOP SPINNING WHILE WE'RE CLEANING, AS IT WILL KEEP ACCEPTING ALL THE NEW SOULS.
MURMUR
BUT IF YOU ACCIDENTALLY GET SUCKED IN, EVEN IF YOU'RE A SHINIGAMI, YOU WILL BE REBORN.
SO NO MATTER WHAT, NO HORSE-PLAY.

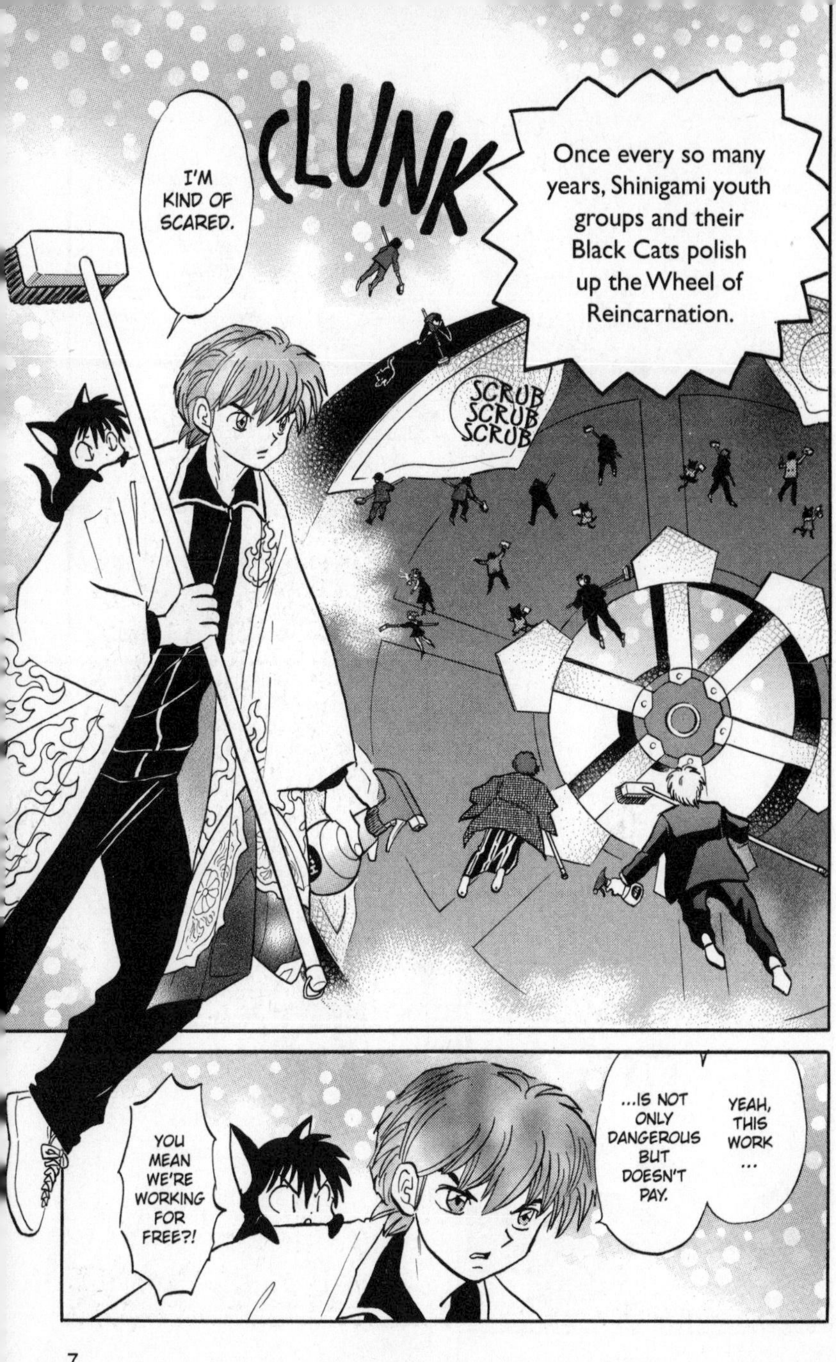
Once every so many years, Shinigami youth groups and their Black Cats polish up the Wheel of Reincarnation.
CLUNK
SCRUB SCRUB SCRUB
I'M KIND OF SCARED.
YEAH, THIS WORK...
...IS NOT ONLY DANGEROUS BUT DOESN'T PAY.
YOU MEAN WE'RE WORKING FOR FREE?!

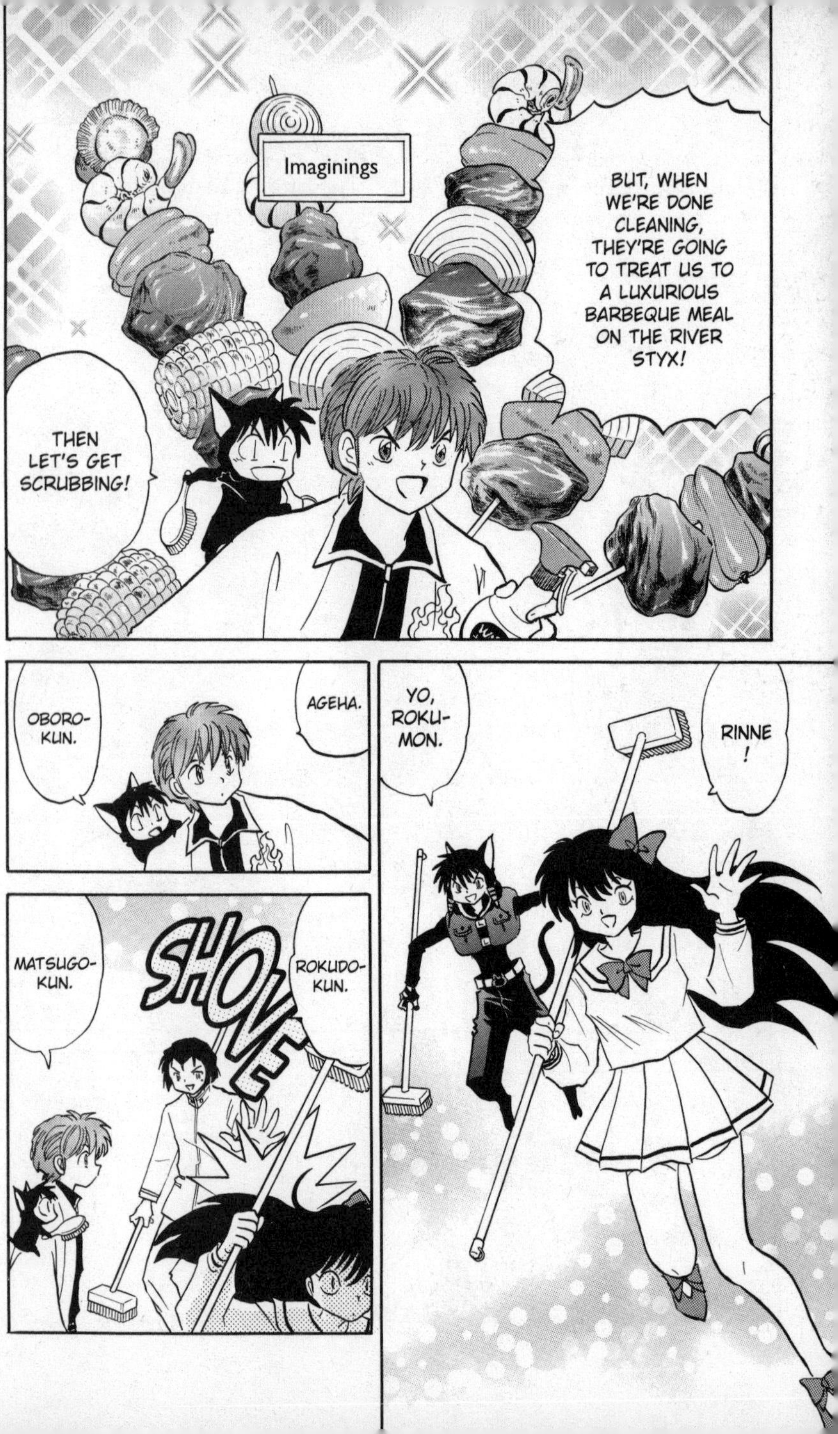
BUT, WHEN WE'RE DONE CLEANING, THEY'RE GOING TO TREAT US TO A LUXURIOUS BARBEQUE MEAL ON THE RIVER STYX!
Imaginings
THEN LET'S GET SCRUBBING!
RINNE!
YO, ROKU-MON.
AGEHA.
OBORO-KUN.
ROKUDO-KUN.
SHOVE
MATSUGO-KUN.

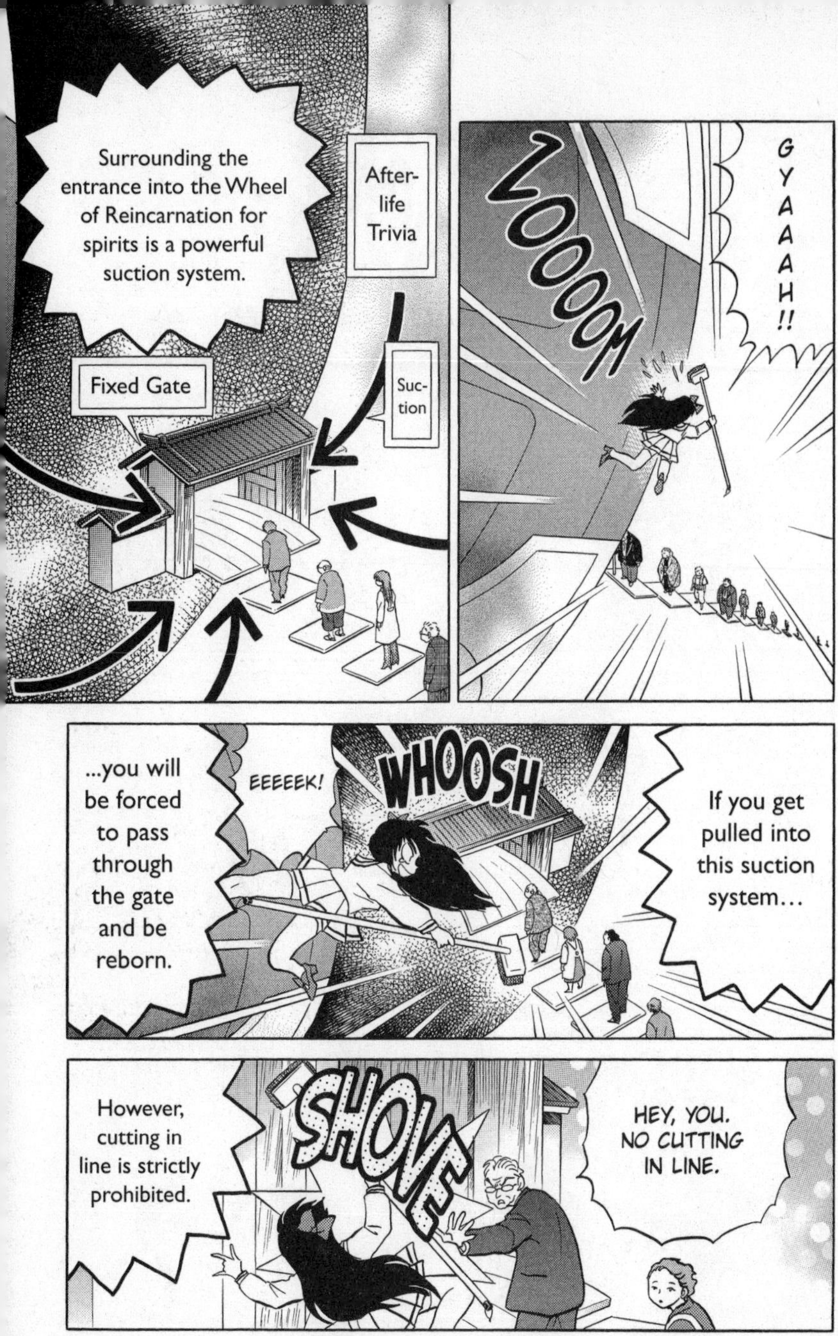
GYAAAAH!!
VOOOOM
After-life Trivia
Surrounding the entrance into the Wheel of Reincarnation for spirits is a powerful suction system.
Suc-tion
Fixed Gate
If you get pulled into this suction system…
WHOOSH
EEEEEK!
...you will be forced to pass through the gate and be reborn.
HEY, YOU. NO CUTTING IN LINE.
SHOVE
However, cutting in line is strictly prohibited.

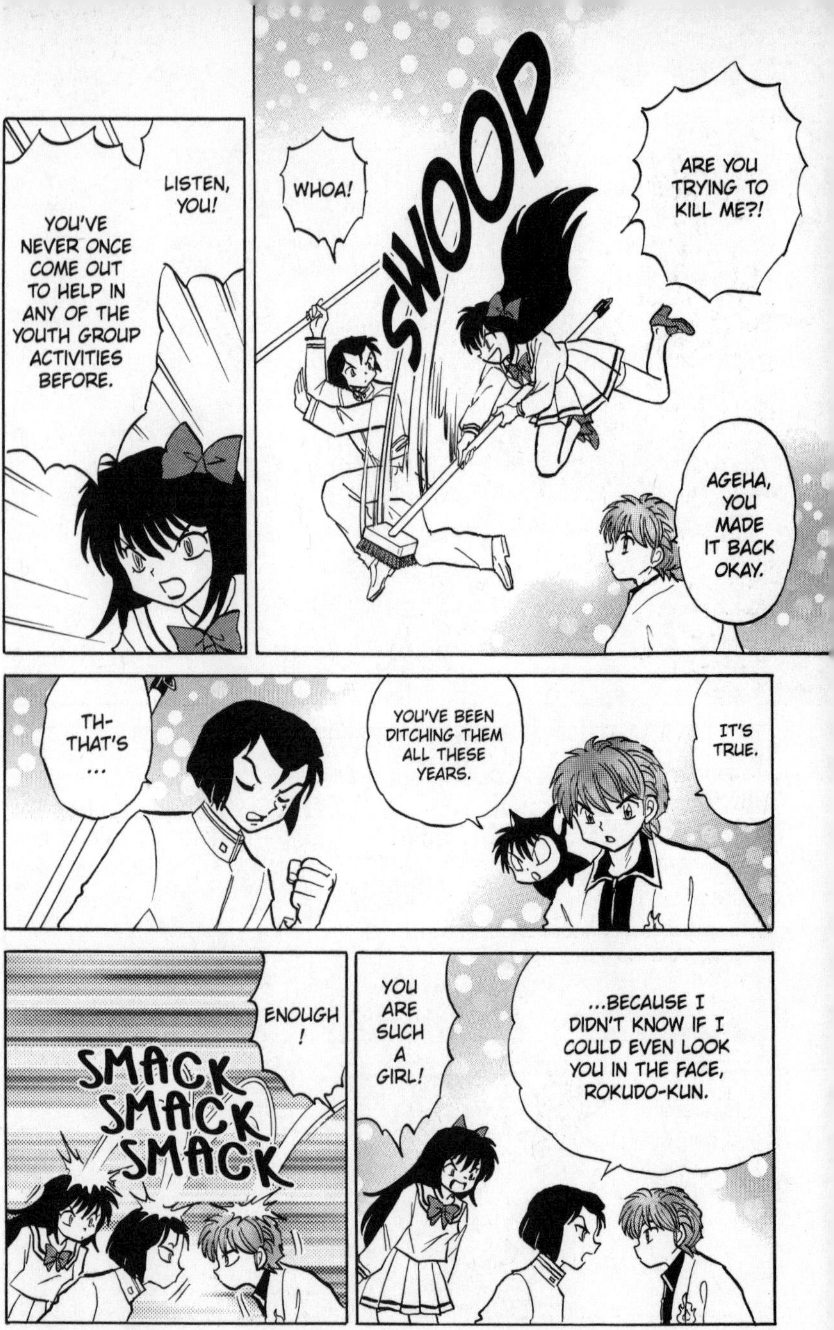
ARE YOU TRYING TO KILL ME?!
SWOOP
WHOA!
AGEHA, YOU MADE IT BACK OKAY.
LISTEN, YOU!
YOU'VE NEVER ONCE COME OUT TO HELP IN ANY OF THE YOUTH GROUP ACTIVITIES BEFORE.
IT'S TRUE.
YOU'VE BEEN DITCHING THEM ALL THESE YEARS.
TH-THAT'S ...
...BECAUSE I DIDN'T KNOW IF I COULD EVEN LOOK YOU IN THE FACE, ROKUDO-KUN.
YOU ARE SUCH A GIRL!
ENOUGH!
SMACK SMACK SMACK

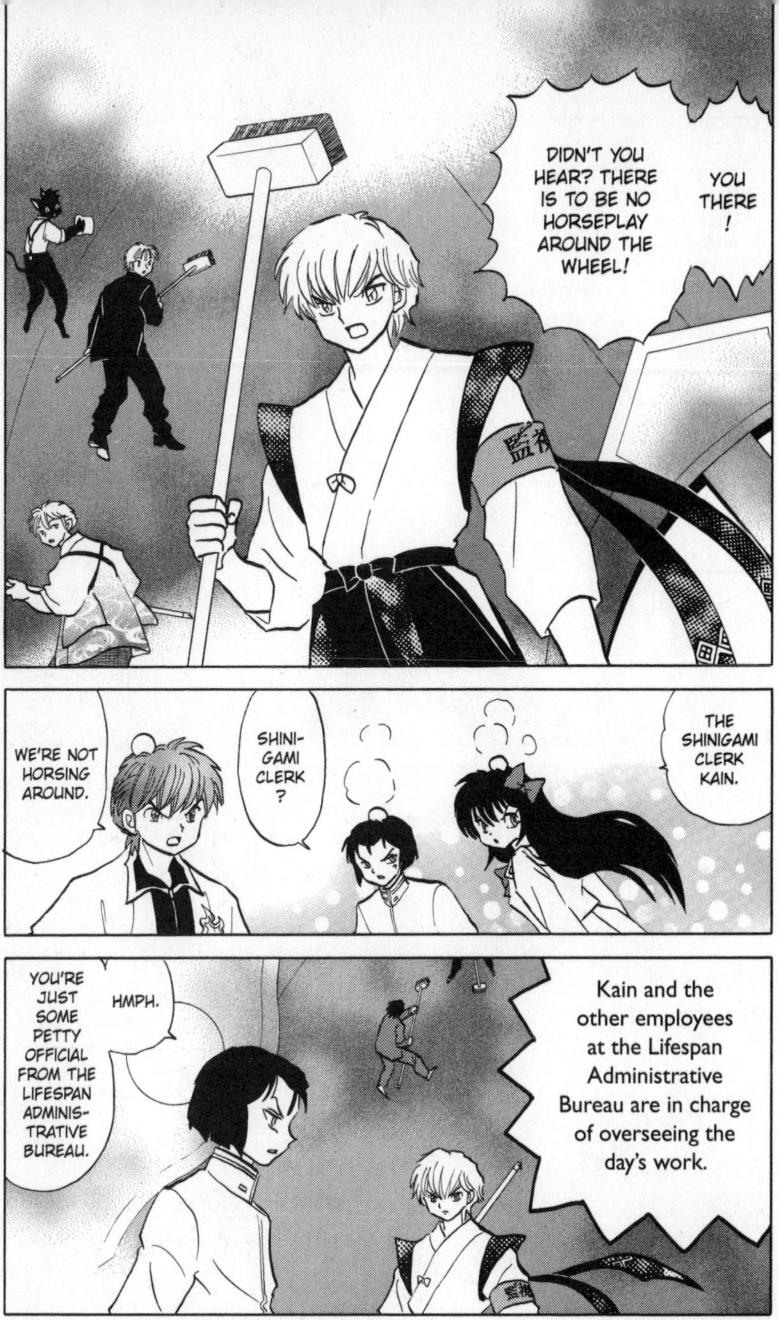
YOU THERE!
DIDN'T YOU HEAR? THERE IS TO BE NO HORSEPLAY AROUND THE WHEEL!
THE SHINIGAMI CLERK KAIN.
SHINIGAMI CLERK?
WE'RE NOT HORSING AROUND.
Kain and the other employees at the Lifespan Administrative Bureau are in charge of overseeing the day's work.
HMPH.
YOU'RE JUST SOME PETTY OFFICIAL FROM THE LIFESPAN ADMINISTRATIVE BUREAU.

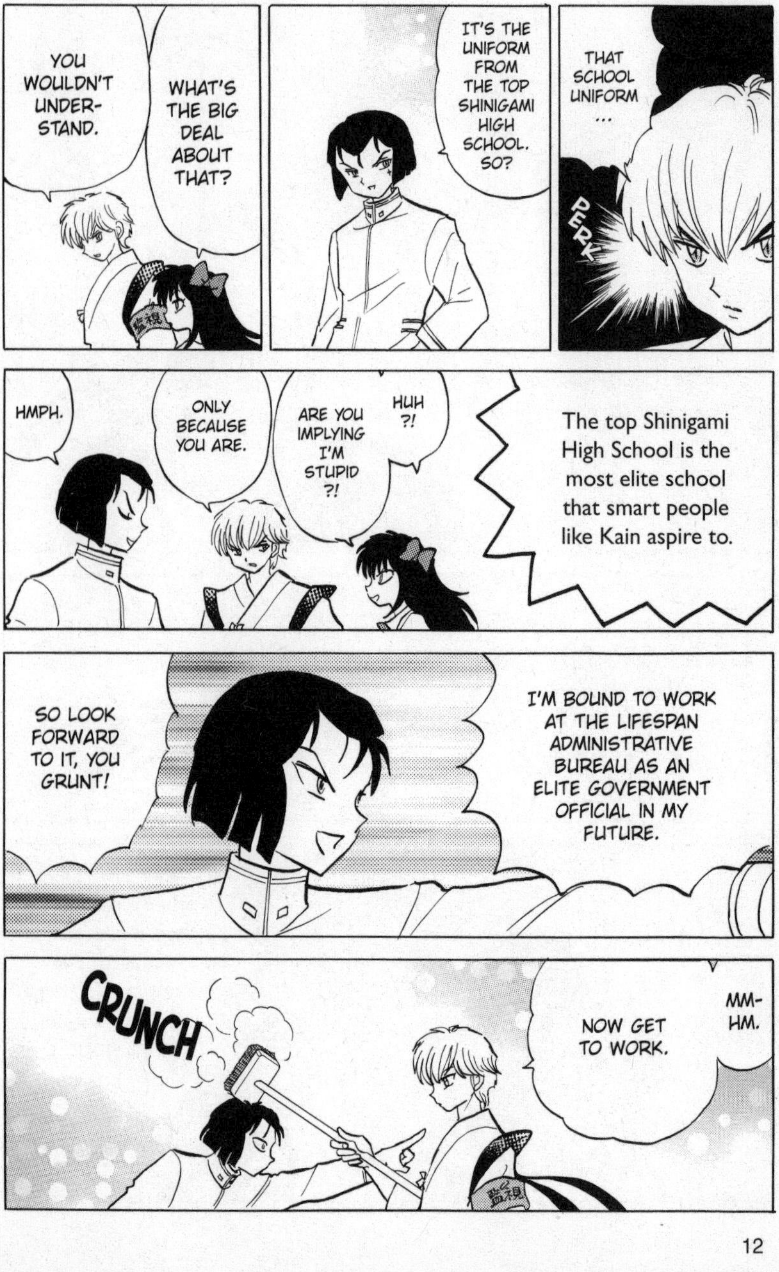
THAT SCHOOL UNIFORM ...
PERK
IT'S THE UNIFORM FROM THE TOP SHINIGAMI HIGH SCHOOL. SO?
WHAT'S THE BIG DEAL ABOUT THAT?
YOU WOULDN'T UNDER-STAND.
The top Shinigami High School is the most elite school that smart people like Kain aspire to.
HUH ?!
ARE YOU IMPLYING I'M STUPID ?!
ONLY BECAUSE YOU ARE.
HMPH.
I'M BOUND TO WORK AT THE LIFESPAN ADMINISTRATIVE BUREAU AS AN ELITE GOVERNMENT OFFICIAL IN MY FUTURE.
SO LOOK FORWARD TO IT, YOU GRUNT!
MM-HM.
NOW GET TO WORK.
CRUNCH

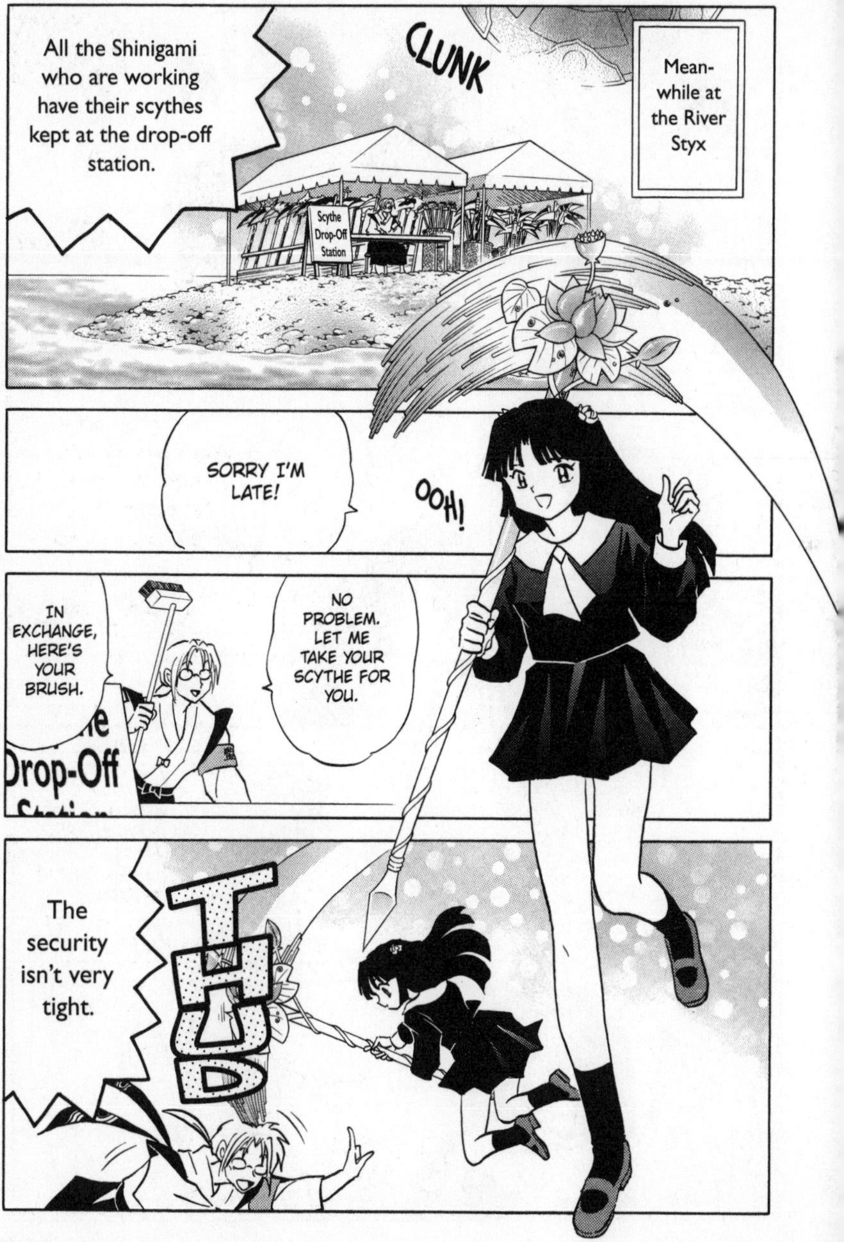
Mean-while at the River Styx
CLUNK
Scythe Drop-Off Station
All the Shinigami who are working have their scythes kept at the drop-off station.
OOH!
SORRY I'M LATE!
NO PROBLEM. LET ME TAKE YOUR SCYTHE FOR YOU.
IN EXCHANGE, HERE'S YOUR BRUSH.
Drop-Off
THUD
The security isn't very tight.

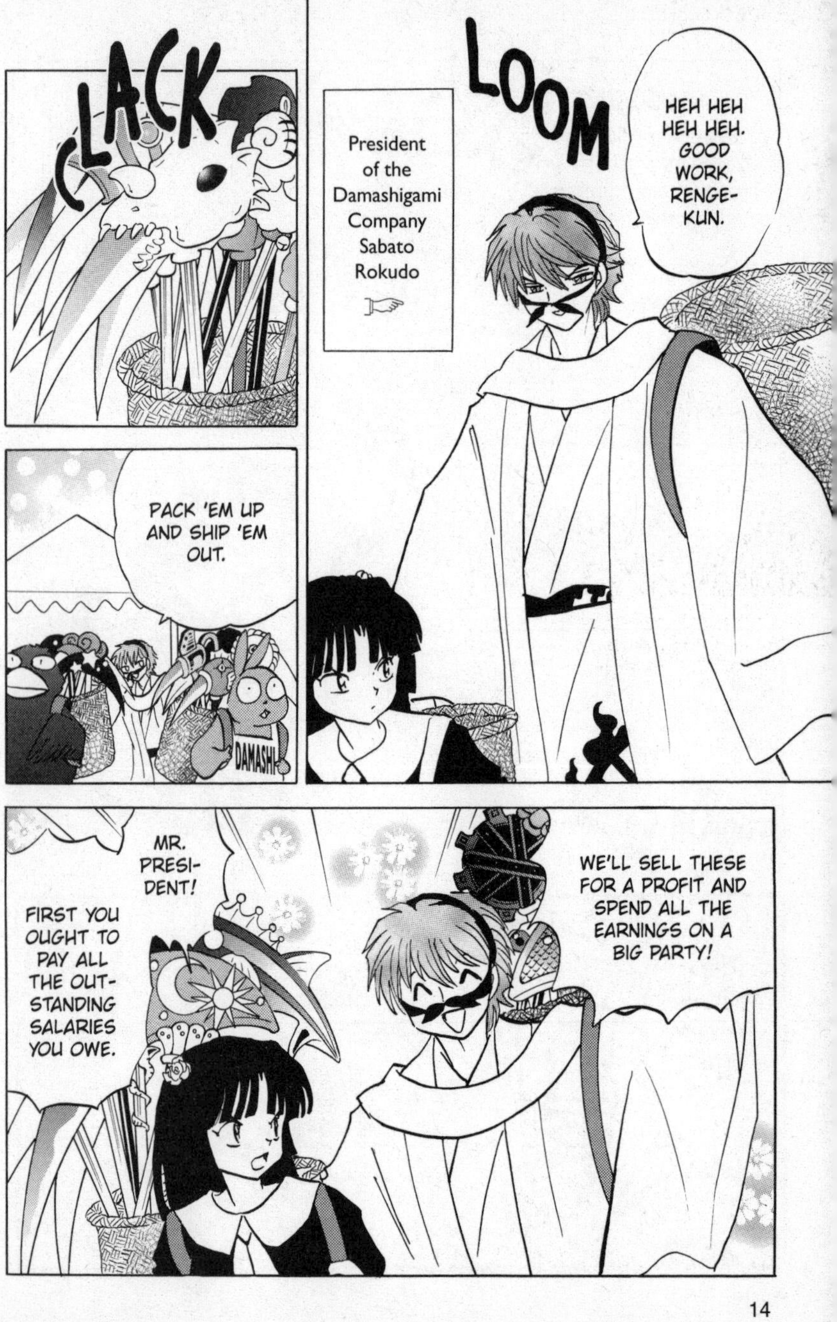
HEH HEH HEH HEH. GOOD WORK, RENGE-KUN.
LOOM
President of the Damashigami Company Sabato Rokudo ☞
CLACK
PACK 'EM UP AND SHIP 'EM OUT.
DAMASHI
WE'LL SELL THESE FOR A PROFIT AND SPEND ALL THE EARNINGS ON A BIG PARTY!
MR. PRESI-DENT!
FIRST YOU OUGHT TO PAY ALL THE OUT-STANDING SALARIES YOU OWE.

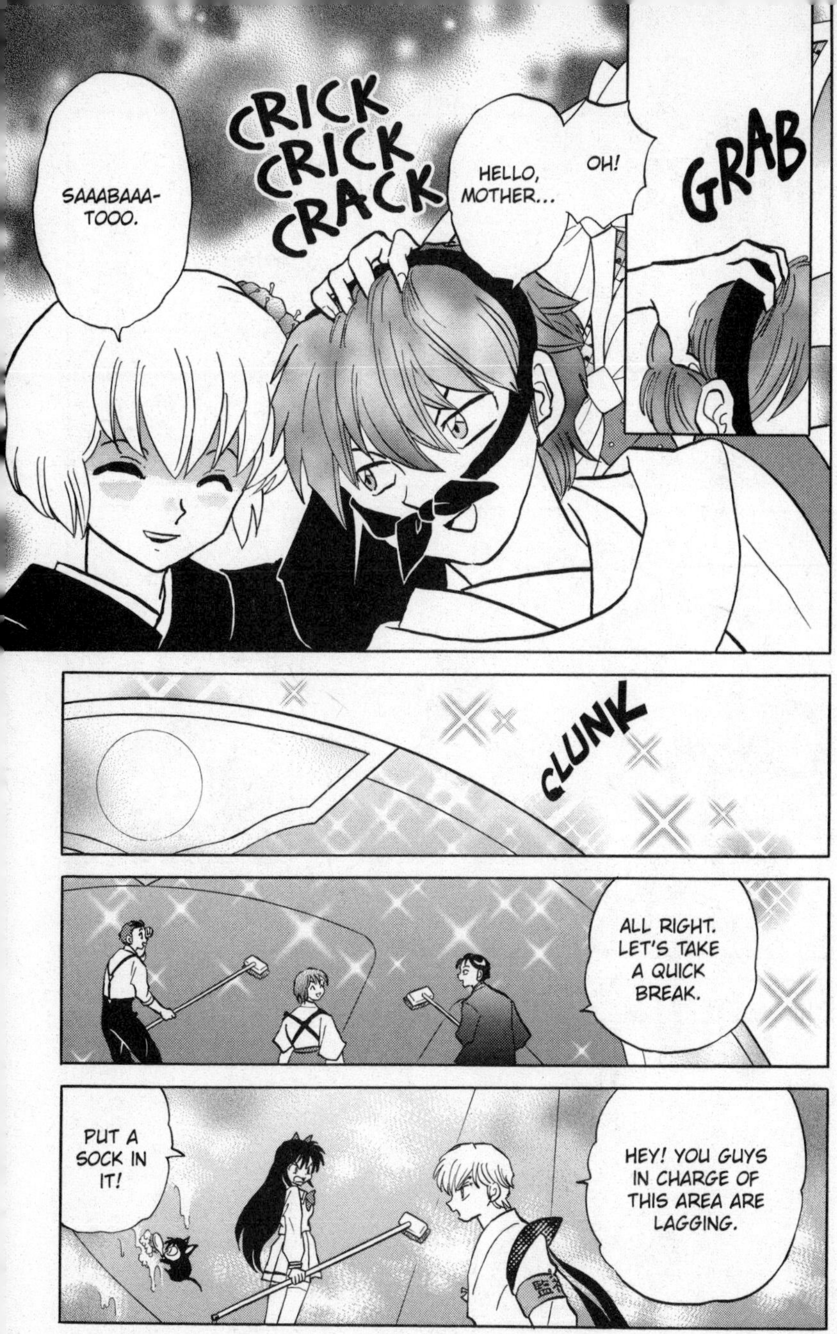
GRAB
OH!
HELLO, MOTHER...
CRICK CRICK CRACK
SAAABAAA-TOOO.
CLUNK
ALL RIGHT. LET'S TAKE A QUICK BREAK.
HEY! YOU GUYS IN CHARGE OF THIS AREA ARE LAGGING.
PUT A SOCK IN IT!

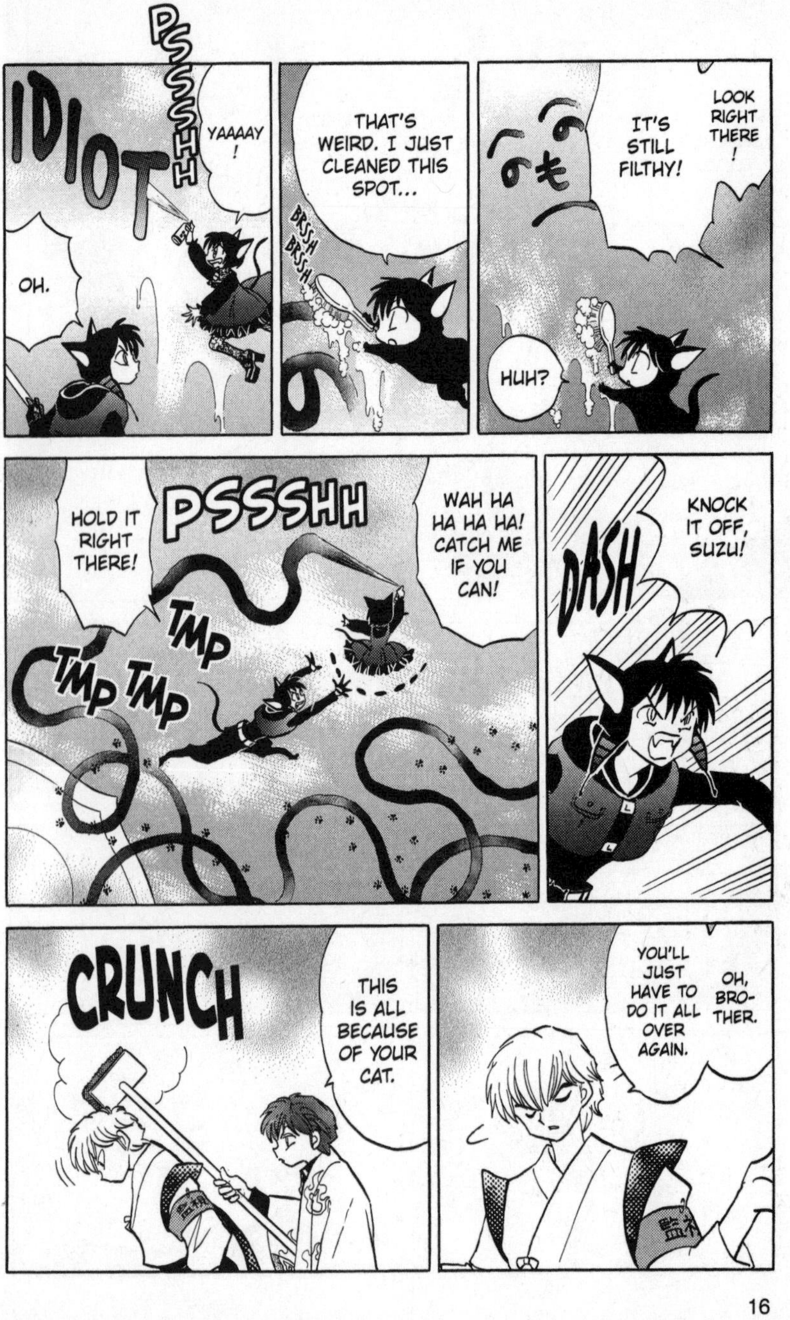

LOOK RIGHT THERE!
IT'S STILL FILTHY!
HUH?
THAT'S WEIRD. I JUST CLEANED THIS SPOT...
BRSSH BRSSH
PSSSSHH
YAAAAY!
IDIOT
OH.
KNOCK IT OFF, SUZU!
DASH
WAH HA HA HA HA! CATCH ME IF YOU CAN!
PSSSHH
HOLD IT RIGHT THERE!
TMP
TMP TMP
OH, BRO-THER.
YOU'LL JUST HAVE TO DO IT ALL OVER AGAIN.
THIS IS ALL BECAUSE OF YOUR CAT.
CRUNCH

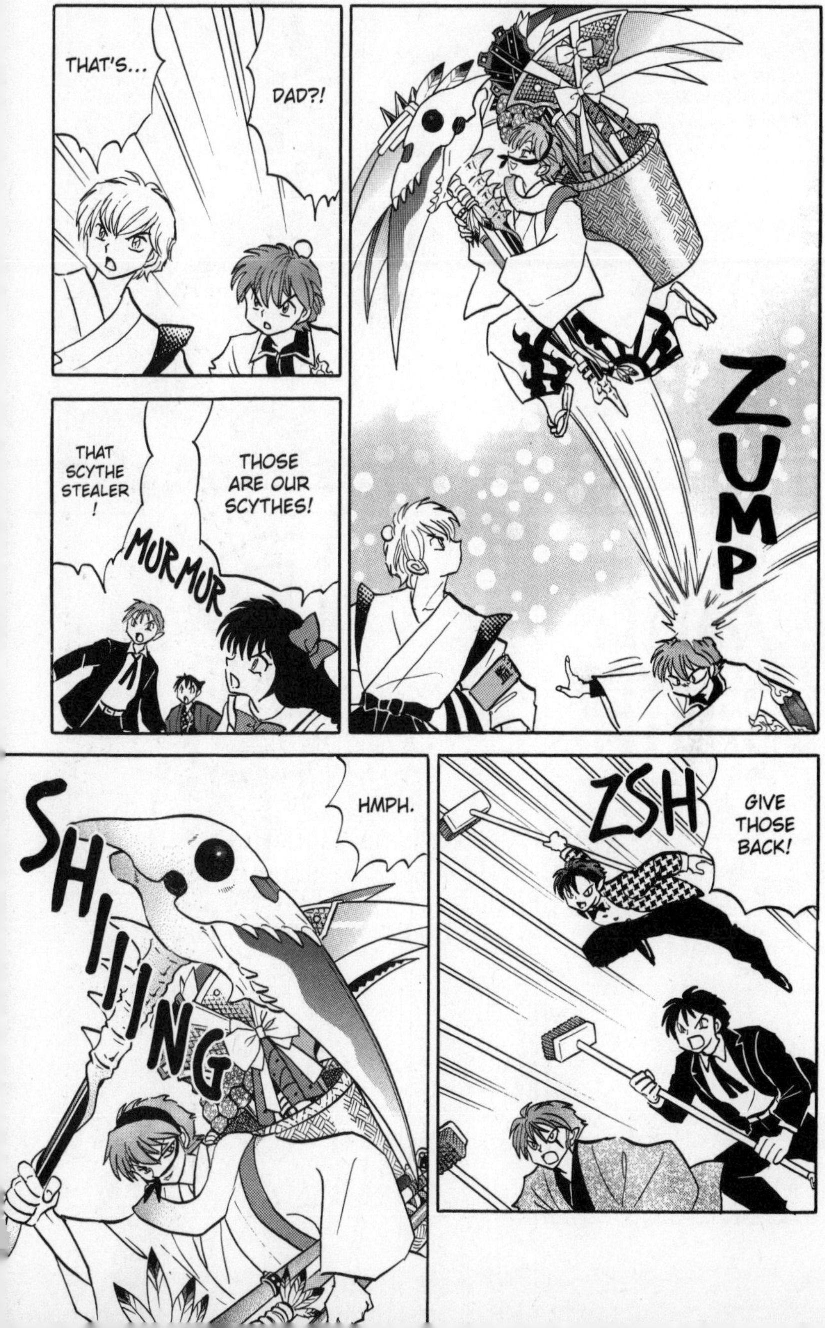
ZUMP
THAT'S...
DAD?!
THOSE ARE OUR SCYTHES!
THAT SCYTHE STEALER!
MURMUR
ZSH
GIVE THOSE BACK!
HMPH.
SHIIING

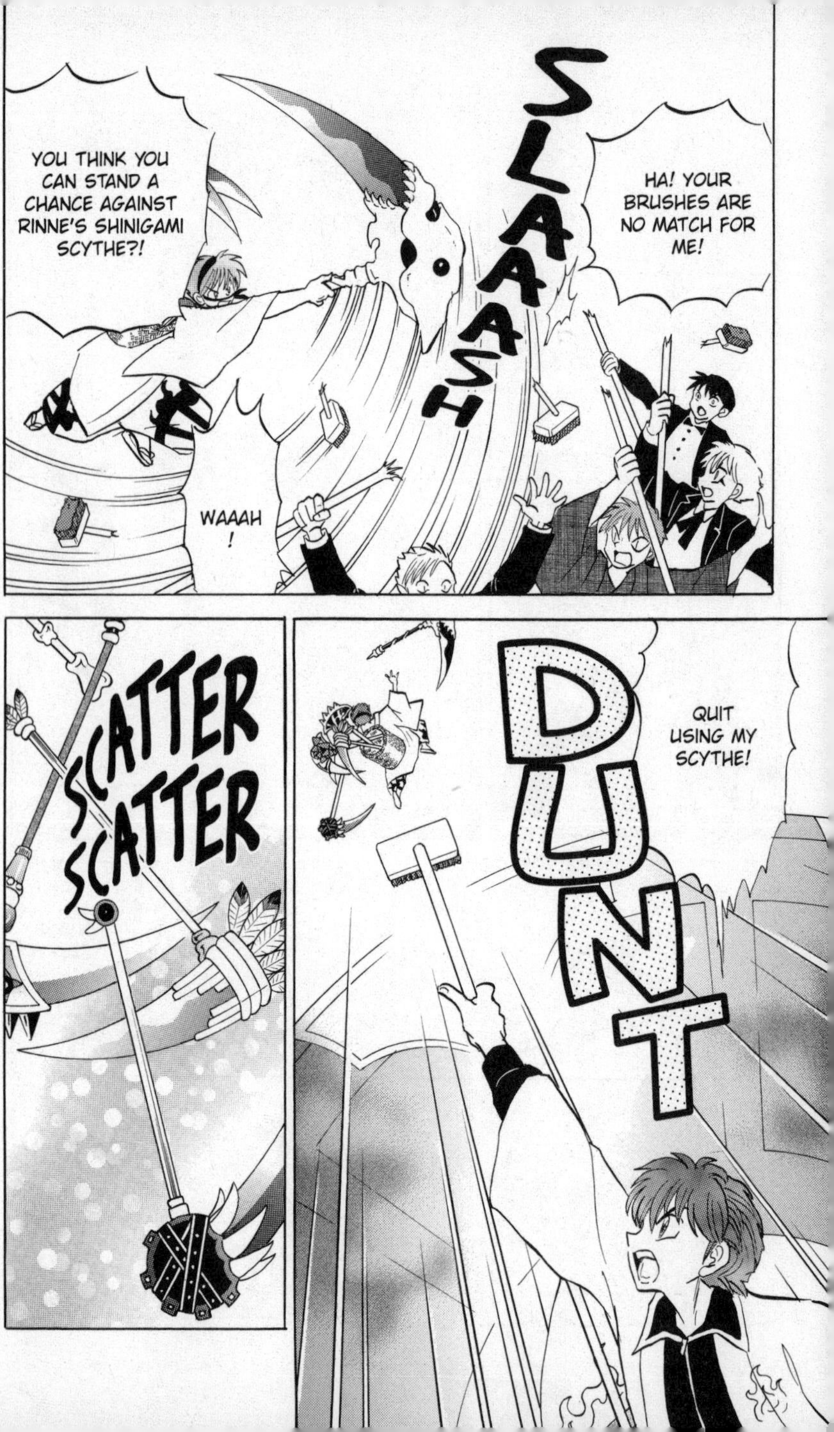
HA! YOUR BRUSHES ARE NO MATCH FOR ME!
SLAAASH
YOU THINK YOU CAN STAND A CHANCE AGAINST RINNE'S SHINIGAMI SCYTHE?!
WAAAH!
QUIT USING MY SCYTHE!
DUNT
SCATTER SCATTER

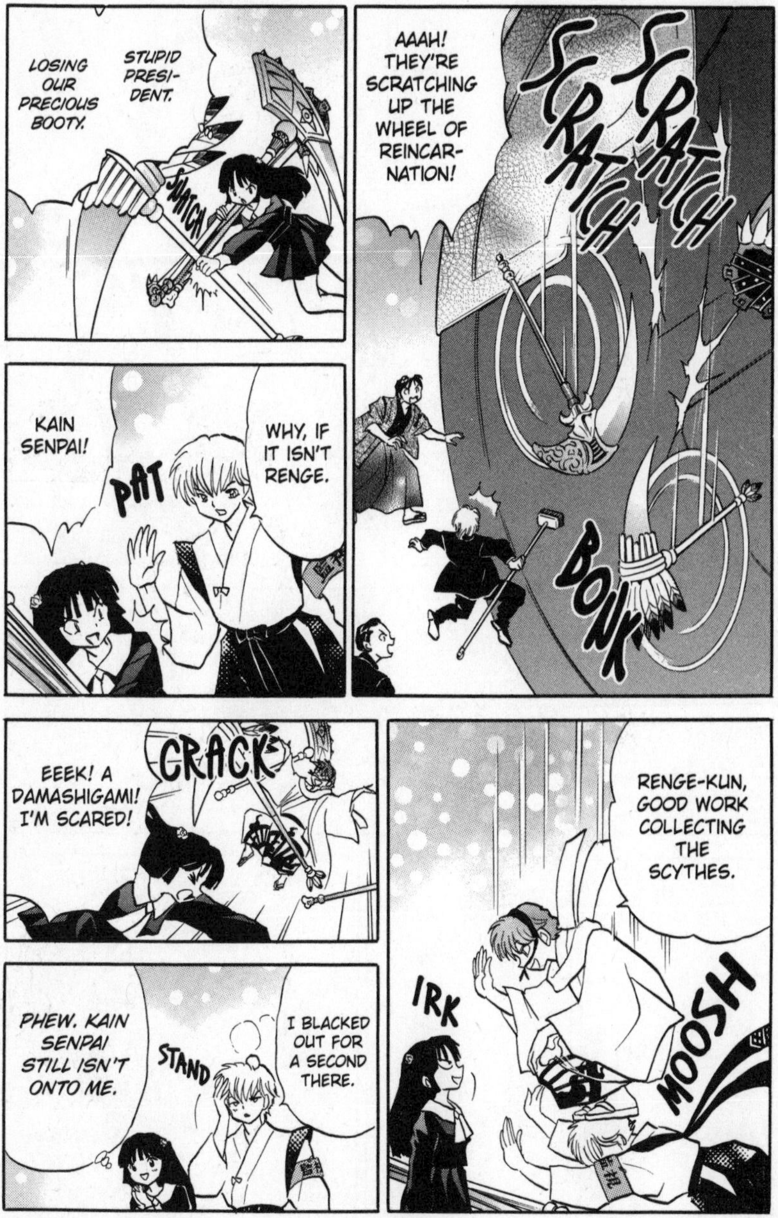
AAAH! THEY'RE SCRATCHING UP THE WHEEL OF REINCARNATION!
SCRATCH
SCRATCH
BONK
STUPID PRESIDENT.
LOSING OUR PRECIOUS BOOTY.
SNATCH
WHY, IF IT ISN'T RENGE.
PAT
KAIN SENPAI!
RENGE-KUN, GOOD WORK COLLECTING THE SCYTHES.
MOOSH
IRK
CRACK
EEEK! A DAMASHIGAMI! I'M SCARED!
I BLACKED OUT FOR A SECOND THERE.
STAND
PHEW. KAIN SENPAI STILL ISN'T ONTO ME.

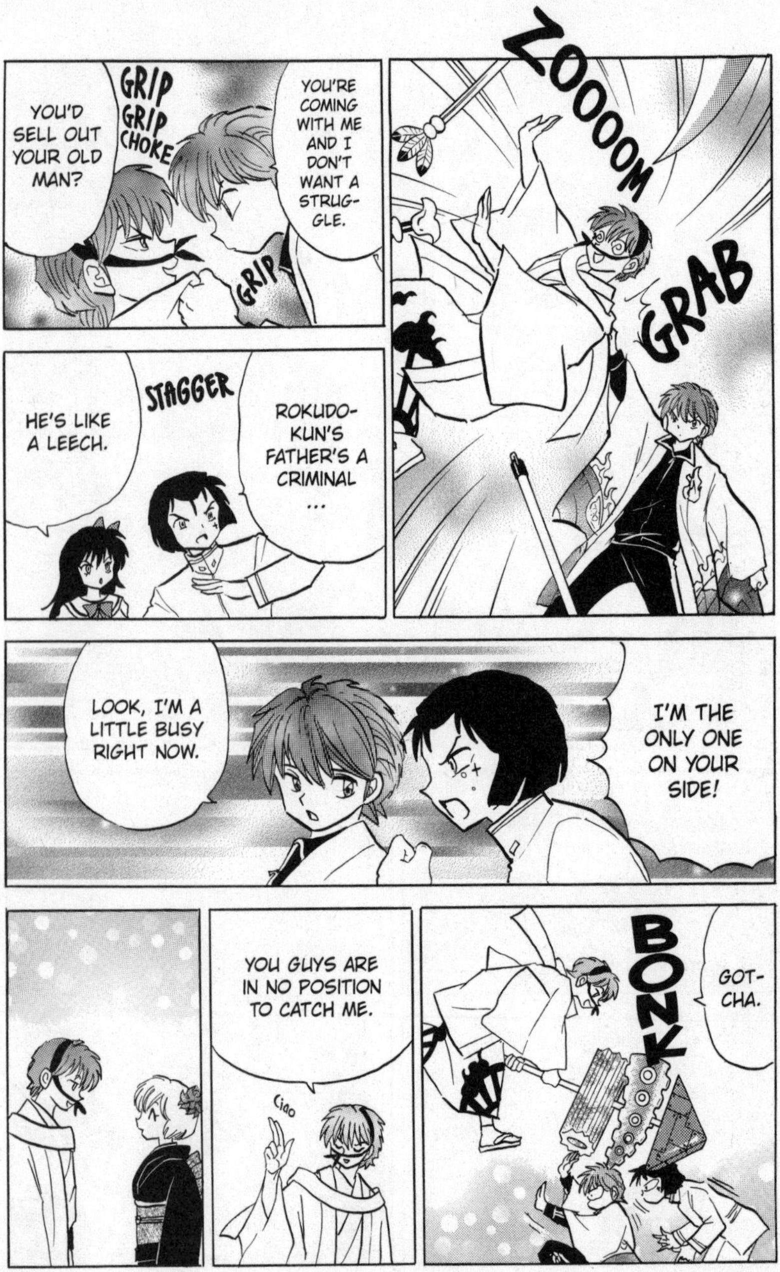
ZOOOOOM
GRAB
YOU'RE COMING WITH ME AND I DON'T WANT A STRUG-GLE.
GRIP GRIP CHOKE
YOU'D SELL OUT YOUR OLD MAN?
GRIP
ROKUDO-KUN'S FATHER'S A CRIMINAL ...
STAGGER
HE'S LIKE A LEECH.
I'M THE ONLY ONE ON YOUR SIDE!
LOOK, I'M A LITTLE BUSY RIGHT NOW.
GOT-CHA.
BONK
YOU GUYS ARE IN NO POSITION TO CATCH ME.
Ciao

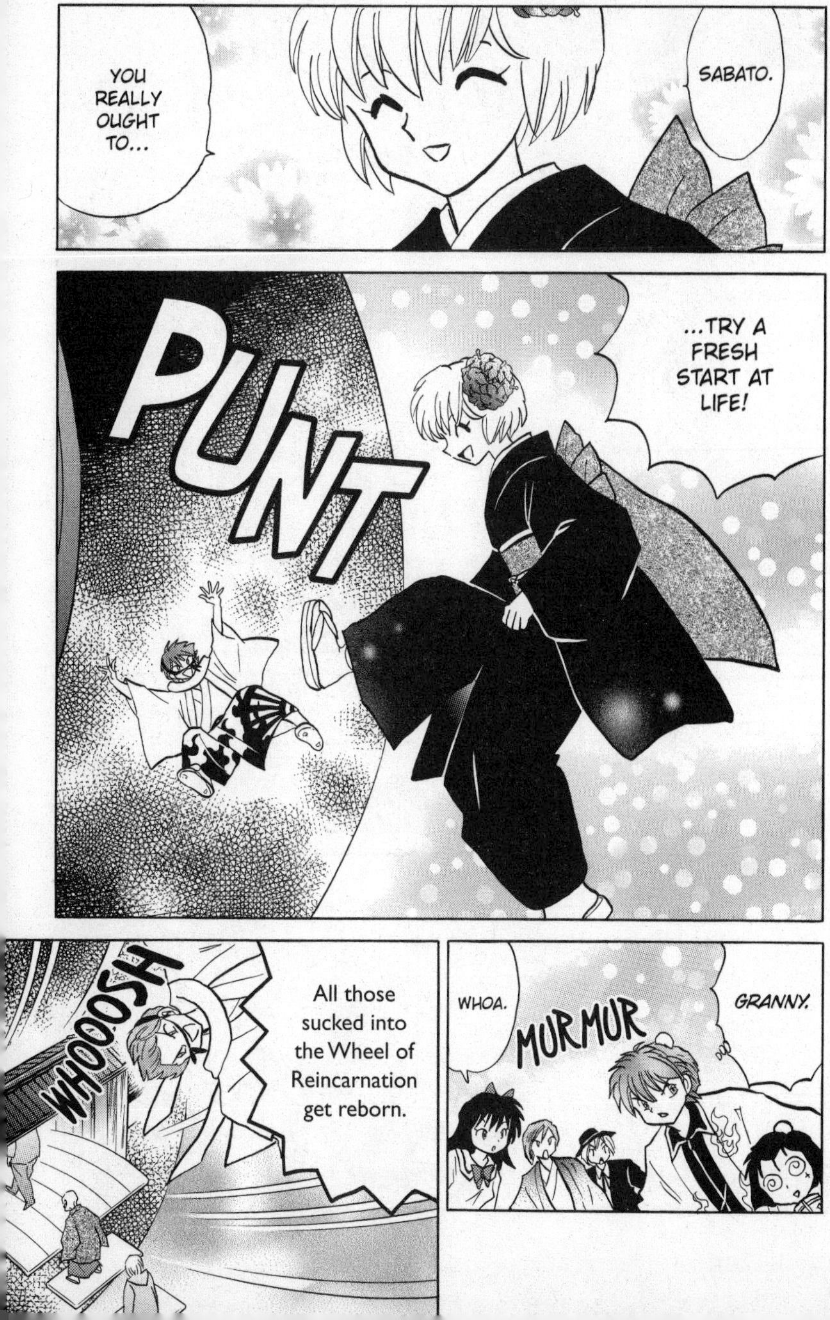
SABATO.
YOU REALLY OUGHT TO...
...TRY A FRESH START AT LIFE!
PUNT
GRANNY.
MURMUR
WHOA.
All those sucked into the Wheel of Reincarnation get reborn.
WHOOOSH

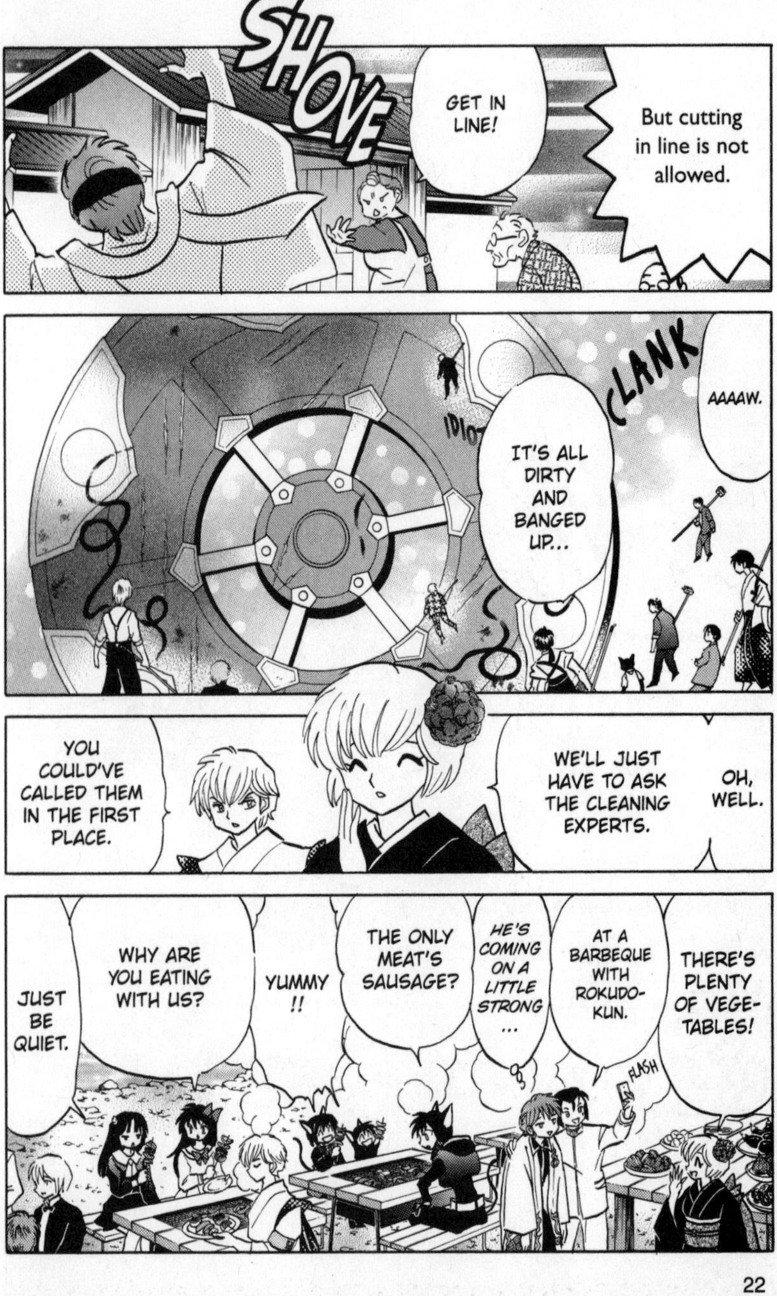
But cutting in line is not allowed.
GET IN LINE!
SHOVE
AAAAW.
CLANK
IT'S ALL DIRTY AND BANGED UP...
IDIOT
OH, WELL.
WE'LL JUST HAVE TO ASK THE CLEANING EXPERTS.
YOU COULD'VE CALLED THEM IN THE FIRST PLACE.
THERE'S PLENTY OF VEGE-TABLES!
AT A BARBEQUE WITH ROKUDO-KUN.
FLASH
HE'S COMING ON A LITTLE STRONG...
THE ONLY MEAT'S SAUSAGE?
YUMMY!!
WHY ARE YOU EATING WITH US?
JUST BE QUIET.

CHAPTER 190: THE SHOP WITH NO CUSTOMERS

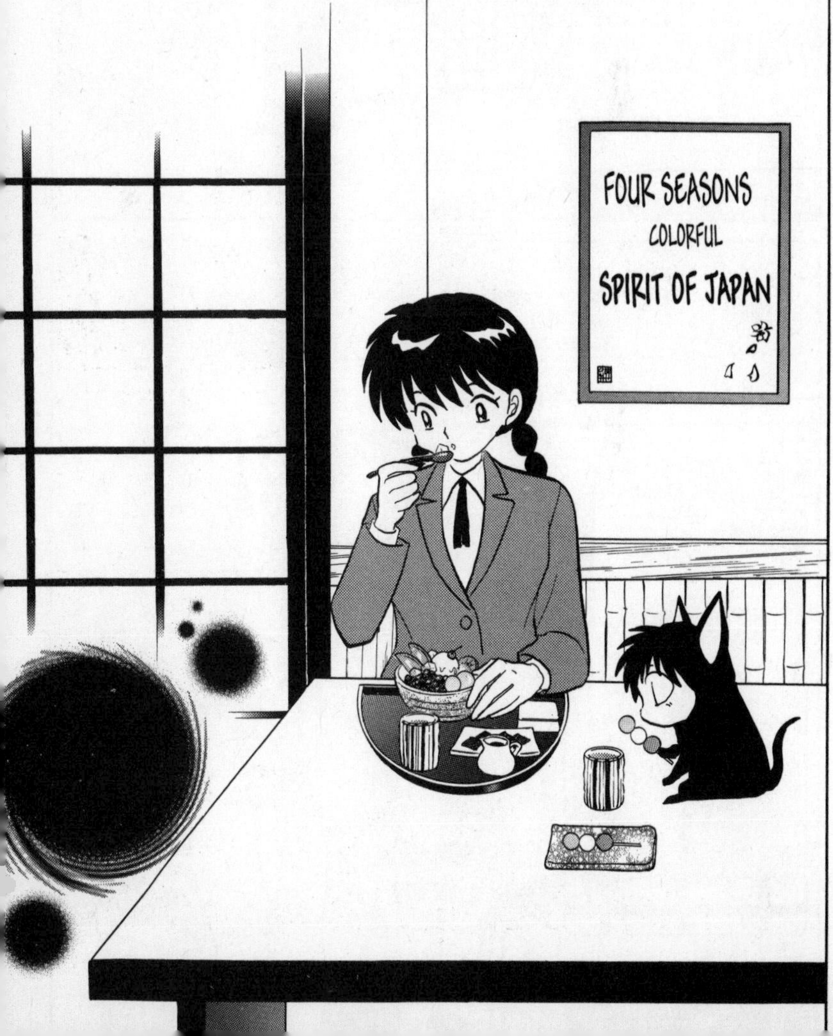
FOUR SEASONS
COLORFUL
SPIRIT OF JAPAN

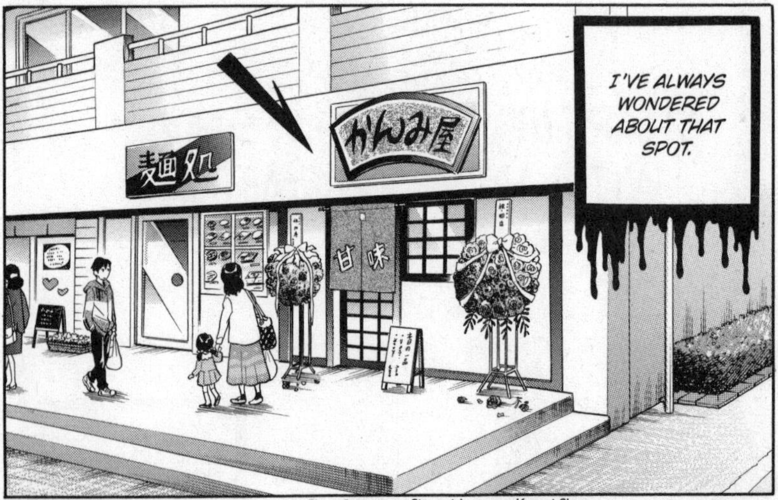
I'VE ALWAYS WONDERED ABOUT THAT SPOT.
かんみ屋
甘味
Flags: Sweets Sign with arrow: Kanmi Shop

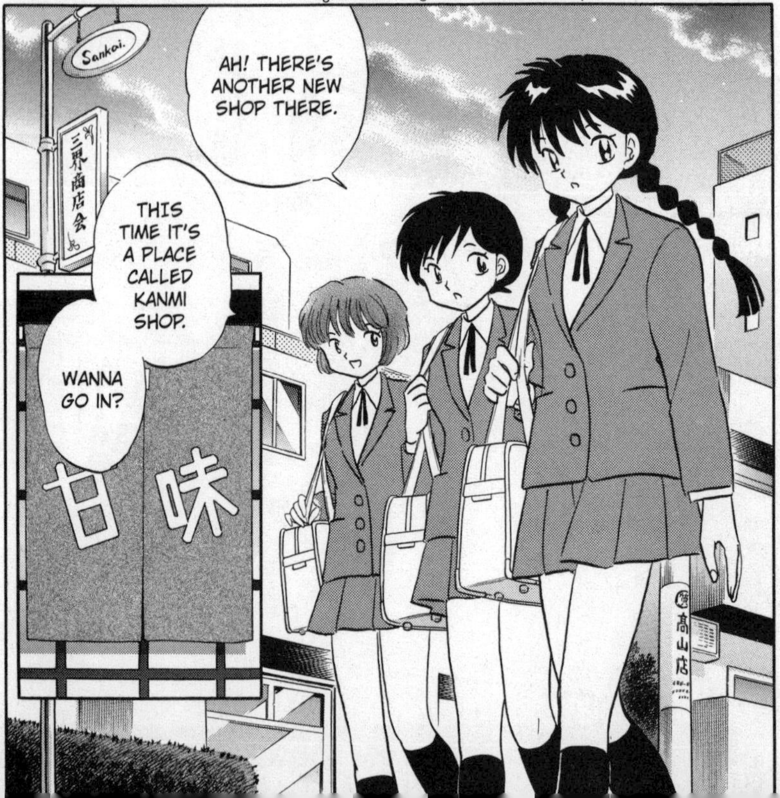
AH! THERE'S ANOTHER NEW SHOP THERE.
THIS TIME IT'S A PLACE CALLED KANMI SHOP.
WANNA GO IN?
Sankai.
三界商店会
甘味
高山店

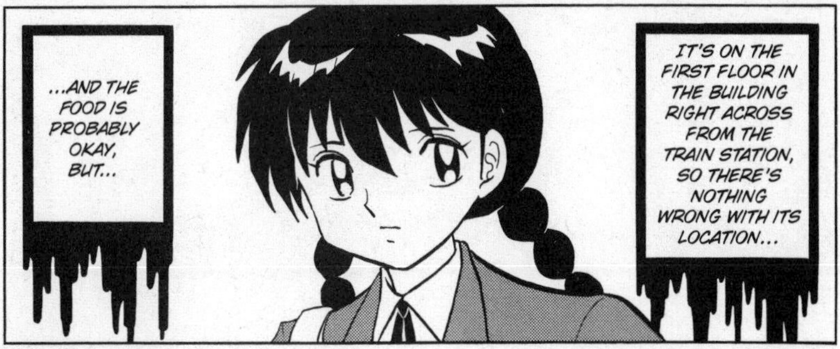
IT'S ON THE FIRST FLOOR IN THE BUILDING RIGHT ACROSS FROM THE TRAIN STATION, SO THERE'S NOTHING WRONG WITH ITS LOCATION...
...AND THE FOOD IS PROBABLY OKAY, BUT...
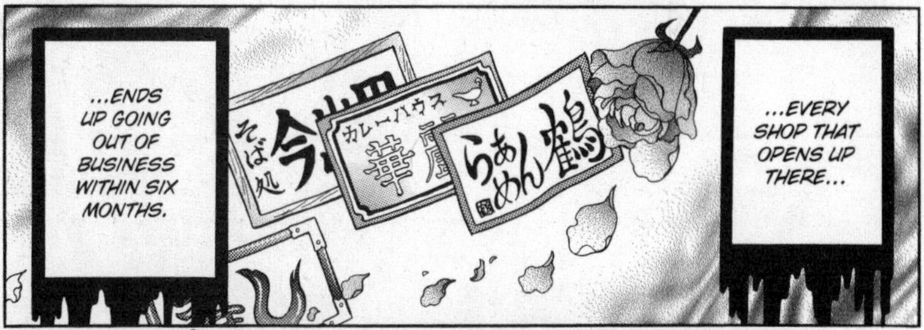
...EVERY SHOP THAT OPENS UP THERE...
らあめん鶴
カレーハウス
そば処
...ENDS UP GOING OUT OF BUSINESS WITHIN SIX MONTHS.
Signs: Ramen Crane   Curry House of Splendor   Soba Stand Imayamada

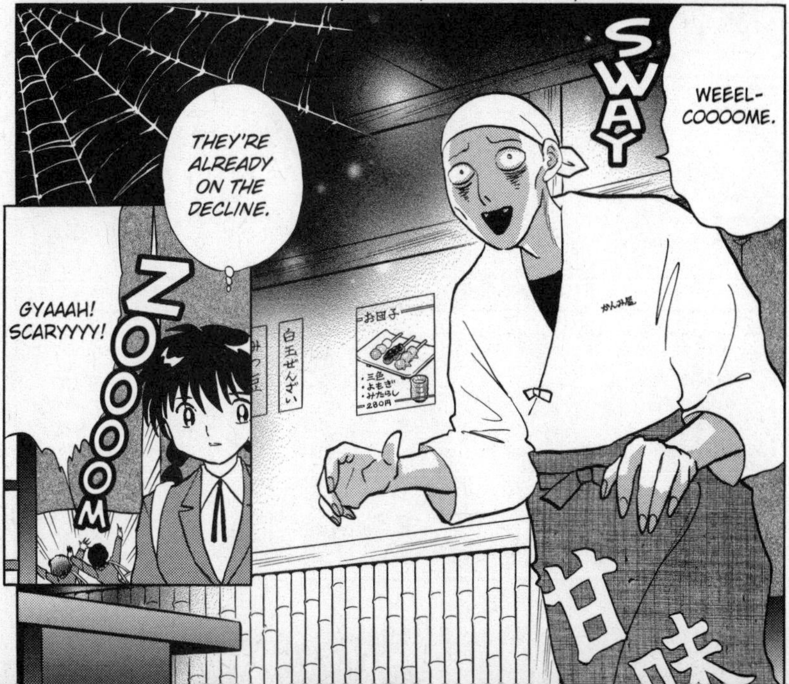
WEEEL-COOOOME.
SWAY
THEY'RE ALREADY ON THE DECLINE.
かんみ屋
お団子
三色
・よもぎ
・みたらし
280円
白玉ぜんざい
甘味
ZOOOOOOM
GYAAAH! SCARYYYY!

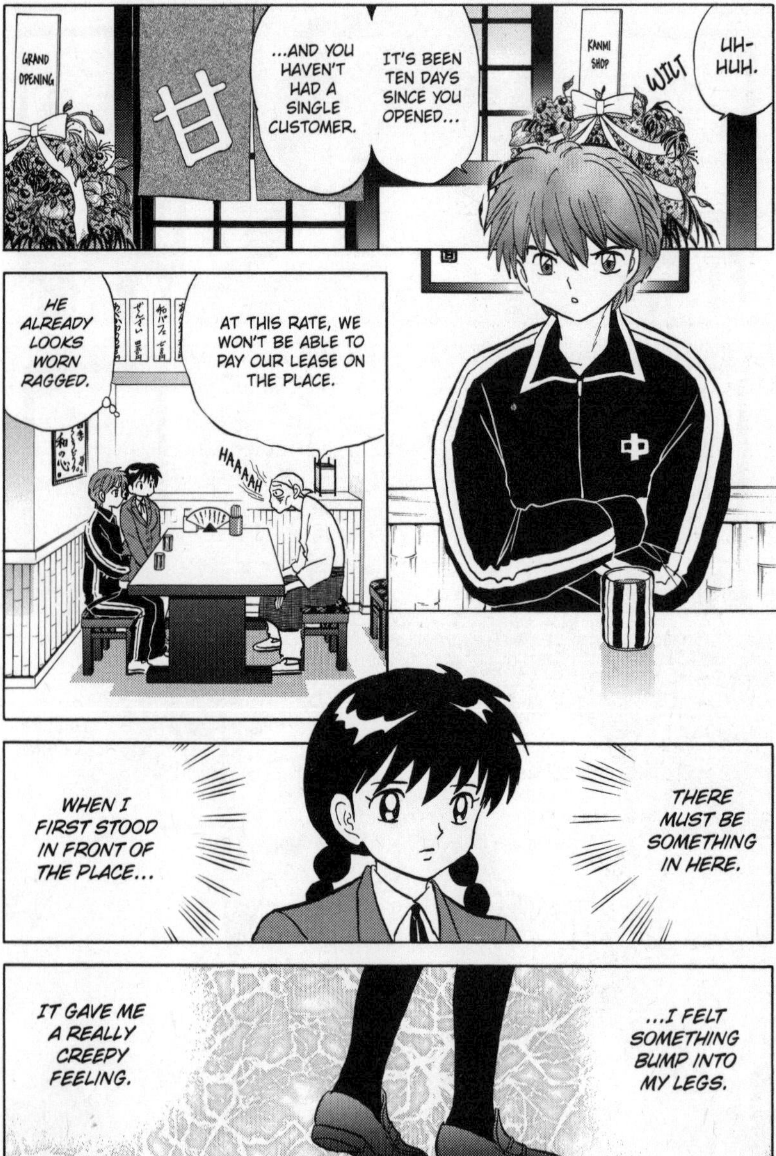
KANMI SHOP
WILT
UH-HUH.
IT'S BEEN TEN DAYS SINCE YOU OPENED...
...AND YOU HAVEN'T HAD A SINGLE CUSTOMER.
GRAND OPENING
AT THIS RATE, WE WON'T BE ABLE TO PAY OUR LEASE ON THE PLACE.
HAAAAH
HE ALREADY LOOKS WORN RAGGED.
THERE MUST BE SOMETHING IN HERE.
WHEN I FIRST STOOD IN FRONT OF THE PLACE...
...I FELT SOMETHING BUMP INTO MY LEGS.
IT GAVE ME A REALLY CREEPY FEELING.

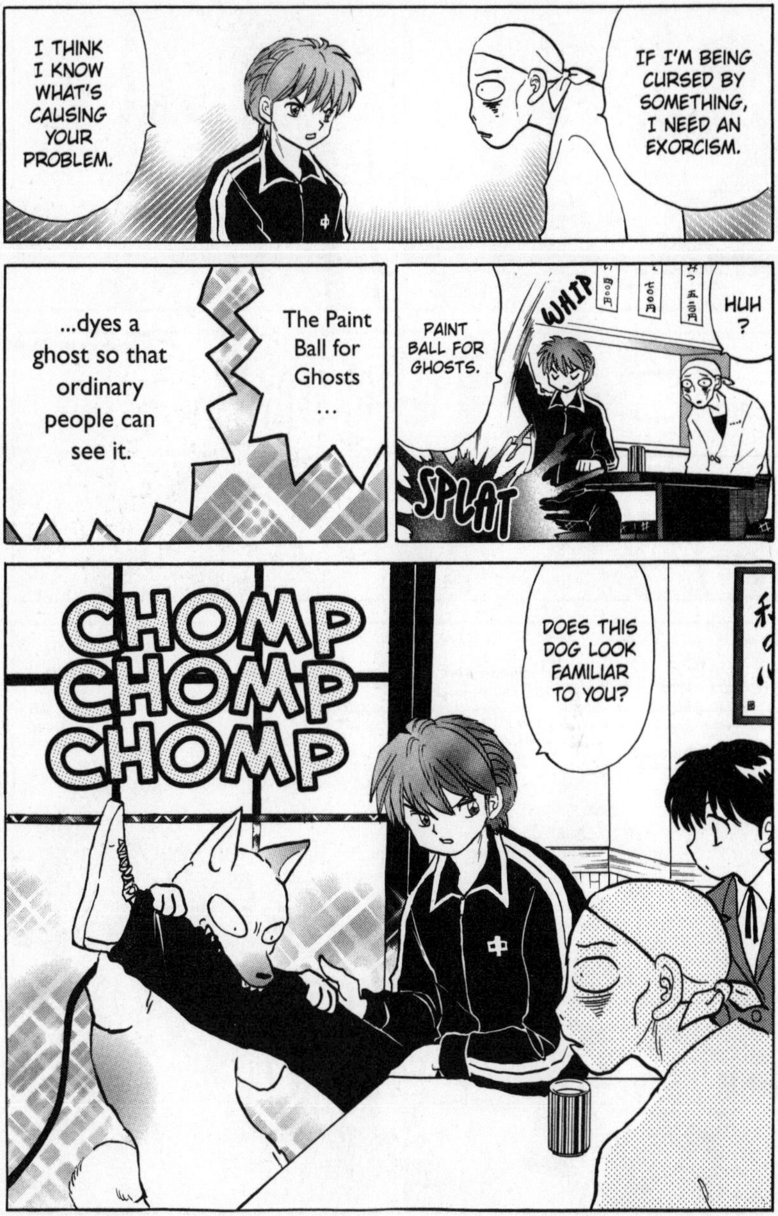
IF I'M BEING CURSED BY SOMETHING, I NEED AN EXORCISM.
I THINK I KNOW WHAT'S CAUSING YOUR PROBLEM.
HUH?
WHIP
PAINT BALL FOR GHOSTS.
SPLAT
The Paint Ball for Ghosts …
...dyes a ghost so that ordinary people can see it.
DOES THIS DOG LOOK FAMILIAR TO YOU?
CHOMP CHOMP CHOMP

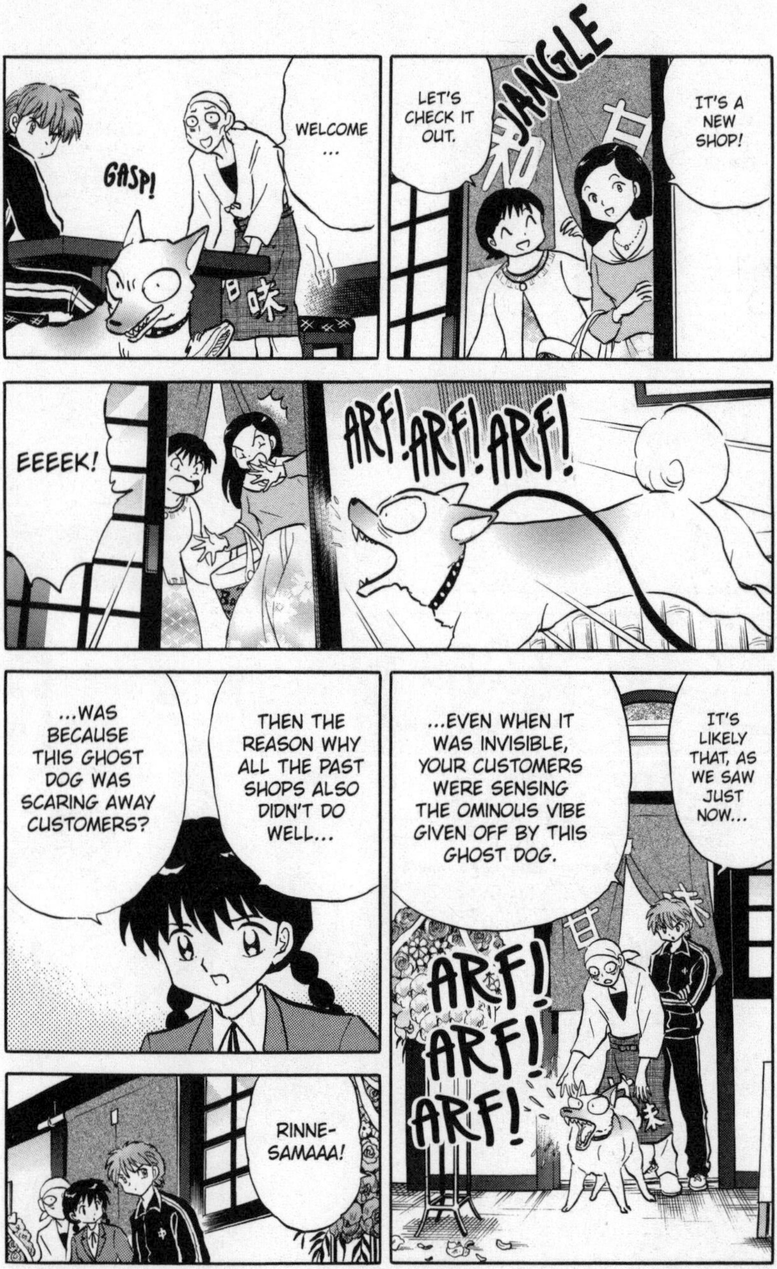
IT'S A NEW SHOP!
LET'S CHECK IT OUT.
JANGLE
WELCOME ...
GASP!
ARF! ARF! ARF!
EEEEK!
IT'S LIKELY THAT, AS WE SAW JUST NOW...
...EVEN WHEN IT WAS INVISIBLE, YOUR CUSTOMERS WERE SENSING THE OMINOUS VIBE GIVEN OFF BY THIS GHOST DOG.
ARF! ARF! ARF!
THEN THE REASON WHY ALL THE PAST SHOPS ALSO DIDN'T DO WELL...
...WAS BECAUSE THIS GHOST DOG WAS SCARING AWAY CUSTOMERS?
RINNE-SAMAAA!

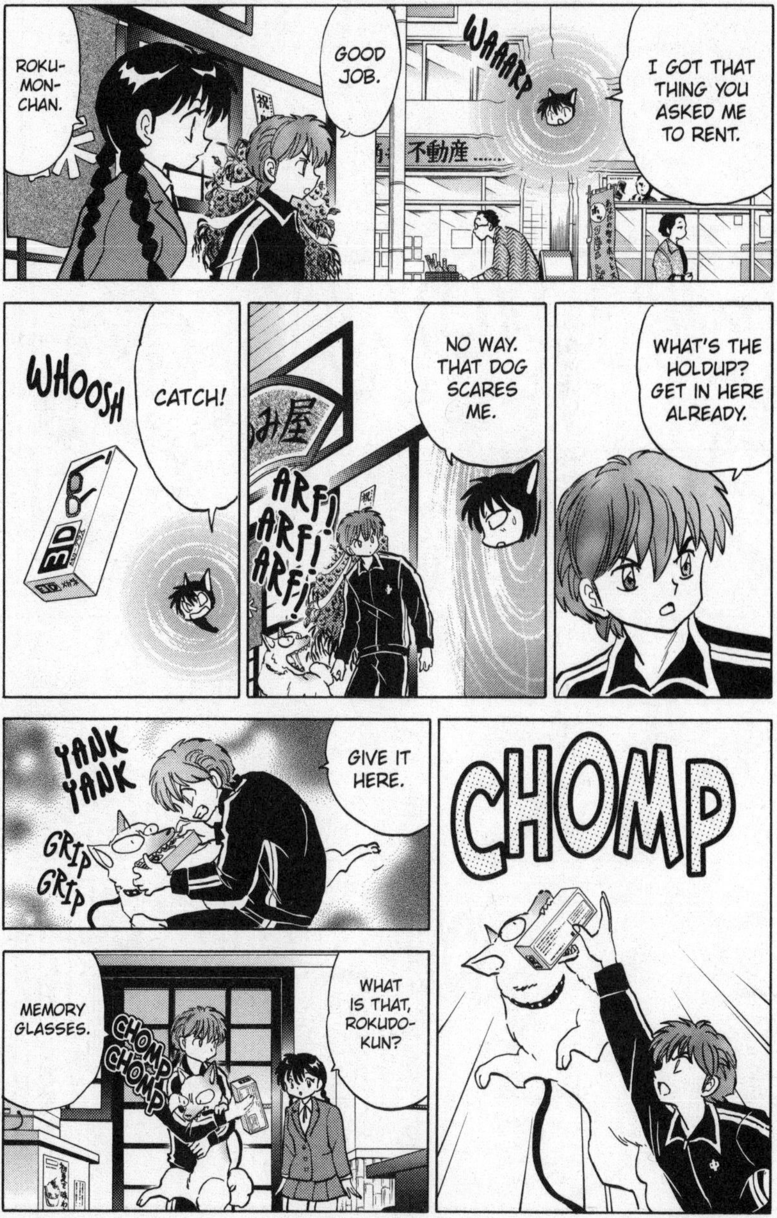
I GOT THAT THING YOU ASKED ME TO RENT.
WAAARP
不動産
GOOD JOB.
ROKU-MON-CHAN.
WHAT'S THE HOLDUP? GET IN HERE ALREADY.
NO WAY. THAT DOG SCARES ME.
ARF! ARF! ARF!
CATCH!
WHOOSH
3D
CHOMP
GIVE IT HERE.
YANK YANK
GRIP GRIP
WHAT IS THAT, ROKUDO-KUN?
CHOMP CHOMP
MEMORY GLASSES.

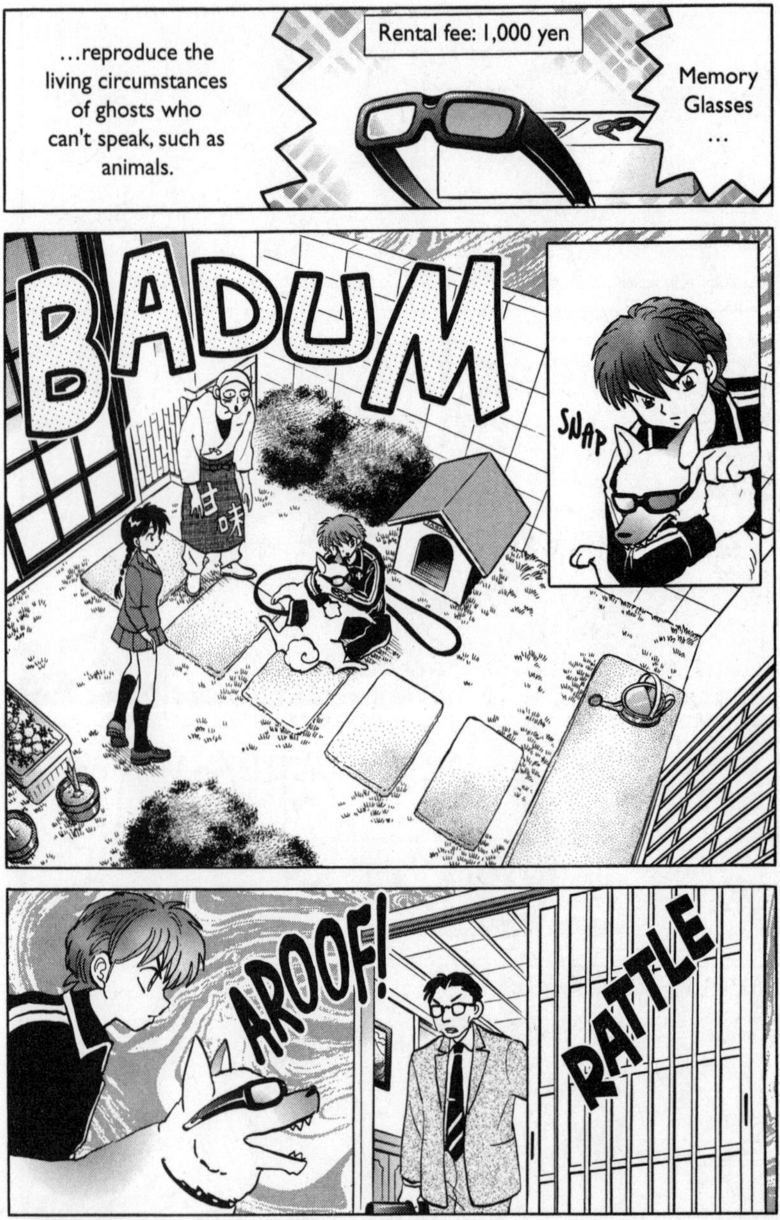
Memory Glasses ...
Rental fee: 1,000 yen
...reproduce the living circumstances of ghosts who can't speak, such as animals.
SNAP
BADUM
RATTLE
AROOF!

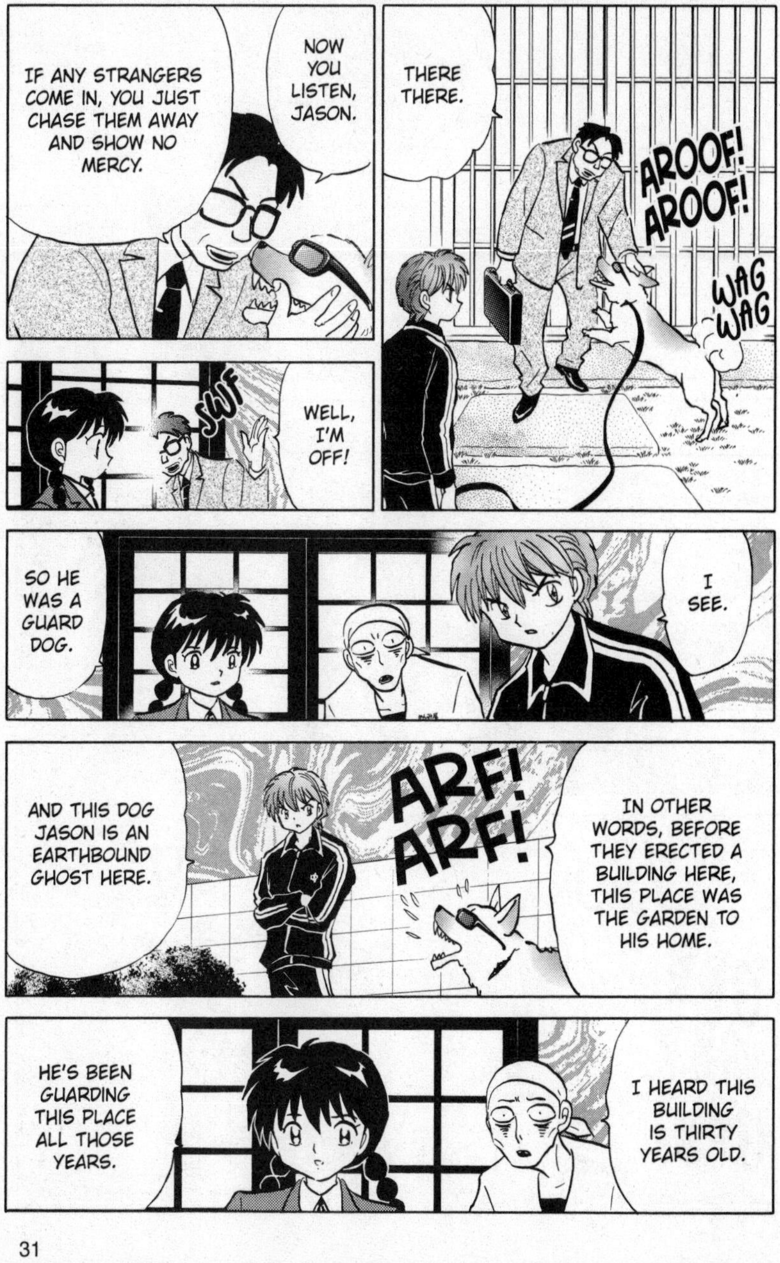
THERE THERE.
AROOF! AROOF!
WAG WAG
NOW YOU LISTEN, JASON.
IF ANY STRANGERS COME IN, YOU JUST CHASE THEM AWAY AND SHOW NO MERCY.
WELL, I'M OFF!
SWF
I SEE.
SO HE WAS A GUARD DOG.
IN OTHER WORDS, BEFORE THEY ERECTED A BUILDING HERE, THIS PLACE WAS THE GARDEN TO HIS HOME.
ARF! ARF!
AND THIS DOG JASON IS AN EARTHBOUND GHOST HERE.
I HEARD THIS BUILDING IS THIRTY YEARS OLD.
HE'S BEEN GUARDING THIS PLACE ALL THOSE YEARS.

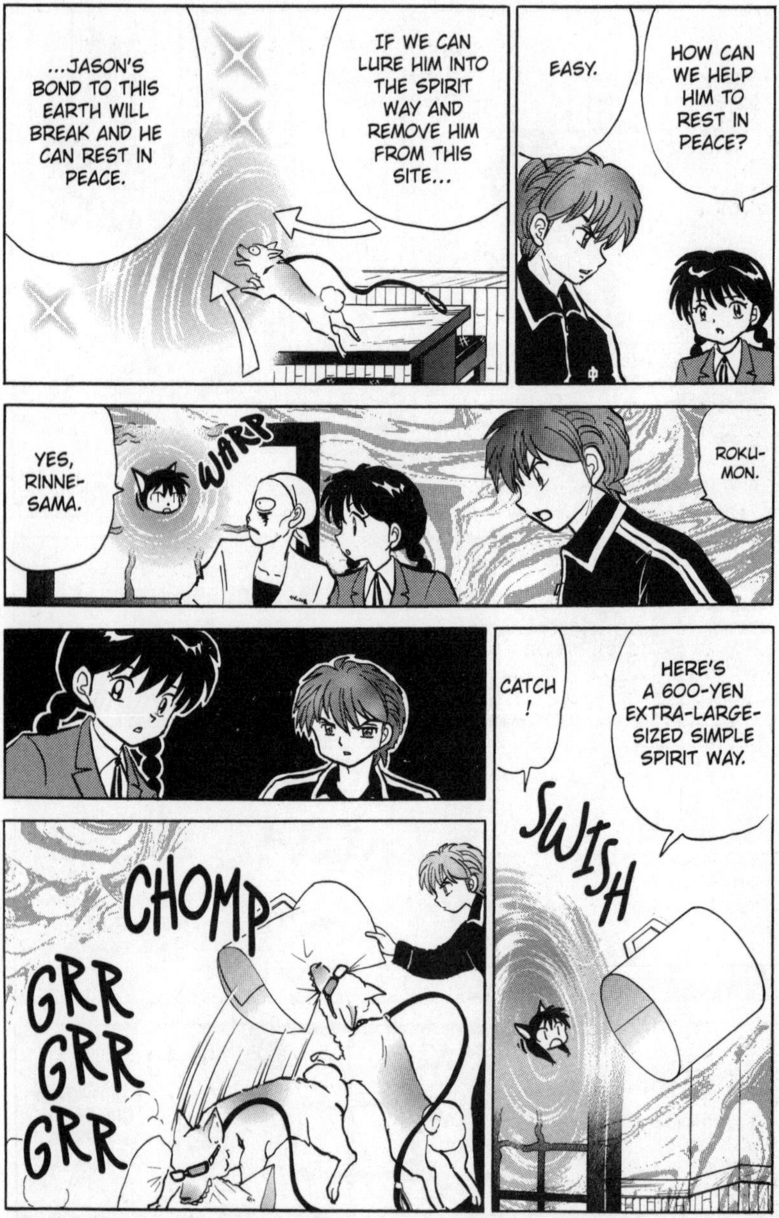
HOW CAN WE HELP HIM TO REST IN PEACE?
EASY.
IF WE CAN LURE HIM INTO THE SPIRIT WAY AND REMOVE HIM FROM THIS SITE...
...JASON'S BOND TO THIS EARTH WILL BREAK AND HE CAN REST IN PEACE.
ROKU-MON.
WARP
YES, RINNE-SAMA.
HERE'S A 600-YEN EXTRA-LARGE-SIZED SIMPLE SPIRIT WAY.
CATCH!
SWISH
CHOMP
GRR
GRR
GRR

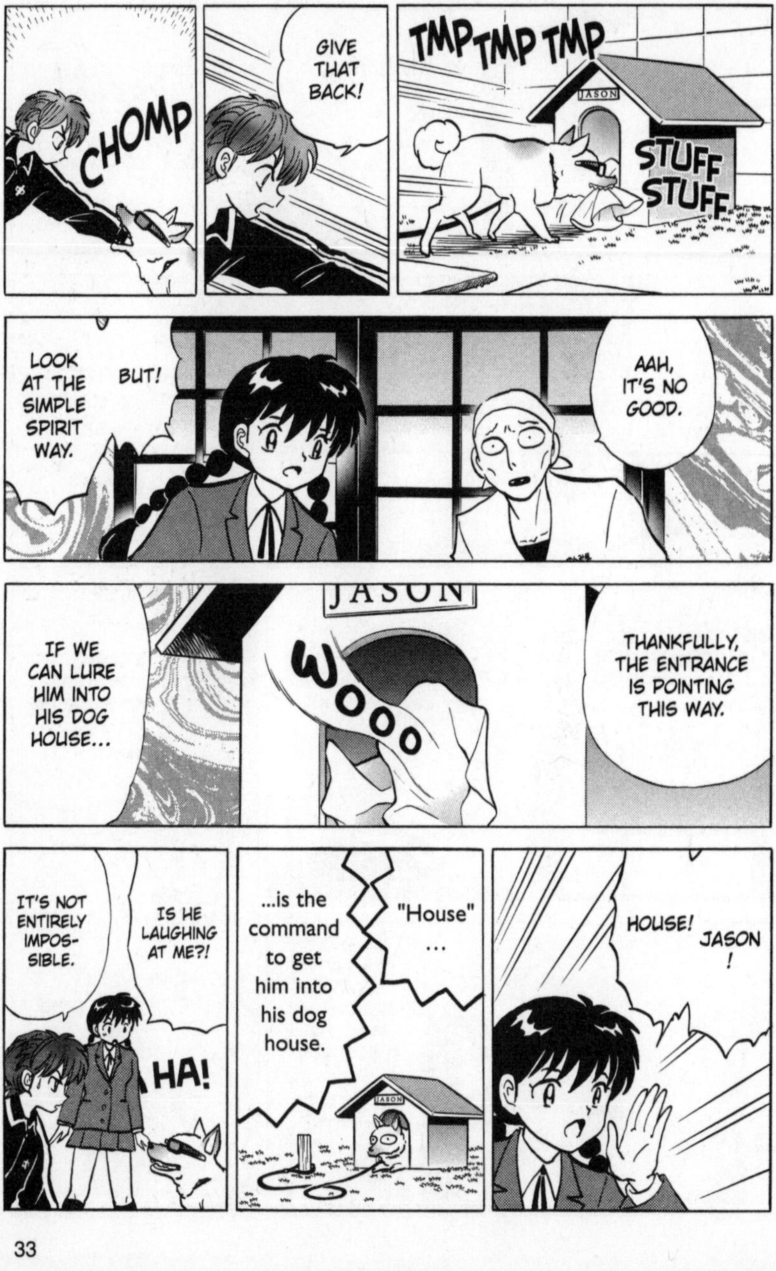
TMP TMP TMP
STUFF STUFF
GIVE THAT BACK!
CHOMP
AAH, IT'S NO GOOD.
BUT!
LOOK AT THE SIMPLE SPIRIT WAY.
THANKFULLY, THE ENTRANCE IS POINTING THIS WAY.
JASON
WOOO
IF WE CAN LURE HIM INTO HIS DOG HOUSE...
JASON !
HOUSE!
"House" ...
...is the command to get him into his dog house.
IS HE LAUGHING AT ME?!
IT'S NOT ENTIRELY IMPOS-SIBLE.
HA!

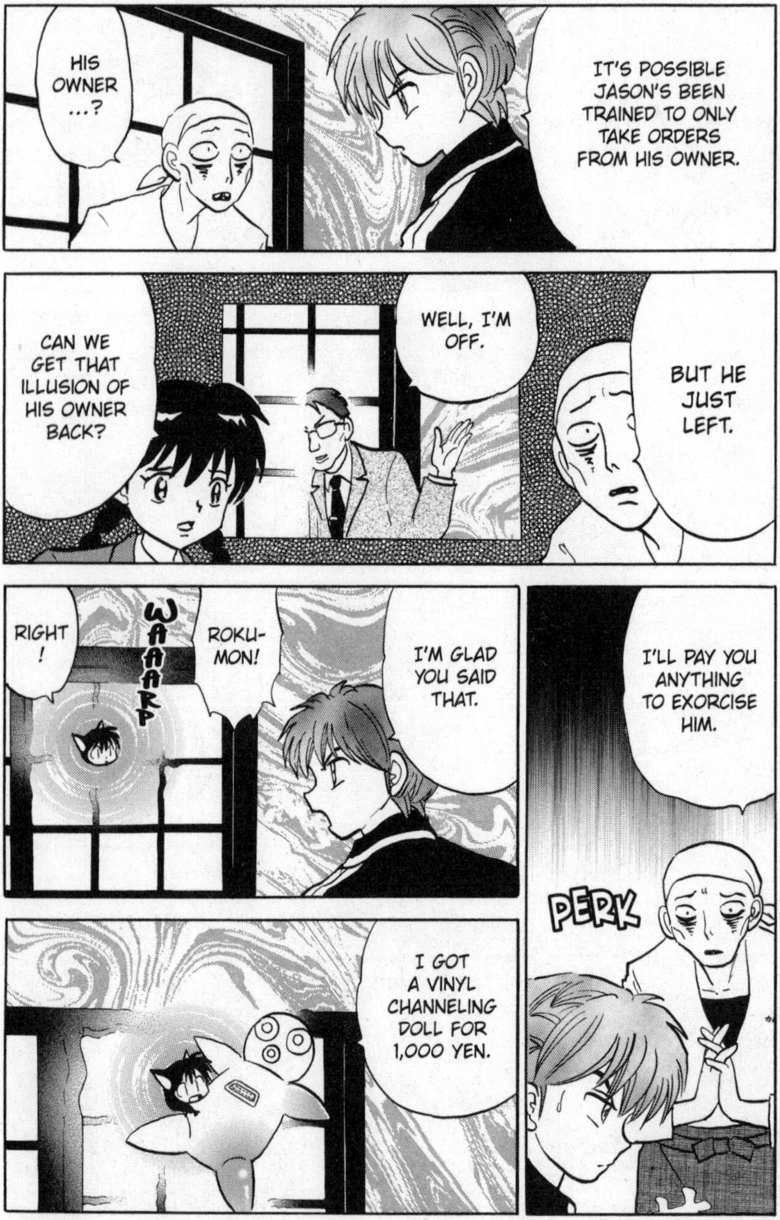
IT'S POSSIBLE JASON'S BEEN TRAINED TO ONLY TAKE ORDERS FROM HIS OWNER.
HIS OWNER ...?
BUT HE JUST LEFT.
WELL, I'M OFF.
CAN WE GET THAT ILLUSION OF HIS OWNER BACK?
I'LL PAY YOU ANYTHING TO EXORCISE HIM.
PERK
I'M GLAD YOU SAID THAT.
ROKU-MON!
WAAARP
RIGHT!
I GOT A VINYL CHANNELING DOLL FOR 1,000 YEN.

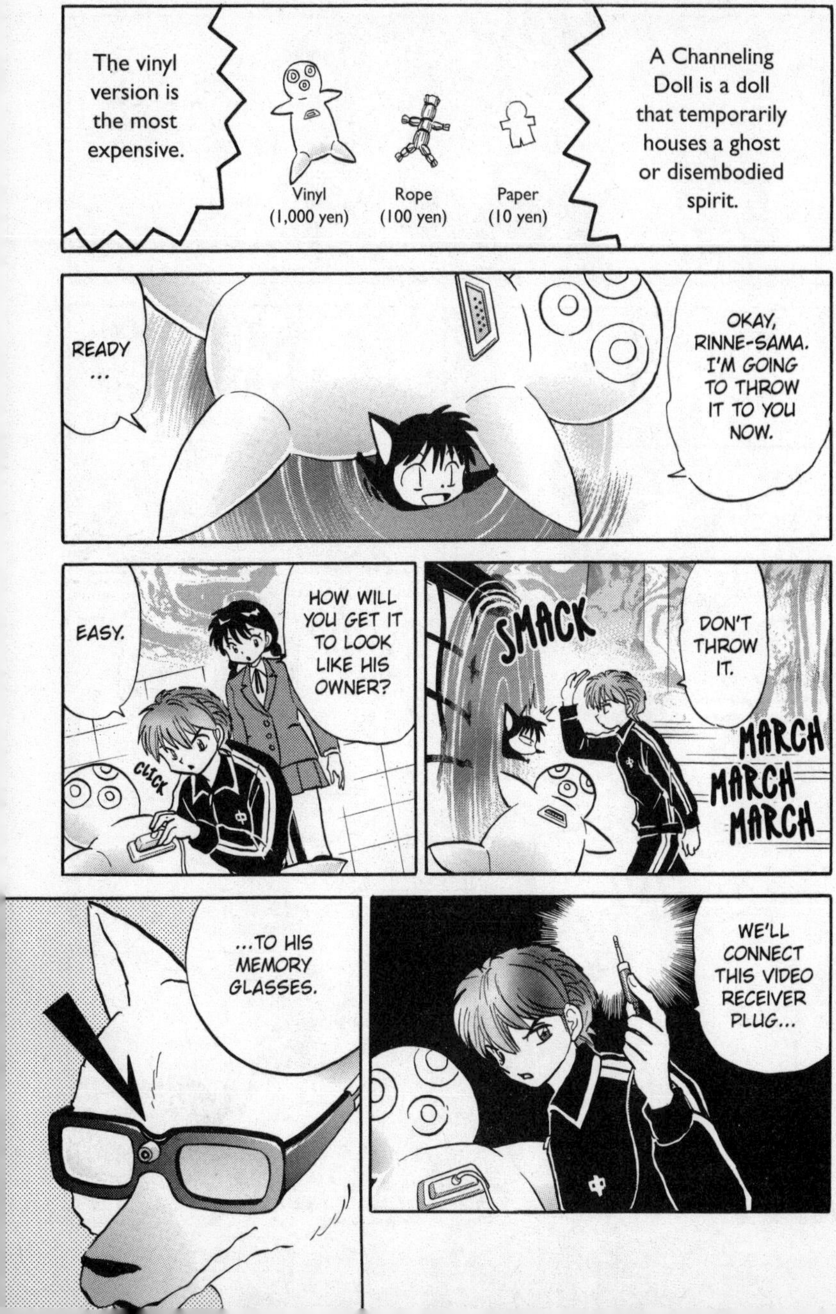
A Channeling Doll is a doll that temporarily houses a ghost or disembodied spirit.
Paper (10 yen)
Rope (100 yen)
Vinyl (1,000 yen)
The vinyl version is the most expensive.
OKAY, RINNE-SAMA. I'M GOING TO THROW IT TO YOU NOW.
READY ...
DON'T THROW IT.
SMACK
MARCH MARCH MARCH
HOW WILL YOU GET IT TO LOOK LIKE HIS OWNER?
EASY.
CLICK
WE'LL CONNECT THIS VIDEO RECEIVER PLUG...
...TO HIS MEMORY GLASSES.

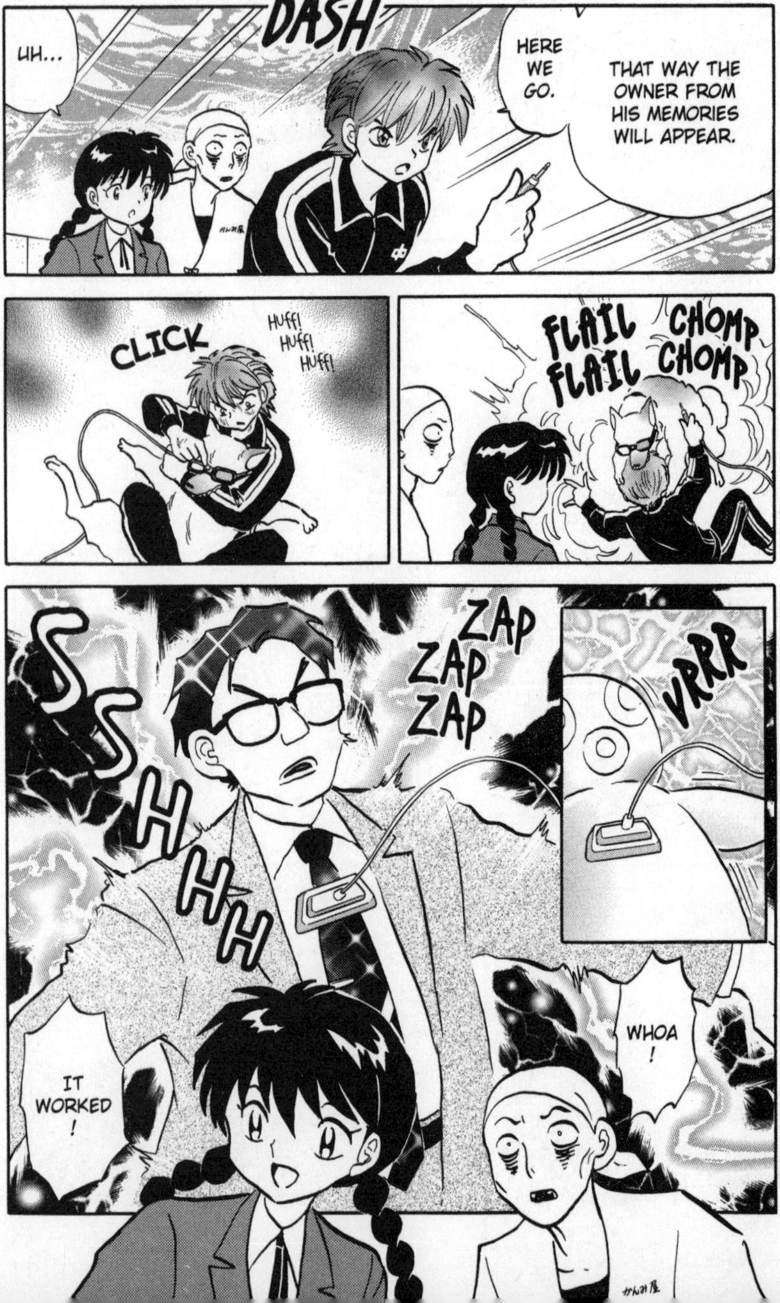
THAT WAY THE OWNER FROM HIS MEMORIES WILL APPEAR.
HERE WE GO.
DASH
UH...
CHOMP CHOMP
FLAIL FLAIL
HUFF! HUFF! HUFF!
CLICK
VRRR
ZAP ZAP ZAP
SSHHHH
WHOA!
IT WORKED!

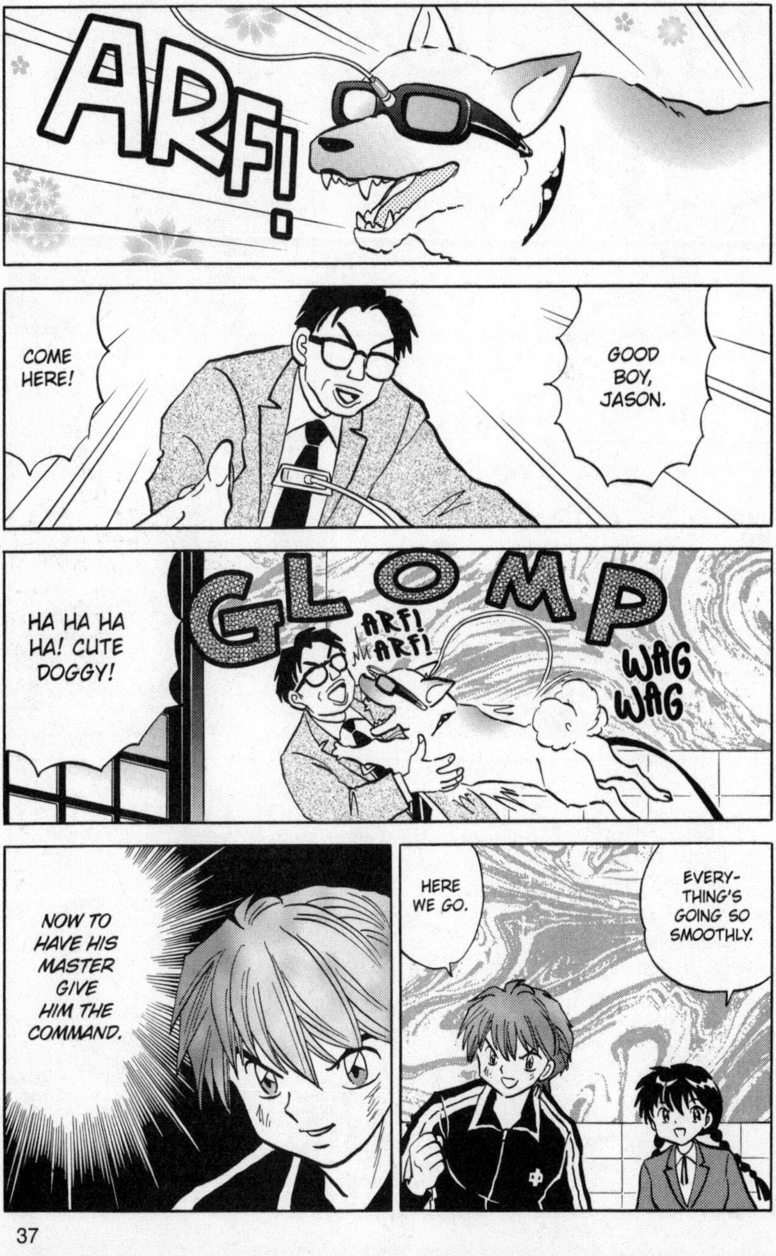
ARF!
GOOD BOY, JASON.
COME HERE!
GLOMP
WAG WAG
ARF! ARF!
HA HA HA HA! CUTE DOGGY!
EVERY-THING'S GOING SO SMOOTHLY.
HERE WE GO.
NOW TO HAVE HIS MASTER GIVE HIM THE COMMAND.

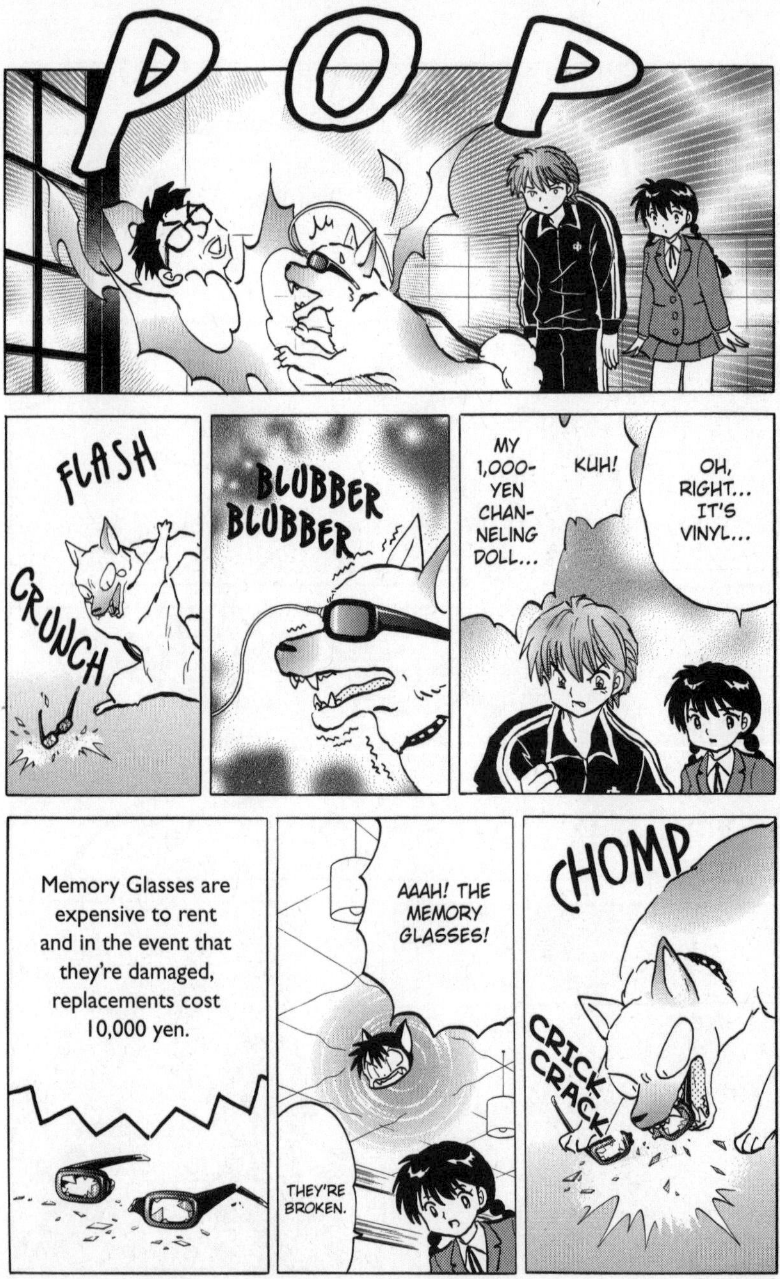
POP
OH, RIGHT... IT'S VINYL...
KUH!
MY 1,000-YEN CHAN-NELING DOLL...
BLUBBER BLUBBER
FLASH
CRUNCH
CHOMP
CRICK CRACK
AAAH! THE MEMORY GLASSES!
THEY'RE BROKEN.
Memory Glasses are expensive to rent and in the event that they're damaged, replacements cost 10,000 yen.

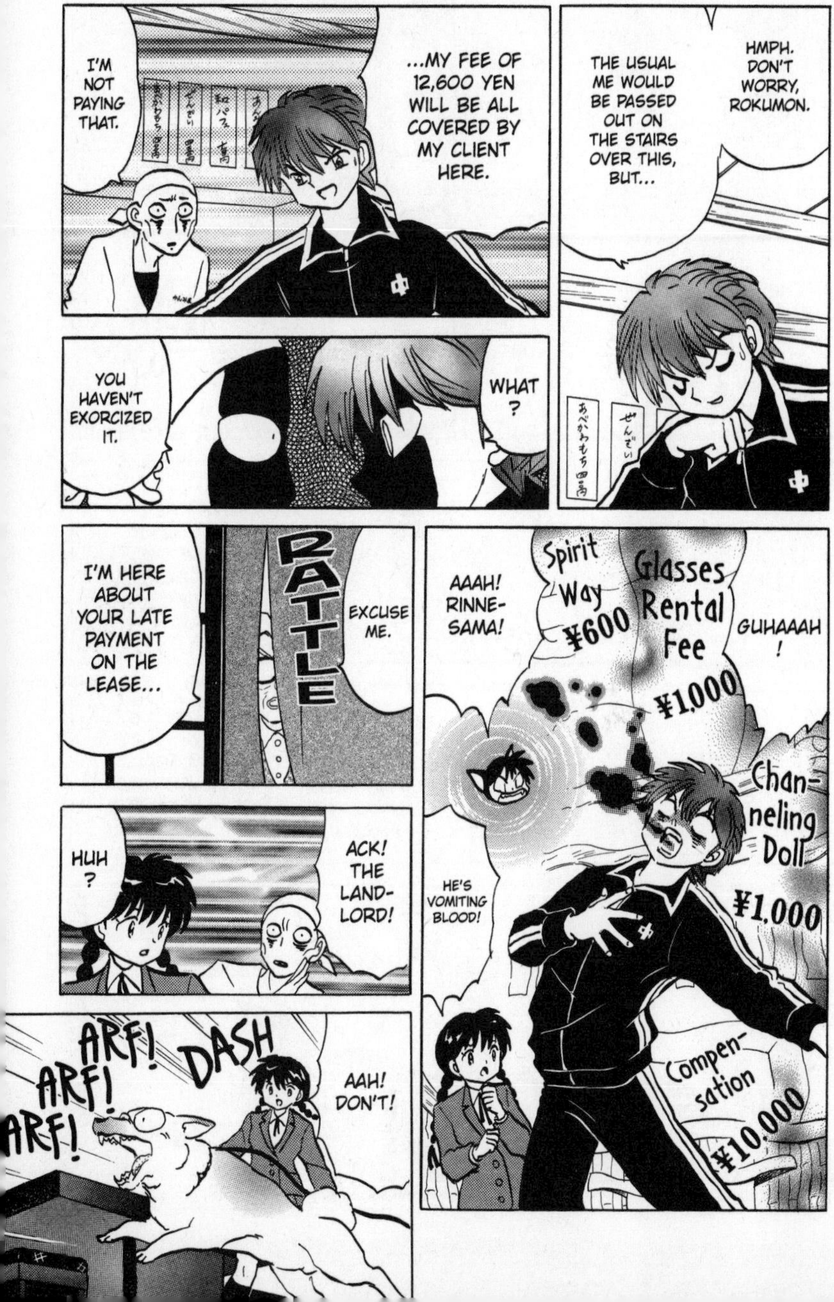
HMPH. DON'T WORRY, ROKUMON.
THE USUAL ME WOULD BE PASSED OUT ON THE STAIRS OVER THIS, BUT...
...MY FEE OF 12,600 YEN WILL BE ALL COVERED BY MY CLIENT HERE.
I'M NOT PAYING THAT.
WHAT?
YOU HAVEN'T EXORCIZED IT.
GUHAAAH!
Glasses Rental Fee ¥1,000
Spirit Way ¥600
AAAH! RINNE-SAMA!
Channeling Doll ¥1,000
HE'S VOMITING BLOOD!
Compensation ¥10,000
EXCUSE ME.
RATTLE
I'M HERE ABOUT YOUR LATE PAYMENT ON THE LEASE...
ACK! THE LANDLORD!
HUH?
AAH! DON'T!
DASH
ARF! ARF! ARF!

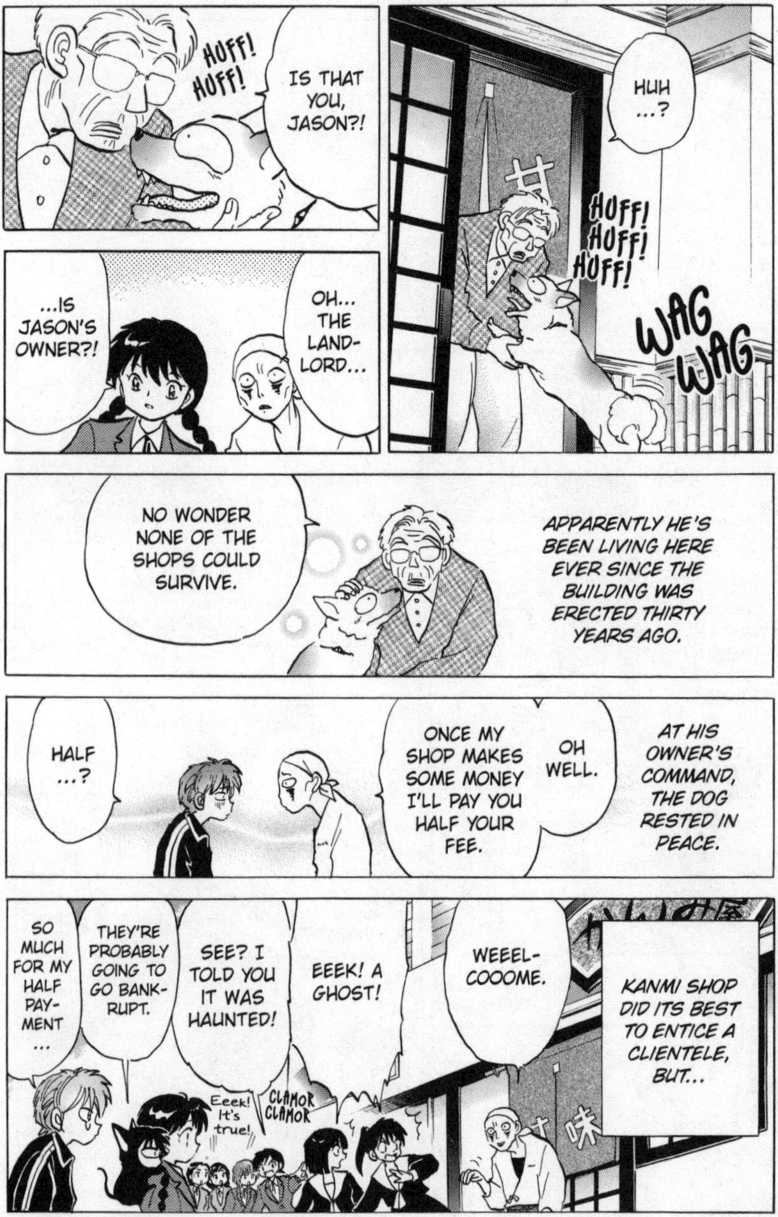
HUH ...?
HUFF! HUFF! HUFF!
WAG WAG
IS THAT YOU, JASON?!
HUFF! HUFF!
OH... THE LANDLORD...
...IS JASON'S OWNER?!
APPARENTLY HE'S BEEN LIVING HERE EVER SINCE THE BUILDING WAS ERECTED THIRTY YEARS AGO.
NO WONDER NONE OF THE SHOPS COULD SURVIVE.
AT HIS OWNER'S COMMAND, THE DOG RESTED IN PEACE.
OH WELL.
ONCE MY SHOP MAKES SOME MONEY I'LL PAY YOU HALF YOUR FEE.
HALF ...?
KANMI SHOP DID ITS BEST TO ENTICE A CLIENTELE, BUT...
WEEEL-COOOME.
EEEK! A GHOST!
SEE? I TOLD YOU IT WAS HAUNTED!
CLAMOR CLAMOR
Eeek! It's true!
THEY'RE PROBABLY GOING TO GO BANK-RUPT.
SO MUCH FOR MY HALF PAY-MENT ...

CHAPTER 191: BRING A DATE

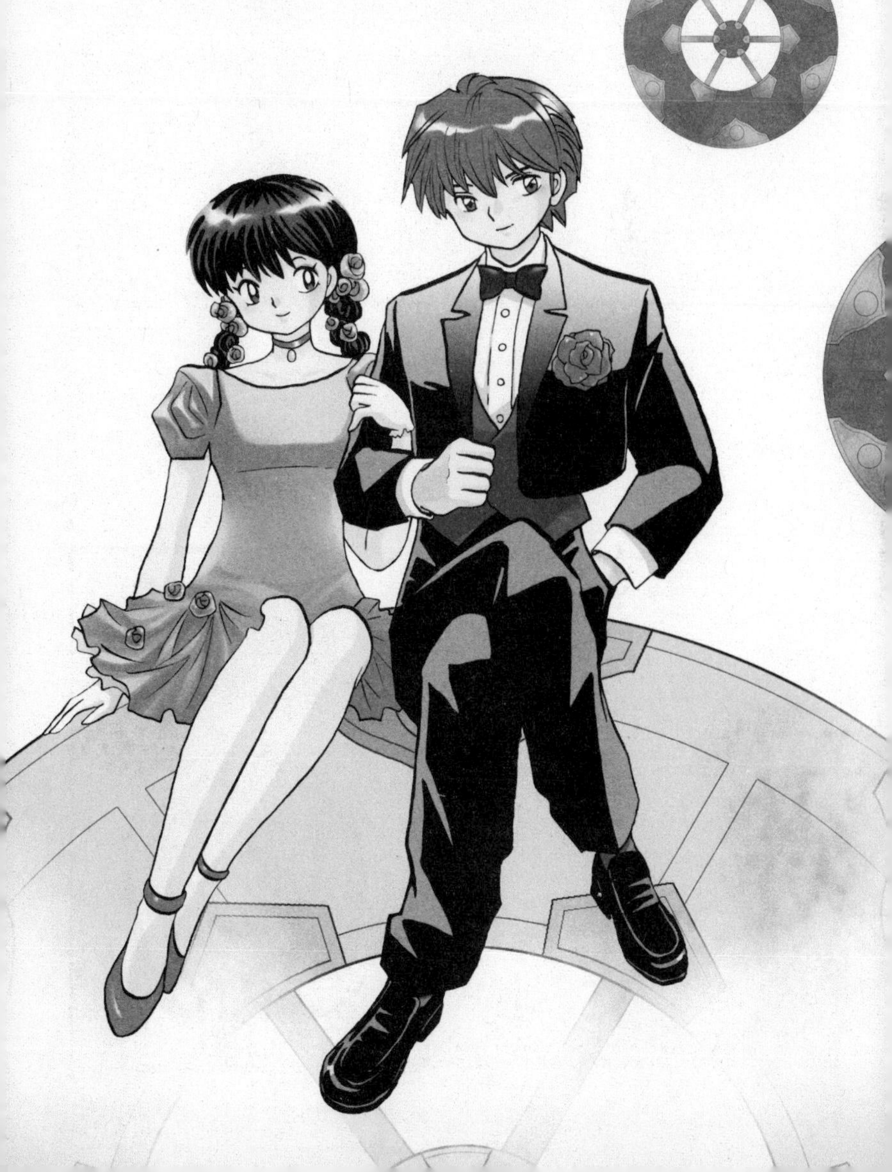

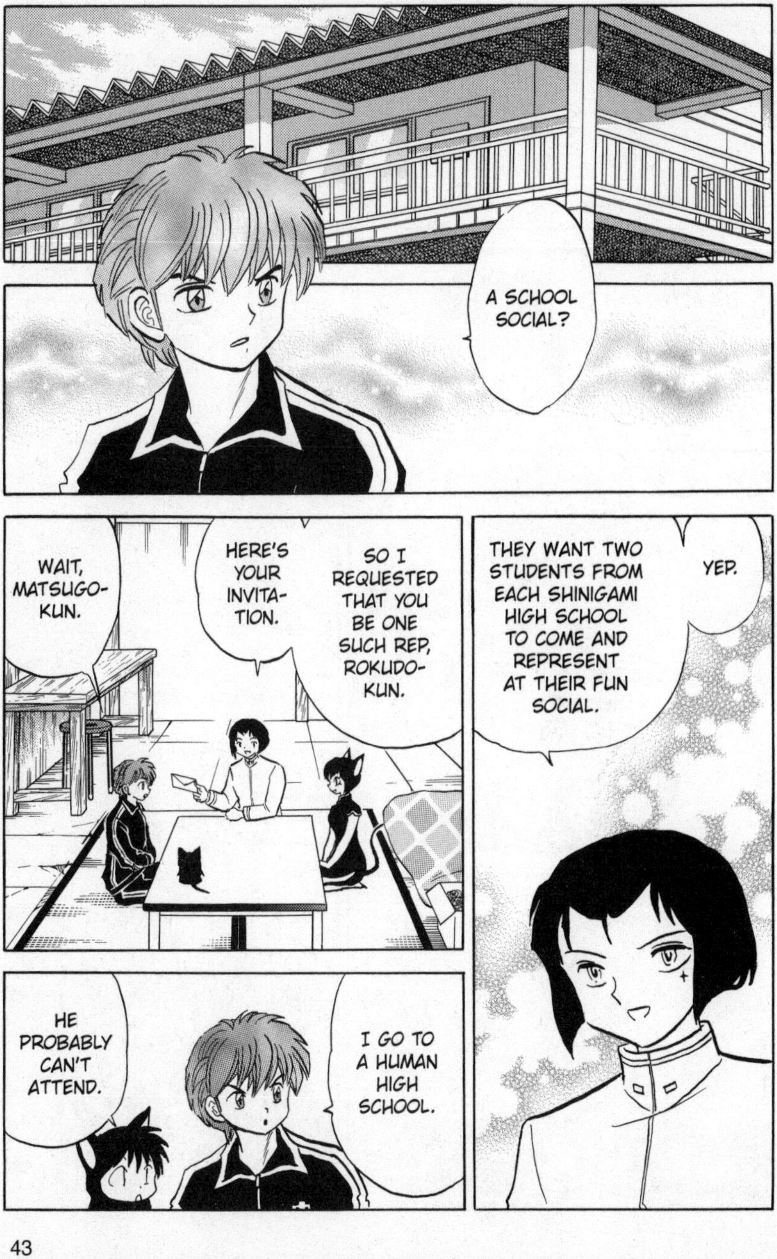
A SCHOOL SOCIAL?
YEP.
THEY WANT TWO STUDENTS FROM EACH SHINIGAMI HIGH SCHOOL TO COME AND REPRESENT AT THEIR FUN SOCIAL.
SO I REQUESTED THAT YOU BE ONE SUCH REP, ROKUDO-KUN.
HERE'S YOUR INVITA-TION.
WAIT, MATSUGO-KUN.
I GO TO A HUMAN HIGH SCHOOL.
HE PROBABLY CAN'T ATTEND.

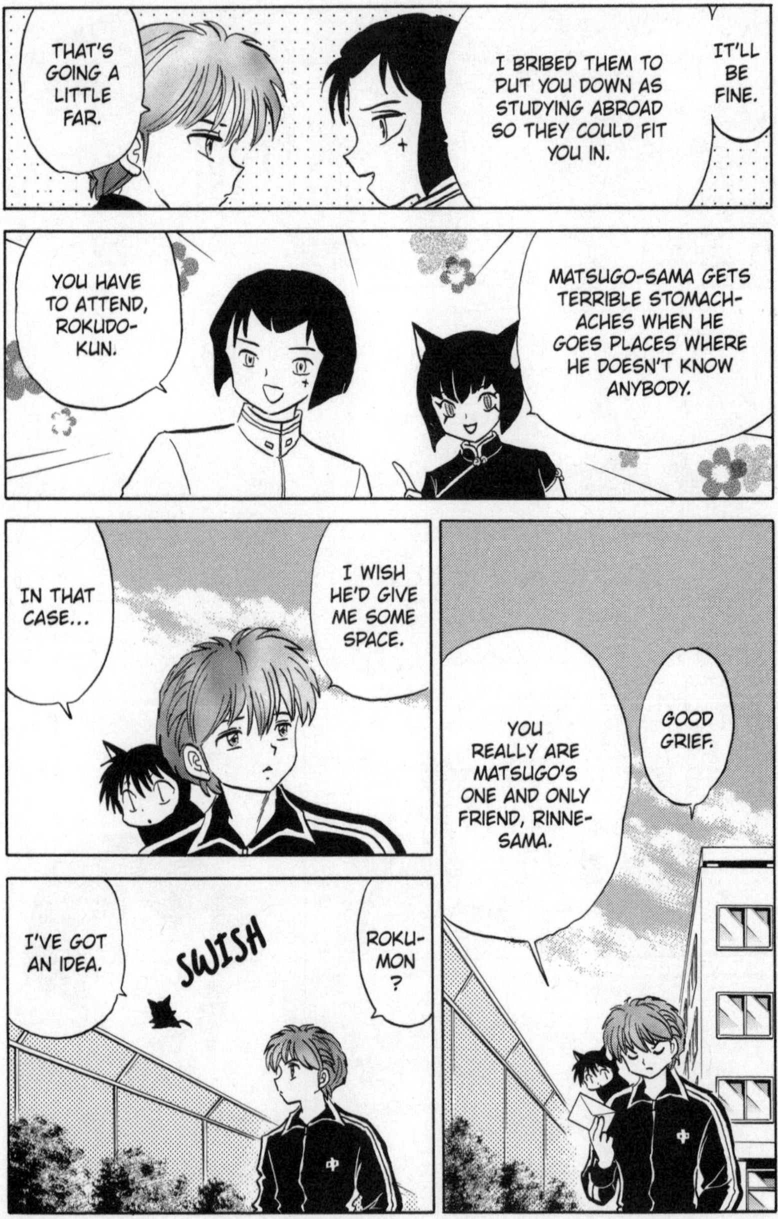
IT'LL BE FINE.
I BRIBED THEM TO PUT YOU DOWN AS STUDYING ABROAD SO THEY COULD FIT YOU IN.
THAT'S GOING A LITTLE FAR.
MATSUGO-SAMA GETS TERRIBLE STOMACH-ACHES WHEN HE GOES PLACES WHERE HE DOESN'T KNOW ANYBODY.
YOU HAVE TO ATTEND, ROKUDO-KUN.
GOOD GRIEF.
YOU REALLY ARE MATSUGO'S ONE AND ONLY FRIEND, RINNE-SAMA.
I WISH HE'D GIVE ME SOME SPACE.
IN THAT CASE...
ROKU-MON?
SWISH
I'VE GOT AN IDEA.

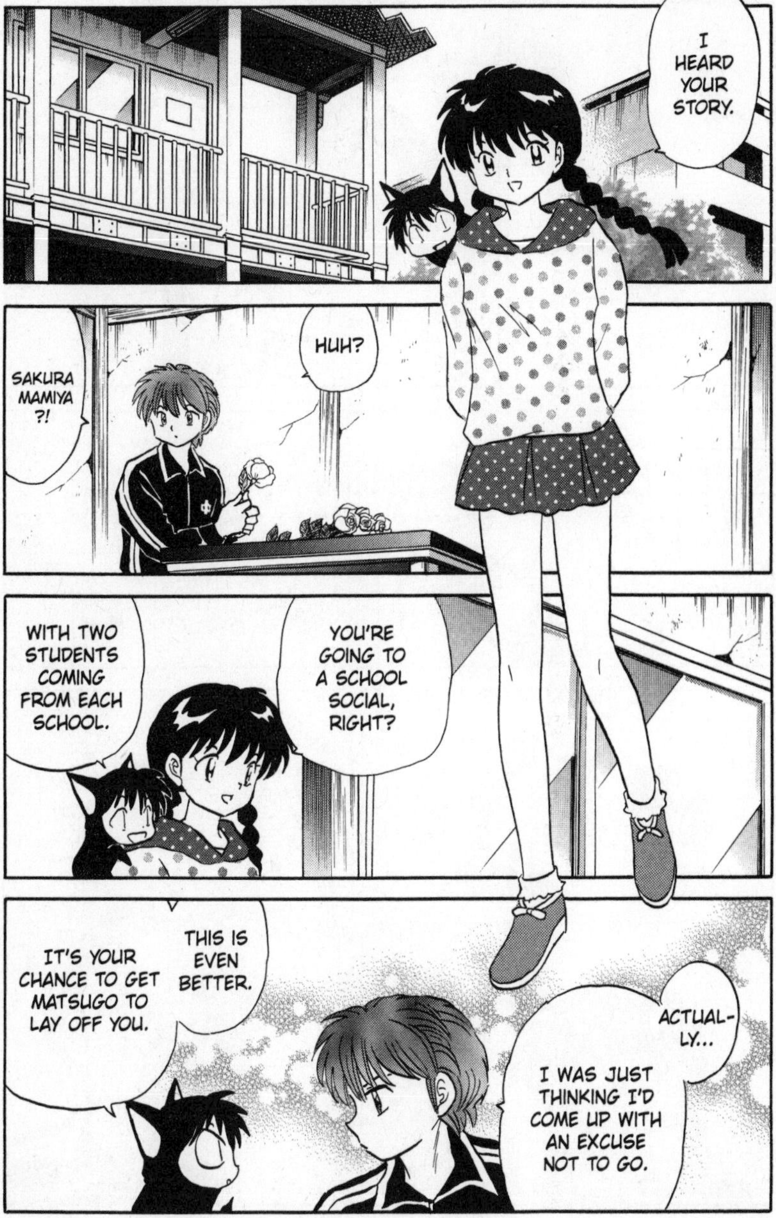
I HEARD YOUR STORY.
HUH?
SAKURA MAMIYA?!
YOU'RE GOING TO A SCHOOL SOCIAL, RIGHT?
WITH TWO STUDENTS COMING FROM EACH SCHOOL.
ACTUAL-LY...
I WAS JUST THINKING I'D COME UP WITH AN EXCUSE NOT TO GO.
THIS IS EVEN BETTER.
IT'S YOUR CHANCE TO GET MATSUGO TO LAY OFF YOU.

I DIDN'T WANT TO MISS THIS OPPORTUNITY TO BRING MY GIRLFRIEND.
G-GIRL-FRIEND ?!
I SEE. WELL, THEN.
I'D HATE TO INTER-RUPT.
MM-HM.
IF YOU BROUGHT A GUY FRIEND IT MIGHT MAKE HIM FEEL RIVALROUS.
WITH A GIRL ON YOUR ARM, HE'S SURE TO BACK DOWN.
S... SAKURA MAMIYA...
...WILL BE MY GIRL-FRIEND ?!
IF...IF IT'S ALL RIGHT WITH YOU!
IT'S FINE.
I'LL DO MY BEST TO ACT LIKE YOUR GIRL-FRIEND.

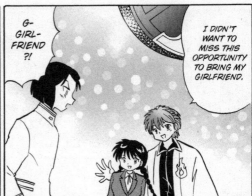

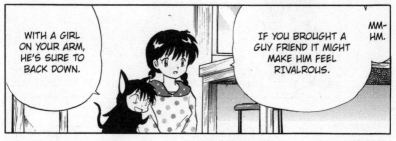

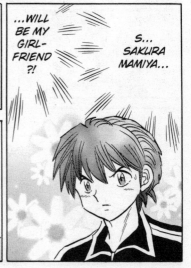

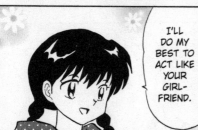

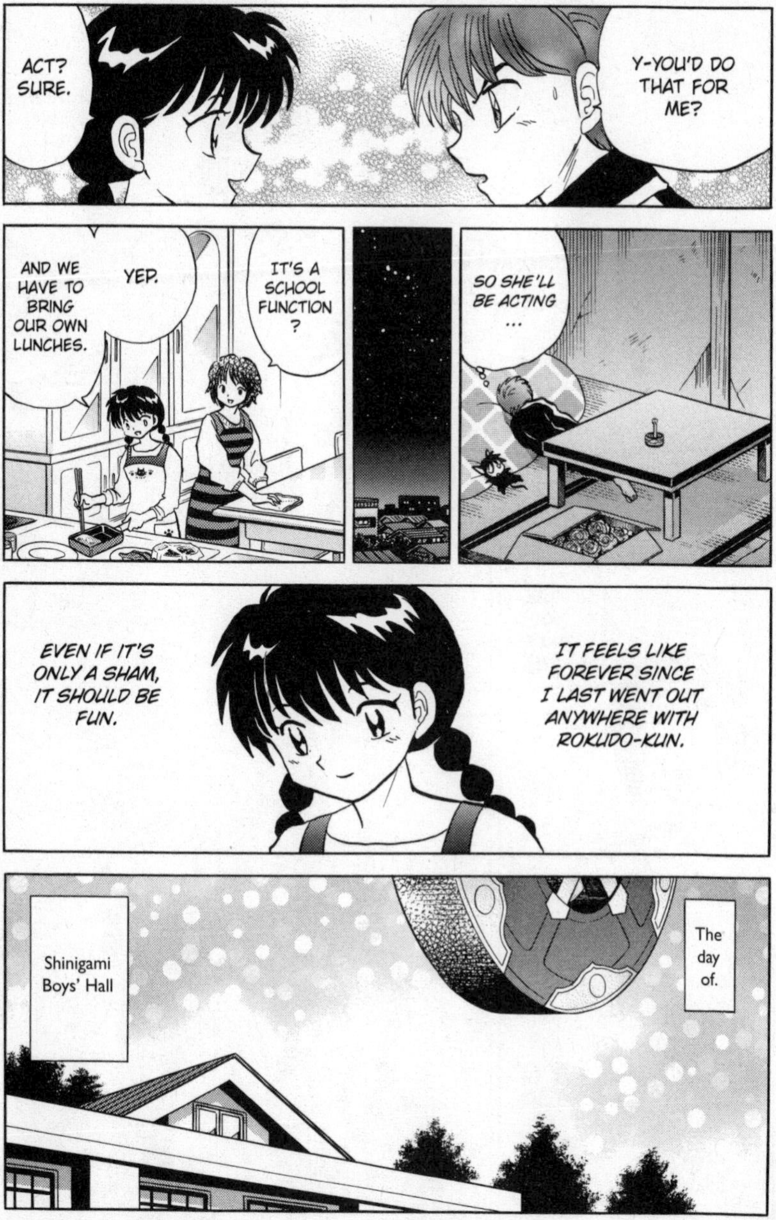
Y-YOU'D DO THAT FOR ME?
ACT? SURE.
SO SHE'LL BE ACTING ...
IT'S A SCHOOL FUNCTION ?
YEP.
AND WE HAVE TO BRING OUR OWN LUNCHES.
IT FEELS LIKE FOREVER SINCE I LAST WENT OUT ANYWHERE WITH ROKUDO-KUN.
EVEN IF IT'S ONLY A SHAM, IT SHOULD BE FUN.
The day of.
Shinigami Boys' Hall

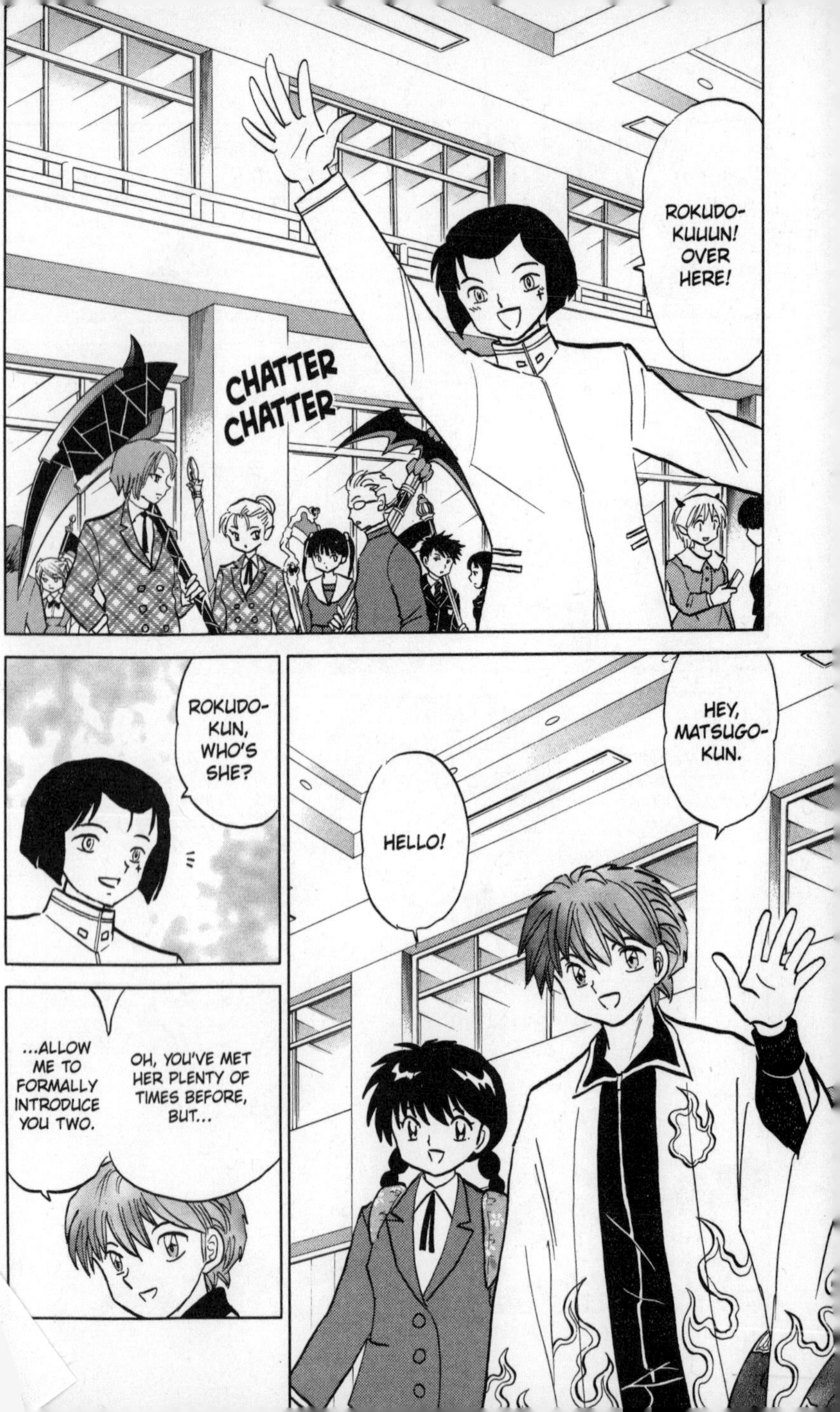
ROKUDO-KUUUN! OVER HERE!
CHATTER CHATTER
HEY, MATSUGO-KUN.
HELLO!
ROKUDO-KUN, WHO'S SHE?
OH, YOU'VE MET HER PLENTY OF TIMES BEFORE, BUT...
...ALLOW ME TO FORMALLY INTRODUCE YOU TWO.

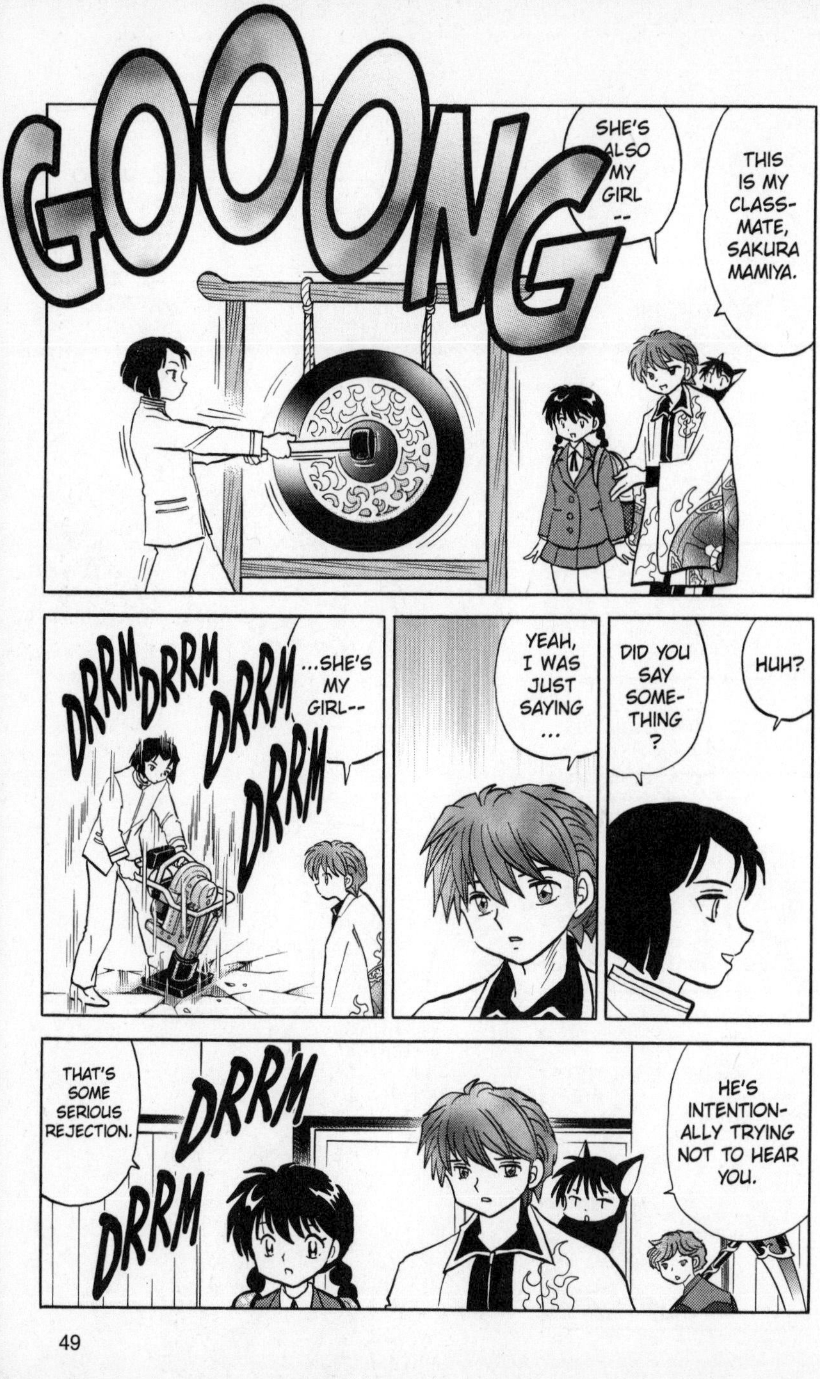
THIS IS MY CLASSMATE, SAKURA MAMIYA.
SHE'S ALSO MY GIRL --
GOOONG
HUH?
DID YOU SAY SOMETHING?
YEAH, I WAS JUST SAYING ...
...SHE'S MY GIRL--
DRRM DRRM DRRM DRRM
HE'S INTENTIONALLY TRYING NOT TO HEAR YOU.
DRRM DRRM
THAT'S SOME SERIOUS REJECTION.

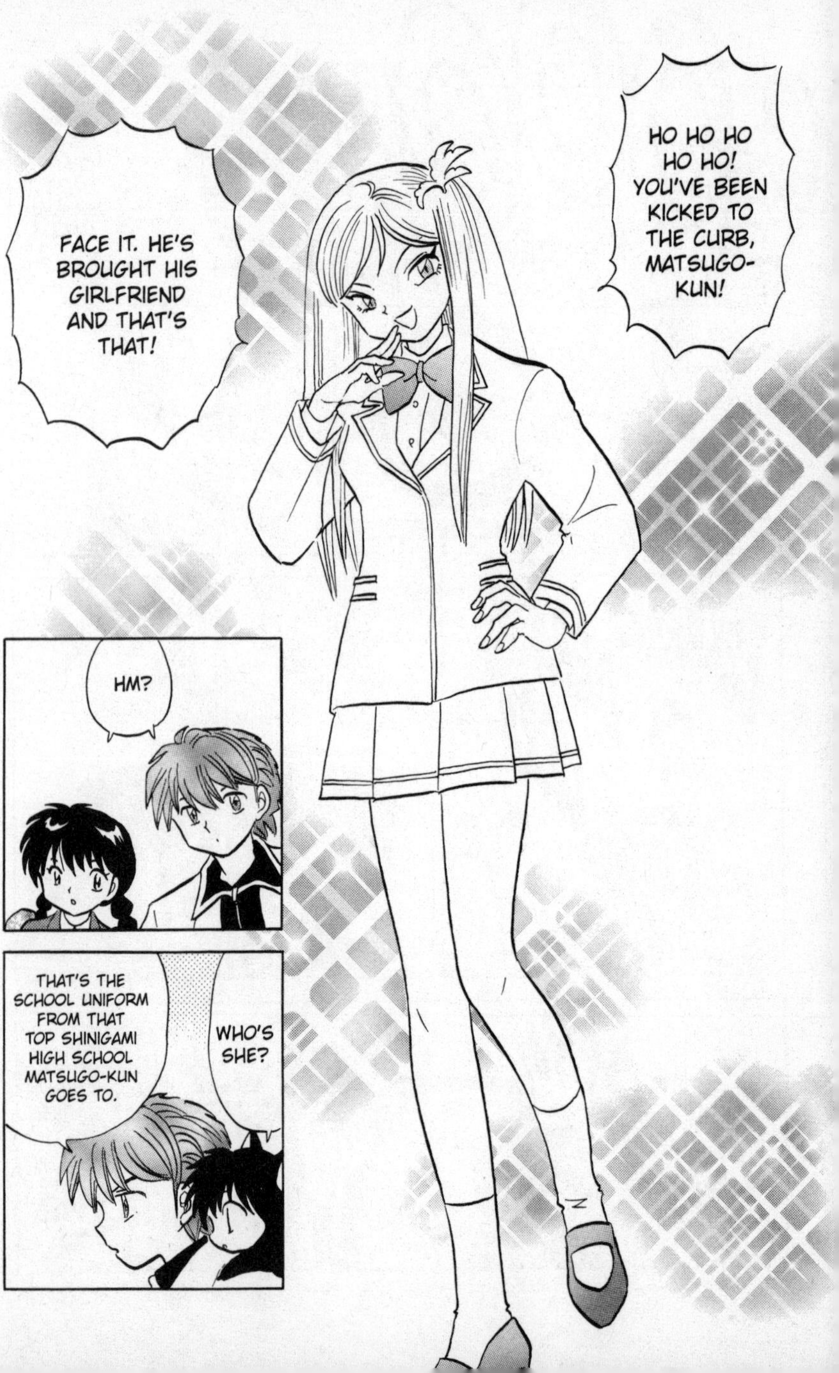
HO HO HO HO HO! YOU'VE BEEN KICKED TO THE CURB, MATSUGO-KUN!
FACE IT. HE'S BROUGHT HIS GIRLFRIEND AND THAT'S THAT!
HM?
WHO'S SHE?
THAT'S THE SCHOOL UNIFORM FROM THAT TOP SHINIGAMI HIGH SCHOOL MATSUGO-KUN GOES TO.

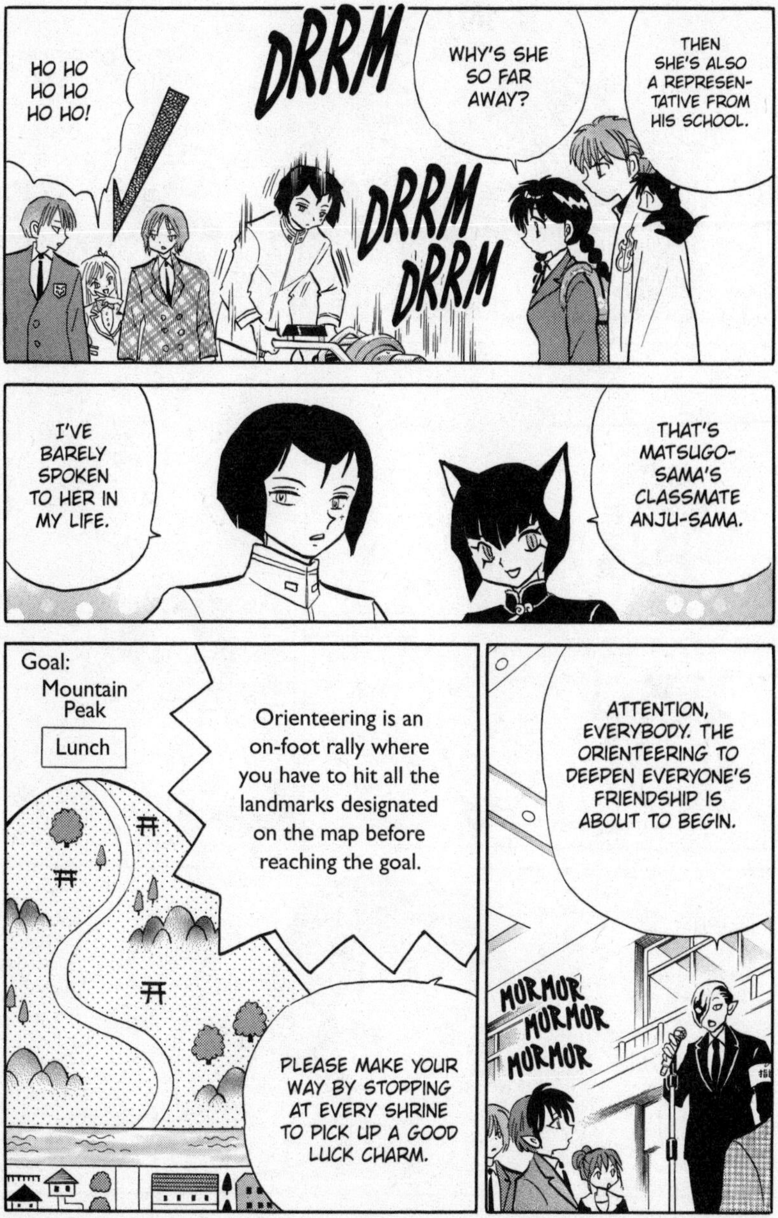
THEN SHE'S ALSO A REPRESENTATIVE FROM HIS SCHOOL.
WHY'S SHE SO FAR AWAY?
DRRM
DRRM DRRM DRRM
HO HO HO HO HO HO!
THAT'S MATSUGO-SAMA'S CLASSMATE ANJU-SAMA.
I'VE BARELY SPOKEN TO HER IN MY LIFE.
ATTENTION, EVERYBODY. THE ORIENTEERING TO DEEPEN EVERYONE'S FRIENDSHIP IS ABOUT TO BEGIN.
MORMOR MORMOR MORMOR
Orienteering is an on-foot rally where you have to hit all the landmarks designated on the map before reaching the goal.
Goal: Mountain Peak
Lunch
PLEASE MAKE YOUR WAY BY STOPPING AT EVERY SHRINE TO PICK UP A GOOD LUCK CHARM.

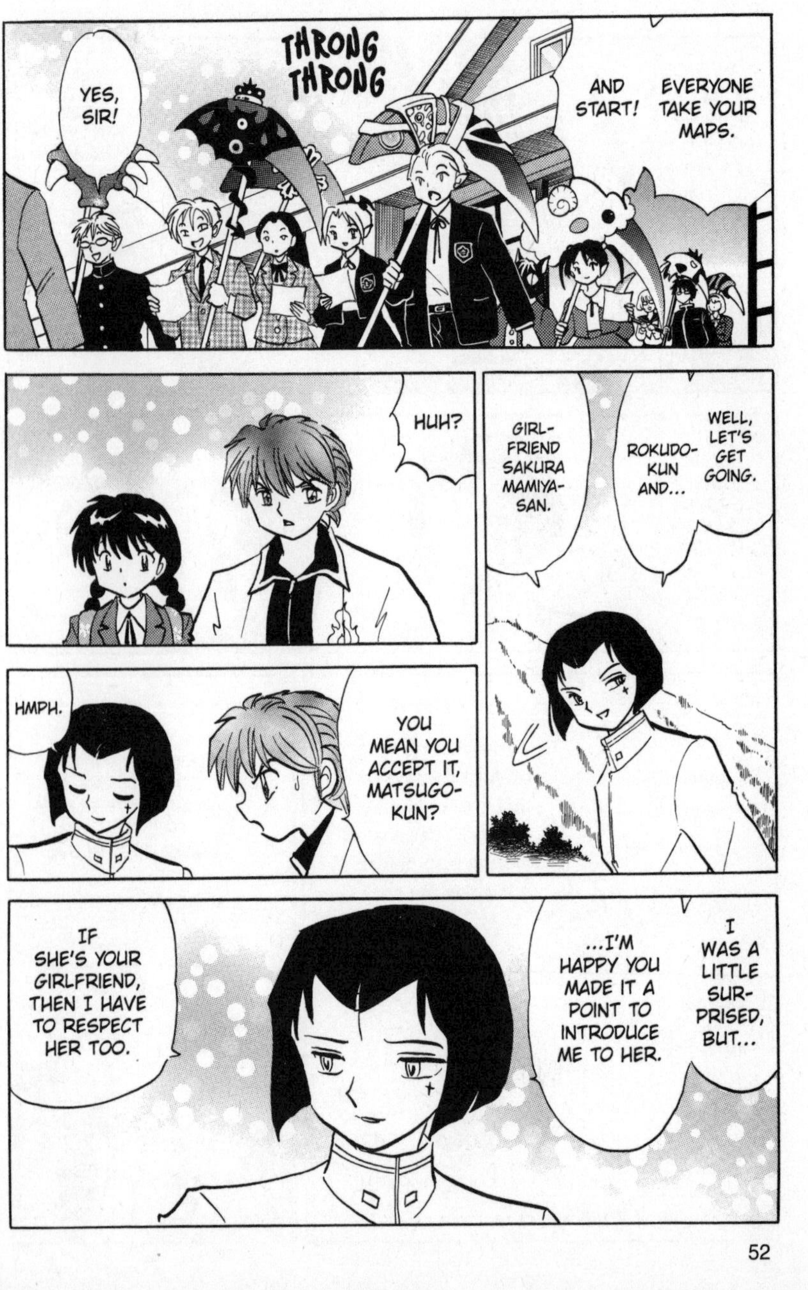
EVERYONE TAKE YOUR MAPS.
AND START!
THRONG THRONG
YES, SIR!
WELL, LET'S GET GOING.
ROKUDO-KUN AND...
GIRL-FRIEND SAKURA MAMIYA-SAN.
HUH?
YOU MEAN YOU ACCEPT IT, MATSUGO-KUN?
HMPH.
I WAS A LITTLE SUR-PRISED, BUT...
...I'M HAPPY YOU MADE IT A POINT TO INTRODUCE ME TO HER.
IF SHE'S YOUR GIRLFRIEND, THEN I HAVE TO RESPECT HER TOO.

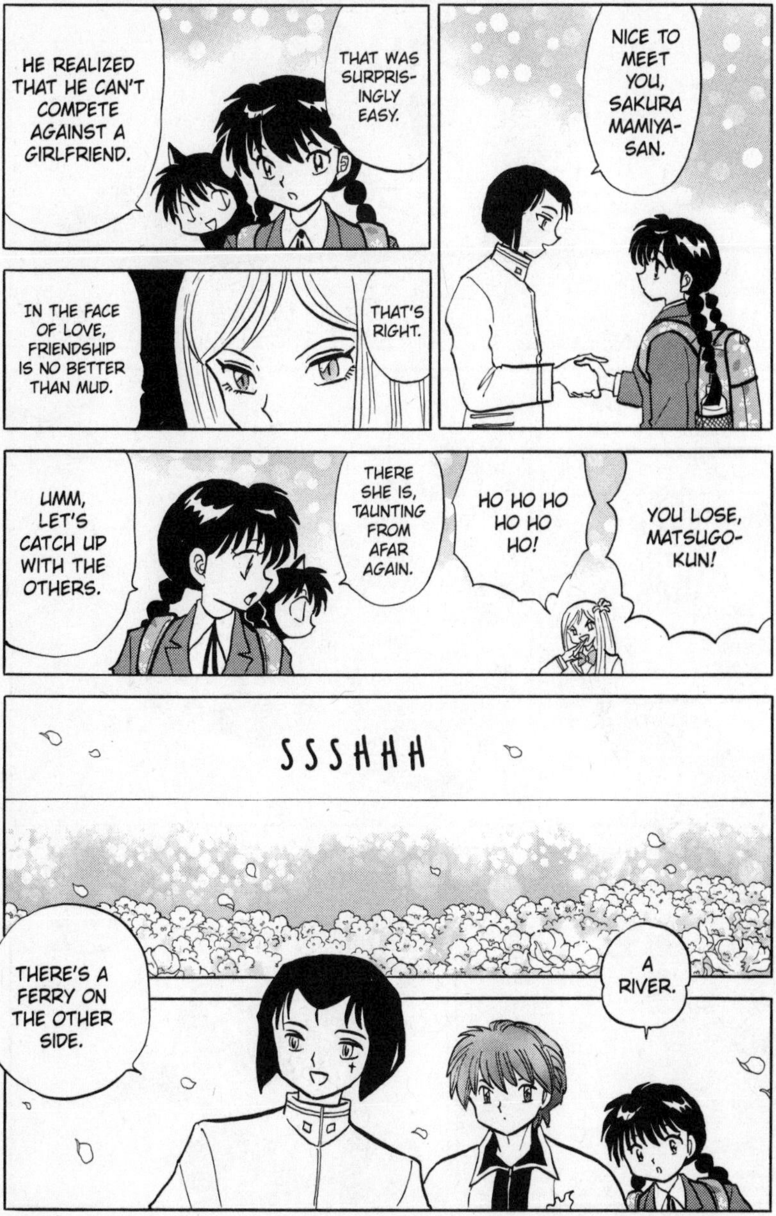
NICE TO MEET YOU, SAKURA MAMIYA-SAN.
THAT WAS SURPRIS-INGLY EASY.
HE REALIZED THAT HE CAN'T COMPETE AGAINST A GIRLFRIEND.
THAT'S RIGHT.
IN THE FACE OF LOVE, FRIENDSHIP IS NO BETTER THAN MUD.
YOU LOSE, MATSUGO-KUN!
HO HO HO HO HO HO!
THERE SHE IS, TAUNTING FROM AFAR AGAIN.
UMM, LET'S CATCH UP WITH THE OTHERS.
SSSHHH
A RIVER.
THERE'S A FERRY ON THE OTHER SIDE.

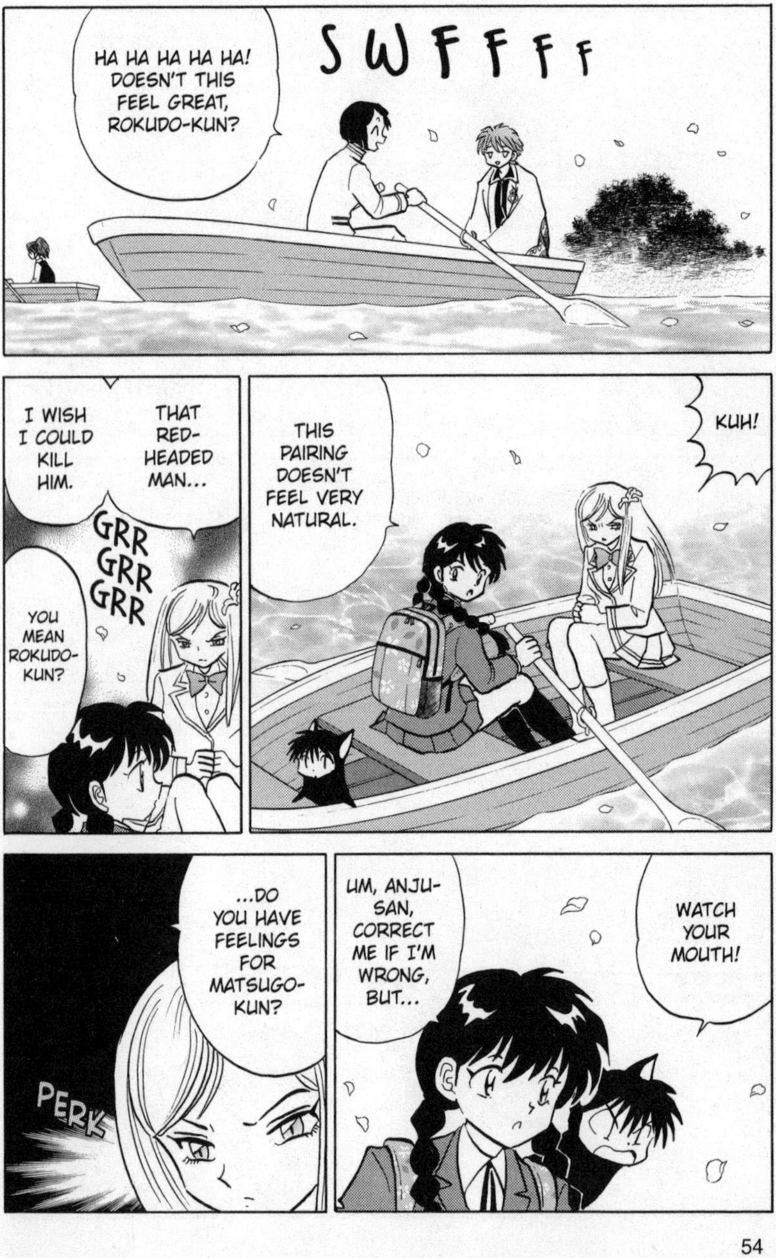
SWFFFF
HA HA HA HA HA! DOESN'T THIS FEEL GREAT, ROKUDO-KUN?
THIS PAIRING DOESN'T FEEL VERY NATURAL.
KUH!
THAT RED-HEADED MAN...
I WISH I COULD KILL HIM.
GRR GRR GRR
YOU MEAN ROKUDO-KUN?
WATCH YOUR MOUTH!
UM, ANJU-SAN, CORRECT ME IF I'M WRONG, BUT...
...DO YOU HAVE FEELINGS FOR MATSUGO-KUN?
PERK

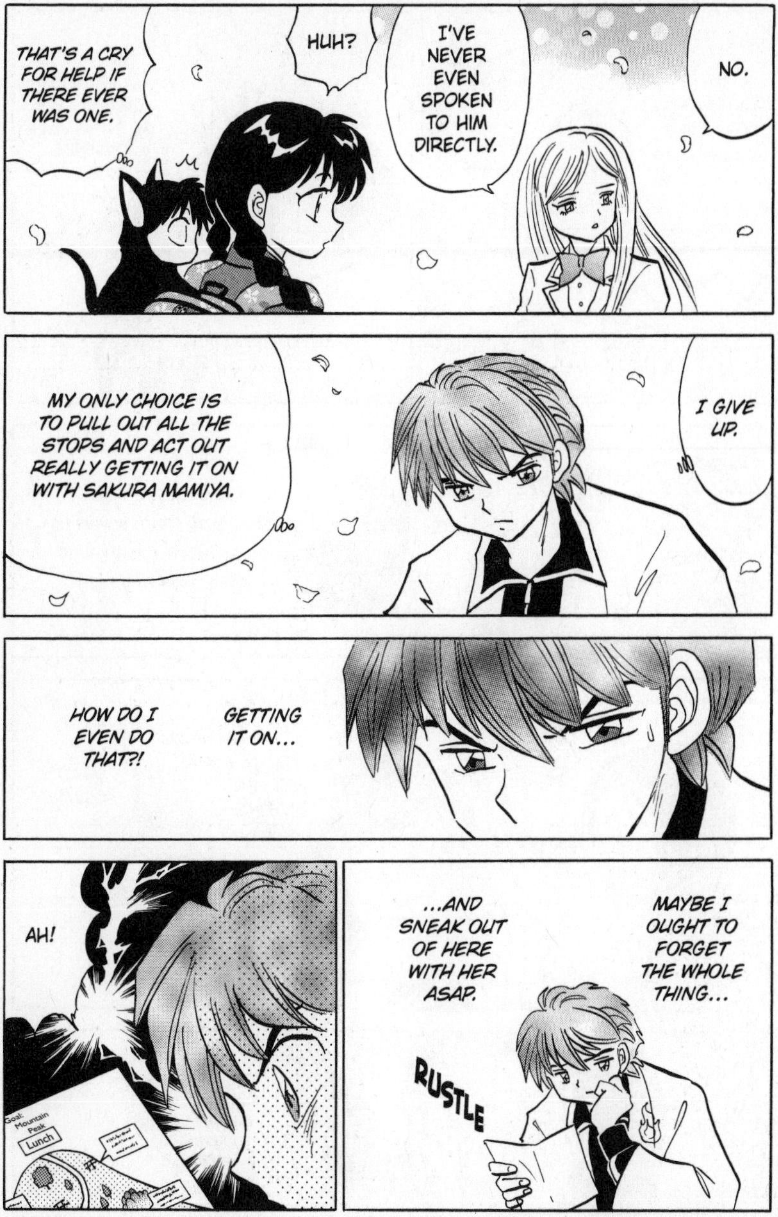
NO.
I'VE NEVER EVEN SPOKEN TO HIM DIRECTLY.
HUH?
THAT'S A CRY FOR HELP IF THERE EVER WAS ONE.
I GIVE UP.
MY ONLY CHOICE IS TO PULL OUT ALL THE STOPS AND ACT OUT REALLY GETTING IT ON WITH SAKURA MAMIYA.
GETTING IT ON...
HOW DO I EVEN DO THAT?!
MAYBE I OUGHT TO FORGET THE WHOLE THING...
...AND SNEAK OUT OF HERE WITH HER ASAP.
RUSTLE
AH!
Goal: Mountain Peak
Lunch

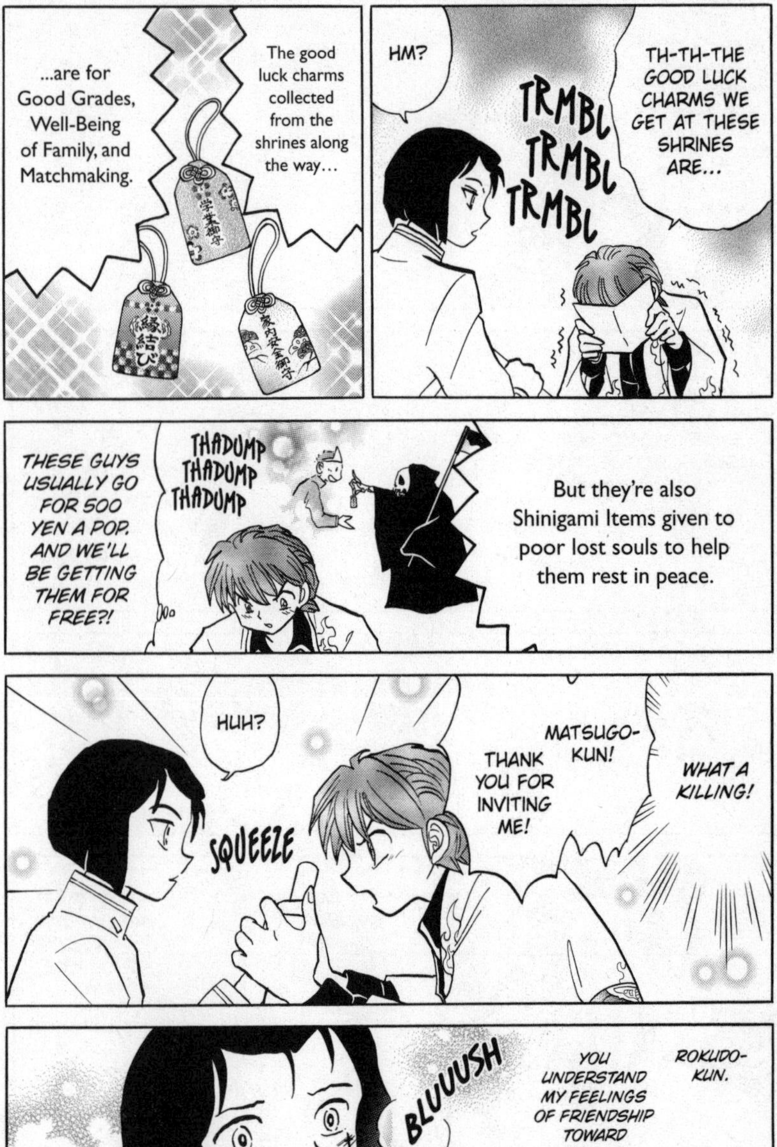
TH-TH-THE GOOD LUCK CHARMS WE GET AT THESE SHRINES ARE…
TRMBL TRMBL TRMBL
HM?
The good luck charms collected from the shrines along the way…
...are for Good Grades, Well-Being of Family, and Matchmaking.
学業御守
家内安全御守
縁結び
But they're also Shinigami Items given to poor lost souls to help them rest in peace.
THADUMP THADUMP THADUMP
THESE GUYS USUALLY GO FOR 500 YEN A POP. AND WE'LL BE GETTING THEM FOR FREE?!
WHAT A KILLING!
MATSUGO-KUN!
THANK YOU FOR INVITING ME!
HUH?
SQUEEZE
ROKUDO-KUN.
YOU UNDERSTAND MY FEELINGS OF FRIENDSHIP TOWARD YOU…?
BLUUUSH

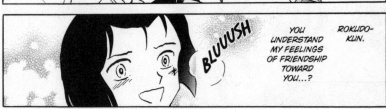

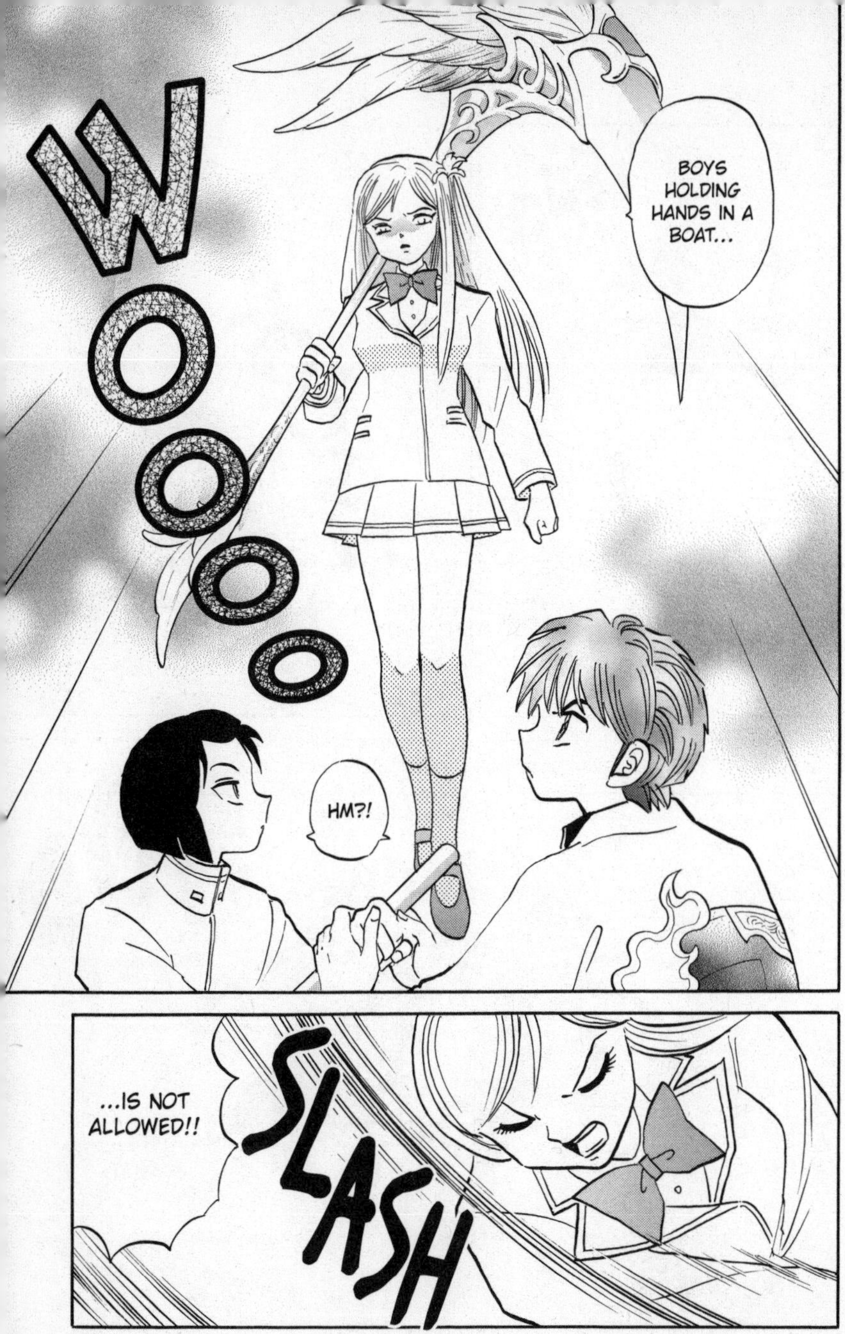
BOYS HOLDING HANDS IN A BOAT...
WOOOOO
HM?!
...IS NOT ALLOWED!!
SLASH

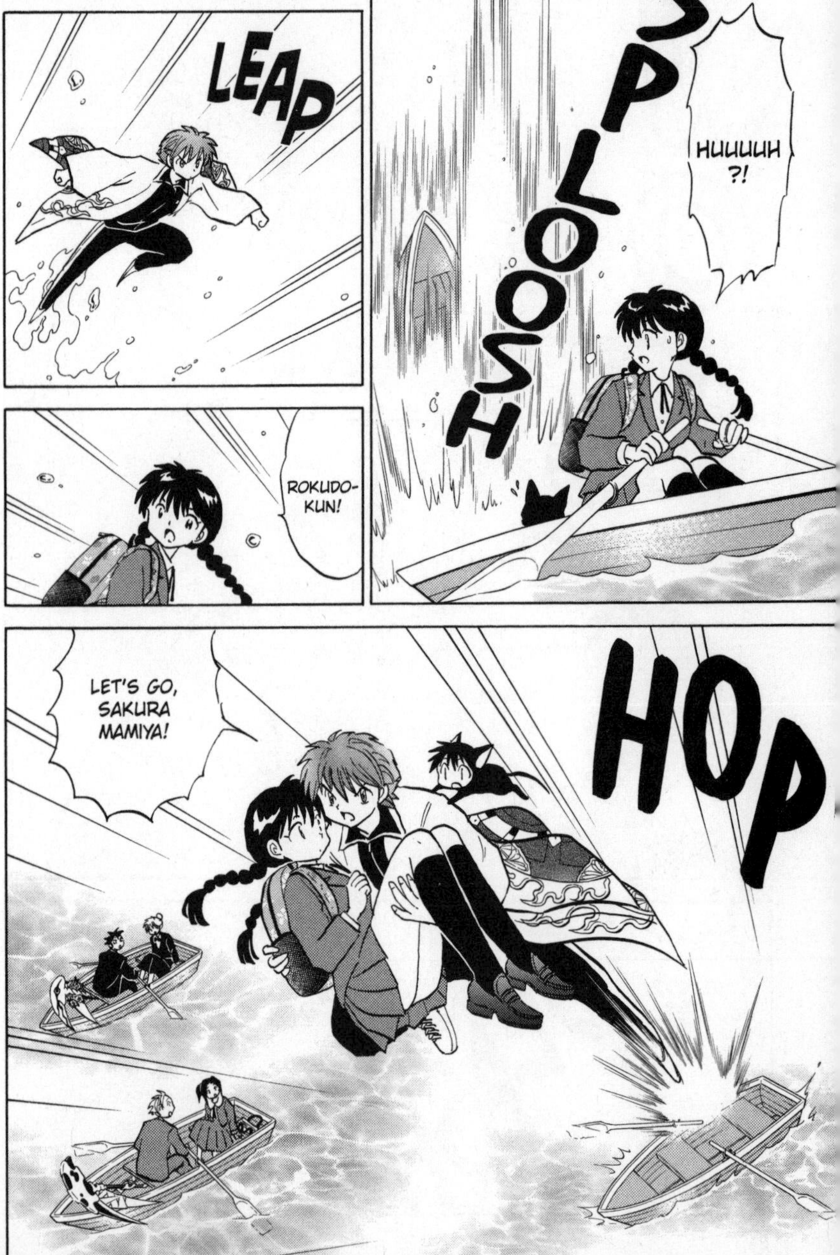
SPLOOSH
HUUUUH ?!
LEAP
ROKUDO-KUN!
HOP
LET'S GO, SAKURA MAMIYA!

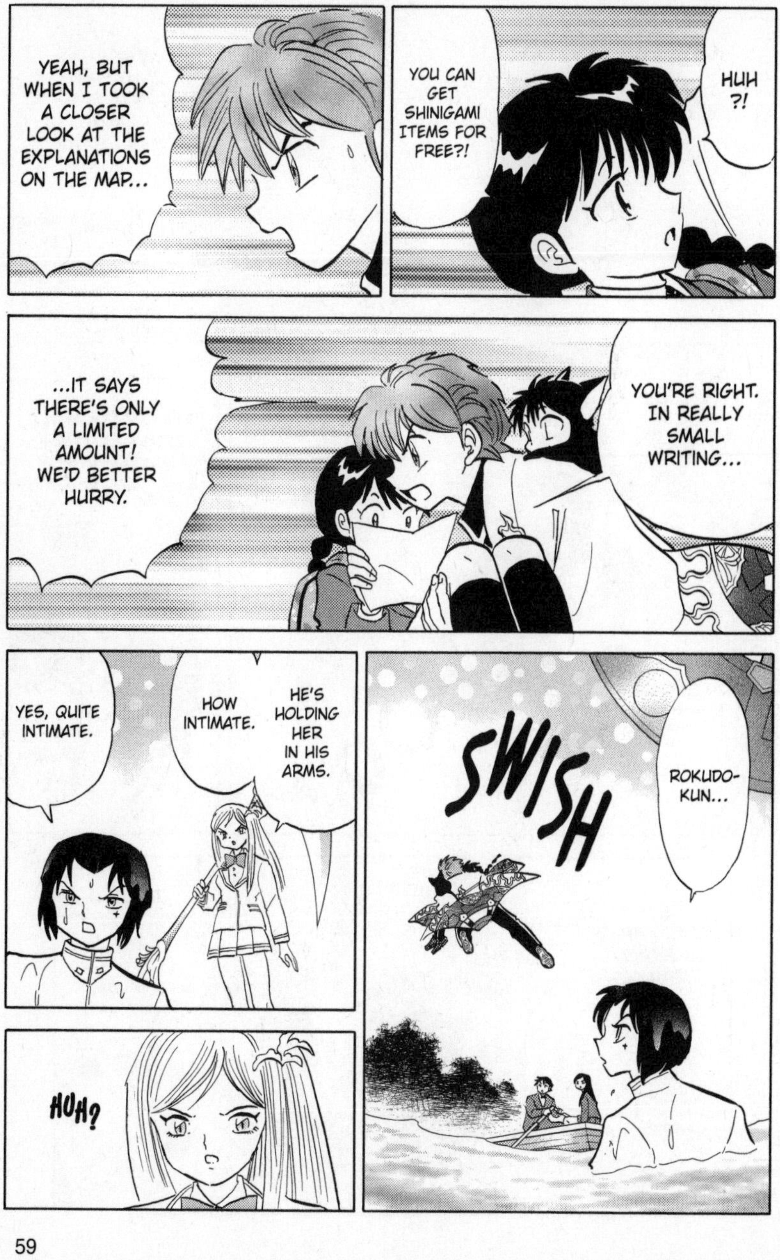
HUH ?!
YOU CAN GET SHINIGAMI ITEMS FOR FREE?!
YEAH, BUT WHEN I TOOK A CLOSER LOOK AT THE EXPLANATIONS ON THE MAP...
YOU'RE RIGHT. IN REALLY SMALL WRITING...
...IT SAYS THERE'S ONLY A LIMITED AMOUNT! WE'D BETTER HURRY.
ROKUDO-KUN...
SWISH
HE'S HOLDING HER IN HIS ARMS.
HOW INTIMATE.
YES, QUITE INTIMATE.
HUH?

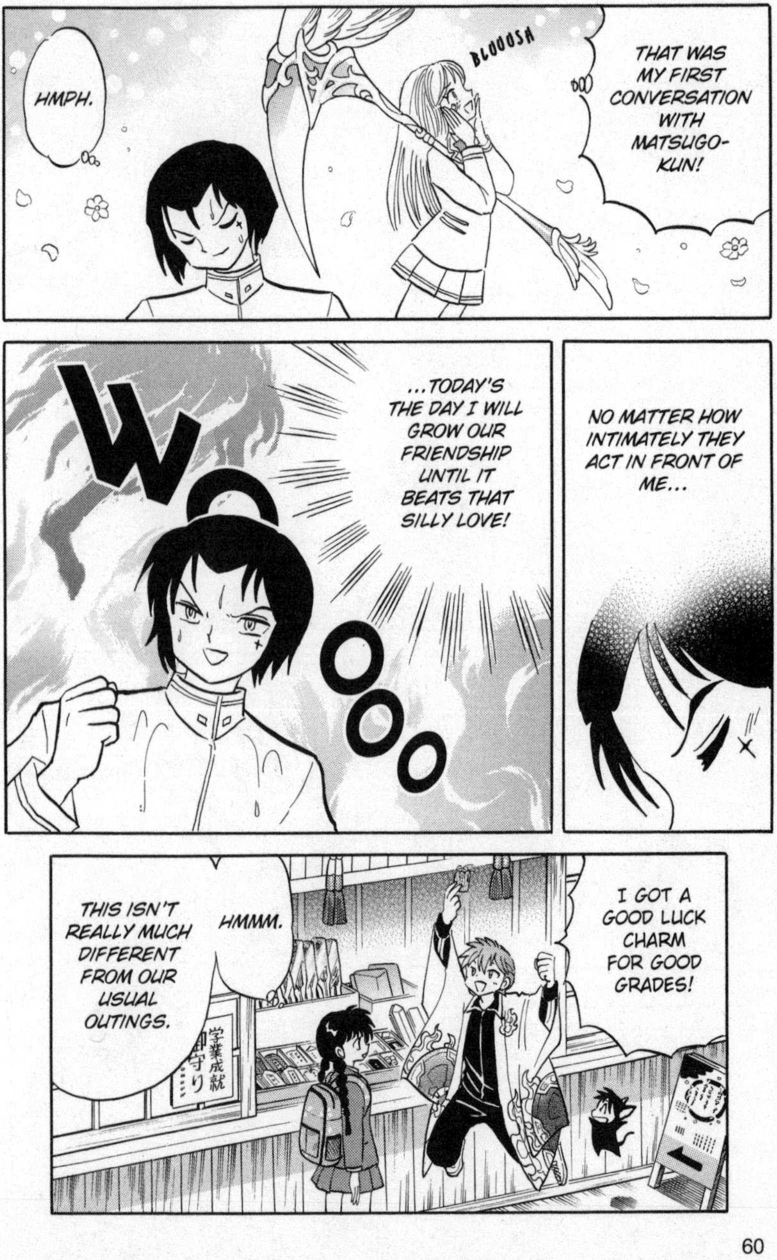
THAT WAS MY FIRST CONVERSATION WITH MATSUGO-KUN!
BLOOOSA
HMPH.
NO MATTER HOW INTIMATELY THEY ACT IN FRONT OF ME...
...TODAY'S THE DAY I WILL GROW OUR FRIENDSHIP UNTIL IT BEATS THAT SILLY LOVE!
WOOOO
I GOT A GOOD LUCK CHARM FOR GOOD GRADES!
HMMM.
THIS ISN'T REALLY MUCH DIFFERENT FROM OUR USUAL OUTINGS.
学業成就
御守り

CHAPTER 192: IT'S ABOUT THE MONEY

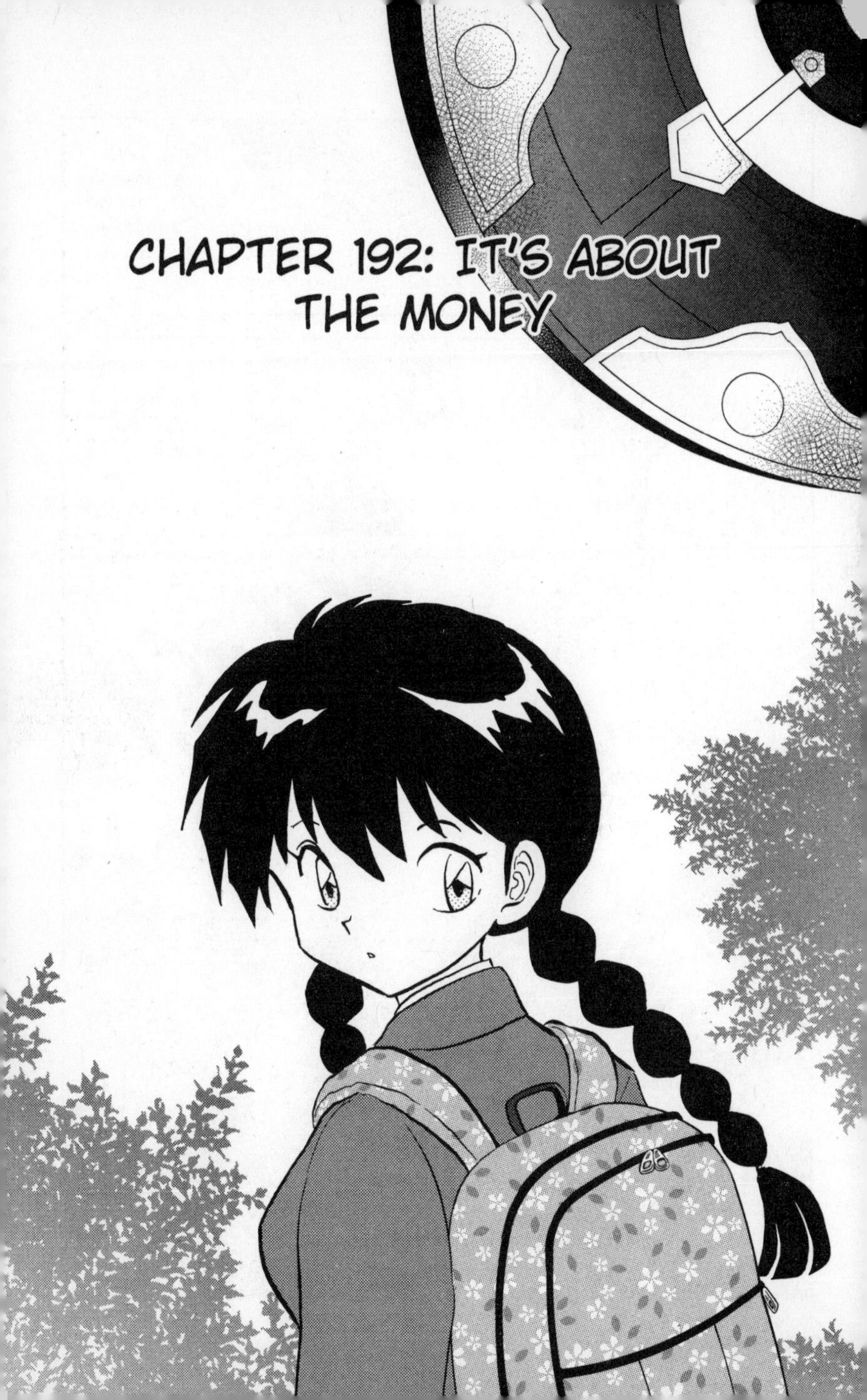

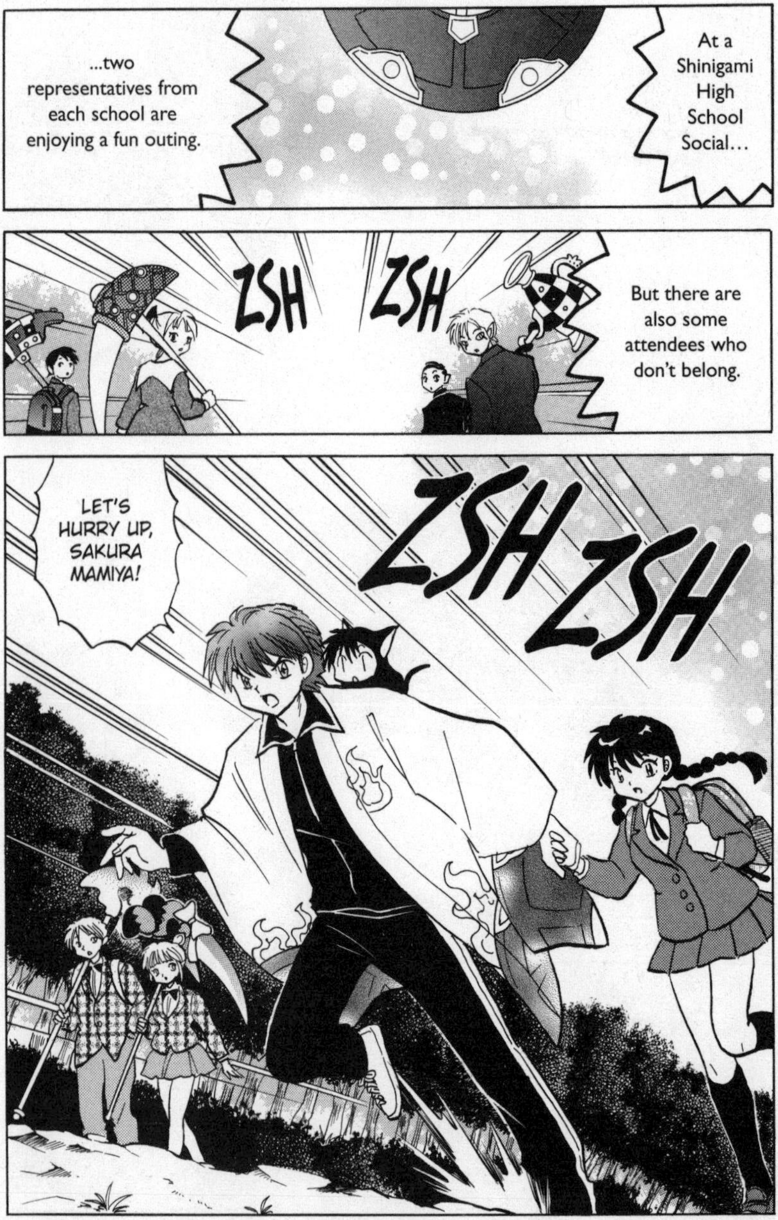

At a Shinigami High School Social…
...two representatives from each school are enjoying a fun outing.
But there are also some attendees who don't belong.
ZSH
ZSH
ZSH
ZSH
LET'S HURRY UP, SAKURA MAMIYA!

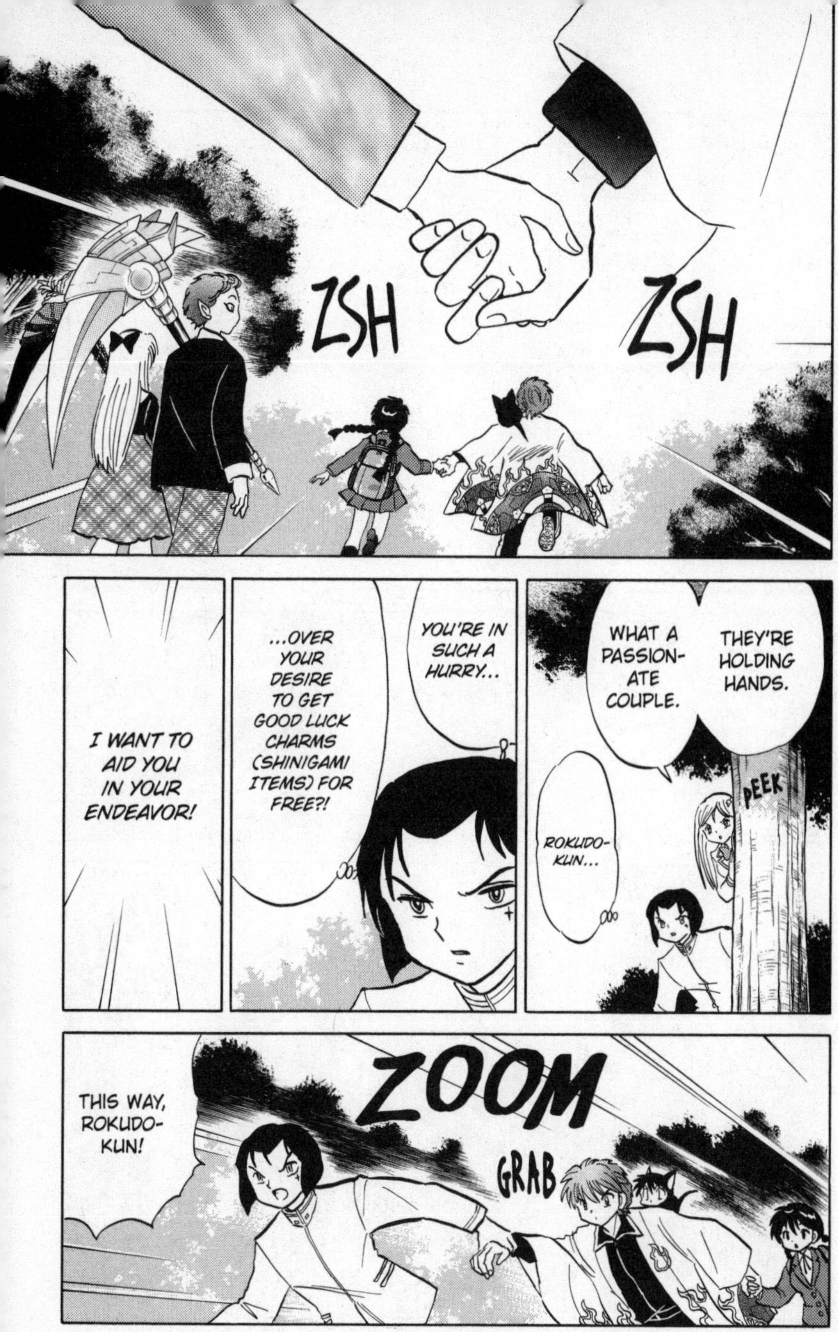
ZSH
ZSH
THEY'RE HOLDING HANDS.
WHAT A PASSION-ATE COUPLE.
PEEK
ROKUDO-KUN...
YOU'RE IN SUCH A HURRY...
...OVER YOUR DESIRE TO GET GOOD LUCK CHARMS (SHINIGAMI ITEMS) FOR FREE?!
I WANT TO AID YOU IN YOUR ENDEAVOR!
ZOOM
GRAB
THIS WAY, ROKUDO-KUN!

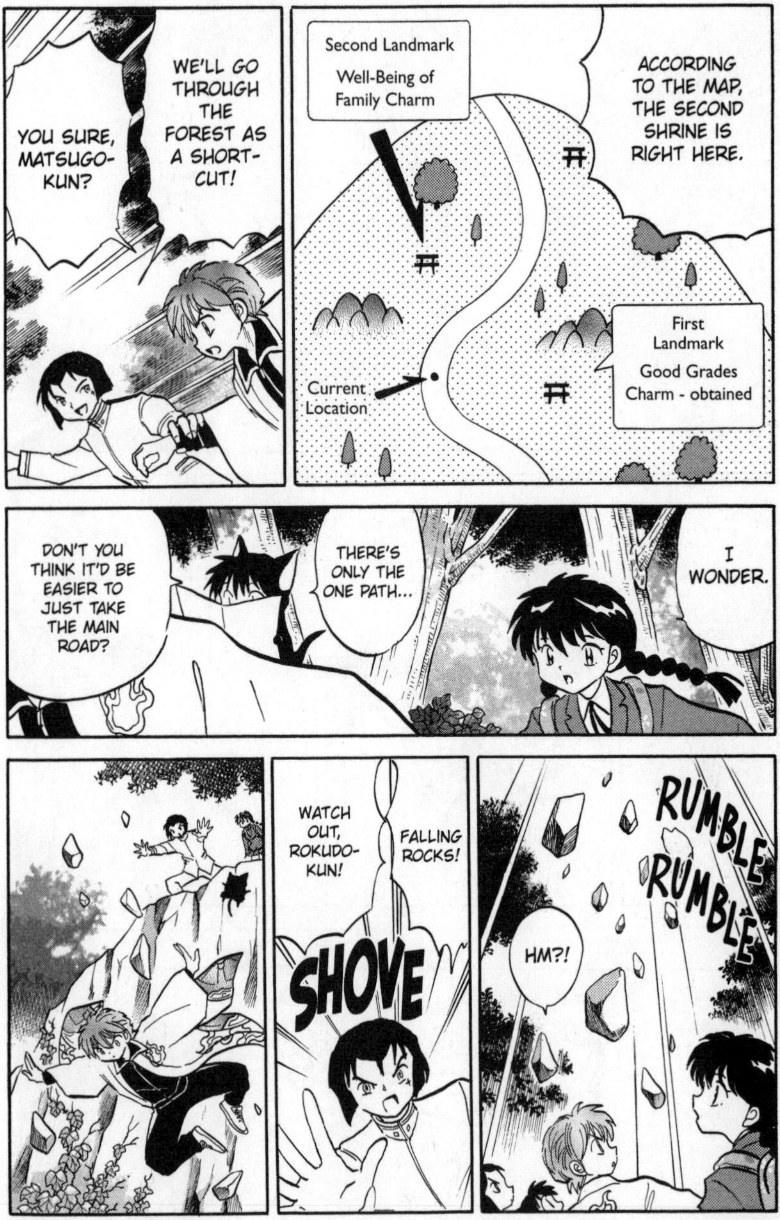
ACCORDING TO THE MAP, THE SECOND SHRINE IS RIGHT HERE.
Second Landmark
Well-Being of Family Charm
First Landmark
Good Grades Charm - obtained
Current Location
WE'LL GO THROUGH THE FOREST AS A SHORT-CUT!
YOU SURE, MATSUGO-KUN?
I WONDER.
THERE'S ONLY THE ONE PATH...
DON'T YOU THINK IT'D BE EASIER TO JUST TAKE THE MAIN ROAD?
RUMBLE RUMBLE
HM?!
FALLING ROCKS!
WATCH OUT, ROKUDO-KUN!
SHOVE

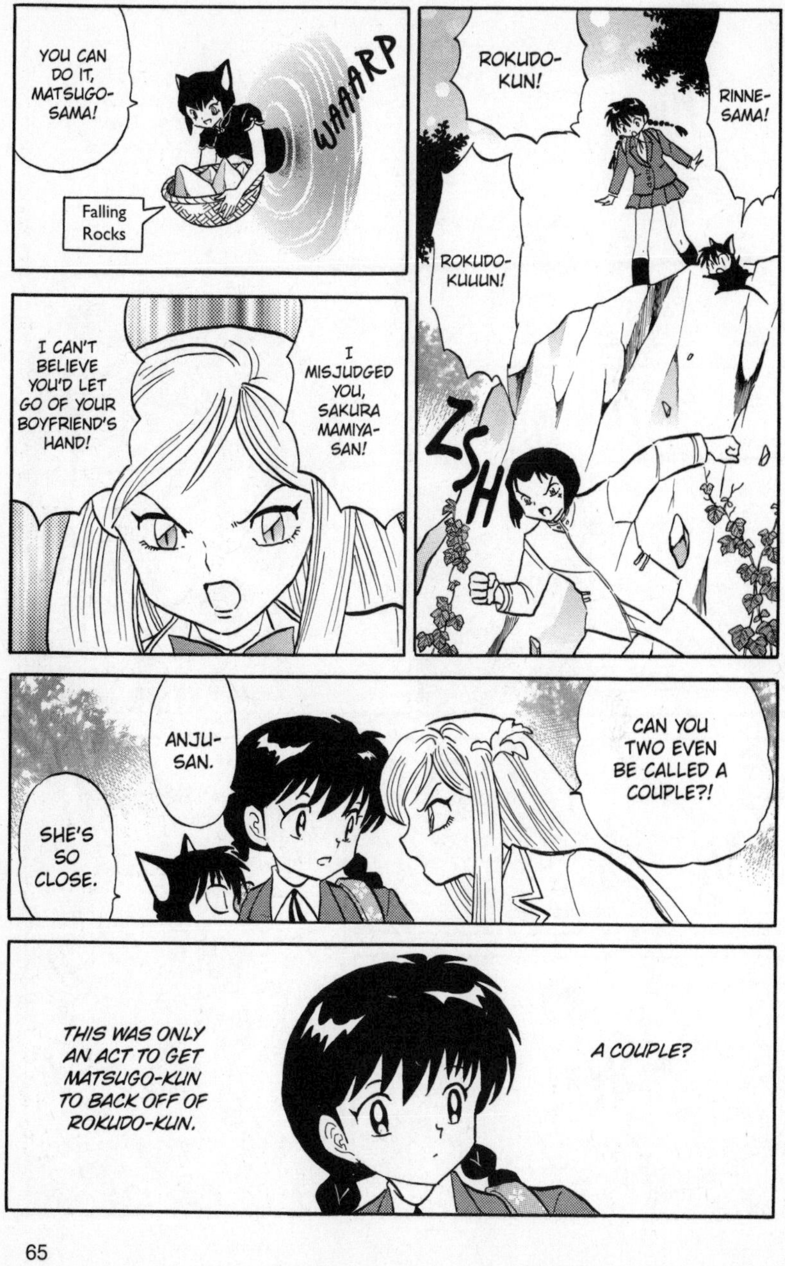
RINNE-SAMA!
ROKUDO-KUN!
ROKUDO-KUUUN!
ZSH
WAAARP
YOU CAN DO IT, MATSUGO-SAMA!
Falling Rocks
I MISJUDGED YOU, SAKURA MAMIYA-SAN!
I CAN'T BELIEVE YOU'D LET GO OF YOUR BOYFRIEND'S HAND!
CAN YOU TWO EVEN BE CALLED A COUPLE?!
ANJU-SAN.
SHE'S SO CLOSE.
A COUPLE?
THIS WAS ONLY AN ACT TO GET MATSUGO-KUN TO BACK OFF OF ROKUDO-KUN.

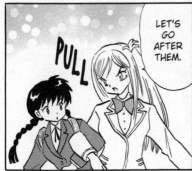

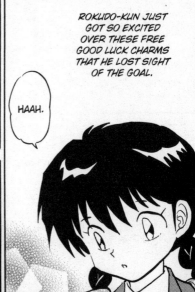

ROKUDO-KUN JUST GOT SO EXCITED OVER THESE FREE GOOD LUCK CHARMS THAT HE LOST SIGHT OF THE GOAL.
HAAH.
PULL
LET'S GO AFTER THEM.
RUSTLE
ZSH
ROKUDO-KUUUN!
HA HA HA HA HA! WAIT UUUP!
ROLL ROLL
BONK
YOU FINALLY STOPPED.
ZSH

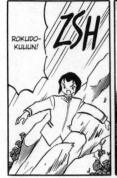

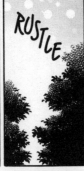

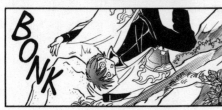

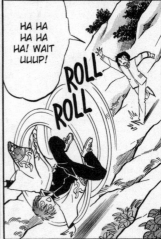

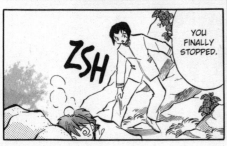

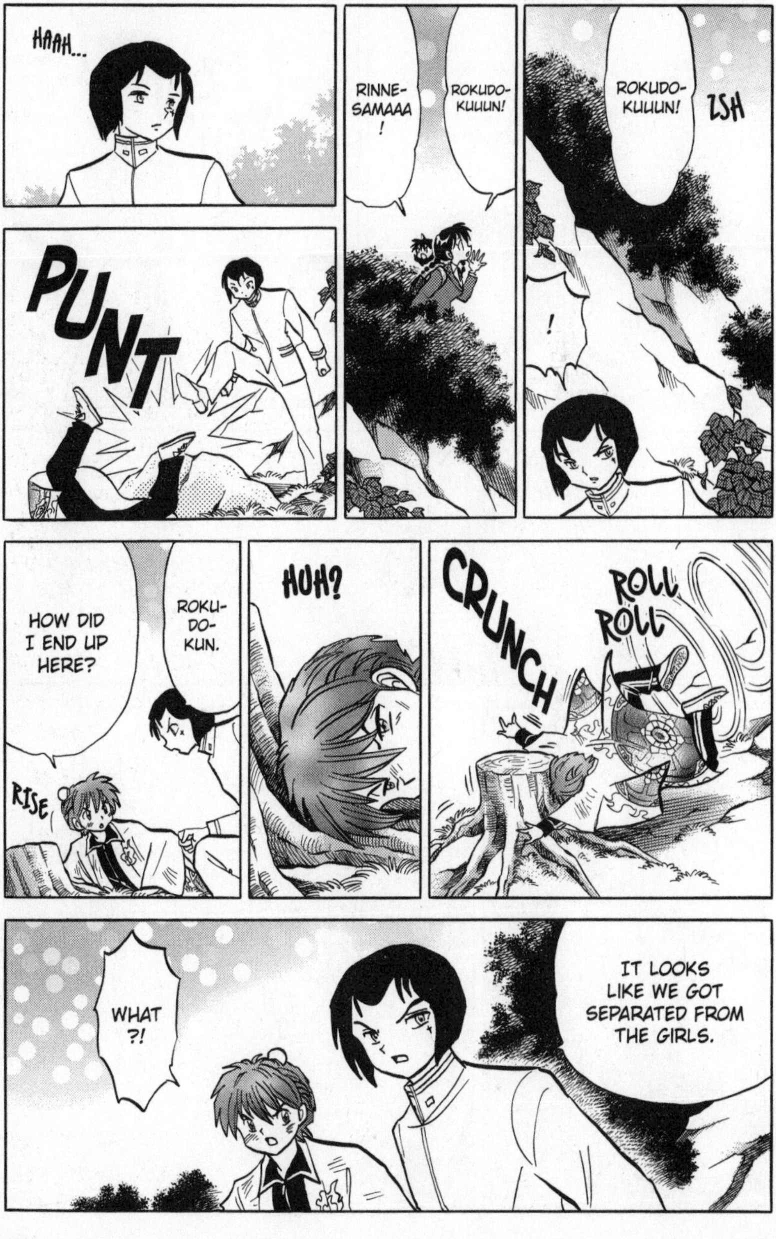
ROKUDO-KUUUN!
ZSH
!
ROKUDO-KUUUN!
RINNE-SAMAAA!
HAAAH...
PUNT
CRUNCH
ROLL ROLL
HUH?
ROKU-DO-KUN.
HOW DID I END UP HERE?
RISE
IT LOOKS LIKE WE GOT SEPARATED FROM THE GIRLS.
WHAT?!

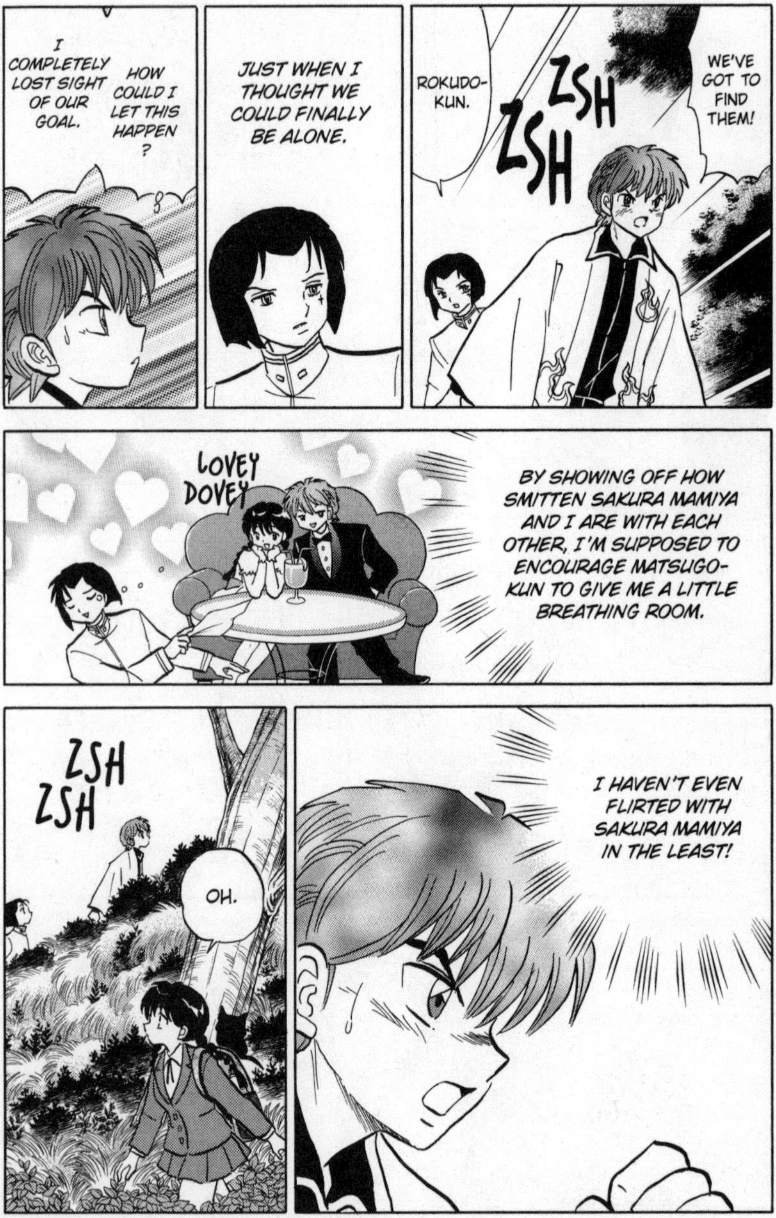
WE'VE GOT TO FIND THEM!
ZSH ZSH
ROKUDO-KUN.
JUST WHEN I THOUGHT WE COULD FINALLY BE ALONE.
HOW COULD I LET THIS HAPPEN?
I COMPLETELY LOST SIGHT OF OUR GOAL.
BY SHOWING OFF HOW SMITTEN SAKURA MAMIYA AND I ARE WITH EACH OTHER, I'M SUPPOSED TO ENCOURAGE MATSUGO-KUN TO GIVE ME A LITTLE BREATHING ROOM.
LOVEY DOVEY
I HAVEN'T EVEN FLIRTED WITH SAKURA MAMIYA IN THE LEAST!
ZSH ZSH
OH.

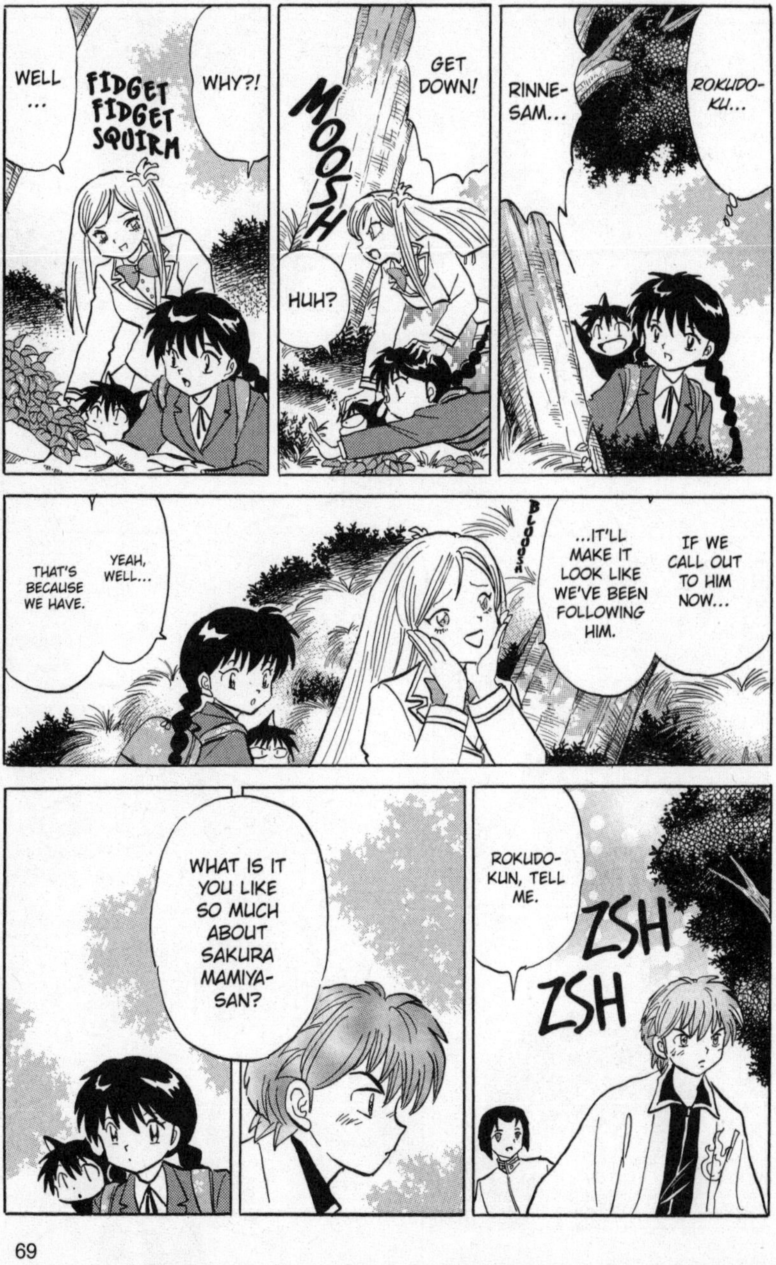
ROKUDO-KU...
RINNE-SAM...
GET DOWN!
MOOSH
HUH?
WHY?!
FIDGET FIDGET SQUIRM
WELL ...
IF WE CALL OUT TO HIM NOW...
...IT'LL MAKE IT LOOK LIKE WE'VE BEEN FOLLOWING HIM.
BLOOOSH
YEAH, WELL...
THAT'S BECAUSE WE HAVE.
ROKUDO-KUN, TELL ME.
ZSH ZSH
WHAT IS IT YOU LIKE SO MUCH ABOUT SAKURA MAMIYA-SAN?

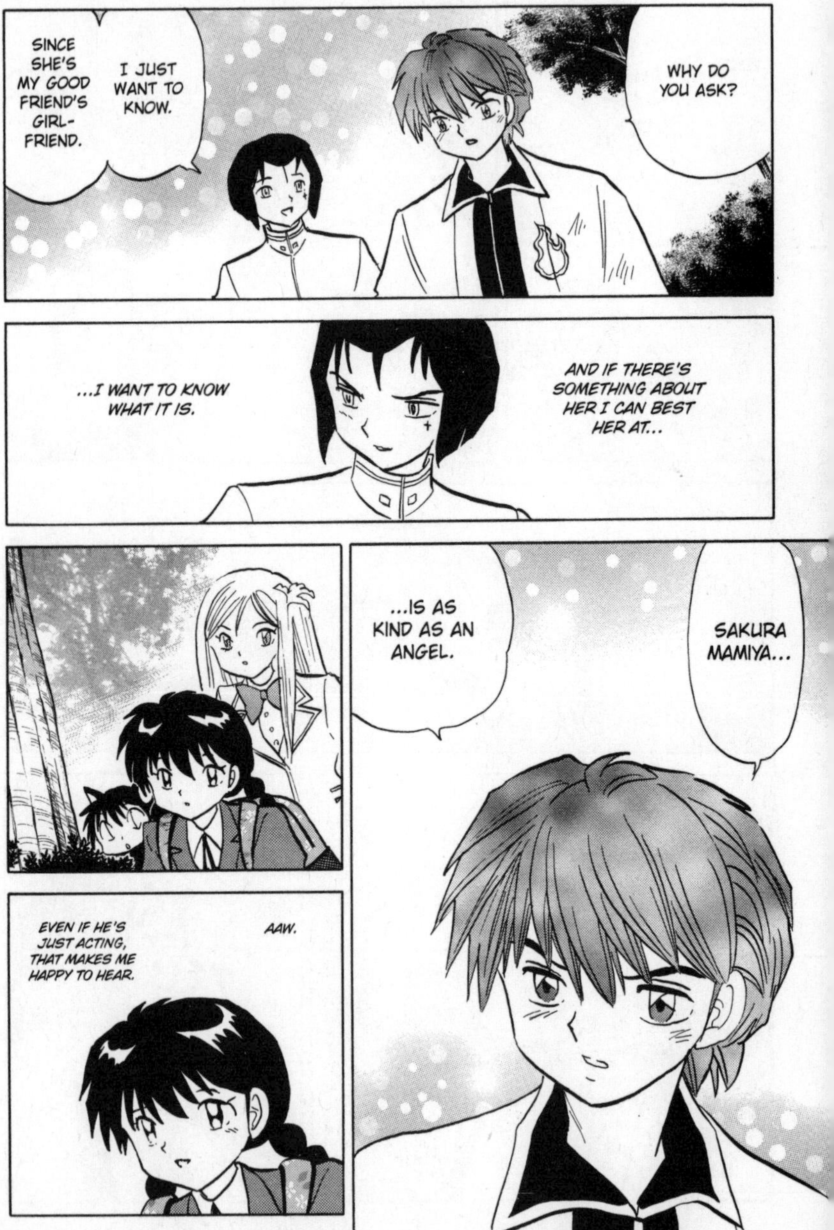
WHY DO YOU ASK?
I JUST WANT TO KNOW.
SINCE SHE'S MY GOOD FRIEND'S GIRL-FRIEND.
AND IF THERE'S SOMETHING ABOUT HER I CAN BEST HER AT...
...I WANT TO KNOW WHAT IT IS.
SAKURA MAMIYA...
...IS AS KIND AS AN ANGEL.
AAW.
EVEN IF HE'S JUST ACTING, THAT MAKES ME HAPPY TO HEAR.

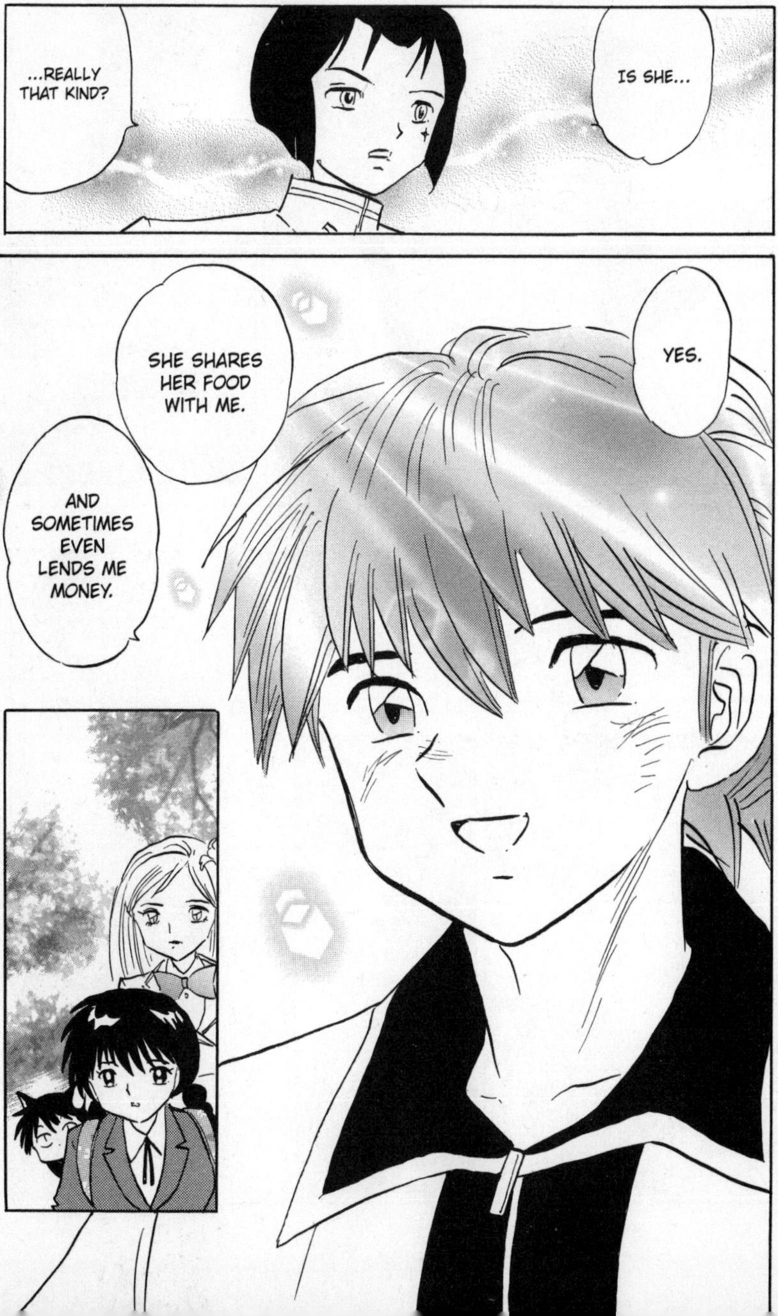
IS SHE...
...REALLY THAT KIND?
YES.
SHE SHARES HER FOOD WITH ME.
AND SOMETIMES EVEN LENDS ME MONEY.

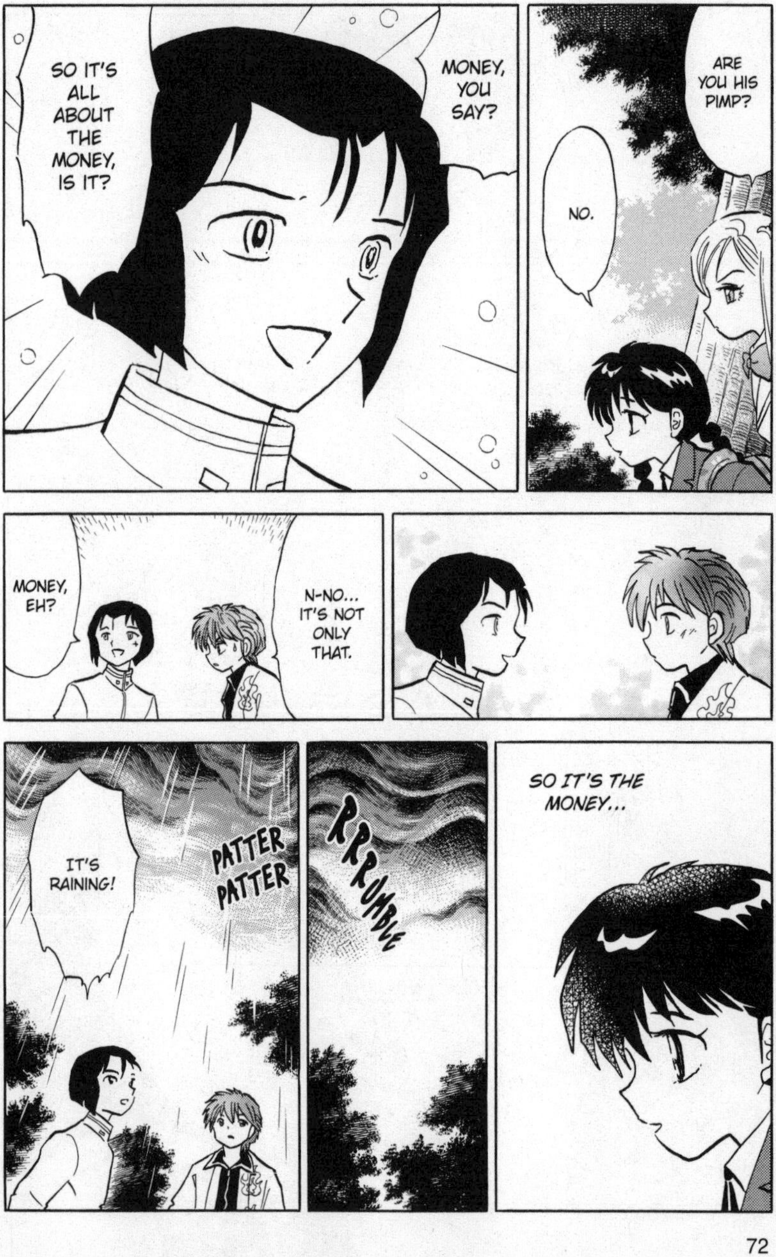
ARE YOU HIS PIMP?
NO.
MONEY, YOU SAY?
SO IT'S ALL ABOUT THE MONEY, IS IT?
MONEY, EH?
N-NO... IT'S NOT ONLY THAT.
SO IT'S THE MONEY...
RRRUMBLE
PATTER PATTER
IT'S RAINING!

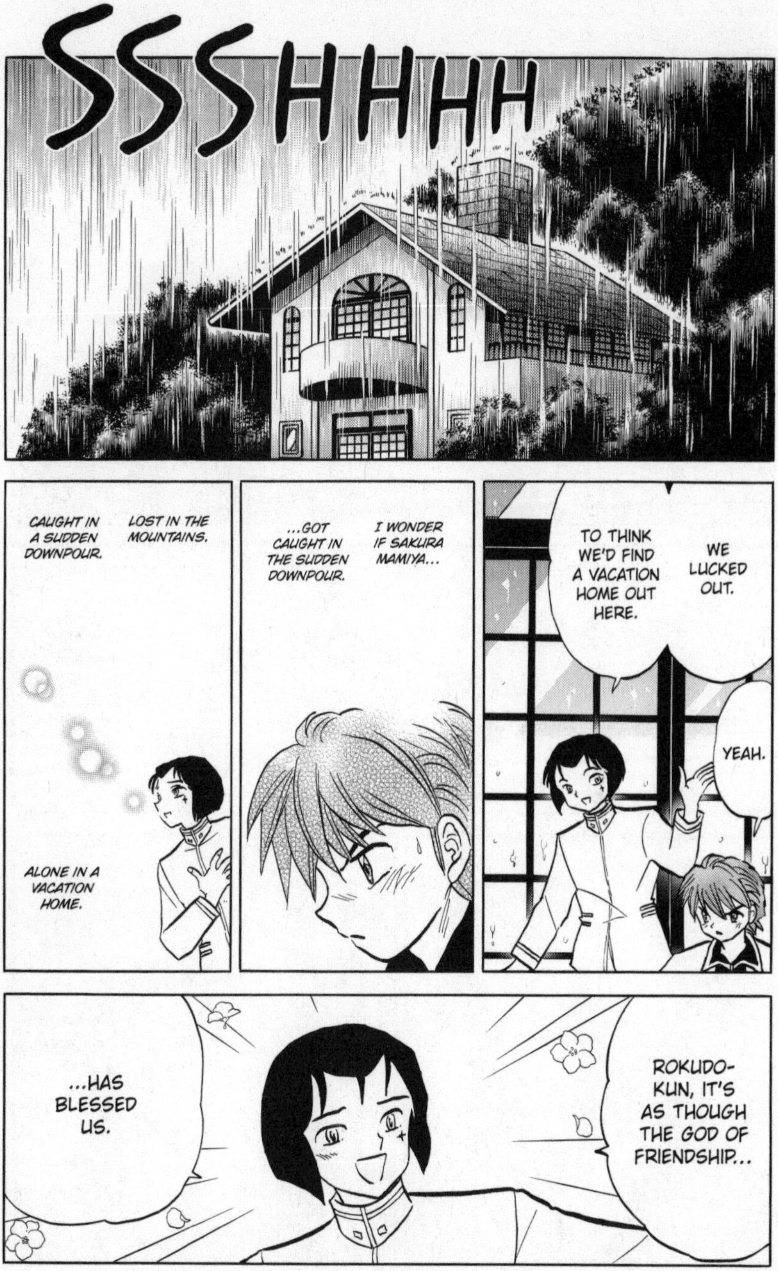
SSSHHHH
WE LUCKED OUT.
TO THINK WE'D FIND A VACATION HOME OUT HERE.
YEAH.
I WONDER IF SAKURA MAMIYA...
...GOT CAUGHT IN THE SUDDEN DOWNPOUR.
LOST IN THE MOUNTAINS.
CAUGHT IN A SUDDEN DOWNPOUR.
ALONE IN A VACATION HOME.
ROKUDO-KUN, IT'S AS THOUGH THE GOD OF FRIENDSHIP...
...HAS BLESSED US.

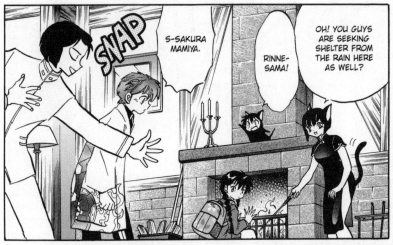

OH! YOU GUYS ARE SEEKING SHELTER FROM THE RAIN HERE AS WELL?
RINNE-SAMA!
S-SAKURA MAMIYA.
SNAP
HO HO HO HO HO! TOO BAD, MATSUGO-KUN.
IT SEEMS THE GOD OF FRIENDSHIP HAS ABANDONED YOU.
HO HO HO HO HO HO!
QUIT ACTING SO DISAPPOINTED.
HAAAAH...
SNEAK
TH- THIS...
...IS MY CHANCE TO ROMANCE SAKURA MAMIYA!

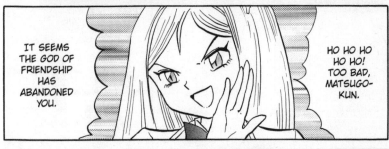

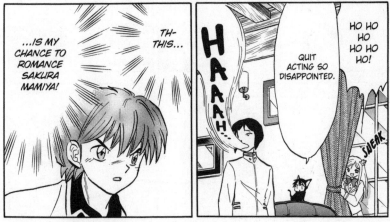

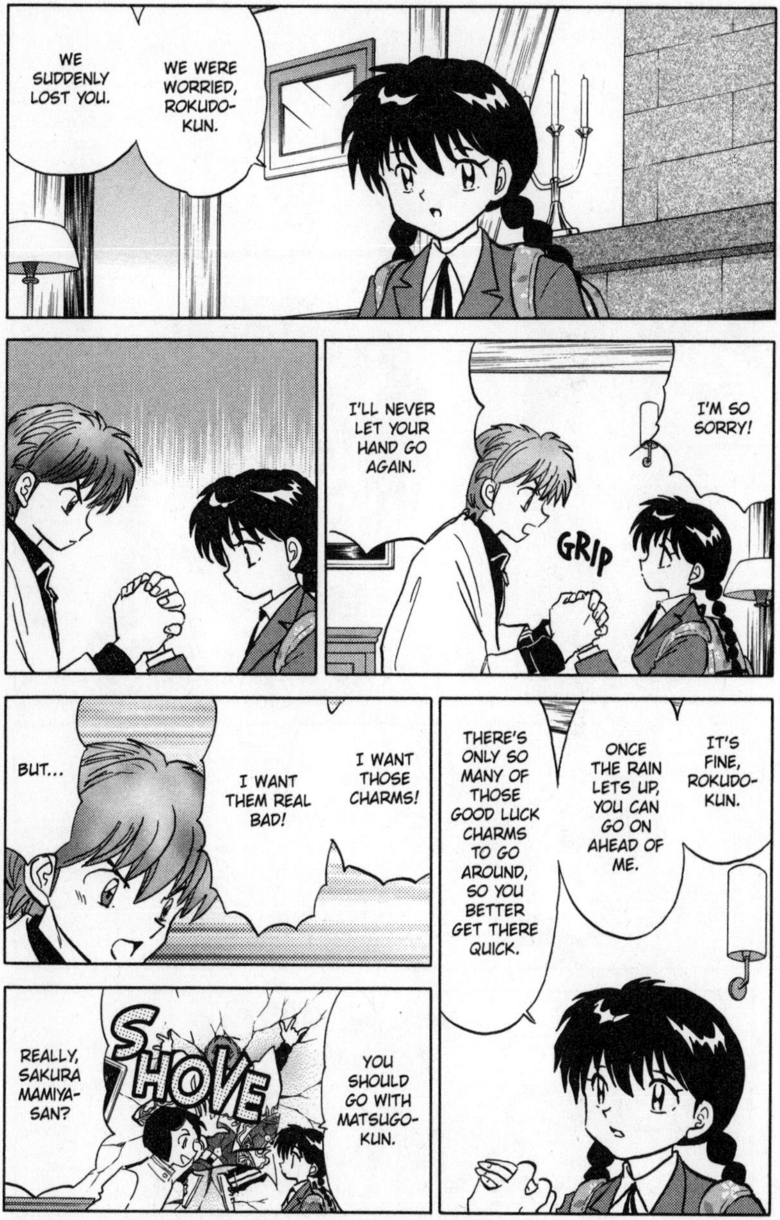
WE WERE WORRIED, ROKUDO-KUN.
WE SUDDENLY LOST YOU.
I'M SO SORRY!
I'LL NEVER LET YOUR HAND GO AGAIN.
GRIP
IT'S FINE, ROKUDO-KUN.
ONCE THE RAIN LETS UP, YOU CAN GO ON AHEAD OF ME.
THERE'S ONLY SO MANY OF THOSE GOOD LUCK CHARMS TO GO AROUND, SO YOU BETTER GET THERE QUICK.
I WANT THOSE CHARMS!
I WANT THEM REAL BAD!
BUT...
YOU SHOULD GO WITH MATSUGO-KUN.
SHOVE
REALLY, SAKURA MAMIYA-SAN?

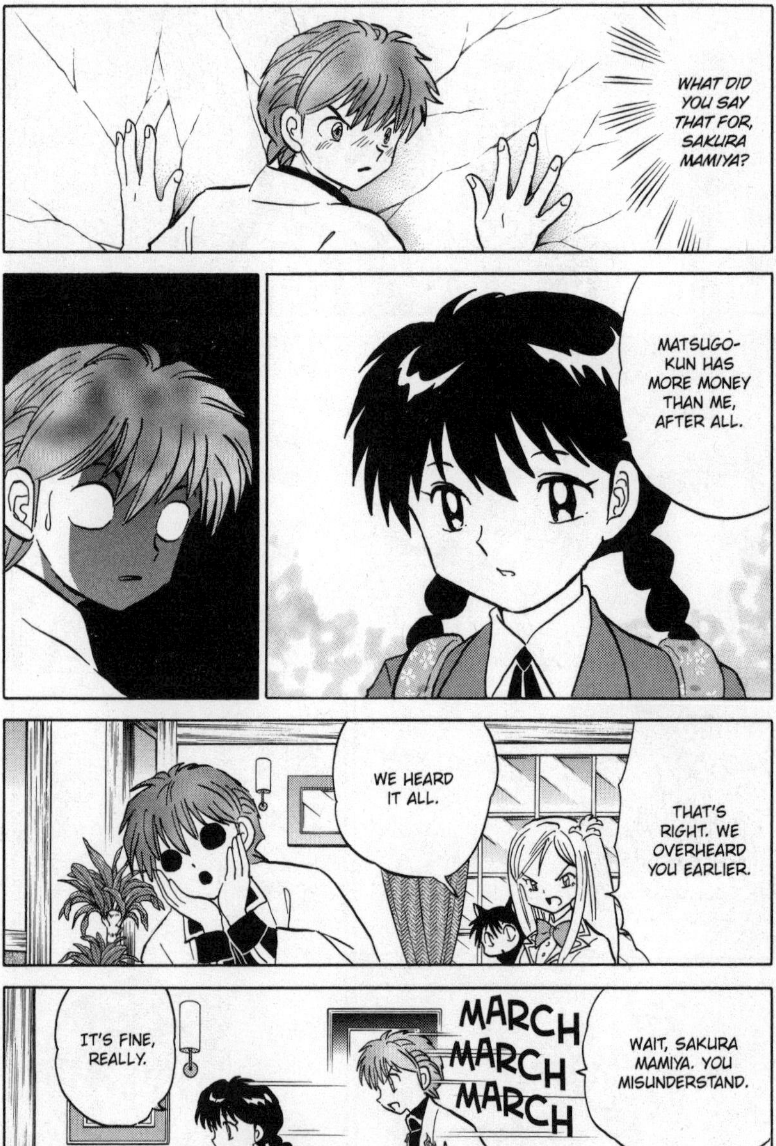
WHAT DID YOU SAY THAT FOR, SAKURA MAMIYA?
MATSUGO-KUN HAS MORE MONEY THAN ME, AFTER ALL.
THAT'S RIGHT. WE OVERHEARD YOU EARLIER.
WE HEARD IT ALL.
WAIT, SAKURA MAMIYA. YOU MISUNDERSTAND.
MARCH MARCH MARCH
IT'S FINE, REALLY.

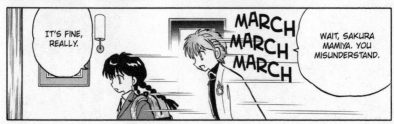

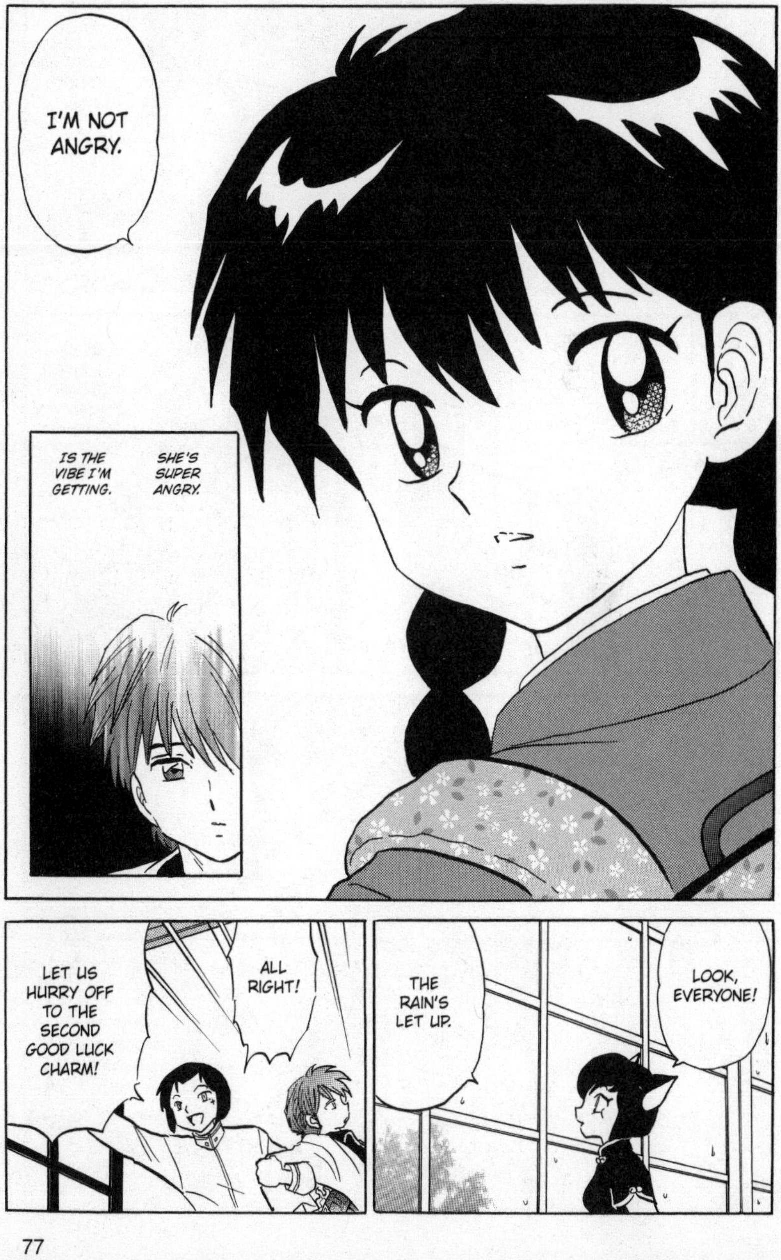
I'M NOT ANGRY.
SHE'S SUPER ANGRY.
IS THE VIBE I'M GETTING.
LOOK, EVERYONE!
THE RAIN'S LET UP.
ALL RIGHT!
LET US HURRY OFF TO THE SECOND GOOD LUCK CHARM!

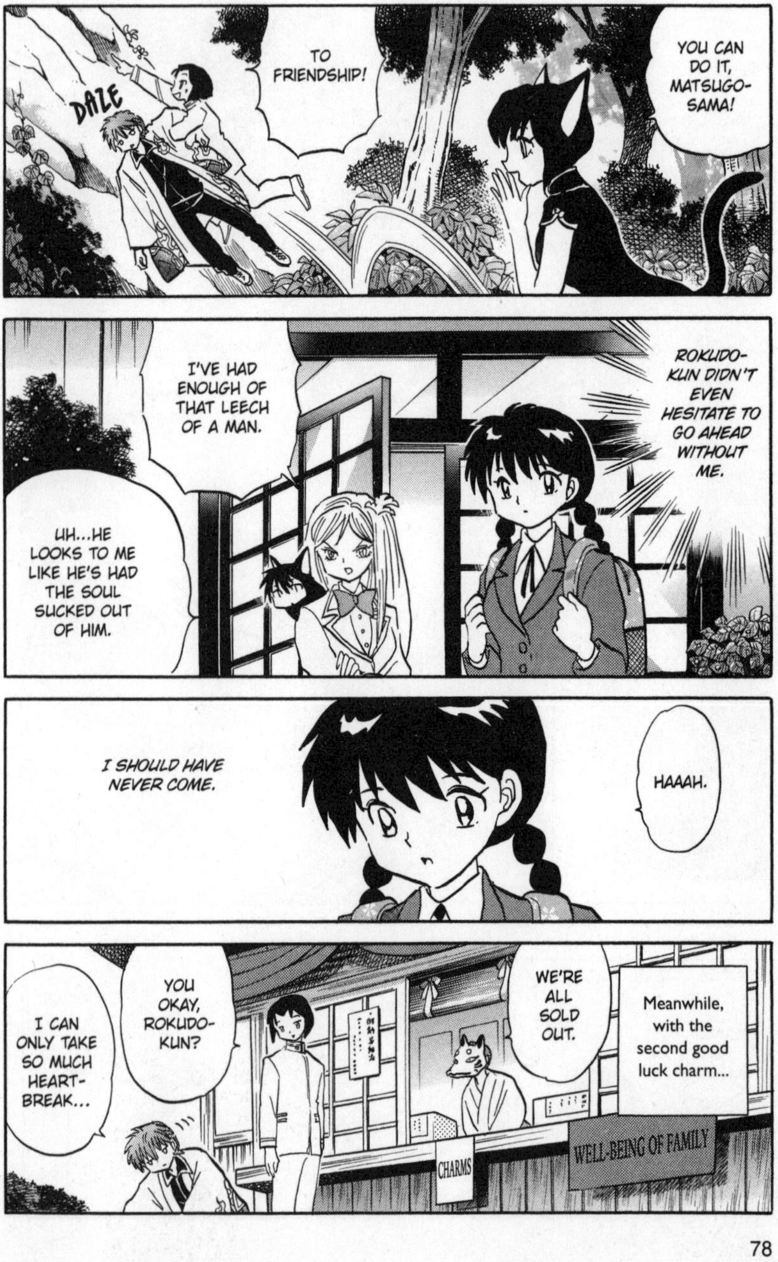
YOU CAN DO IT, MATSUGO-SAMA!
TO FRIENDSHIP!
DAZE
ROKUDO-KUN DIDN'T EVEN HESITATE TO GO AHEAD WITHOUT ME.
I'VE HAD ENOUGH OF THAT LEECH OF A MAN.
UH...HE LOOKS TO ME LIKE HE'S HAD THE SOUL SUCKED OUT OF HIM.
HAAAH.
I SHOULD HAVE NEVER COME.
Meanwhile, with the second good luck charm...
WE'RE ALL SOLD OUT.
WELL-BEING OF FAMILY
CHARMS
YOU OKAY, ROKUDO-KUN?
I CAN ONLY TAKE SO MUCH HEART-BREAK...

Chapter 193: Are You Too Good for It?

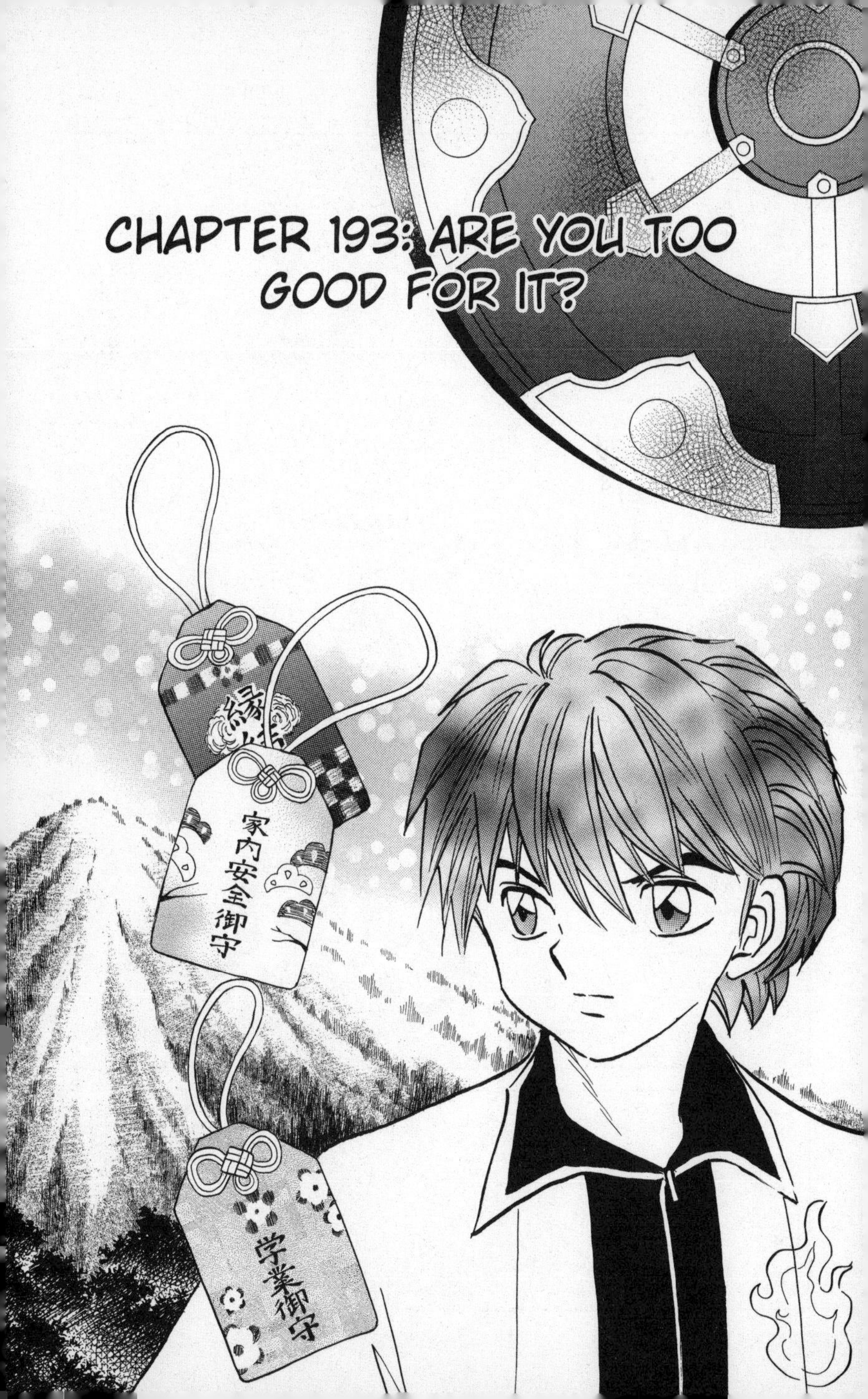
家内安全御守
学業御守

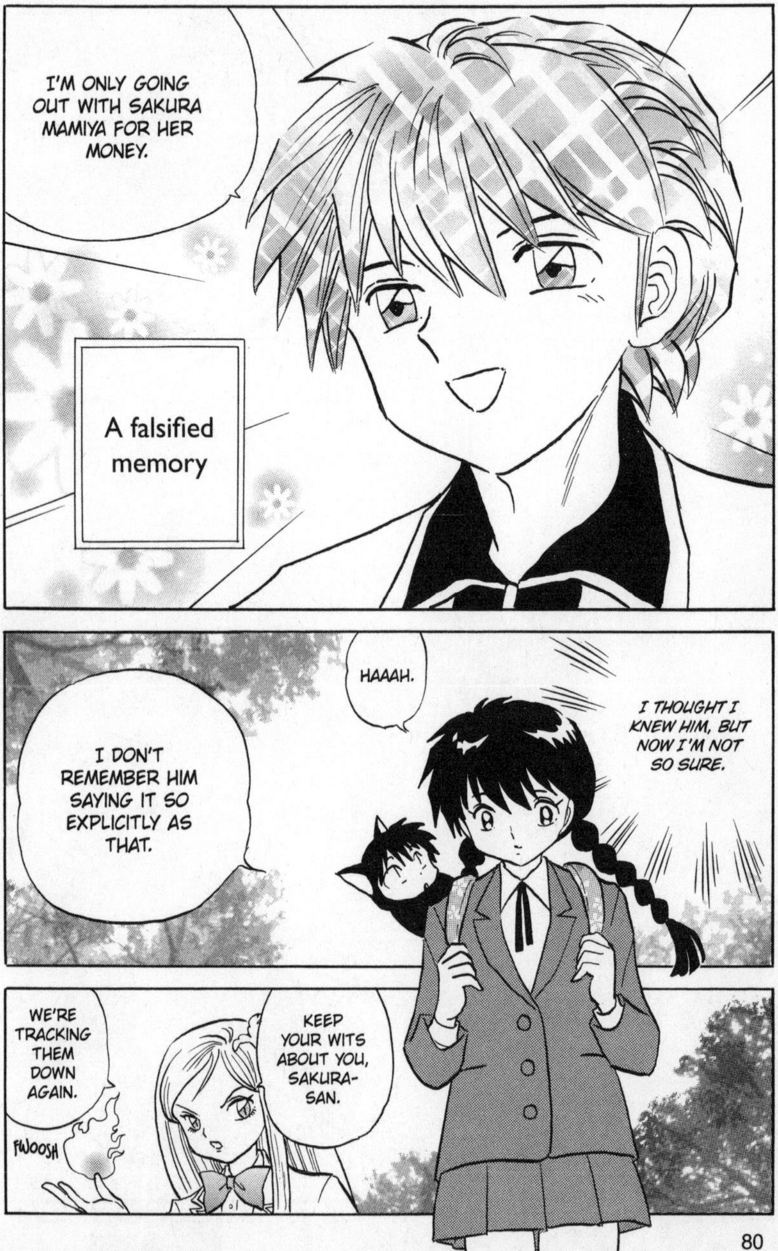
I'M ONLY GOING OUT WITH SAKURA MAMIYA FOR HER MONEY.
A falsified memory
I THOUGHT I KNEW HIM, BUT NOW I'M NOT SO SURE.
HAAAH.
I DON'T REMEMBER HIM SAYING IT SO EXPLICITLY AS THAT.
KEEP YOUR WITS ABOUT YOU, SAKURA-SAN.
WE'RE TRACKING THEM DOWN AGAIN.
FWOOSH

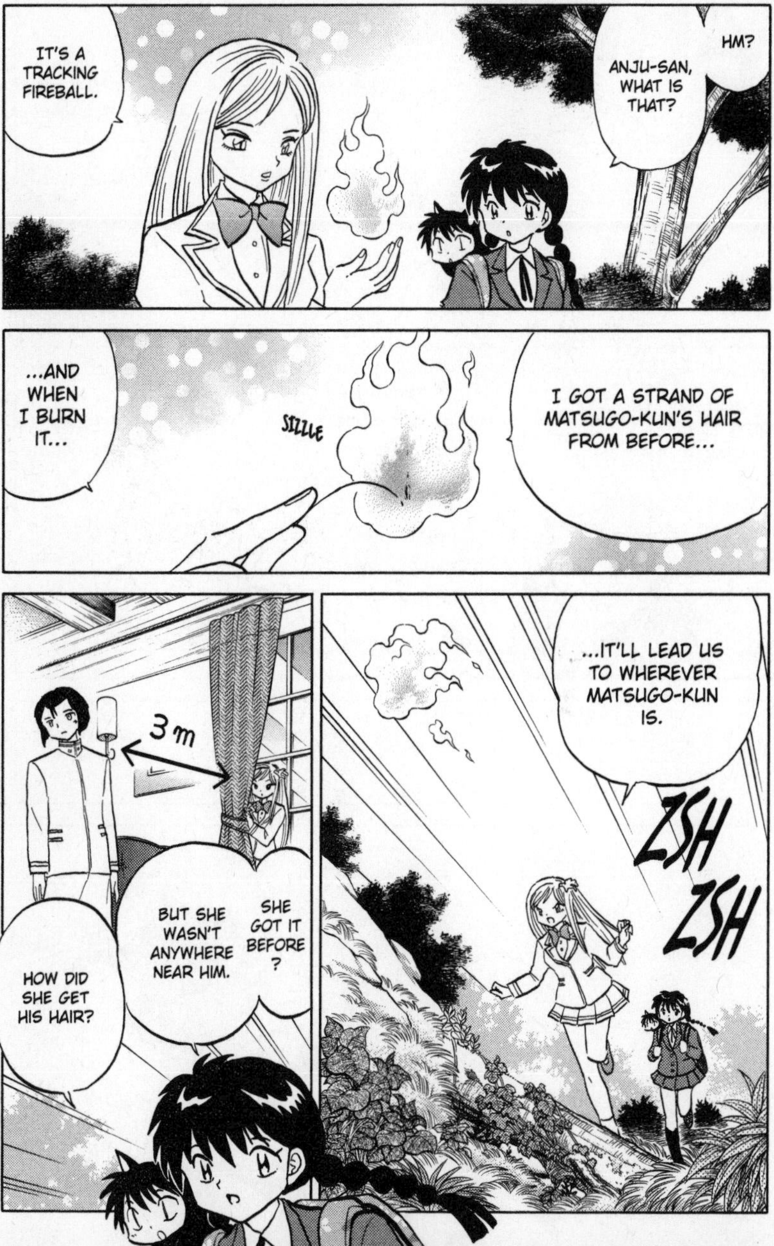
HM?
ANJU-SAN, WHAT IS THAT?
IT'S A TRACKING FIREBALL.
I GOT A STRAND OF MATSUGO-KUN'S HAIR FROM BEFORE...
SIZZLE
...AND WHEN I BURN IT...
...IT'LL LEAD US TO WHEREVER MATSUGO-KUN IS.
ZSH
ZSH
3 m
SHE GOT IT BEFORE?
BUT SHE WASN'T ANYWHERE NEAR HIM.
HOW DID SHE GET HIS HAIR?

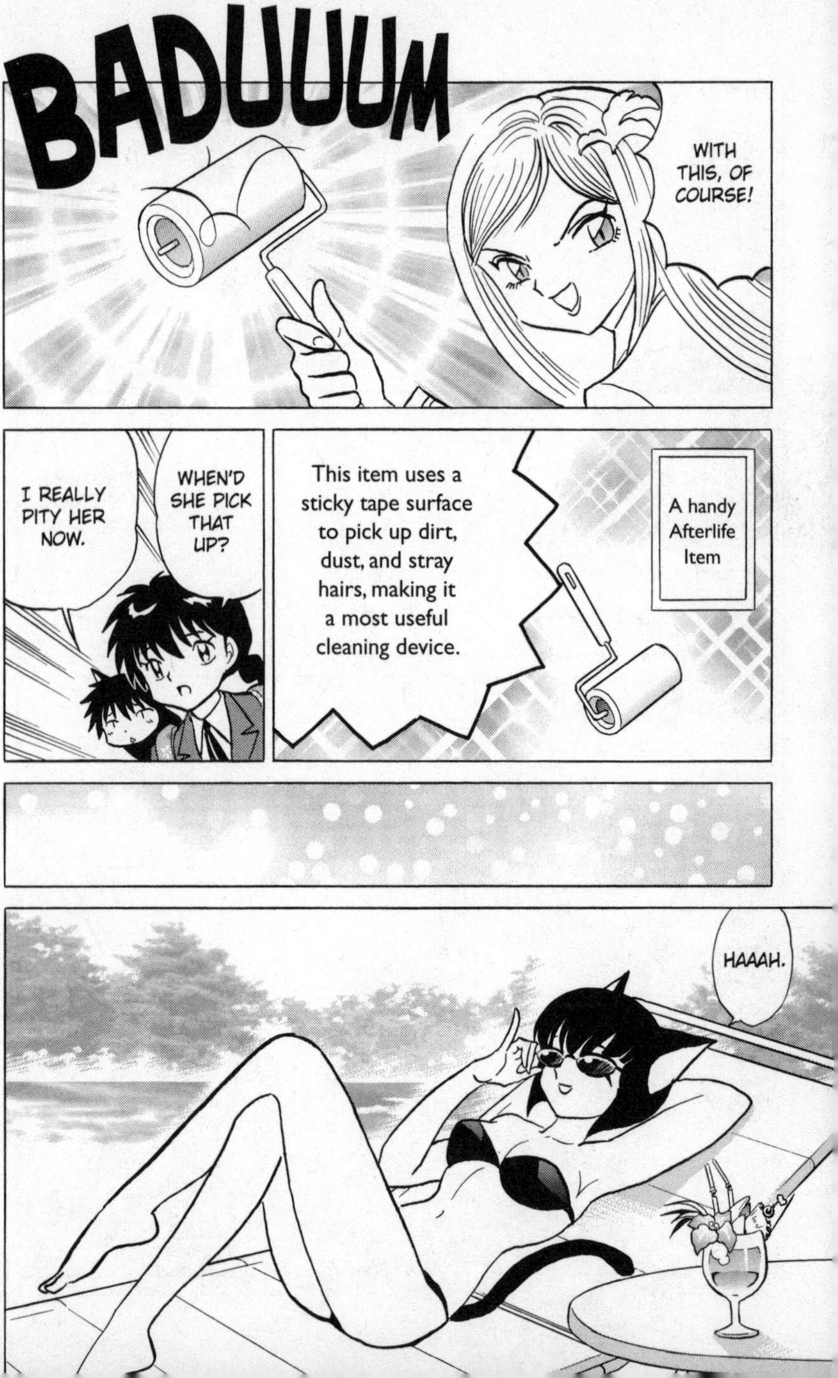
BADUUUM
WITH THIS, OF COURSE!
A handy Afterlife Item
This item uses a sticky tape surface to pick up dirt, dust, and stray hairs, making it a most useful cleaning device.
WHEN'D SHE PICK THAT UP?
I REALLY PITY HER NOW.
HAAAH.

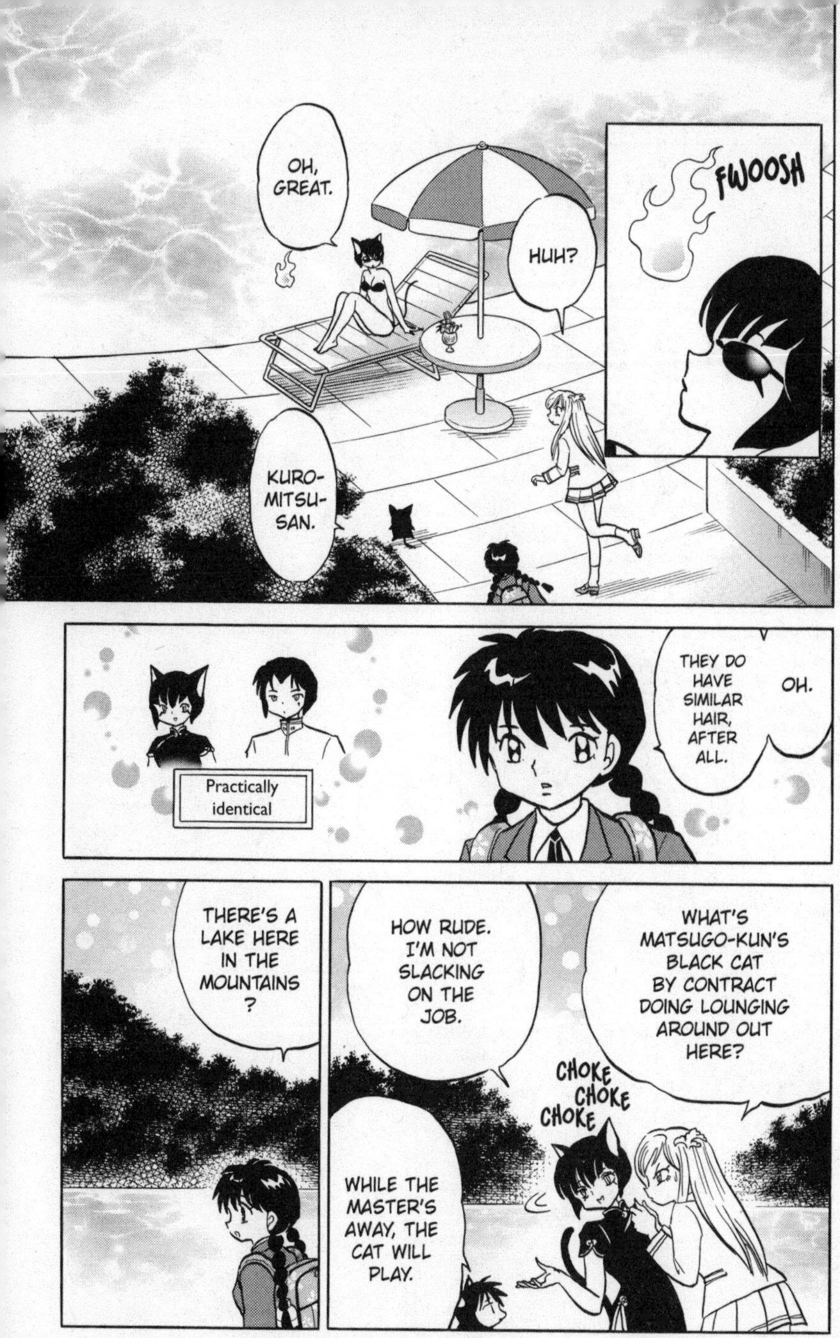
FWOOSH
HUH?
OH, GREAT.
KURO-MITSU-SAN.
OH.
THEY DO HAVE SIMILAR HAIR, AFTER ALL.
Practically identical
WHAT'S MATSUGO-KUN'S BLACK CAT BY CONTRACT DOING LOUNGING AROUND OUT HERE?
HOW RUDE. I'M NOT SLACKING ON THE JOB.
CHOKE CHOKE CHOKE
WHILE THE MASTER'S AWAY, THE CAT WILL PLAY.
THERE'S A LAKE HERE IN THE MOUNTAINS?

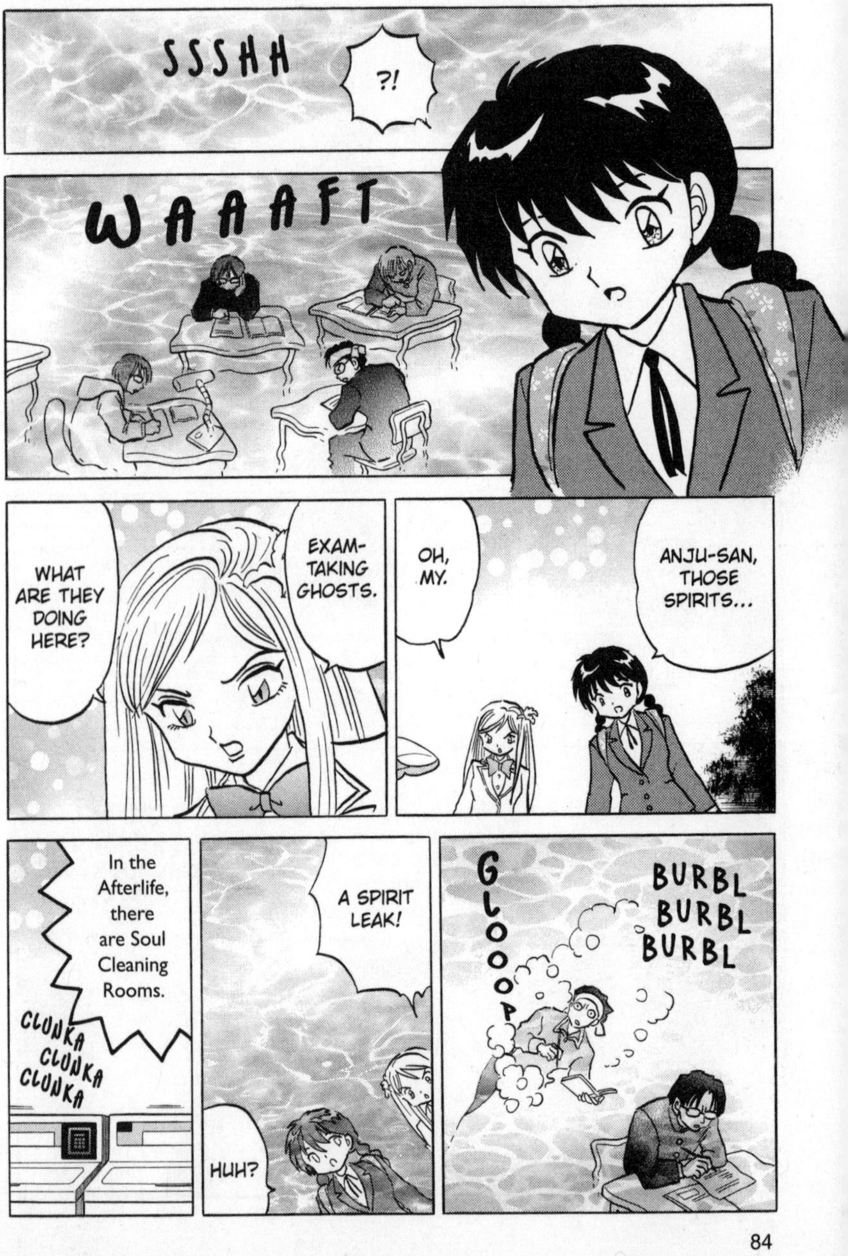
?!
SSSHH
WAAAFT
ANJU-SAN, THOSE SPIRITS...
OH, MY.
EXAM-TAKING GHOSTS.
WHAT ARE THEY DOING HERE?
BURBL BURBL BURBL
GLOOOP
A SPIRIT LEAK!
HUH?
In the Afterlife, there are Soul Cleaning Rooms.
CLUNKA CLUNKA CLUNKA

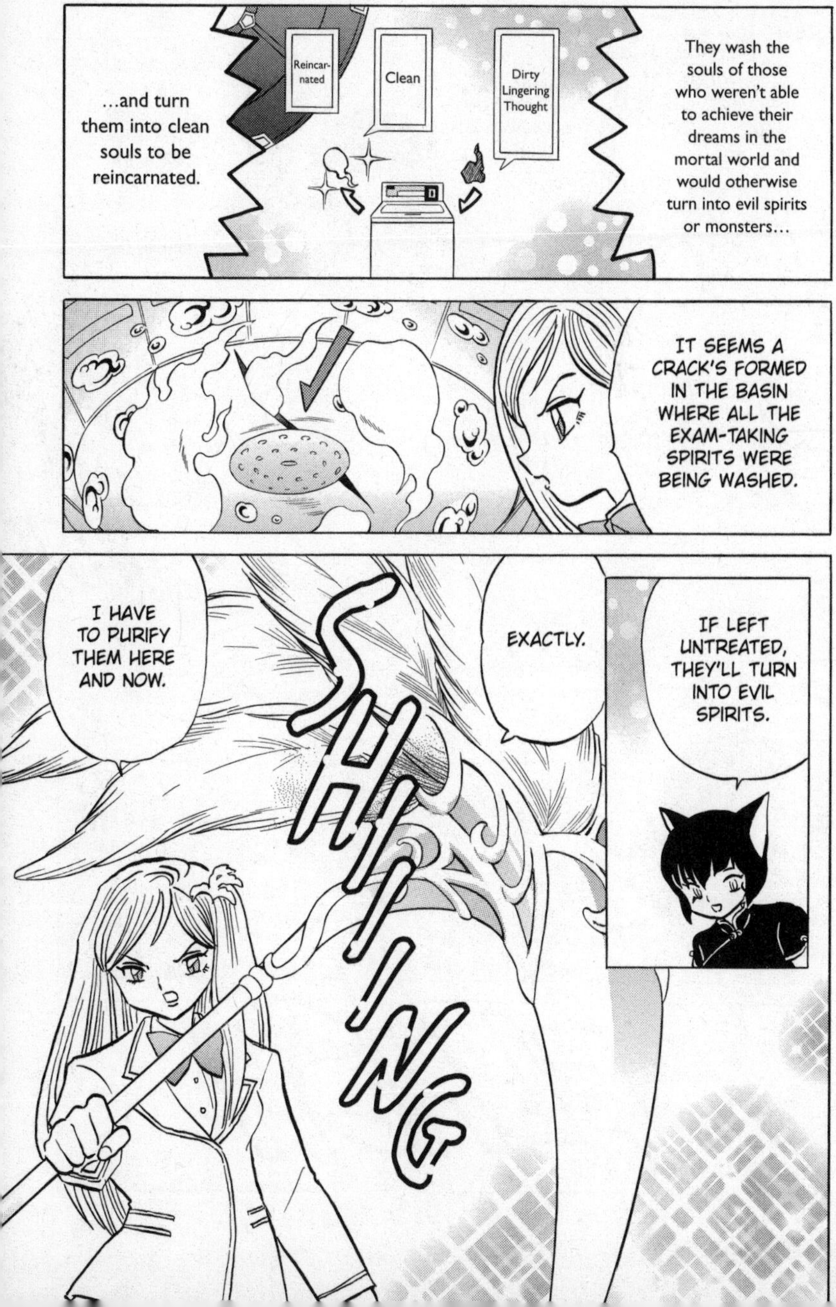
They wash the souls of those who weren't able to achieve their dreams in the mortal world and would otherwise turn into evil spirits or monsters...
Dirty Lingering Thought
Clean
Reincar-nated
...and turn them into clean souls to be reincarnated.
IT SEEMS A CRACK'S FORMED IN THE BASIN WHERE ALL THE EXAM-TAKING SPIRITS WERE BEING WASHED.
IF LEFT UNTREATED, THEY'LL TURN INTO EVIL SPIRITS.
EXACTLY.
I HAVE TO PURIFY THEM HERE AND NOW.
SHIIING

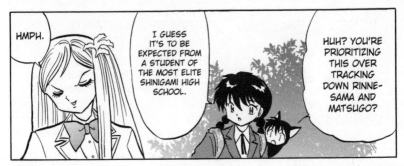

HUH? YOU'RE PRIORITIZING THIS OVER TRACKING DOWN RINNE-SAMA AND MATSUGO?
I GUESS IT'S TO BE EXPECTED FROM A STUDENT OF THE MOST ELITE SHINIGAMI HIGH SCHOOL.
HMPH.
I'LL BE DONE WITH THEM IN AN INSTANT!
BEGONE, YOU FAILURES!
SWISH
HUH?!
GLARE
FLASH
Headband: Pass

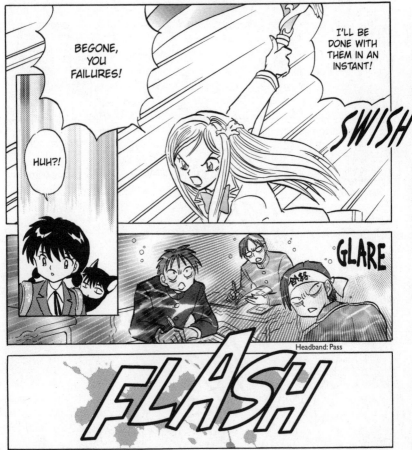

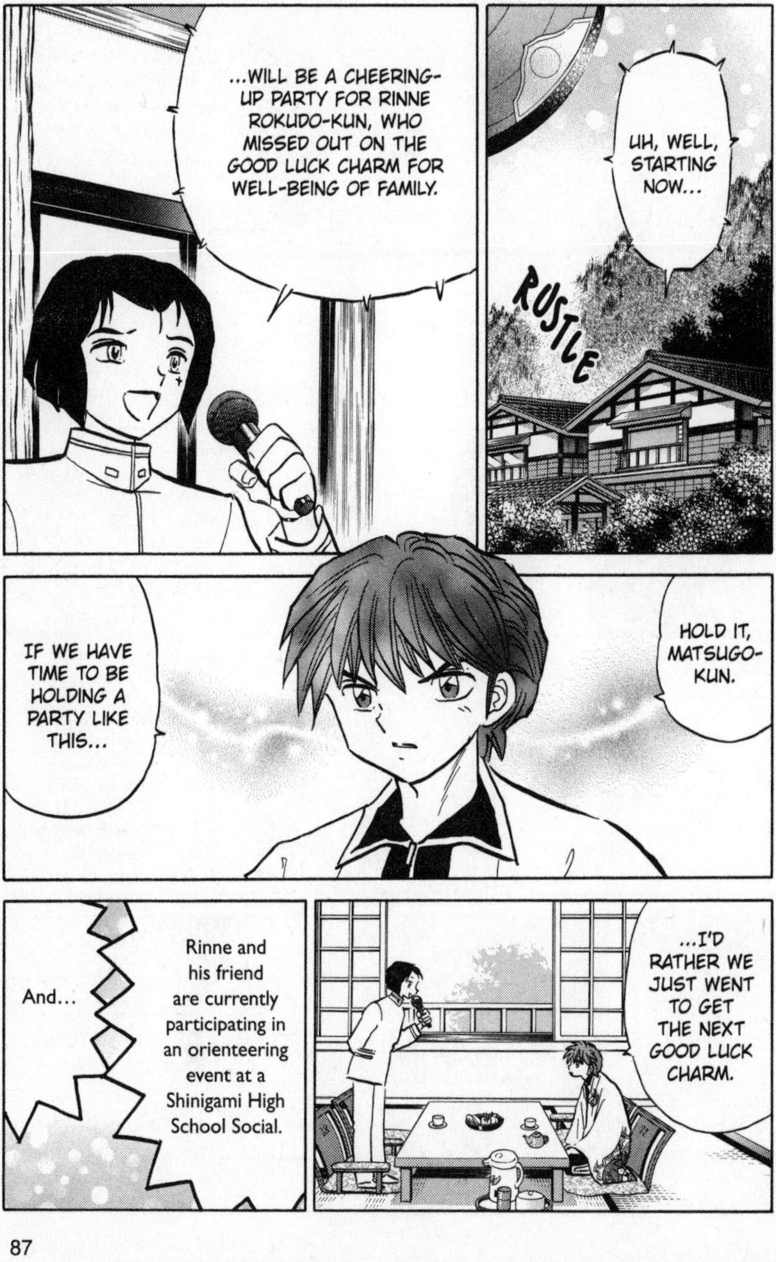
UH, WELL, STARTING NOW...
RUSTLE
...WILL BE A CHEERING-UP PARTY FOR RINNE ROKUDO-KUN, WHO MISSED OUT ON THE GOOD LUCK CHARM FOR WELL-BEING OF FAMILY.
HOLD IT, MATSUGO-KUN.
IF WE HAVE TIME TO BE HOLDING A PARTY LIKE THIS...
...I'D RATHER WE JUST WENT TO GET THE NEXT GOOD LUCK CHARM.
Rinne and his friend are currently participating in an orienteering event at a Shinigami High School Social.
And...

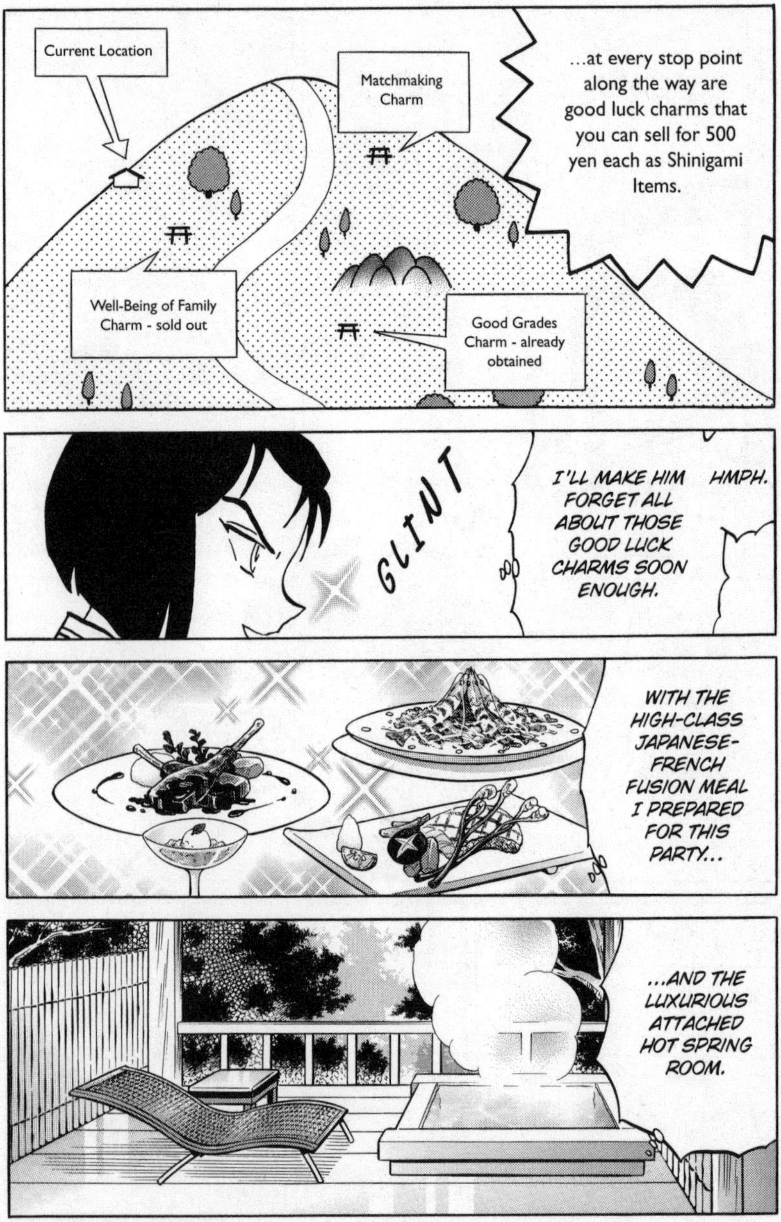
...at every stop point along the way are good luck charms that you can sell for 500 yen each as Shinigami Items.
Matchmaking Charm
Current Location
Well-Being of Family Charm - sold out
Good Grades Charm - already obtained
HMPH.
I'LL MAKE HIM FORGET ALL ABOUT THOSE GOOD LUCK CHARMS SOON ENOUGH.
GLINT
WITH THE HIGH-CLASS JAPANESE-FRENCH FUSION MEAL I PREPARED FOR THIS PARTY...
...AND THE LUXURIOUS ATTACHED HOT SPRING ROOM.

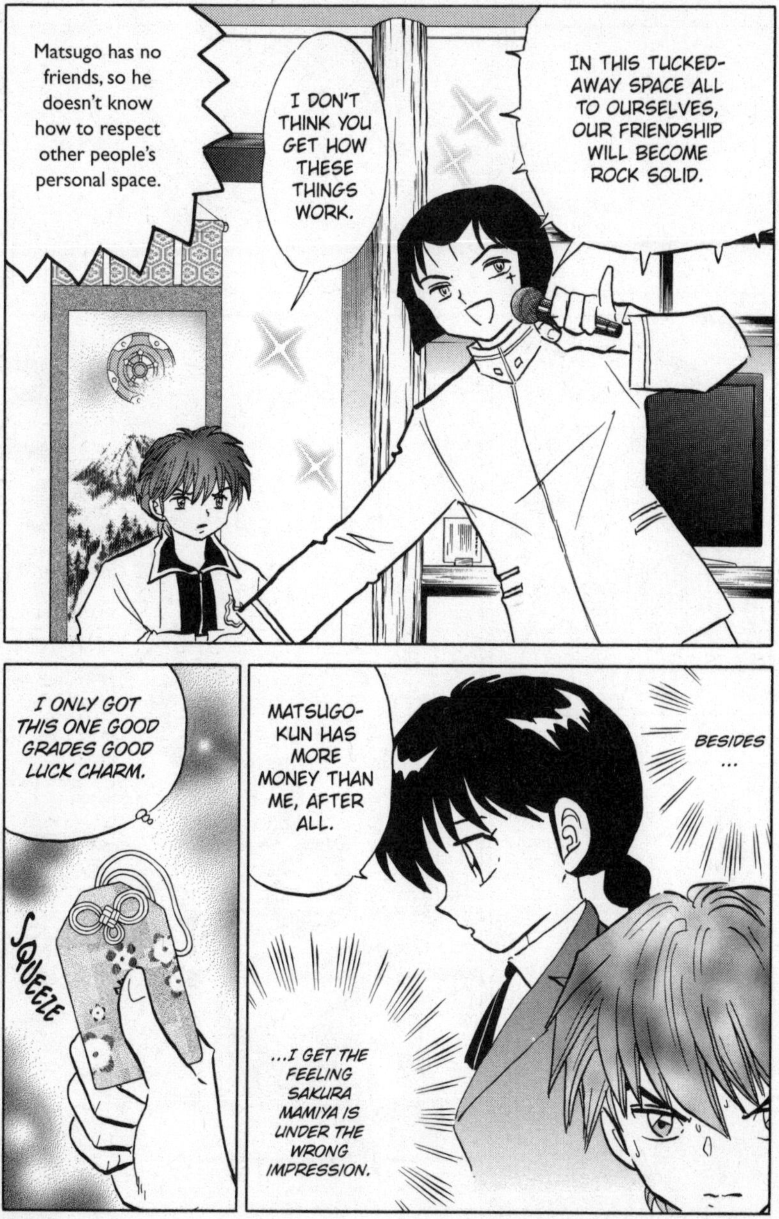
IN THIS TUCKED-AWAY SPACE ALL TO OURSELVES, OUR FRIENDSHIP WILL BECOME ROCK SOLID.
I DON'T THINK YOU GET HOW THESE THINGS WORK.
Matsugo has no friends, so he doesn't know how to respect other people's personal space.
BESIDES...
MATSUGO-KUN HAS MORE MONEY THAN ME, AFTER ALL.
...I GET THE FEELING SAKURA MAMIYA IS UNDER THE WRONG IMPRESSION.
I ONLY GOT THIS ONE GOOD GRADES GOOD LUCK CHARM.
SQUEEZE

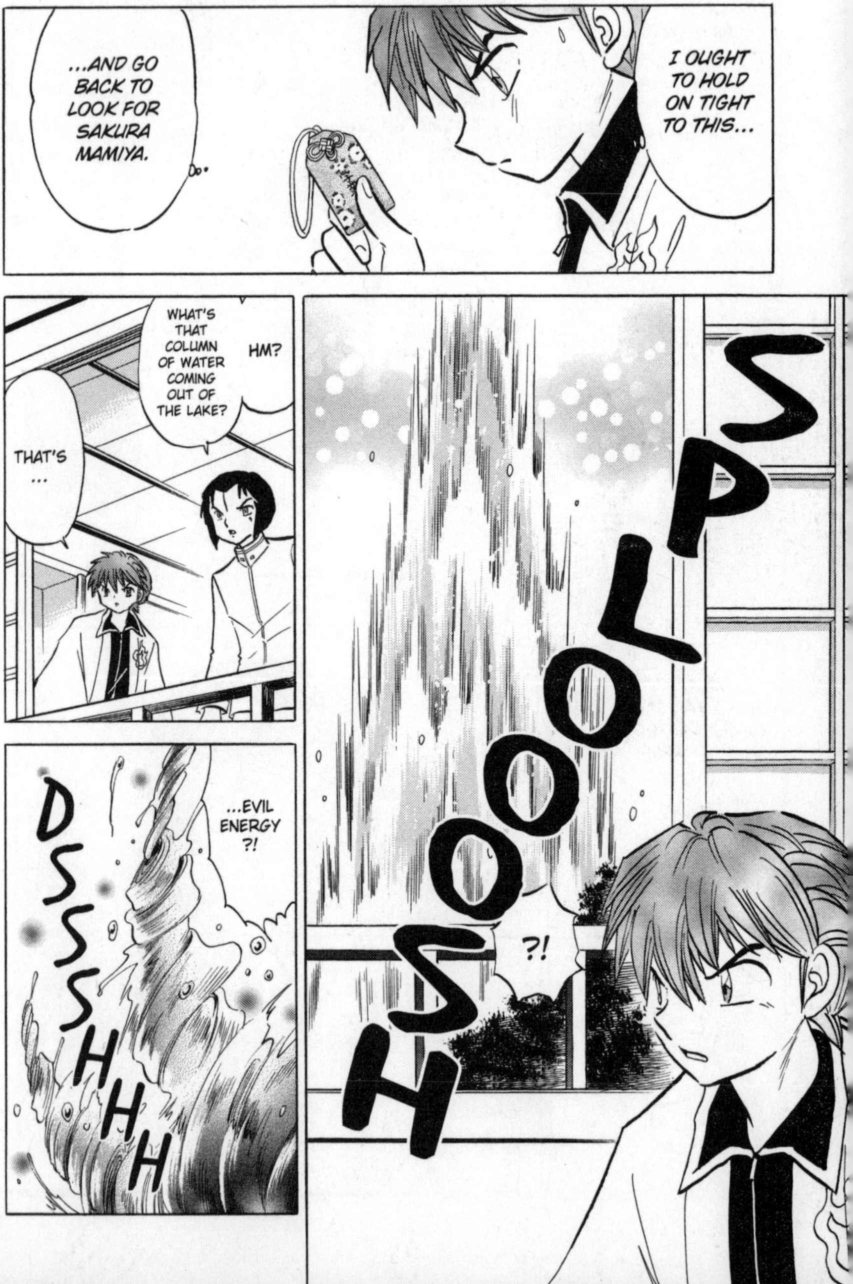
I OUGHT TO HOLD ON TIGHT TO THIS...
...AND GO BACK TO LOOK FOR SAKURA MAMIYA.
SPLOOOOSH
?!
HM?
WHAT'S THAT COLUMN OF WATER COMING OUT OF THE LAKE?
THAT'S...
...EVIL ENERGY?!
DSSSHHHH

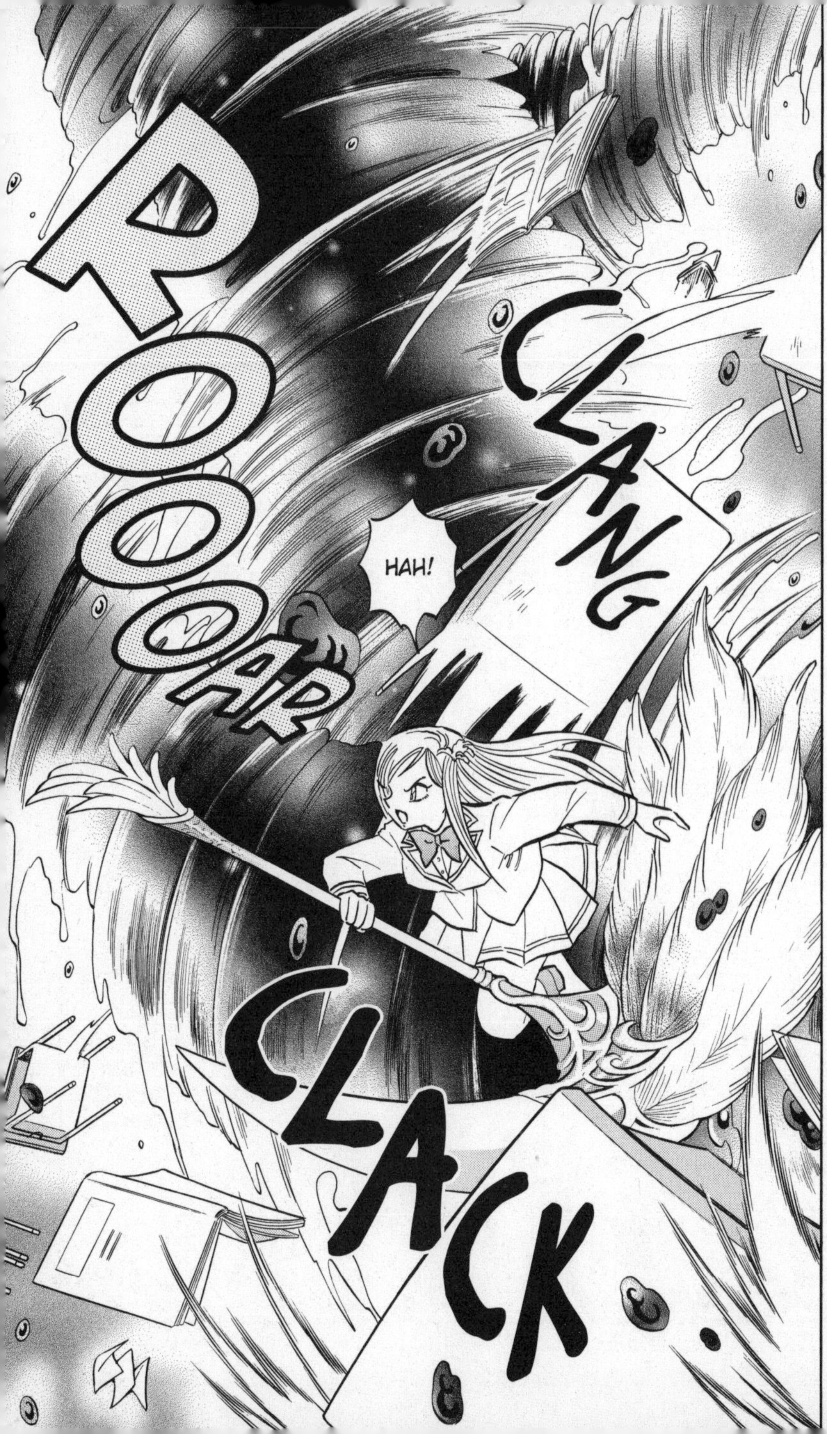
CLANG
HAH!
ROOOOAR
CLACK

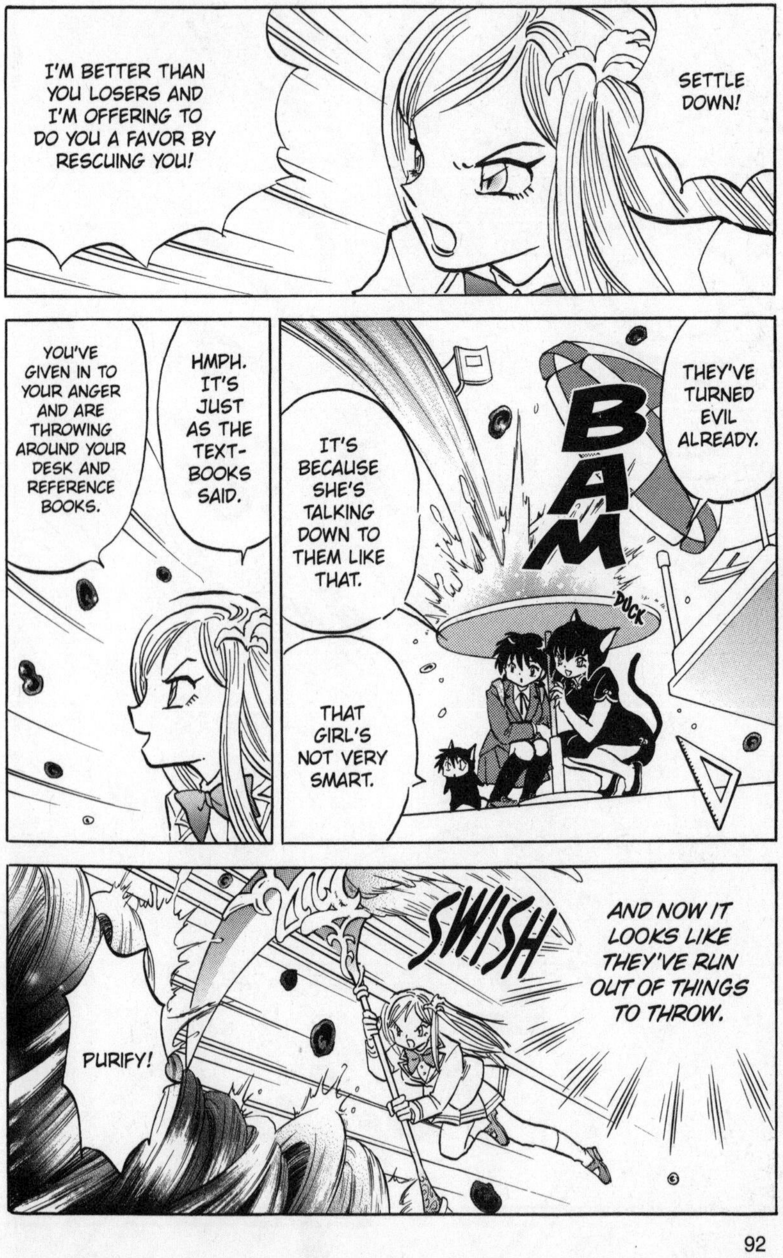
SETTLE DOWN!
I'M BETTER THAN YOU LOSERS AND I'M OFFERING TO DO YOU A FAVOR BY RESCUING YOU!
THEY'VE TURNED EVIL ALREADY.
BAM
IT'S BECAUSE SHE'S TALKING DOWN TO THEM LIKE THAT.
DUCK
THAT GIRL'S NOT VERY SMART.
HMPH. IT'S JUST AS THE TEXT-BOOKS SAID.
YOU'VE GIVEN IN TO YOUR ANGER AND ARE THROWING AROUND YOUR DESK AND REFERENCE BOOKS.
AND NOW IT LOOKS LIKE THEY'VE RUN OUT OF THINGS TO THROW.
SWISH
PURIFY!

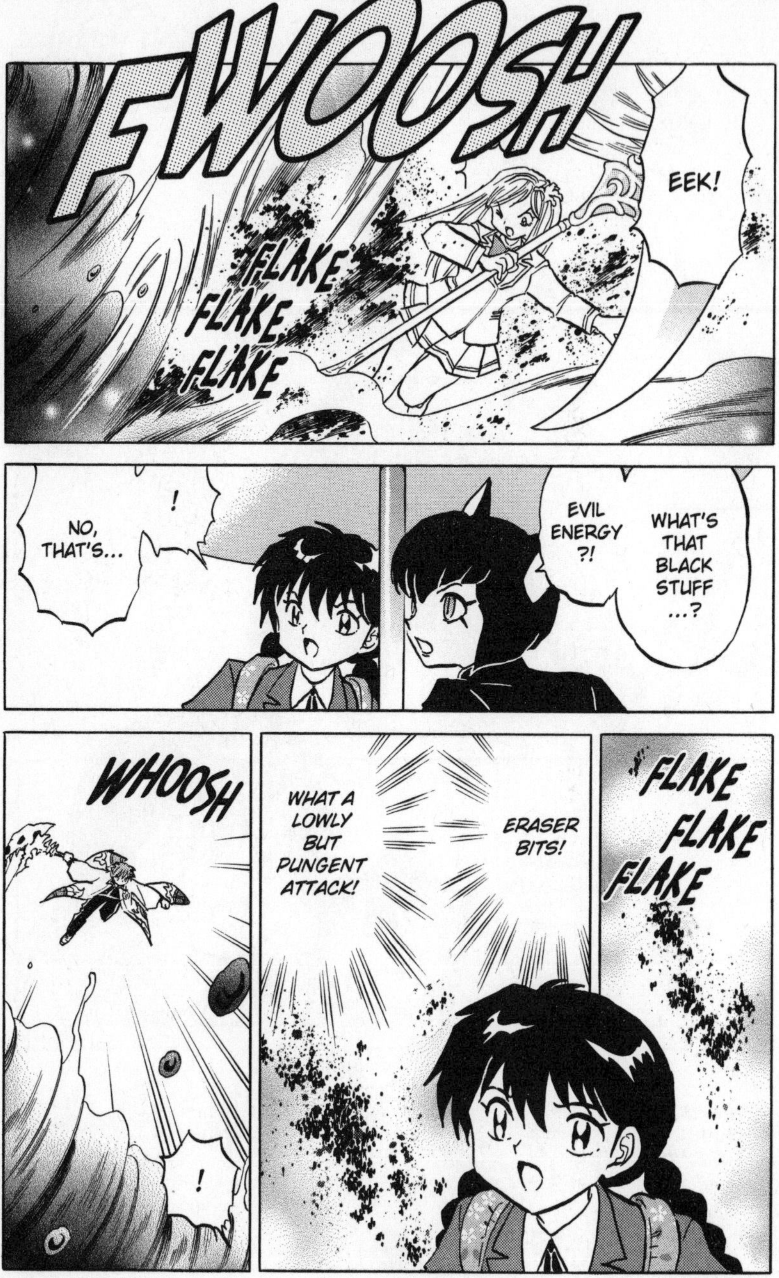
FWOOSH
EEK!
FLAKE FLAKE FLAKE
WHAT'S THAT BLACK STUFF ...?
EVIL ENERGY ?!
!
NO, THAT'S...
FLAKE FLAKE FLAKE
ERASER BITS!
WHAT A LOWLY BUT PUNGENT ATTACK!
WHOOSH
!

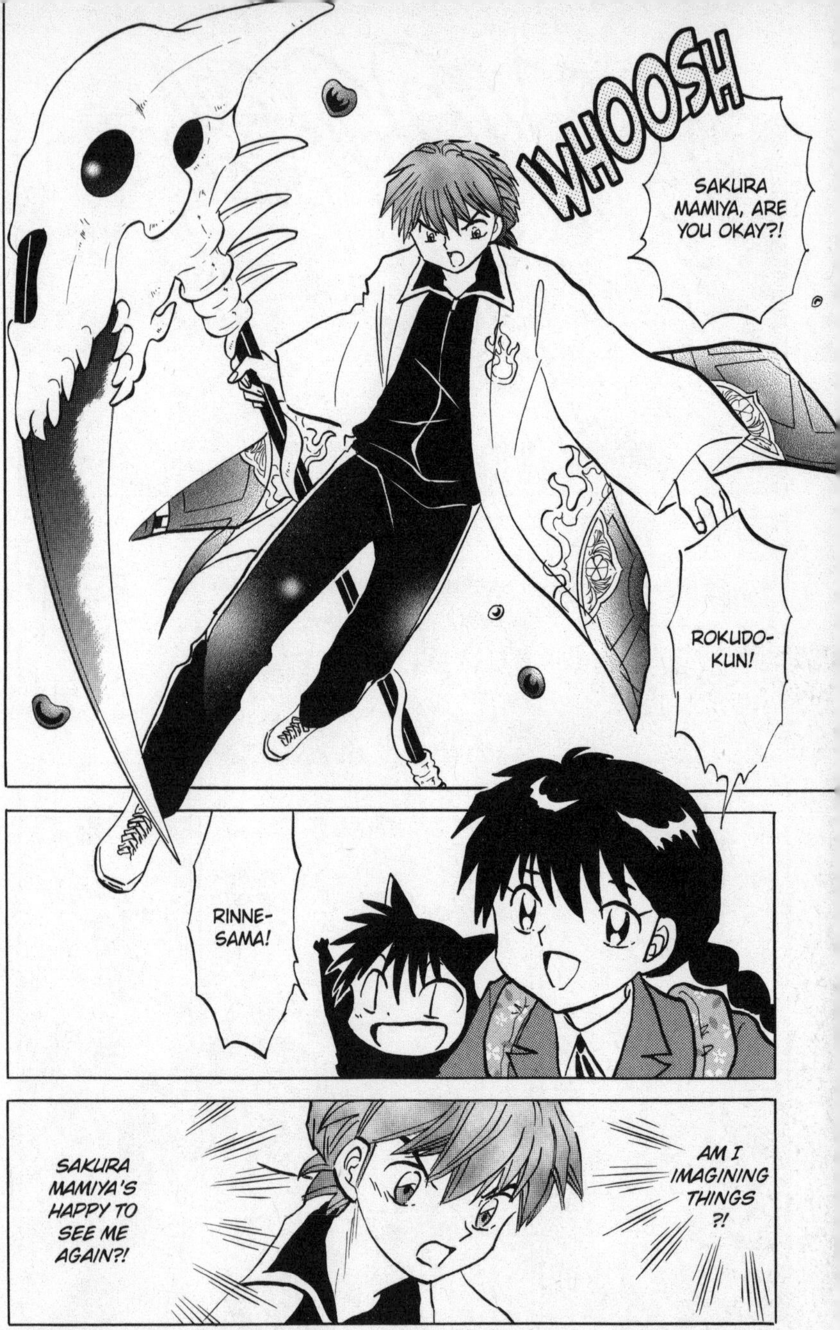
WHOOSH
SAKURA MAMIYA, ARE YOU OKAY?!
ROKUDO-KUN!
RINNE-SAMA!
AM I IMAGINING THINGS?!
SAKURA MAMIYA'S HAPPY TO SEE ME AGAIN?!

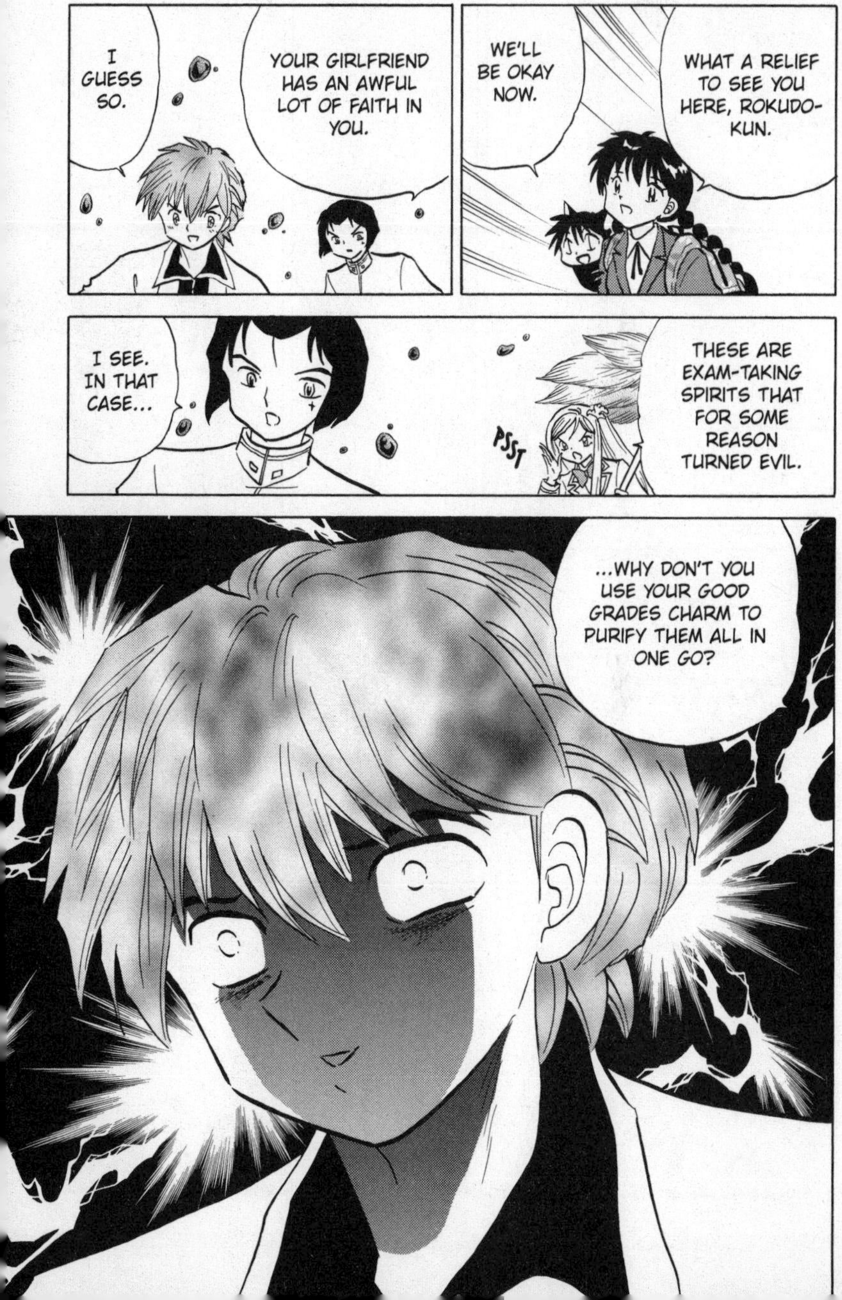
WHAT A RELIEF TO SEE YOU HERE, ROKUDO-KUN.
WE'LL BE OKAY NOW.
YOUR GIRLFRIEND HAS AN AWFUL LOT OF FAITH IN YOU.
I GUESS SO.
THESE ARE EXAM-TAKING SPIRITS THAT FOR SOME REASON TURNED EVIL.
PSST
I SEE. IN THAT CASE...
...WHY DON'T YOU USE YOUR GOOD GRADES CHARM TO PURIFY THEM ALL IN ONE GO?

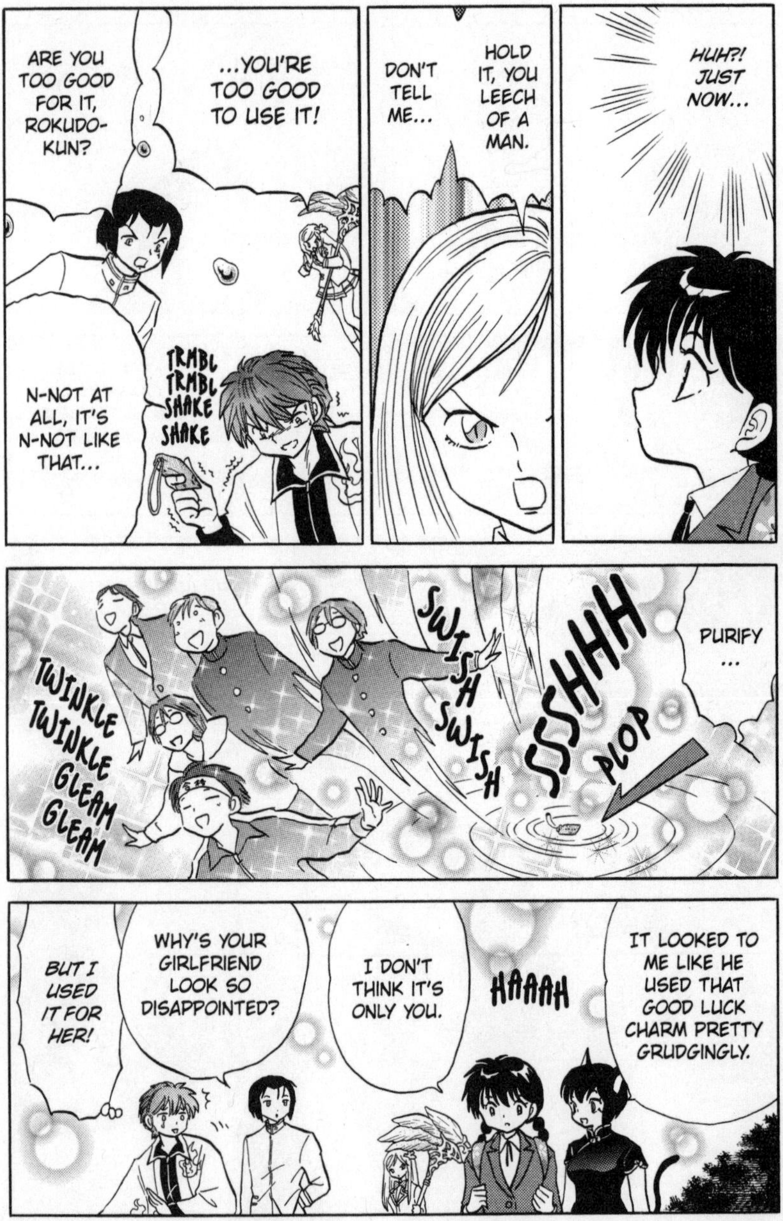
HUH?! JUST NOW...
HOLD IT, YOU LEECH OF A MAN.
DON'T TELL ME...
...YOU'RE TOO GOOD TO USE IT!
ARE YOU TOO GOOD FOR IT, ROKUDO-KUN?
TRMBL TRMBL SHAKE SHAKE
N-NOT AT ALL, IT'S N-NOT LIKE THAT...
PURIFY ...
SSSHHH
PLOP
SWISH SWISH SWISH SWISH
TWINKLE TWINKLE GLEAM GLEAM
IT LOOKED TO ME LIKE HE USED THAT GOOD LUCK CHARM PRETTY GRUDGINGLY.
HAAAH
I DON'T THINK IT'S ONLY YOU.
WHY'S YOUR GIRLFRIEND LOOK SO DISAPPOINTED?
BUT I USED IT FOR HER!

CHAPTER 194: SAKURA'S MOOD

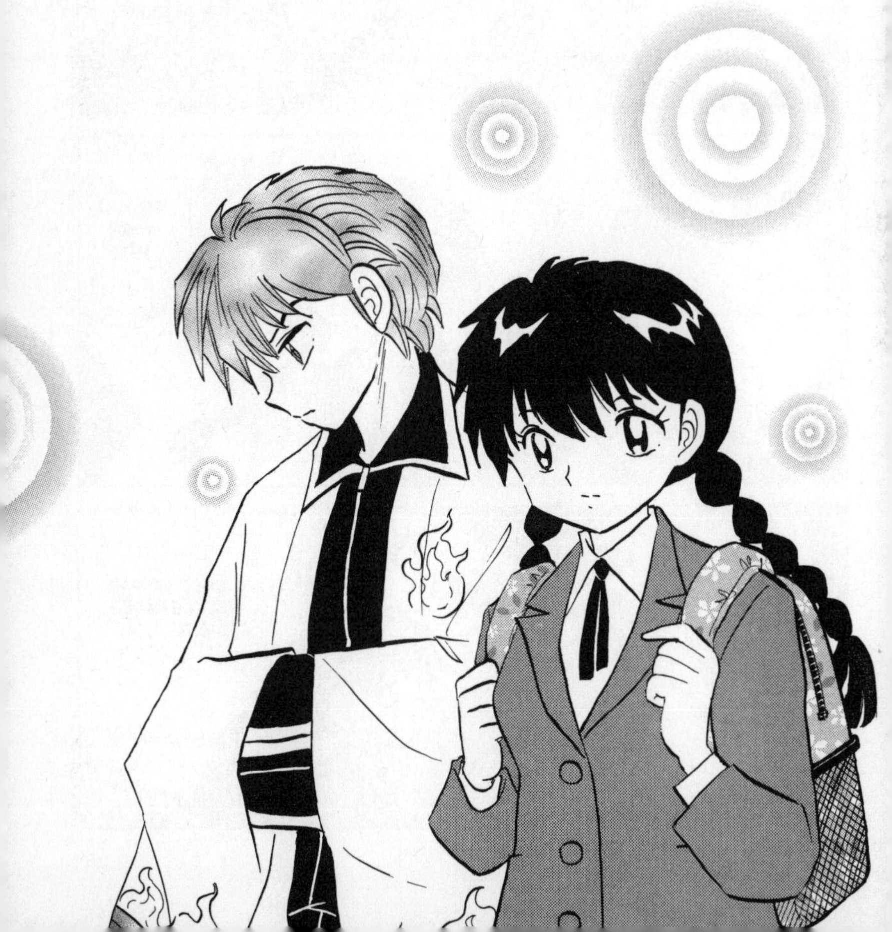

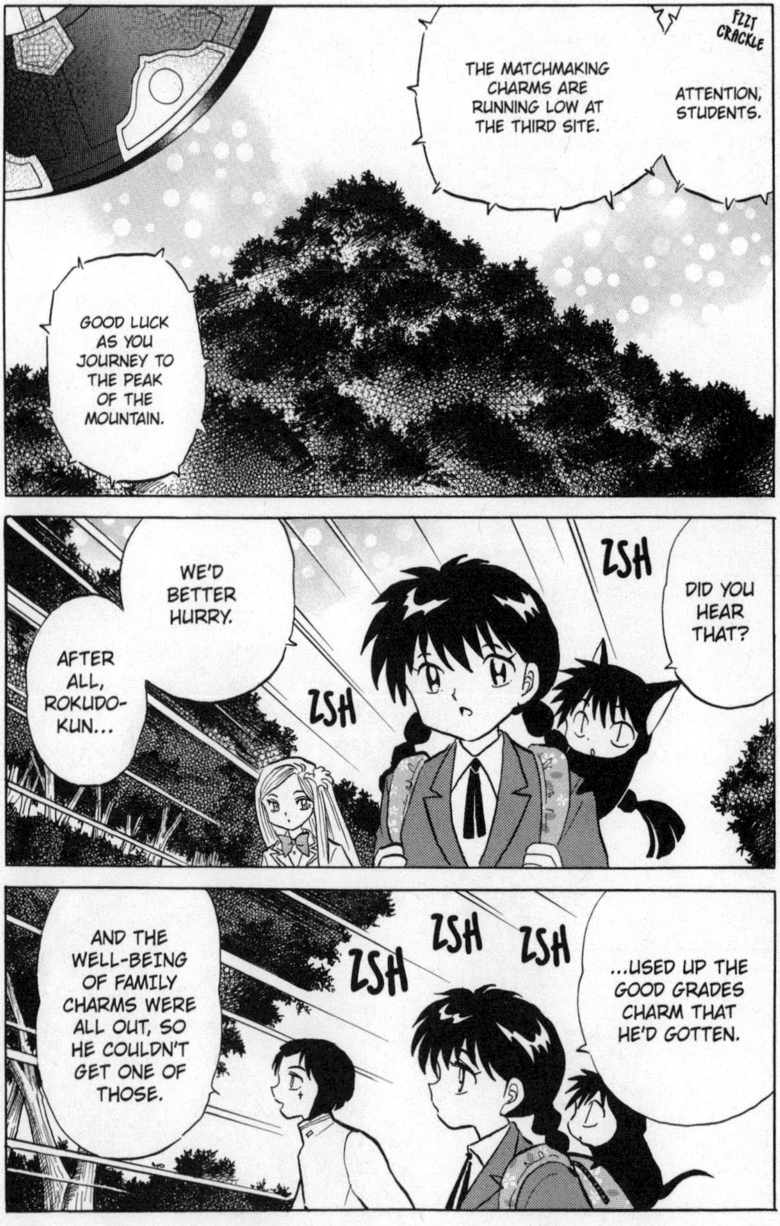
FZZT CRACKLE
ATTENTION, STUDENTS.
THE MATCHMAKING CHARMS ARE RUNNING LOW AT THE THIRD SITE.
GOOD LUCK AS YOU JOURNEY TO THE PEAK OF THE MOUNTAIN.
ZSH
DID YOU HEAR THAT?
ZSH
WE'D BETTER HURRY.
AFTER ALL, ROKUDO-KUN...
...USED UP THE GOOD GRADES CHARM THAT HE'D GOTTEN.
ZSH
ZSH
ZSH
AND THE WELL-BEING OF FAMILY CHARMS WERE ALL OUT, SO HE COULDN'T GET ONE OF THOSE.

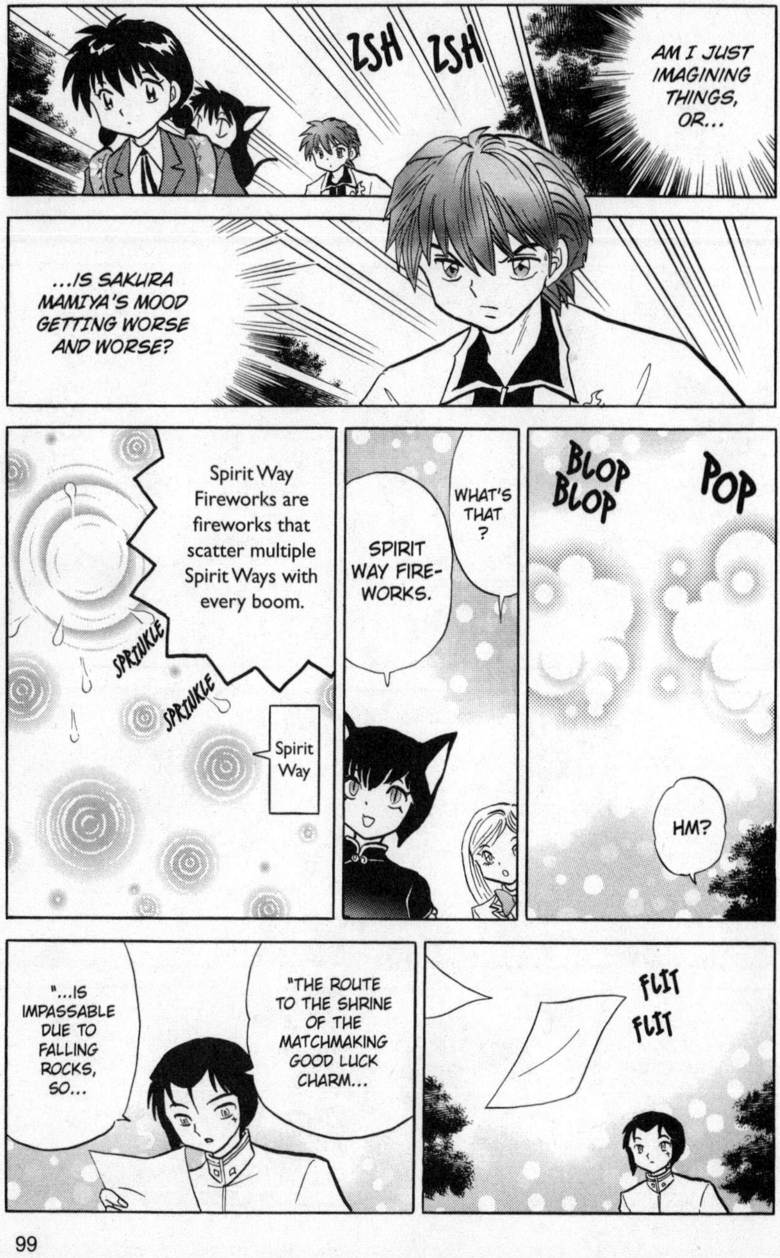
AM I JUST IMAGINING THINGS, OR...
ZSH ZSH
...IS SAKURA MAMIYA'S MOOD GETTING WORSE AND WORSE?
POP
BLOP BLOP
HM?
WHAT'S THAT?
SPIRIT WAY FIRE-WORKS.
Spirit Way Fireworks are fireworks that scatter multiple Spirit Ways with every boom.
SPRINKLE
SPRINKLE
Spirit Way
FLIT
FLIT
"THE ROUTE TO THE SHRINE OF THE MATCHMAKING GOOD LUCK CHARM...
"...IS IMPASSABLE DUE TO FALLING ROCKS, SO...

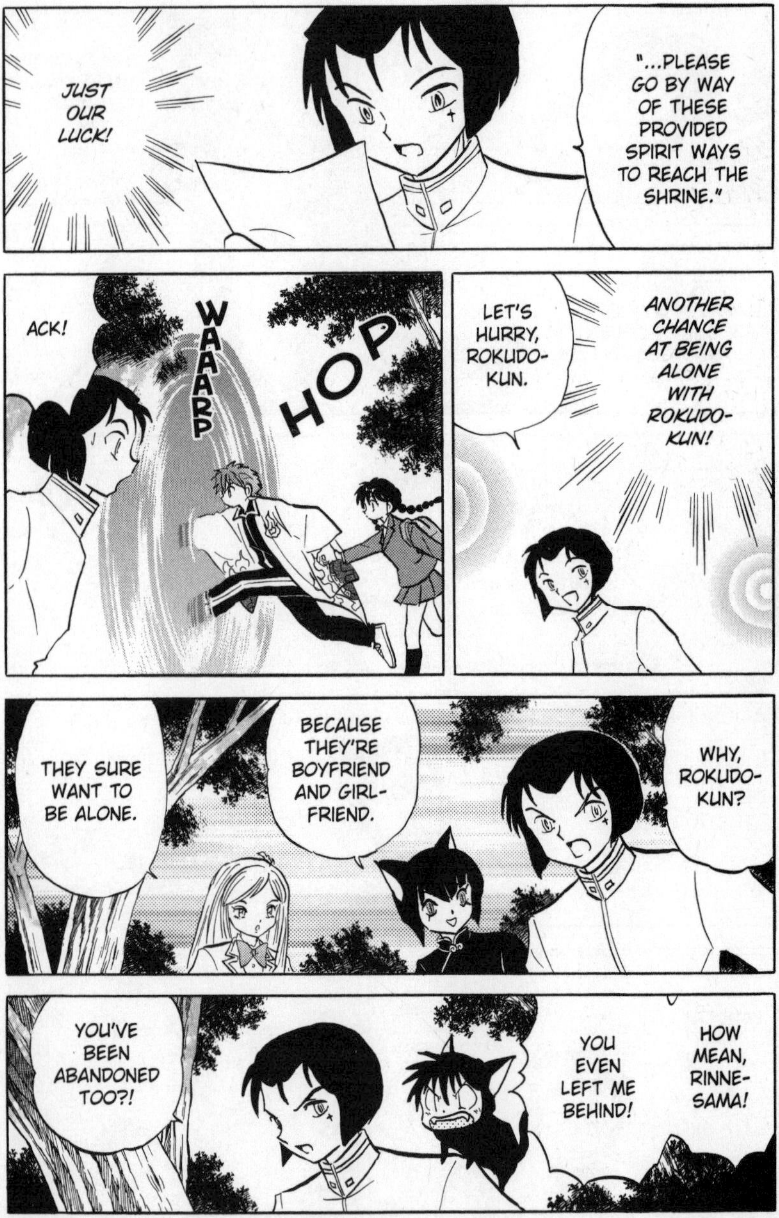
"...PLEASE GO BY WAY OF THESE PROVIDED SPIRIT WAYS TO REACH THE SHRINE."
JUST OUR LUCK!
ANOTHER CHANCE AT BEING ALONE WITH ROKUDO-KUN!
LET'S HURRY, ROKUDO-KUN.
HOP
WAAARP
ACK!
WHY, ROKUDO-KUN?
BECAUSE THEY'RE BOYFRIEND AND GIRL-FRIEND.
THEY SURE WANT TO BE ALONE.
HOW MEAN, RINNE-SAMA!
YOU EVEN LEFT ME BEHIND!
YOU'VE BEEN ABANDONED TOO?!

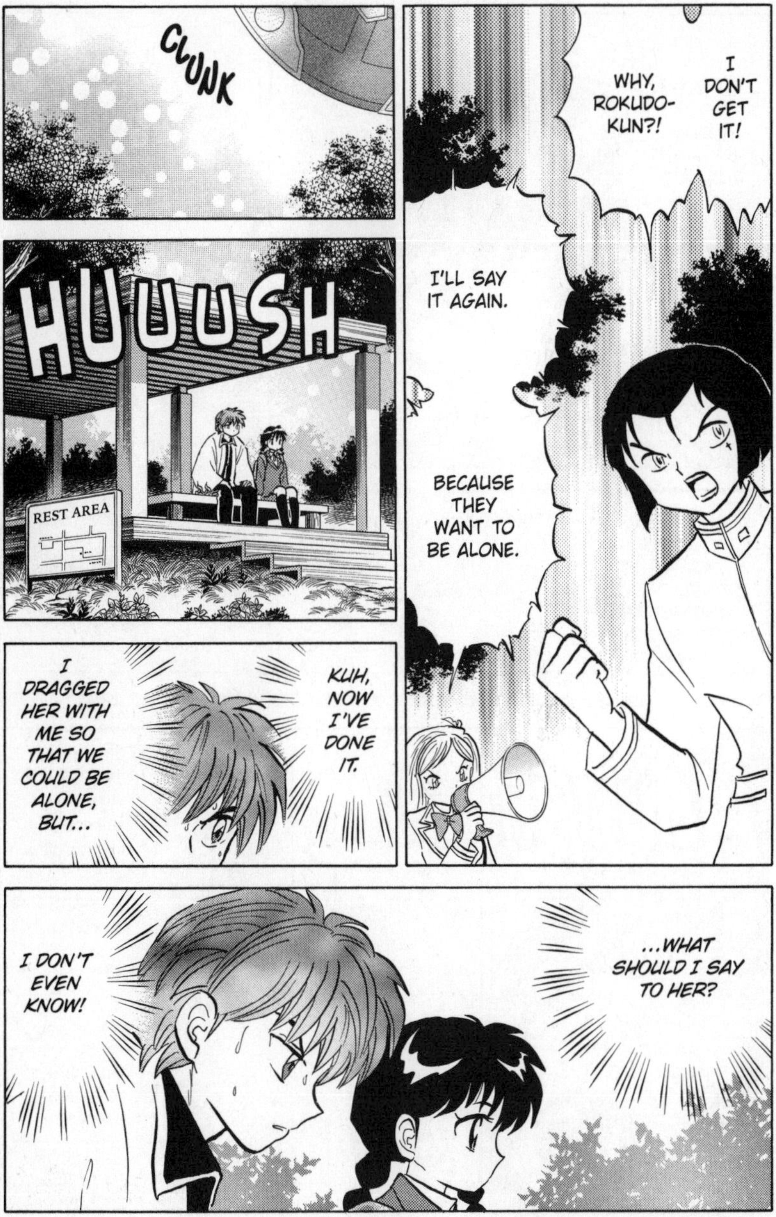
I DON'T GET IT!
WHY, ROKUDO-KUN?!
I'LL SAY IT AGAIN.
BECAUSE THEY WANT TO BE ALONE.
CLUNK
HUUUSH
REST AREA
KUH, NOW I'VE DONE IT.
I DRAGGED HER WITH ME SO THAT WE COULD BE ALONE, BUT...
...WHAT SHOULD I SAY TO HER?
I DON'T EVEN KNOW!

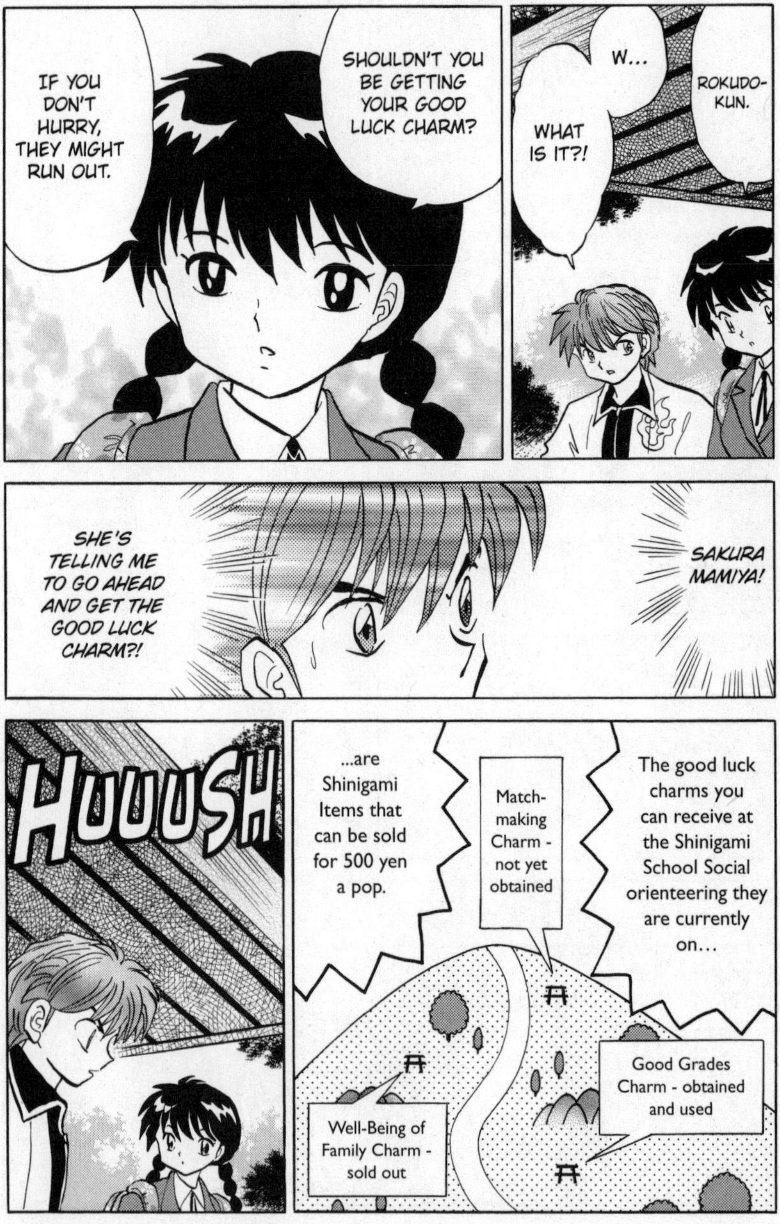
ROKUDO-KUN.
W...
WHAT IS IT?!
SHOULDN'T YOU BE GETTING YOUR GOOD LUCK CHARM?
IF YOU DON'T HURRY, THEY MIGHT RUN OUT.
SAKURA MAMIYA!
SHE'S TELLING ME TO GO AHEAD AND GET THE GOOD LUCK CHARM?!
The good luck charms you can receive at the Shinigami School Social orienteering they are currently on...
Match-making Charm - not yet obtained
...are Shinigami Items that can be sold for 500 yen a pop.
Good Grades Charm - obtained and used
Well-Being of Family Charm - sold out
HUUUSH

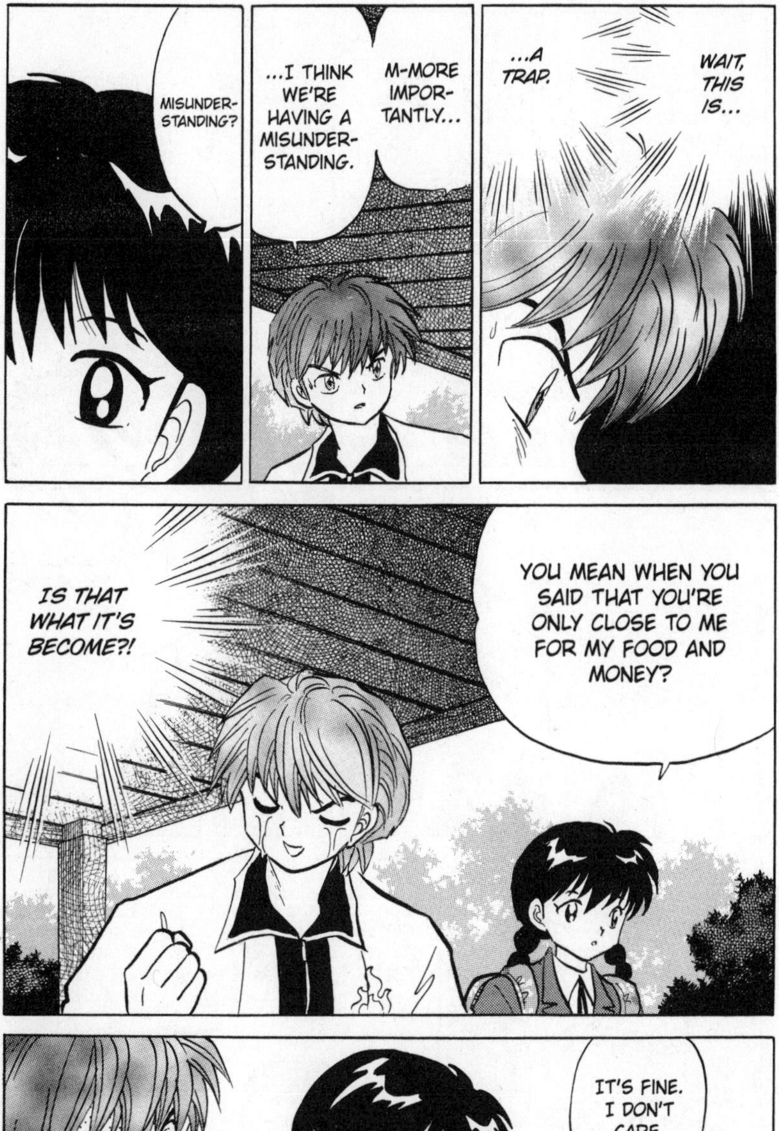
WAIT, THIS IS...
...A TRAP.
M-MORE IMPORTANTLY...
...I THINK WE'RE HAVING A MISUNDERSTANDING.
MISUNDERSTANDING?
YOU MEAN WHEN YOU SAID THAT YOU'RE ONLY CLOSE TO ME FOR MY FOOD AND MONEY?
IS THAT WHAT IT'S BECOME?!
IT'S FINE. I DON'T CARE.

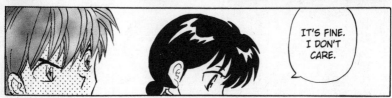

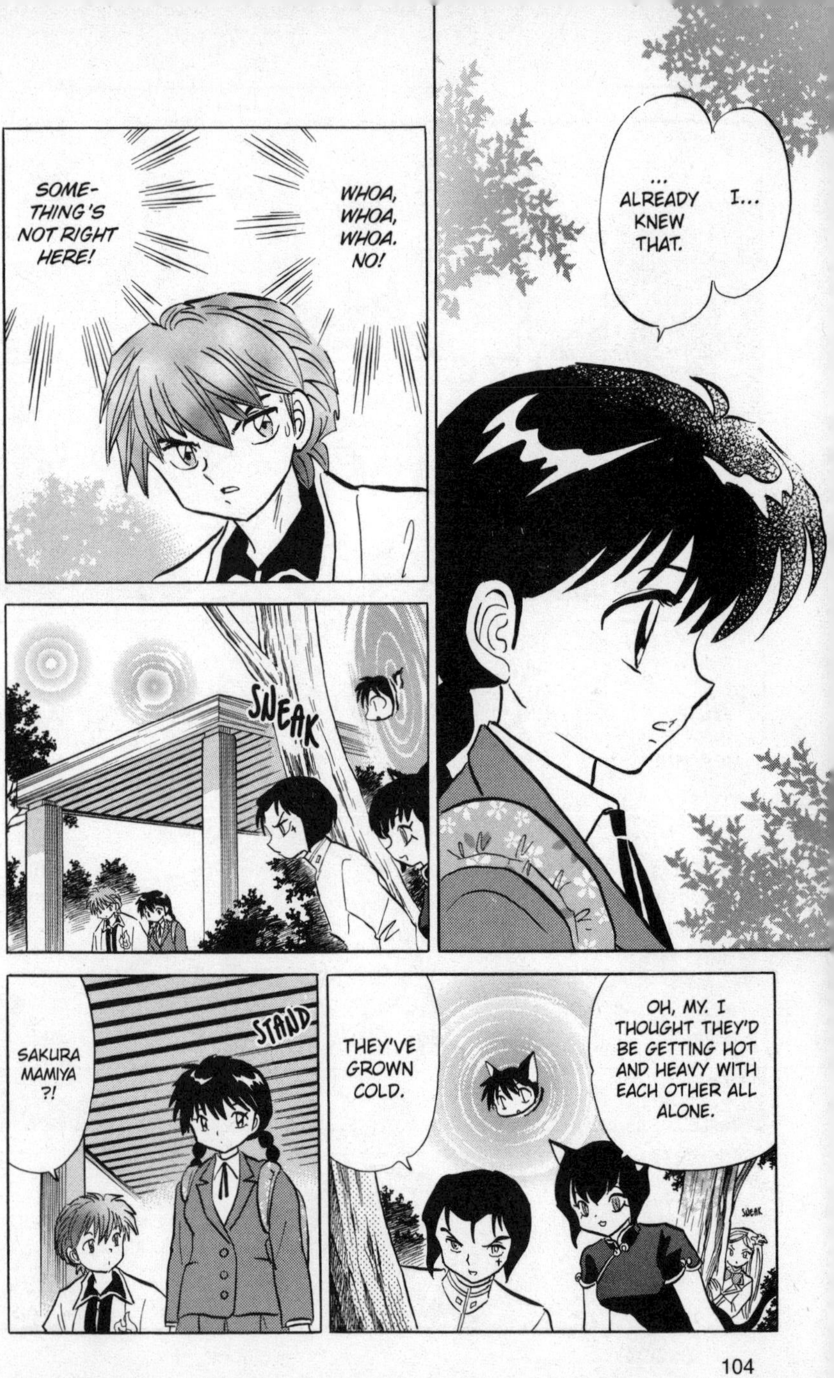
I... ...ALREADY KNEW THAT.
WHOA, WHOA, WHOA. NO!
SOME-THING'S NOT RIGHT HERE!
SNEAK
OH, MY. I THOUGHT THEY'D BE GETTING HOT AND HEAVY WITH EACH OTHER ALL ALONE.
THEY'VE GROWN COLD.
SNEAK
STAND
SAKURA MAMIYA ?!

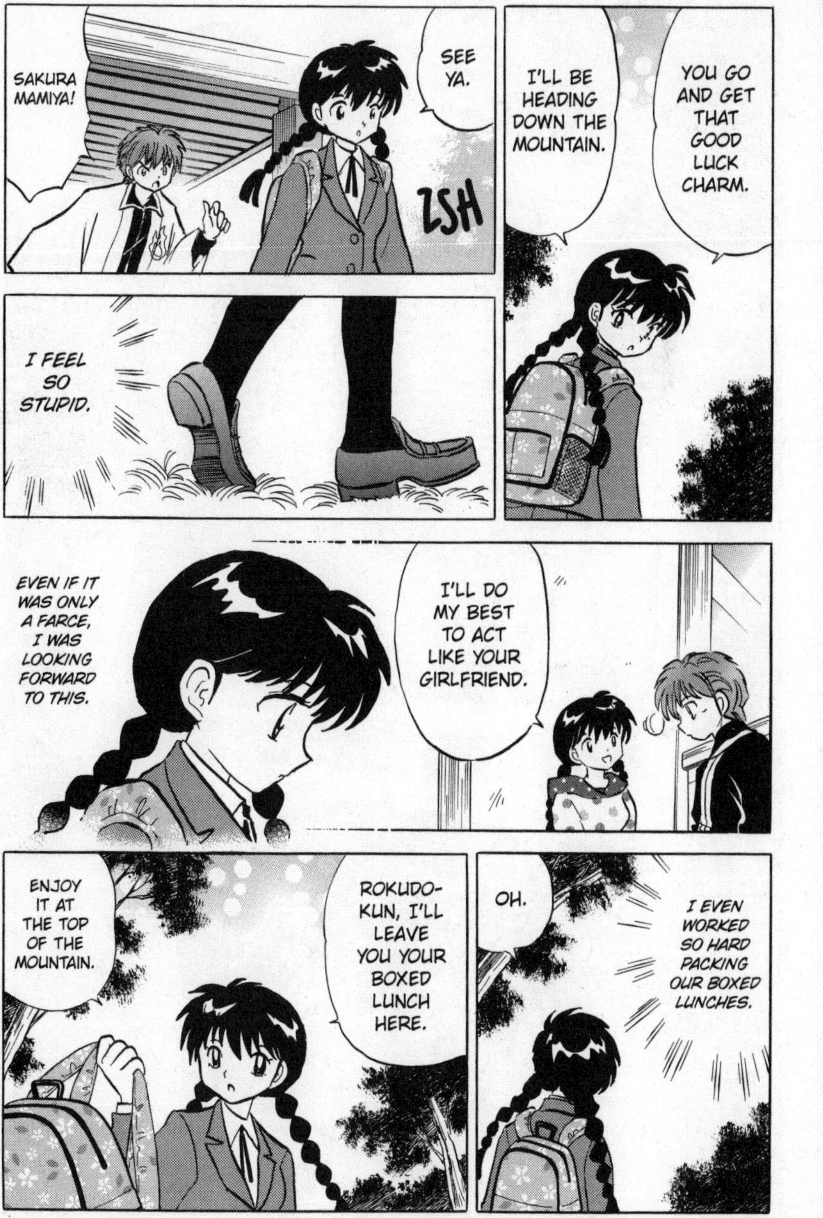
YOU GO AND GET THAT GOOD LUCK CHARM.
I'LL BE HEADING DOWN THE MOUNTAIN.
SEE YA.
SAKURA MAMIYA!
ZSH
I FEEL SO STUPID.
I'LL DO MY BEST TO ACT LIKE YOUR GIRLFRIEND.
EVEN IF IT WAS ONLY A FARCE, I WAS LOOKING FORWARD TO THIS.
I EVEN WORKED SO HARD PACKING OUR BOXED LUNCHES.
OH.
ROKUDO-KUN, I'LL LEAVE YOU YOUR BOXED LUNCH HERE.
ENJOY IT AT THE TOP OF THE MOUNTAIN.

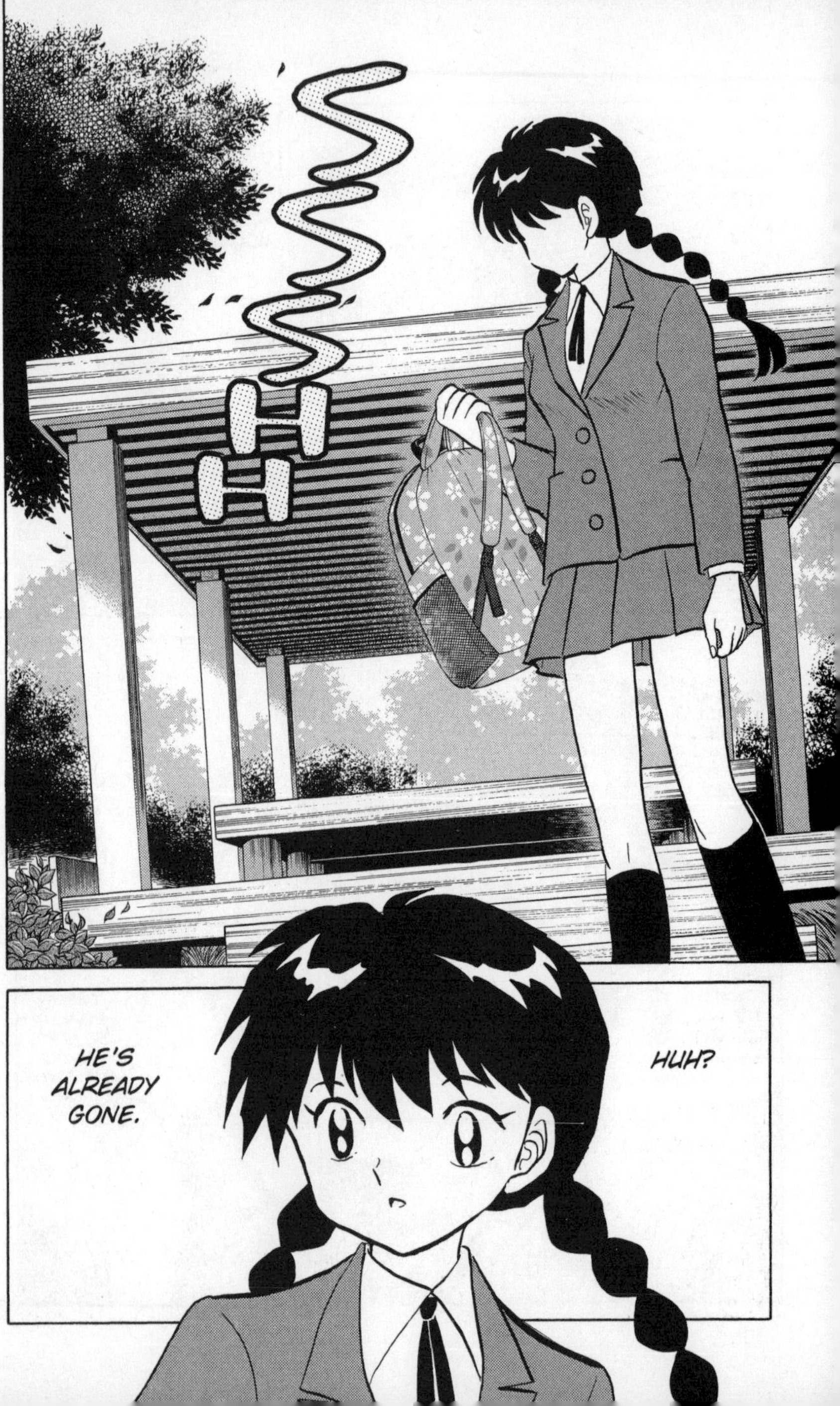
HH
HUH?
HE'S ALREADY GONE.

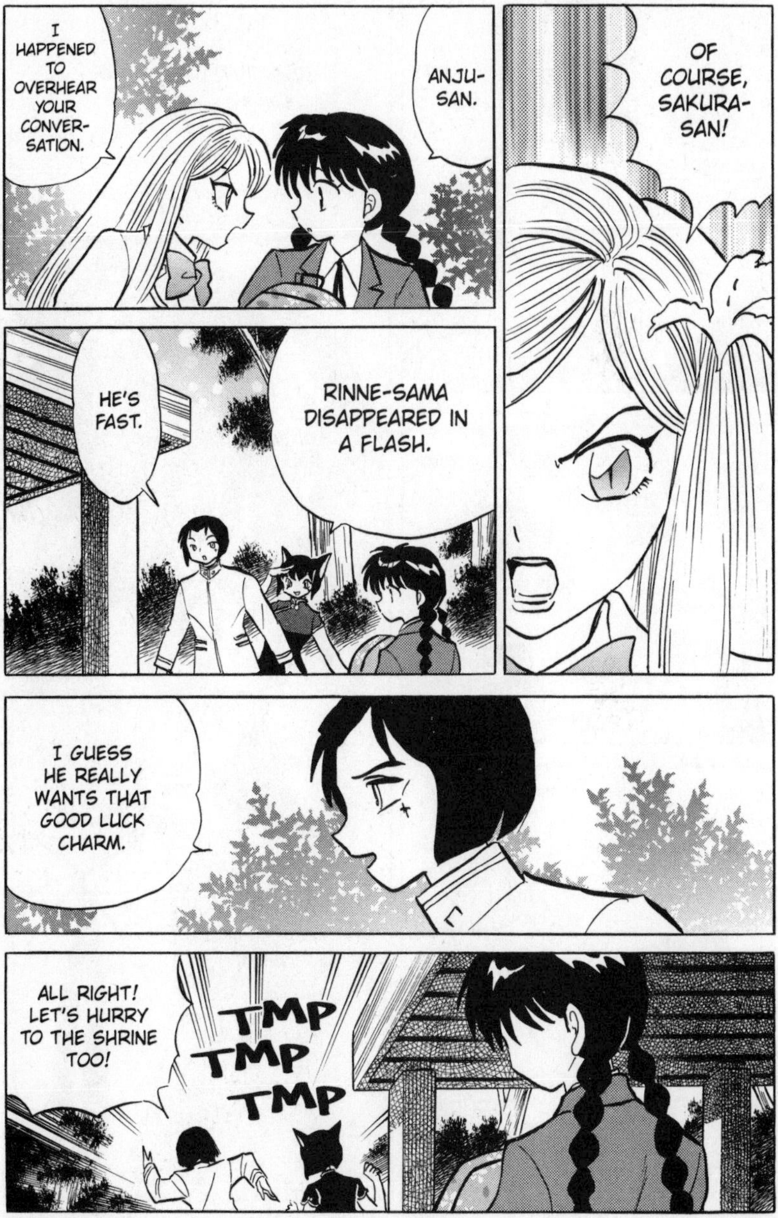
OF COURSE, SAKURA-SAN!
ANJU-SAN.
I HAPPENED TO OVERHEAR YOUR CONVERSATION.
RINNE-SAMA DISAPPEARED IN A FLASH.
HE'S FAST.
I GUESS HE REALLY WANTS THAT GOOD LUCK CHARM.
ALL RIGHT! LET'S HURRY TO THE SHRINE TOO!
TMP TMP TMP

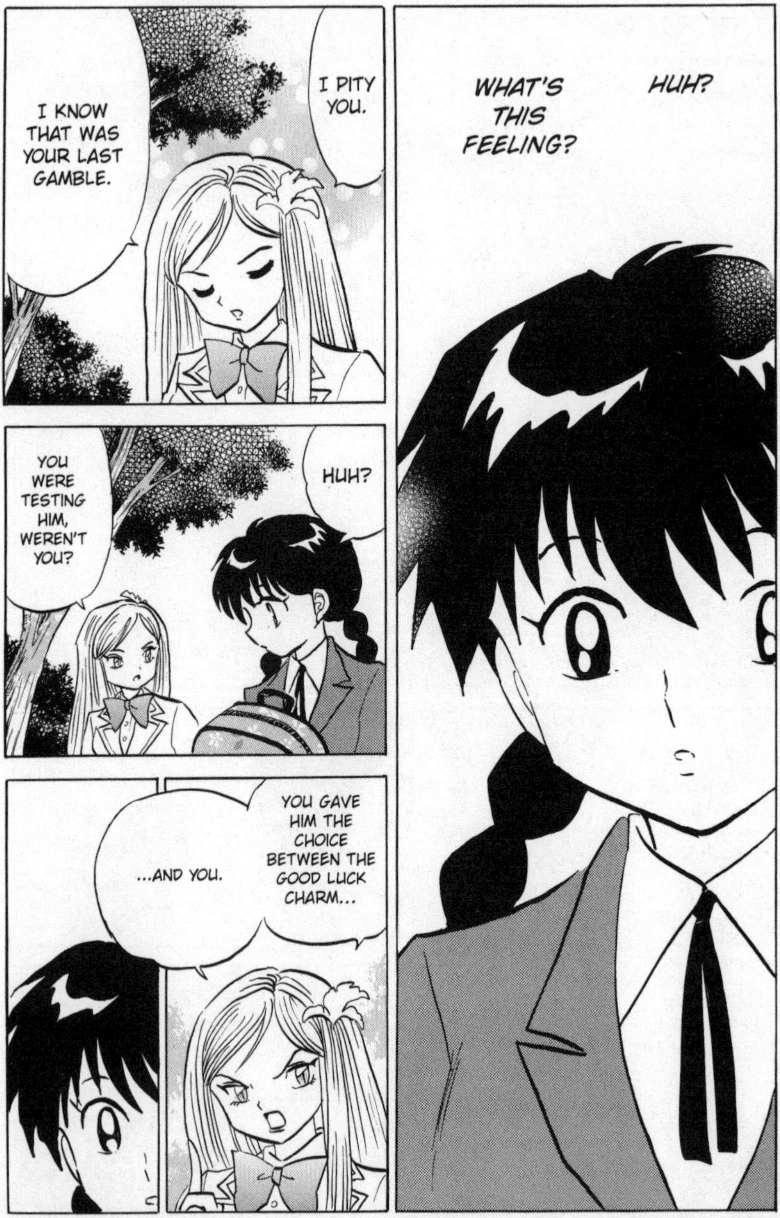
HUH?
WHAT'S THIS FEELING?
I PITY YOU.
I KNOW THAT WAS YOUR LAST GAMBLE.
HUH?
YOU WERE TESTING HIM, WEREN'T YOU?
YOU GAVE HIM THE CHOICE BETWEEN THE GOOD LUCK CHARM...
...AND YOU.

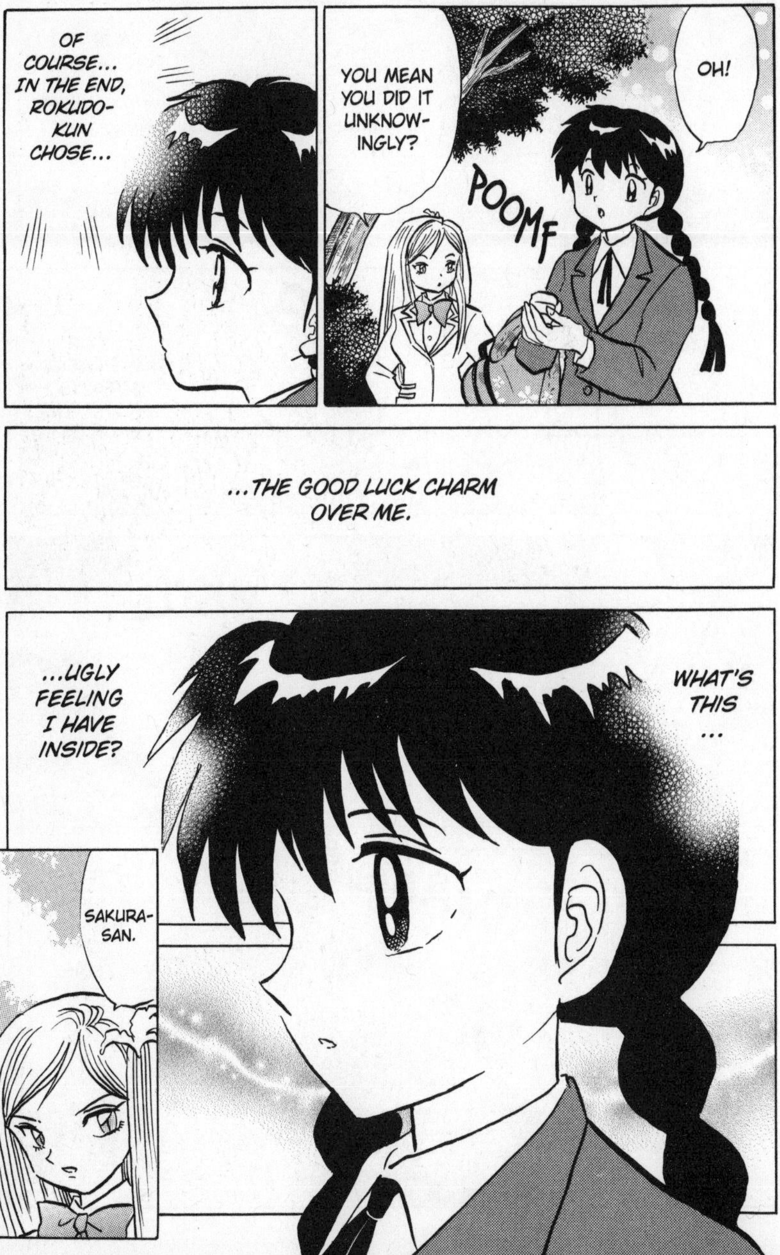
OH!
YOU MEAN YOU DID IT UNKNOWINGLY?
POOMF
OF COURSE... IN THE END, ROKUDO-KUN CHOSE...
...THE GOOD LUCK CHARM OVER ME.
WHAT'S THIS ...
...UGLY FEELING I HAVE INSIDE?
SAKURA-SAN.

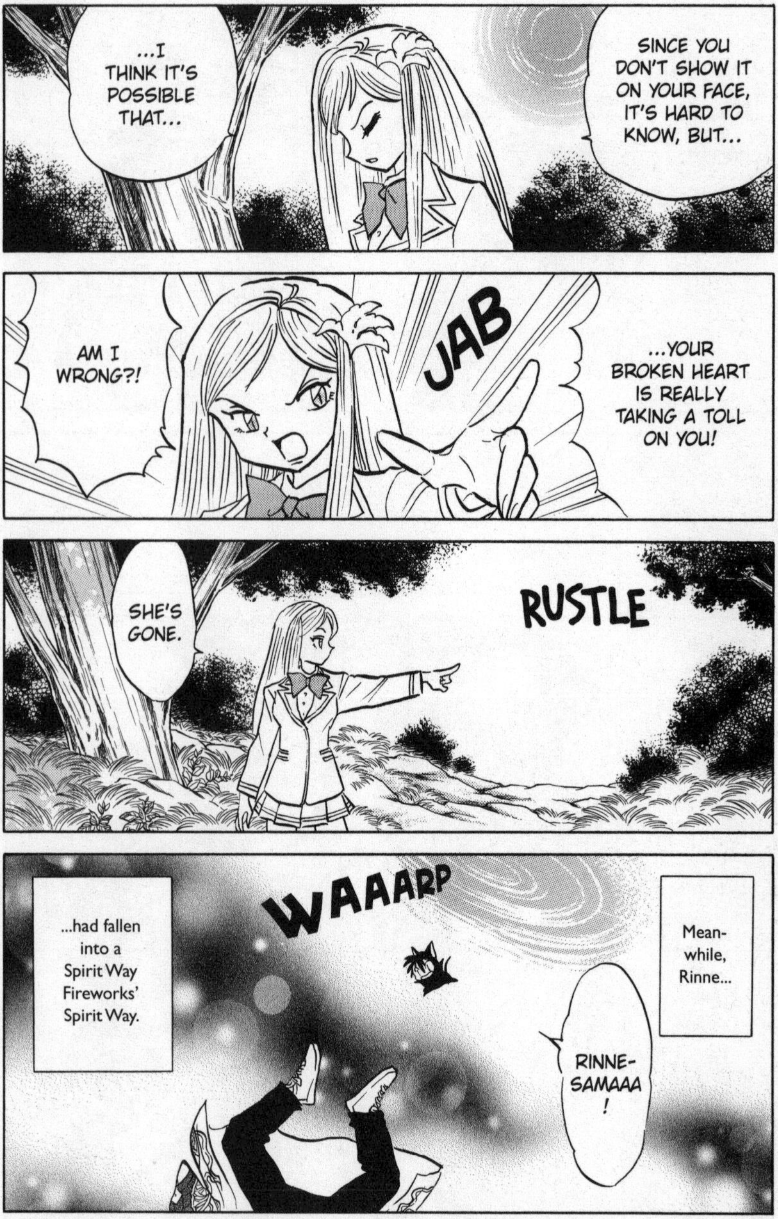
SINCE YOU DON'T SHOW IT ON YOUR FACE, IT'S HARD TO KNOW, BUT...
...I THINK IT'S POSSIBLE THAT...
...YOUR BROKEN HEART IS REALLY TAKING A TOLL ON YOU!
JAB
AM I WRONG?!
RUSTLE
SHE'S GONE.
Mean-while, Rinne...
RINNE-SAMAAA!
WAAARP
...had fallen into a Spirit Way Fireworks' Spirit Way.

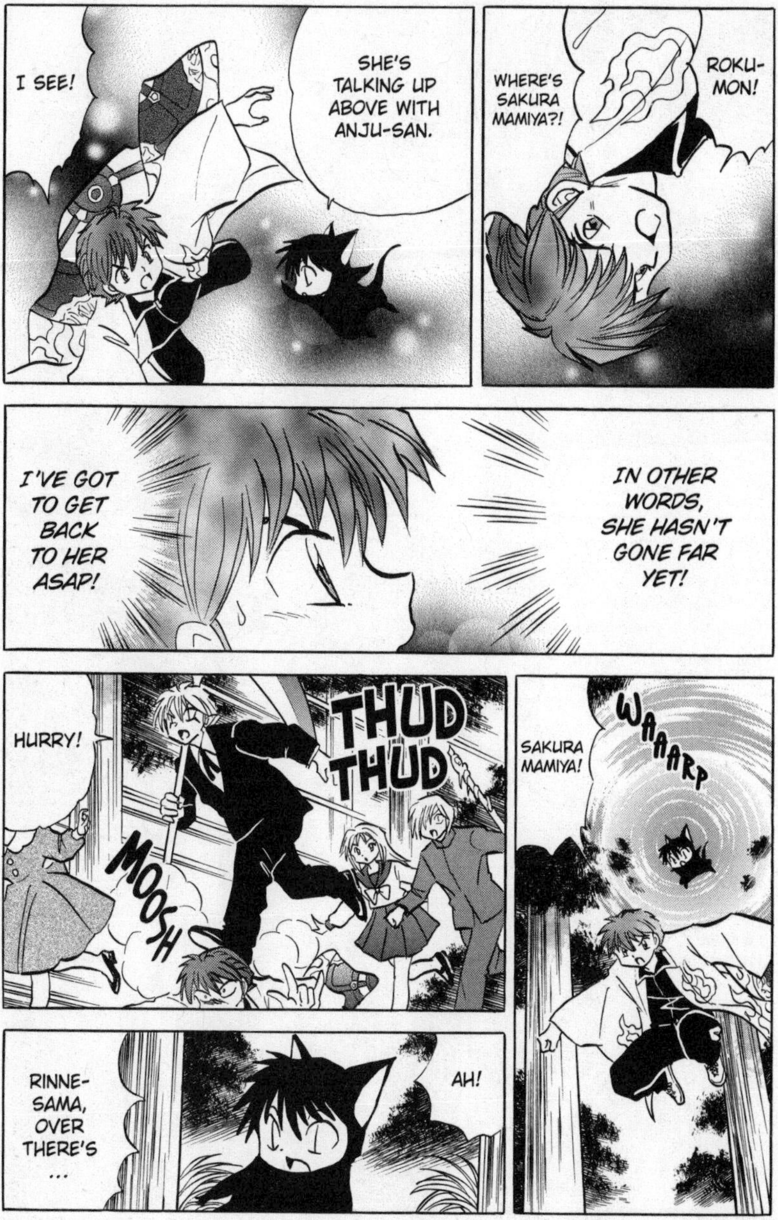
ROKU-MON!
WHERE'S SAKURA MAMIYA?!
SHE'S TALKING UP ABOVE WITH ANJU-SAN.
I SEE!
IN OTHER WORDS, SHE HASN'T GONE FAR YET!
I'VE GOT TO GET BACK TO HER ASAP!
WAAAARP
SAKURA MAMIYA!
THUD THUD
HURRY!
MOOSH
AH!
RINNE-SAMA, OVER THERE'S ...

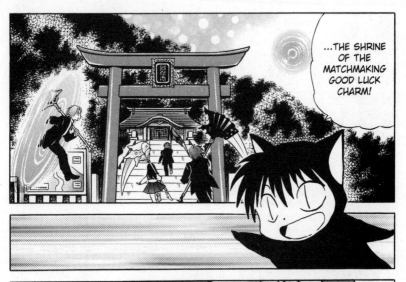

...THE SHRINE OF THE MATCHMAKING GOOD LUCK CHARM!
WHAT?!
Once you fall into a Spirit Way, there's no guarantee that you'll come out where you originally were.
HOW LUCKY OF US, RINNE-SAMA.
KUH!
UNDER NORMAL CIRCUM-STANCES, YES.
BUT RIGHT NOW...
...I NEED TO FIND SAKURA MAMIYA.

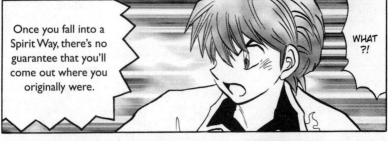

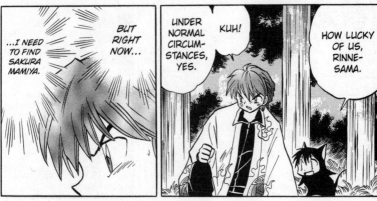

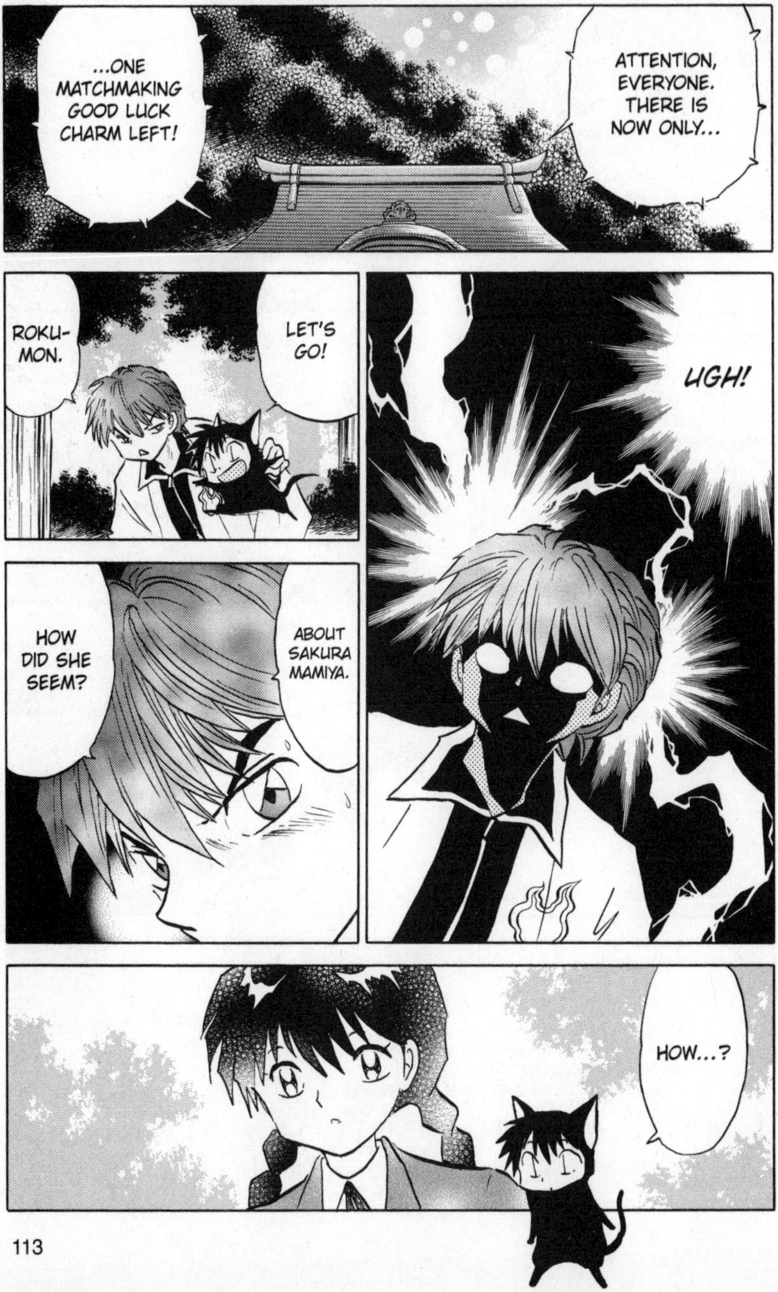
ATTENTION, EVERYONE. THERE IS NOW ONLY...
...ONE MATCHMAKING GOOD LUCK CHARM LEFT!
UGH!
LET'S GO!
ROKU-MON.
ABOUT SAKURA MAMIYA.
HOW DID SHE SEEM?
HOW...?

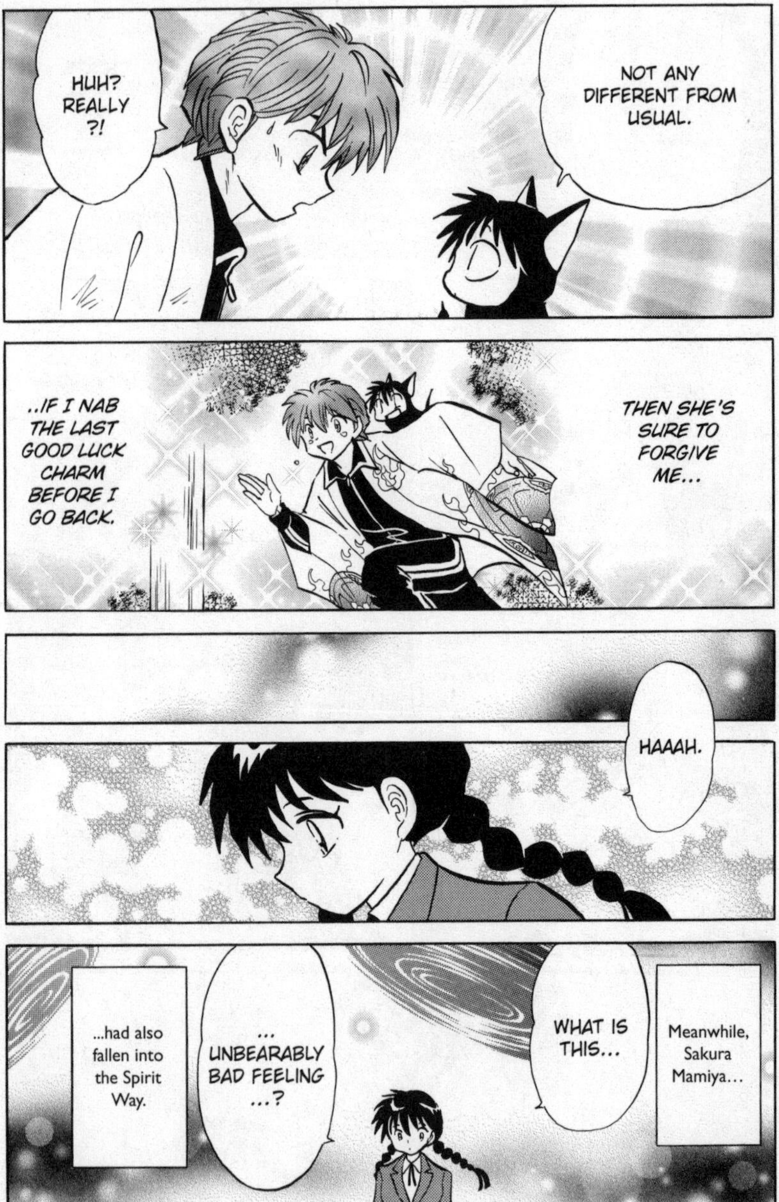
NOT ANY DIFFERENT FROM USUAL.
HUH? REALLY ?!
THEN SHE'S SURE TO FORGIVE ME...
..IF I NAB THE LAST GOOD LUCK CHARM BEFORE I GO BACK.
HAAAH.
Meanwhile, Sakura Mamiya...
WHAT IS THIS...
... UNBEARABLY BAD FEELING ...?
...had also fallen into the Spirit Way.

CHAPTER 195: WE'RE NOT GOING OUT

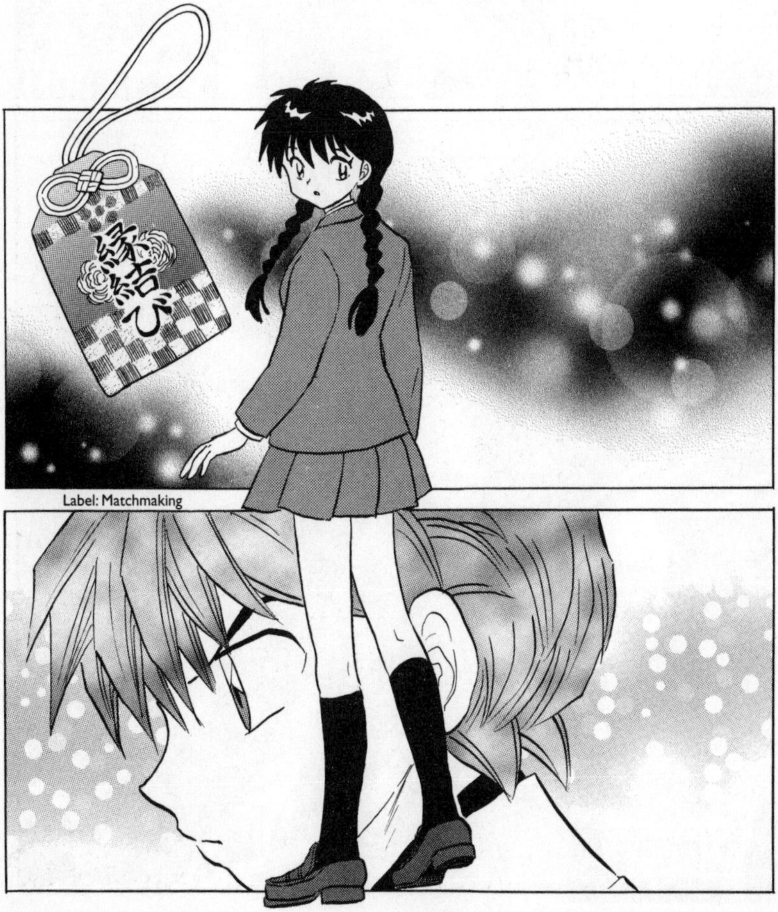
縁結び
Label: Matchmaking

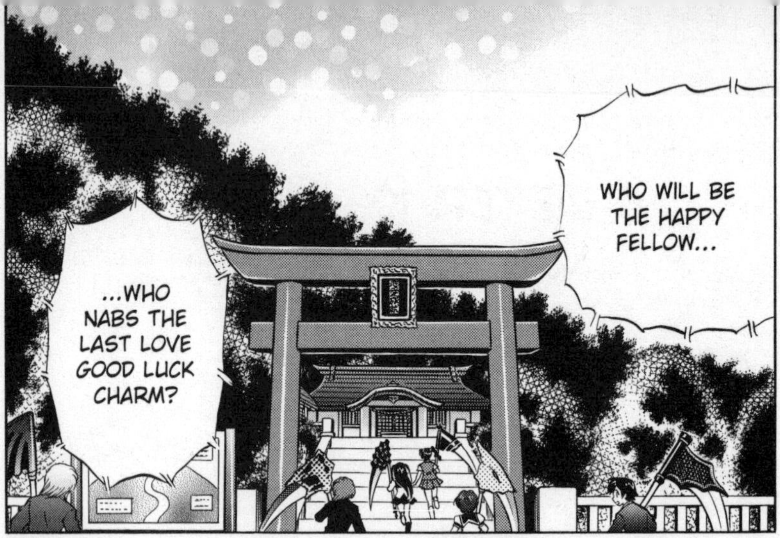
WHO WILL BE THE HAPPY FELLOW...
...WHO NABS THE LAST LOVE GOOD LUCK CHARM?

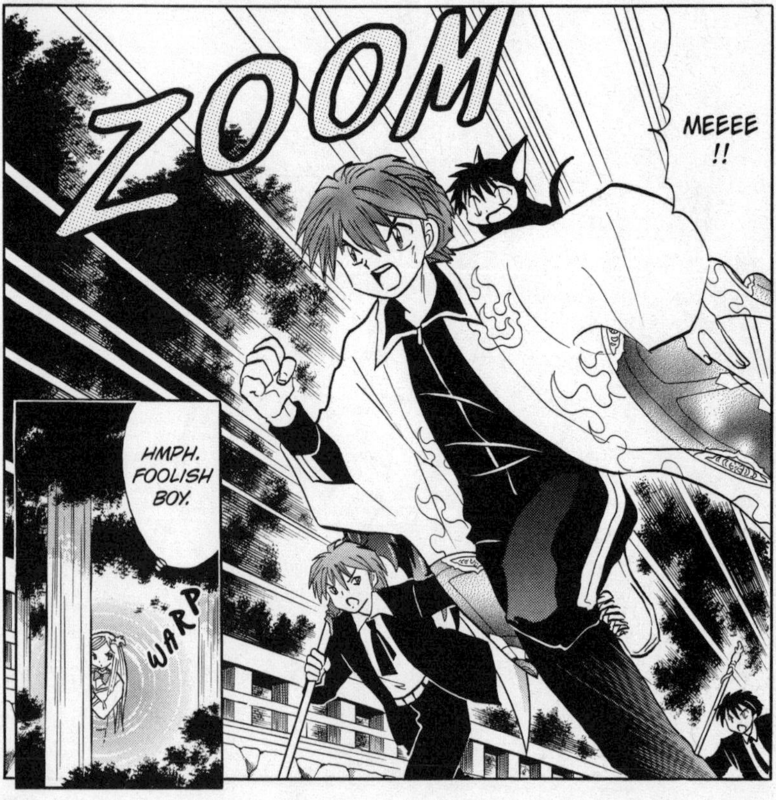
MEEEE !!
ZOOM
HMPH. FOOLISH BOY.
WARP

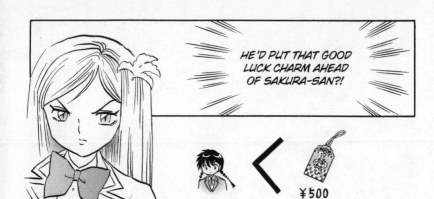

HE'D PUT THAT GOOD LUCK CHARM AHEAD OF SAKURA-SAN?!
¥500
THE MOMENT HE GETS THAT CHARM...
...THEIR RELATIONSHIP IS OVER!
THE CHAAAARM !
ZSH
HERE YOU GO.
LAST ONE.
WHOOSH
?!

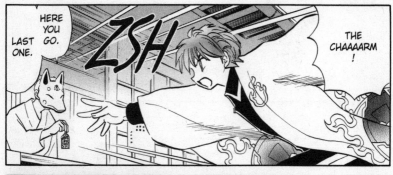

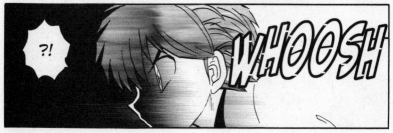

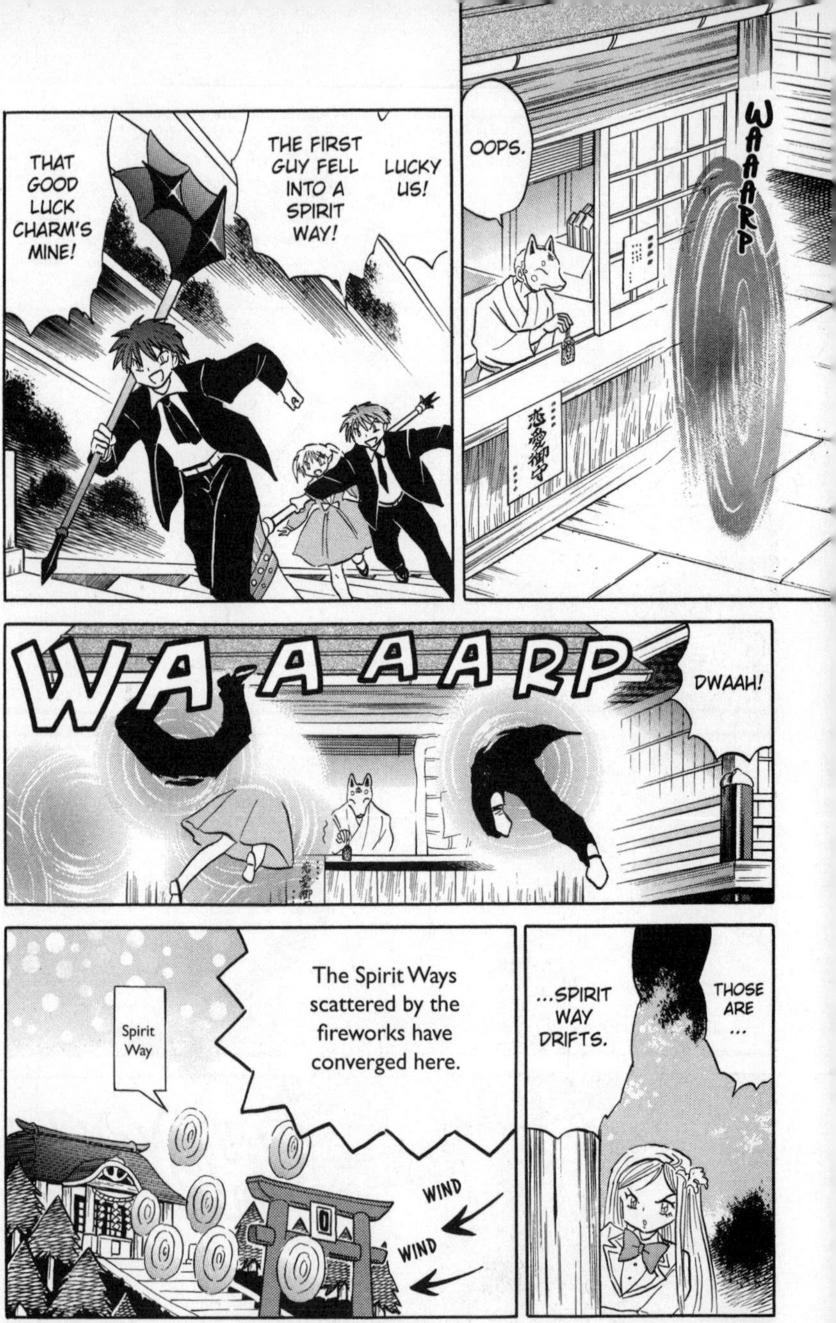
OOPS.
WAAAARP
恋愛御守
LUCKY US!
THE FIRST GUY FELL INTO A SPIRIT WAY!
THAT GOOD LUCK CHARM'S MINE!
WA-A A A ARP
DWAAH!
THOSE ARE ...
...SPIRIT WAY DRIFTS.
The Spirit Ways scattered by the fireworks have converged here.
Spirit Way
WIND
WIND

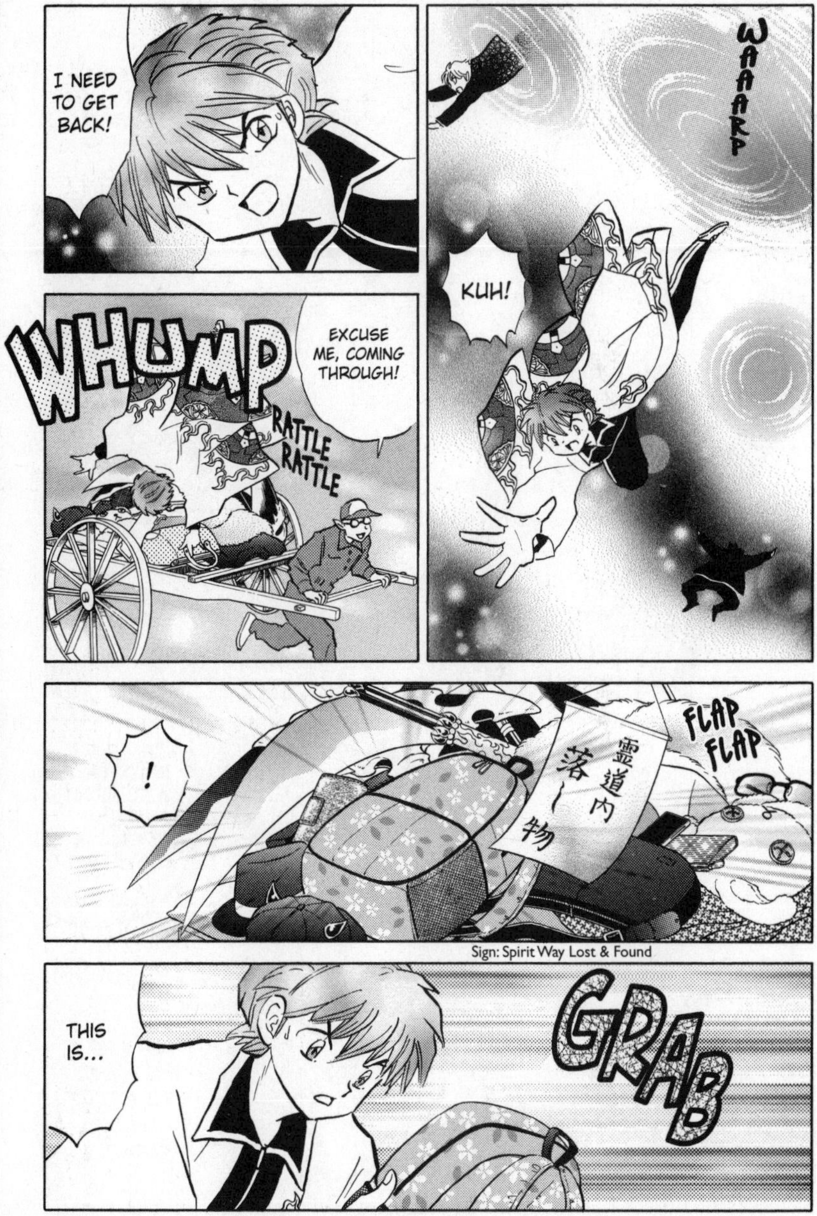
WAAARP
KUH!
I NEED TO GET BACK!
WHUMP
EXCUSE ME, COMING THROUGH!
RATTLE RATTLE
FLAP FLAP
霊道内
落し物
!
GRAB
THIS IS...
Sign: Spirit Way Lost & Found

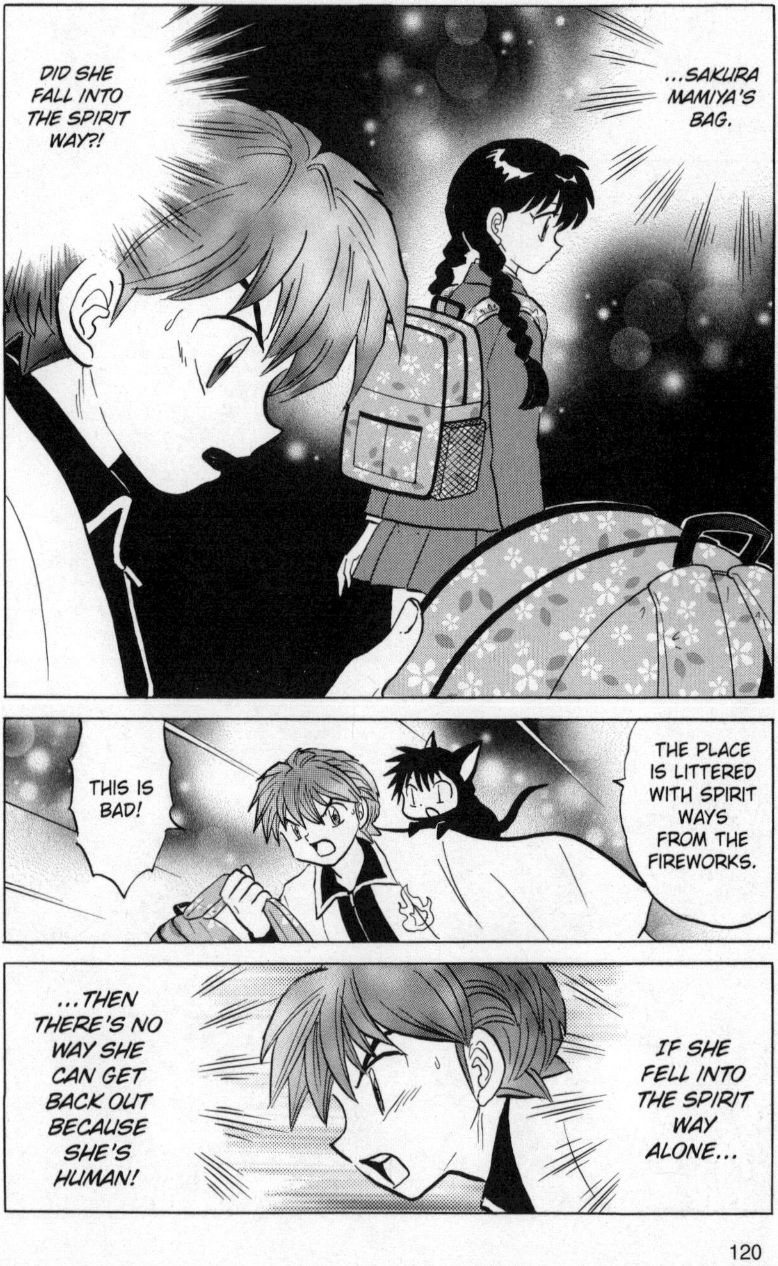
...SAKURA MAMIYA'S BAG.
DID SHE FALL INTO THE SPIRIT WAY?!
THE PLACE IS LITTERED WITH SPIRIT WAYS FROM THE FIREWORKS.
THIS IS BAD!
IF SHE FELL INTO THE SPIRIT WAY ALONE...
...THEN THERE'S NO WAY SHE CAN GET BACK OUT BECAUSE SHE'S HUMAN!

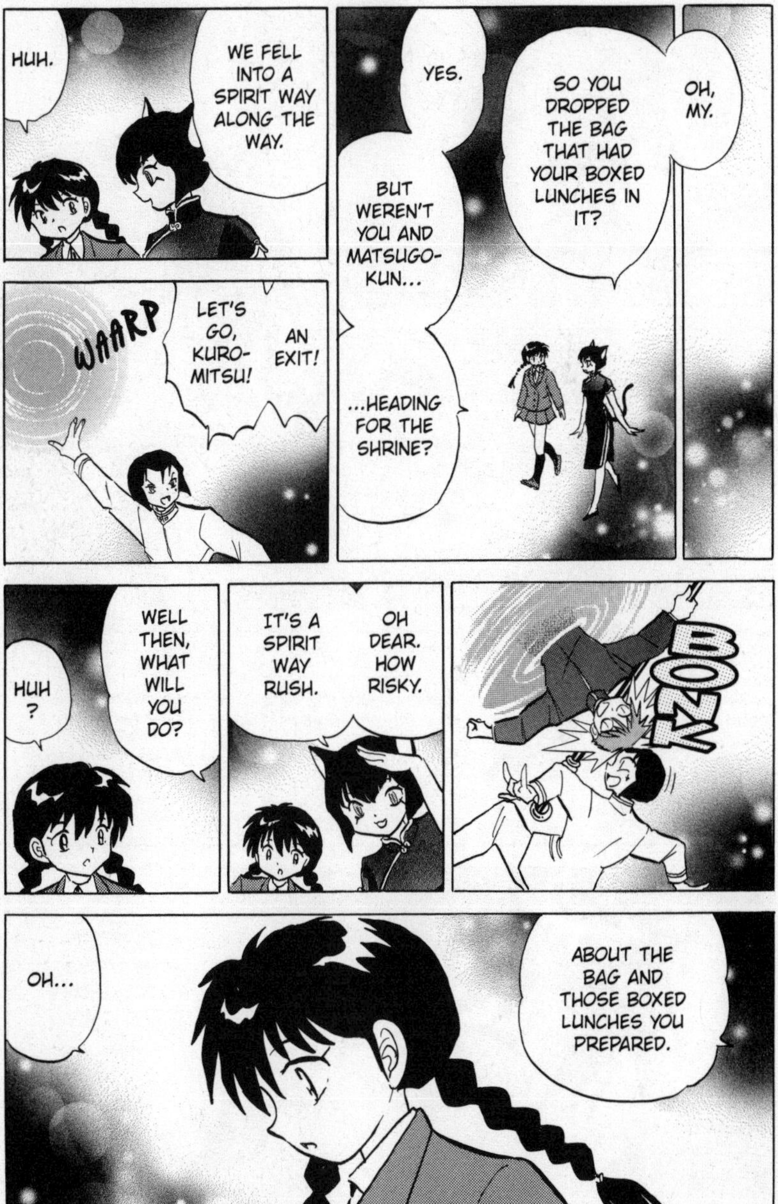
OH, MY.
SO YOU DROPPED THE BAG THAT HAD YOUR BOXED LUNCHES IN IT?
YES.
BUT WEREN'T YOU AND MATSUGO-KUN...
...HEADING FOR THE SHRINE?
WE FELL INTO A SPIRIT WAY ALONG THE WAY.
HUH.
AN EXIT!
LET'S GO, KURO-MITSU!
WAARP
BONK
OH DEAR. HOW RISKY.
IT'S A SPIRIT WAY RUSH.
WELL THEN, WHAT WILL YOU DO?
HUH ?
ABOUT THE BAG AND THOSE BOXED LUNCHES YOU PREPARED.
OH...

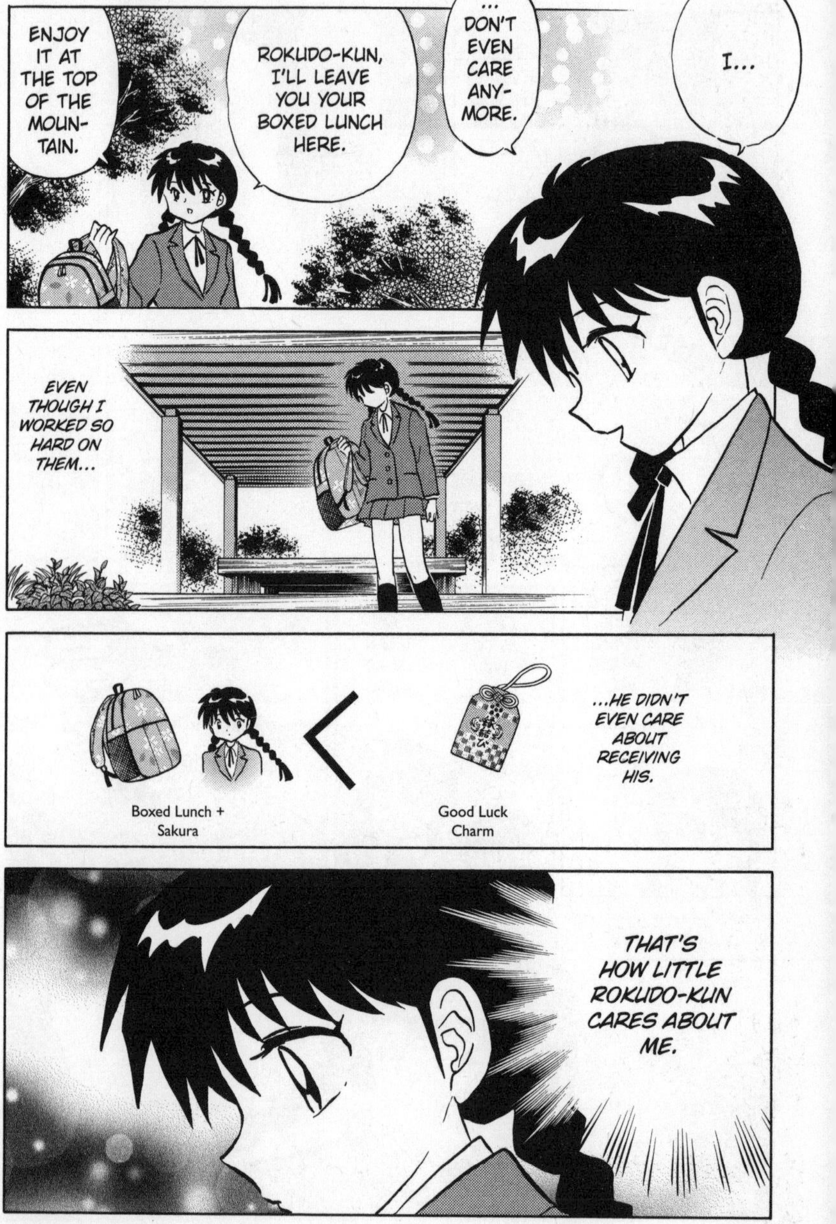
I...
...DON'T EVEN CARE ANYMORE.
ROKUDO-KUN, I'LL LEAVE YOU YOUR BOXED LUNCH HERE.
ENJOY IT AT THE TOP OF THE MOUNTAIN.
EVEN THOUGH I WORKED SO HARD ON THEM...
...HE DIDN'T EVEN CARE ABOUT RECEIVING HIS.
Good Luck Charm
Boxed Lunch + Sakura
THAT'S HOW LITTLE ROKUDO-KUN CARES ABOUT ME.

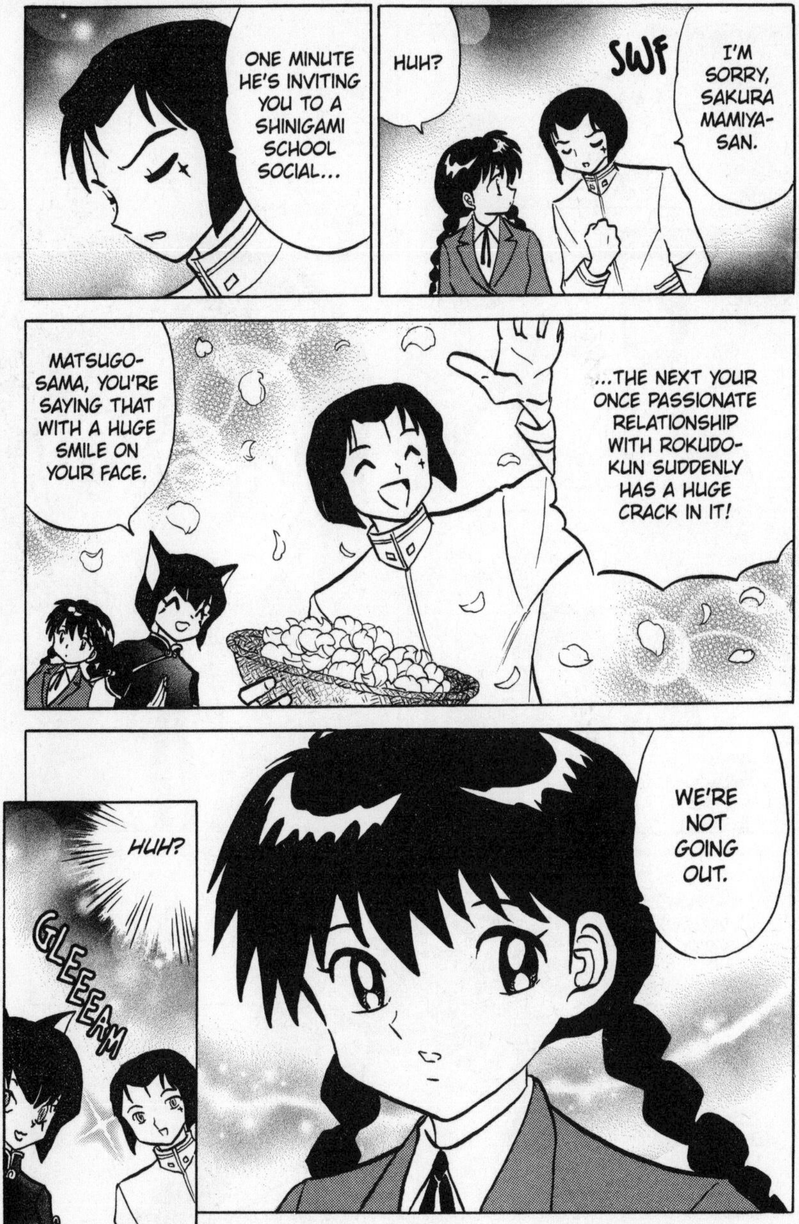
SWF
I'M SORRY, SAKURA MAMIYA-SAN.
HUH?
ONE MINUTE HE'S INVITING YOU TO A SHINIGAMI SCHOOL SOCIAL...
...THE NEXT YOUR ONCE PASSIONATE RELATIONSHIP WITH ROKUDO-KUN SUDDENLY HAS A HUGE CRACK IN IT!
MATSUGO-SAMA, YOU'RE SAYING THAT WITH A HUGE SMILE ON YOUR FACE.
WE'RE NOT GOING OUT.
HUH?
GLEEEAM

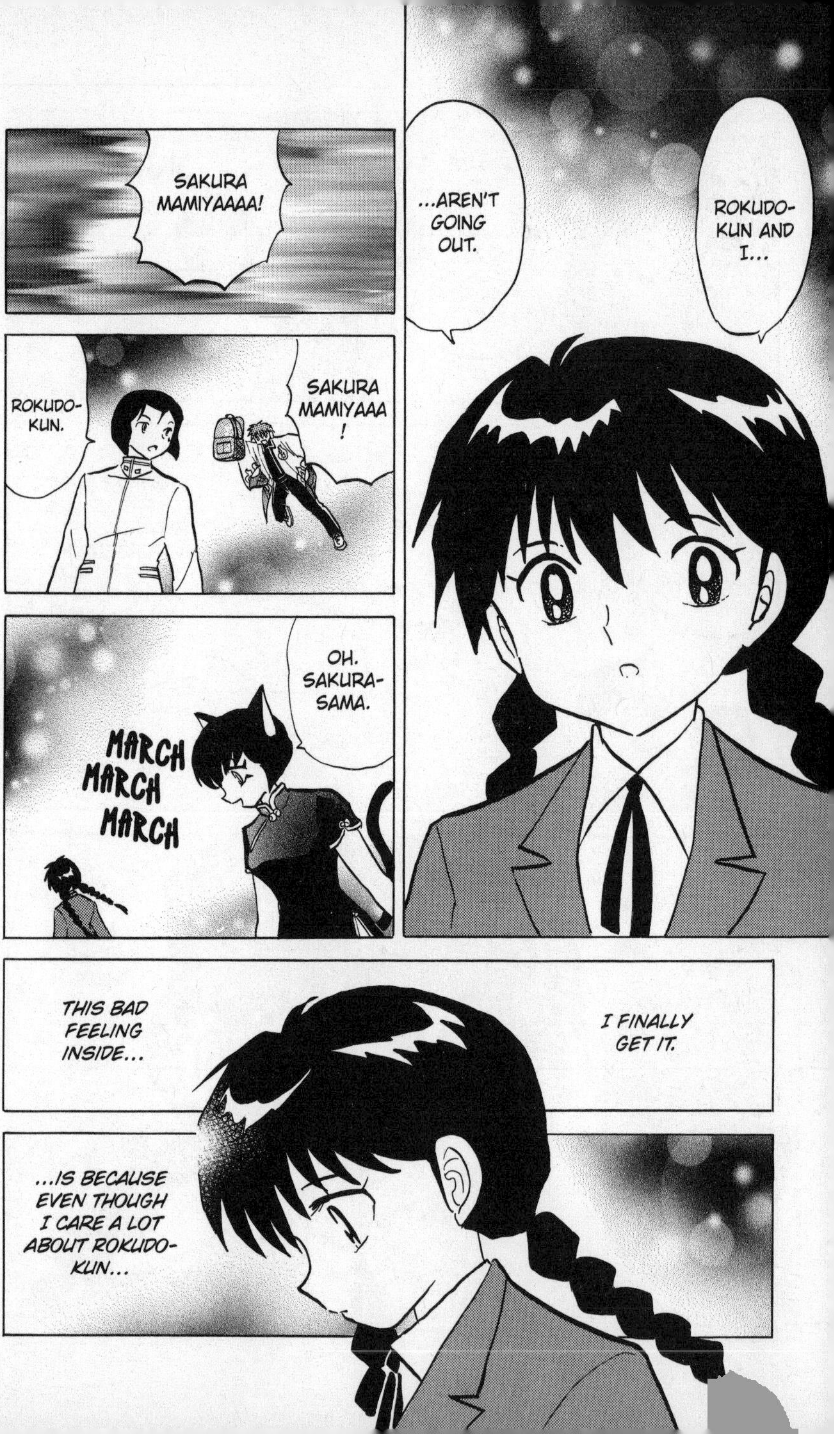
ROKUDO-KUN AND I...
...AREN'T GOING OUT.
SAKURA MAMIYAAAA!
SAKURA MAMIYAAA!
ROKUDO-KUN.
OH. SAKURA-SAMA.
MARCH MARCH MARCH
I FINALLY GET IT.
THIS BAD FEELING INSIDE...
...IS BECAUSE EVEN THOUGH I CARE A LOT ABOUT ROKUDO-KUN...

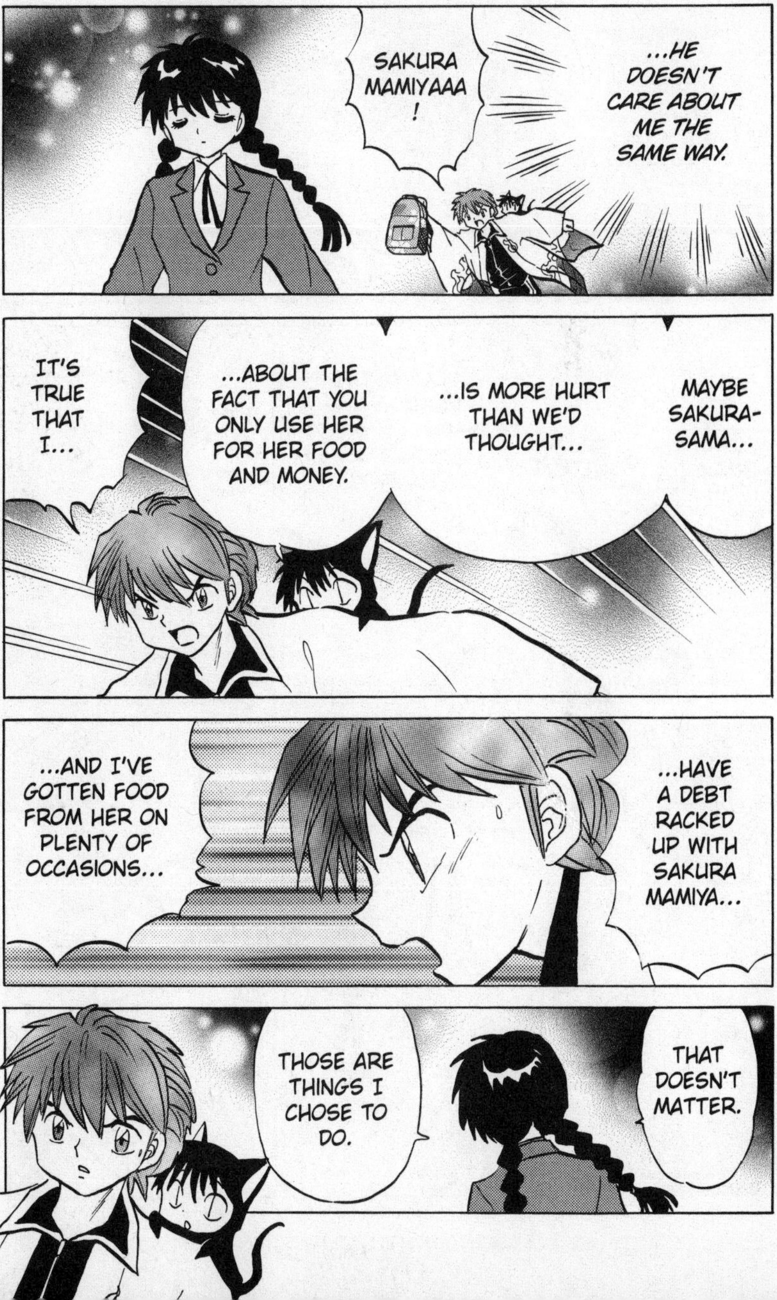
...HE DOESN'T CARE ABOUT ME THE SAME WAY.
SAKURA MAMIYAAA!
MAYBE SAKURA-SAMA...
...IS MORE HURT THAN WE'D THOUGHT...
...ABOUT THE FACT THAT YOU ONLY USE HER FOR HER FOOD AND MONEY.
IT'S TRUE THAT I...
...HAVE A DEBT RACKED UP WITH SAKURA MAMIYA...
...AND I'VE GOTTEN FOOD FROM HER ON PLENTY OF OCCASIONS...
THAT DOESN'T MATTER.
THOSE ARE THINGS I CHOSE TO DO.

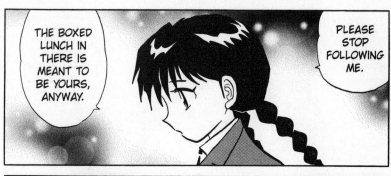

PLEASE STOP FOLLOWING ME.
THE BOXED LUNCH IN THERE IS MEANT TO BE YOURS, ANYWAY.
I WON'T HEAR IT!
HUH?! DOES ROKUDO-KUN INTEND ON GIVING BACK THE BOXED LUNCH?!
GIDDY GIDDY
EVEN THOUGH SHE WORKED SO HARD ON IT?
...YOU DON'T WANT IT?
I DO!

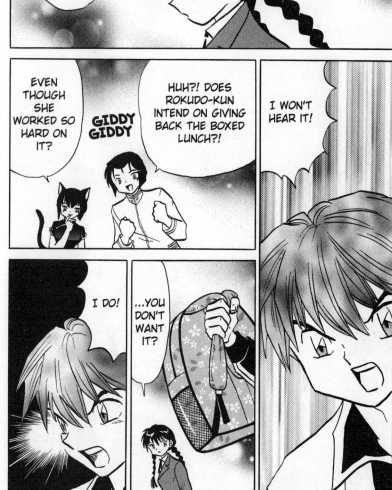

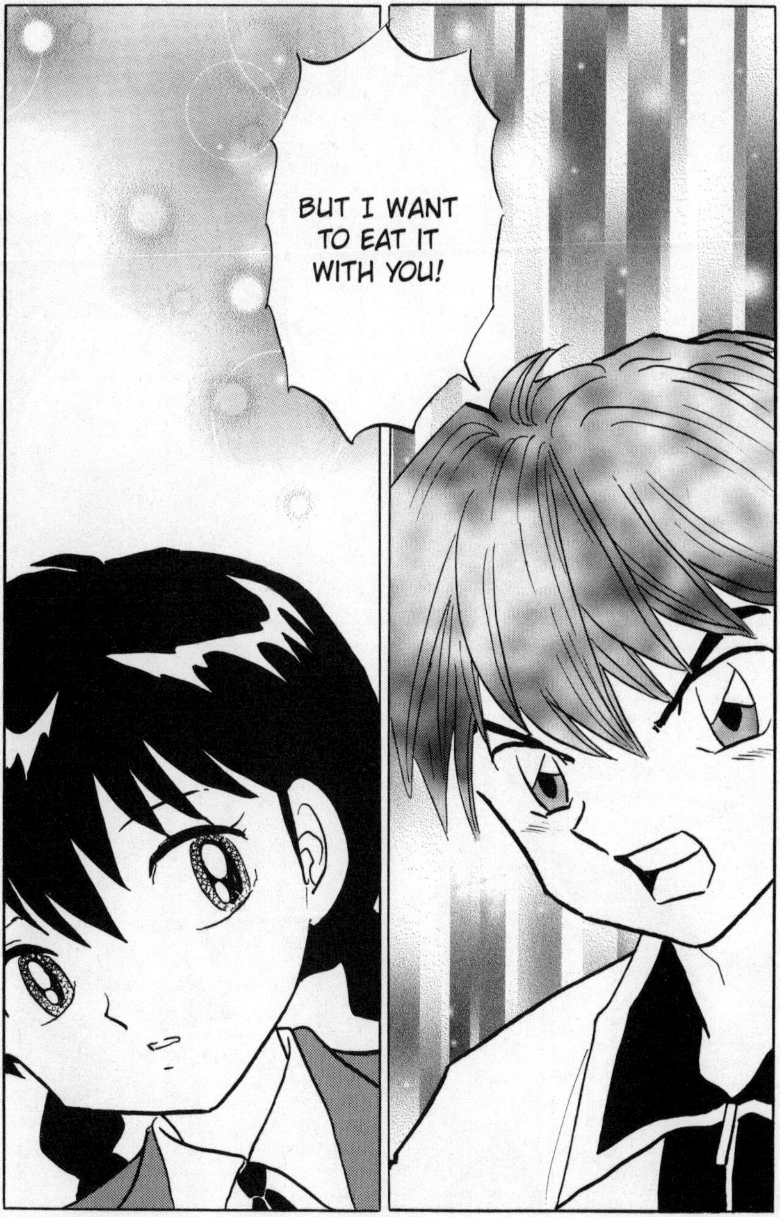
BUT I WANT
TO EAT IT
WITH YOU!

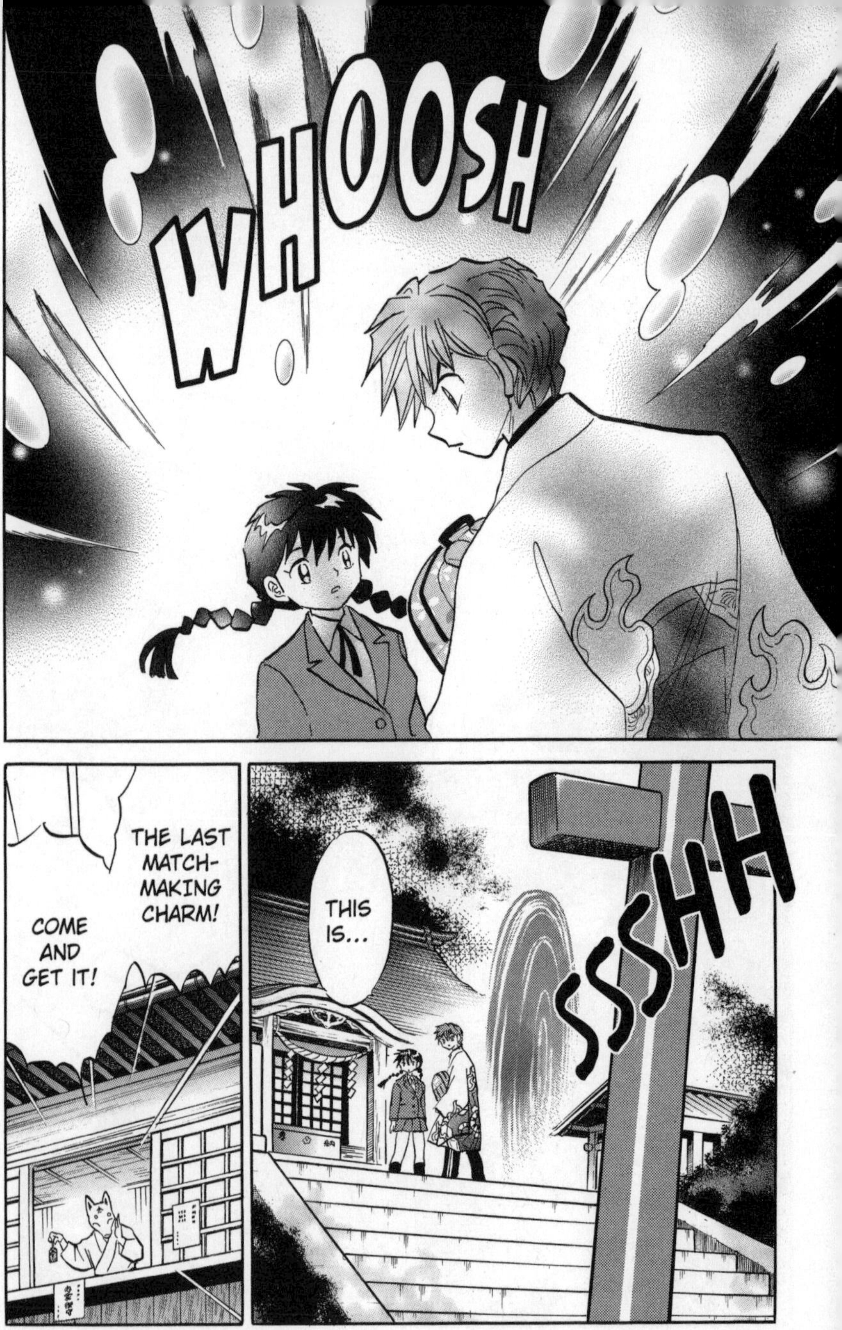
WHOOSH
SSSHH
THIS IS...
THE LAST MATCH-MAKING CHARM!
COME AND GET IT!

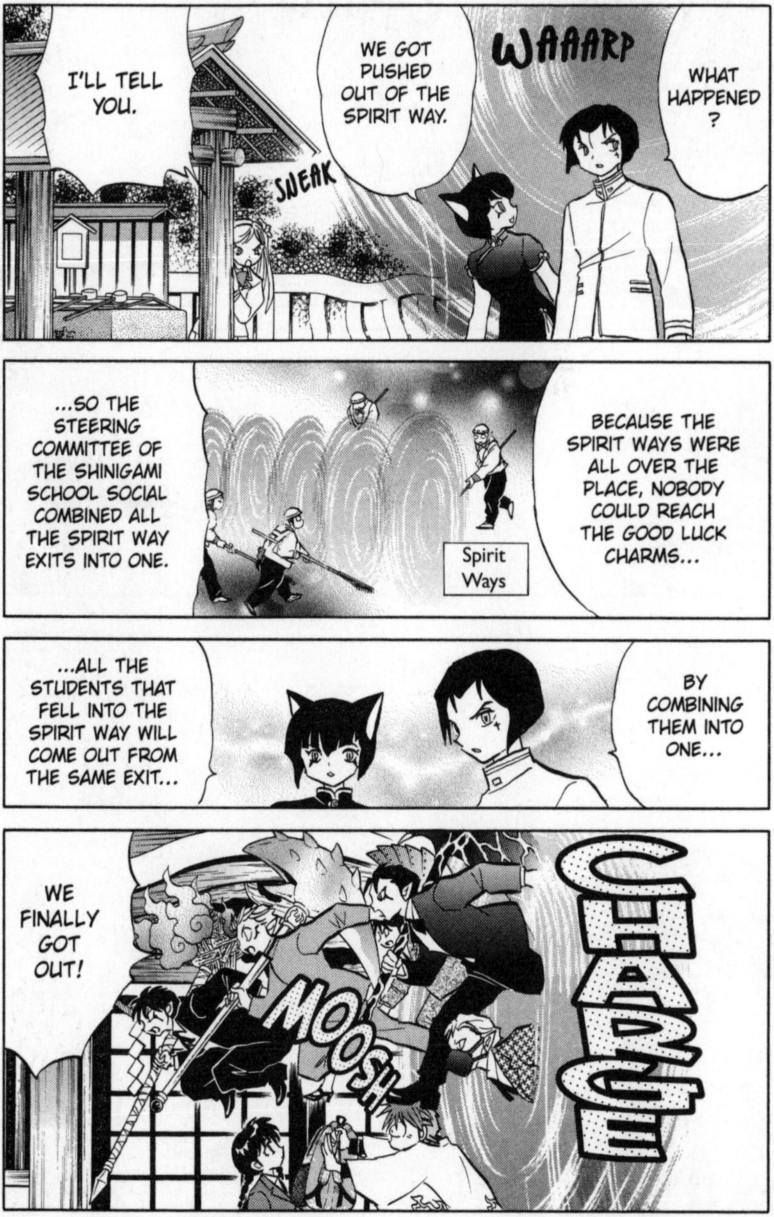
WHAT HAPPENED ?
WAAARP
WE GOT PUSHED OUT OF THE SPIRIT WAY.
SNEAK
I'LL TELL YOU.
BECAUSE THE SPIRIT WAYS WERE ALL OVER THE PLACE, NOBODY COULD REACH THE GOOD LUCK CHARMS...
Spirit Ways
...SO THE STEERING COMMITTEE OF THE SHINIGAMI SCHOOL SOCIAL COMBINED ALL THE SPIRIT WAY EXITS INTO ONE.
BY COMBINING THEM INTO ONE...
...ALL THE STUDENTS THAT FELL INTO THE SPIRIT WAY WILL COME OUT FROM THE SAME EXIT...
CHARGE
MOOSH
WE FINALLY GOT OUT!

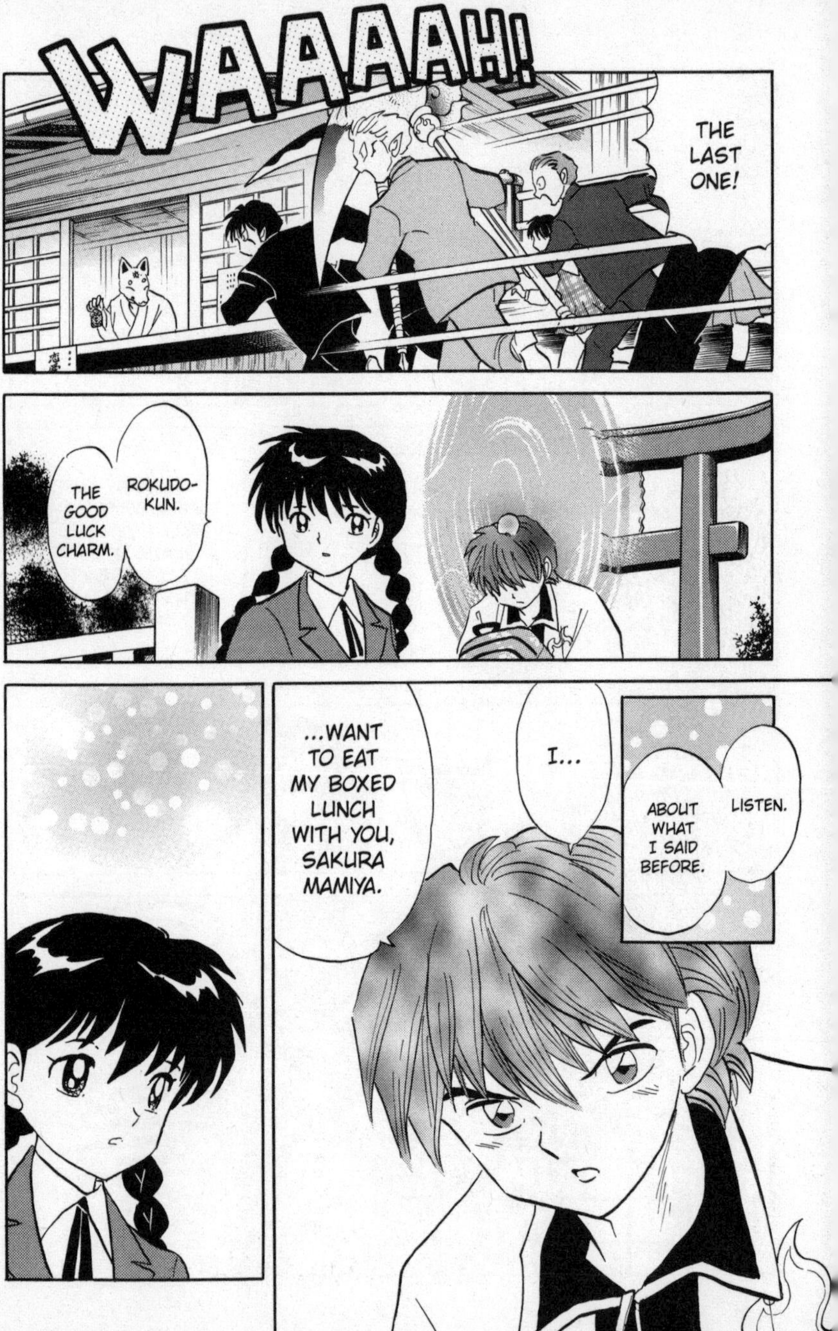
WAAAAAH!
THE LAST ONE!
ROKUDO-KUN.
THE GOOD LUCK CHARM.
LISTEN.
ABOUT WHAT I SAID BEFORE.
I...
...WANT TO EAT MY BOXED LUNCH WITH YOU, SAKURA MAMIYA.

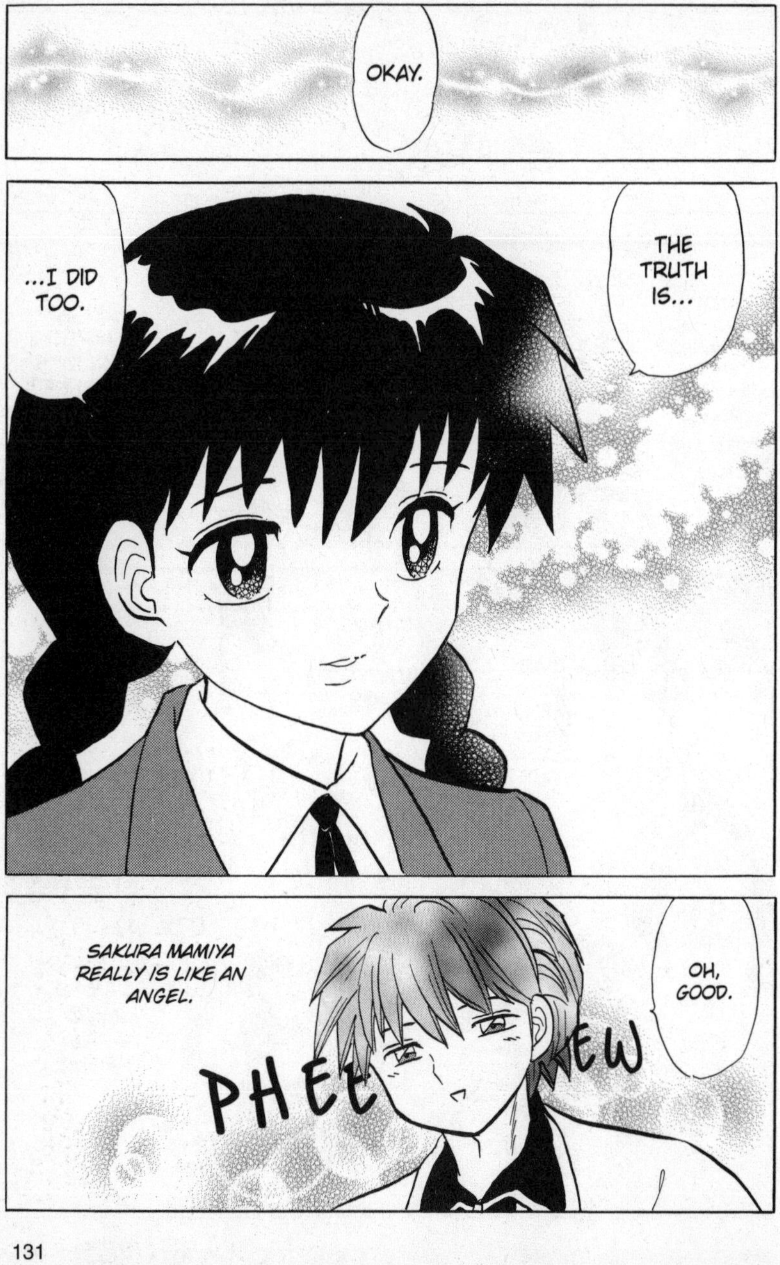
OKAY.
THE TRUTH IS...
...I DID TOO.
OH, GOOD.
PHEE EW
SAKURA MAMIYA REALLY IS LIKE AN ANGEL.

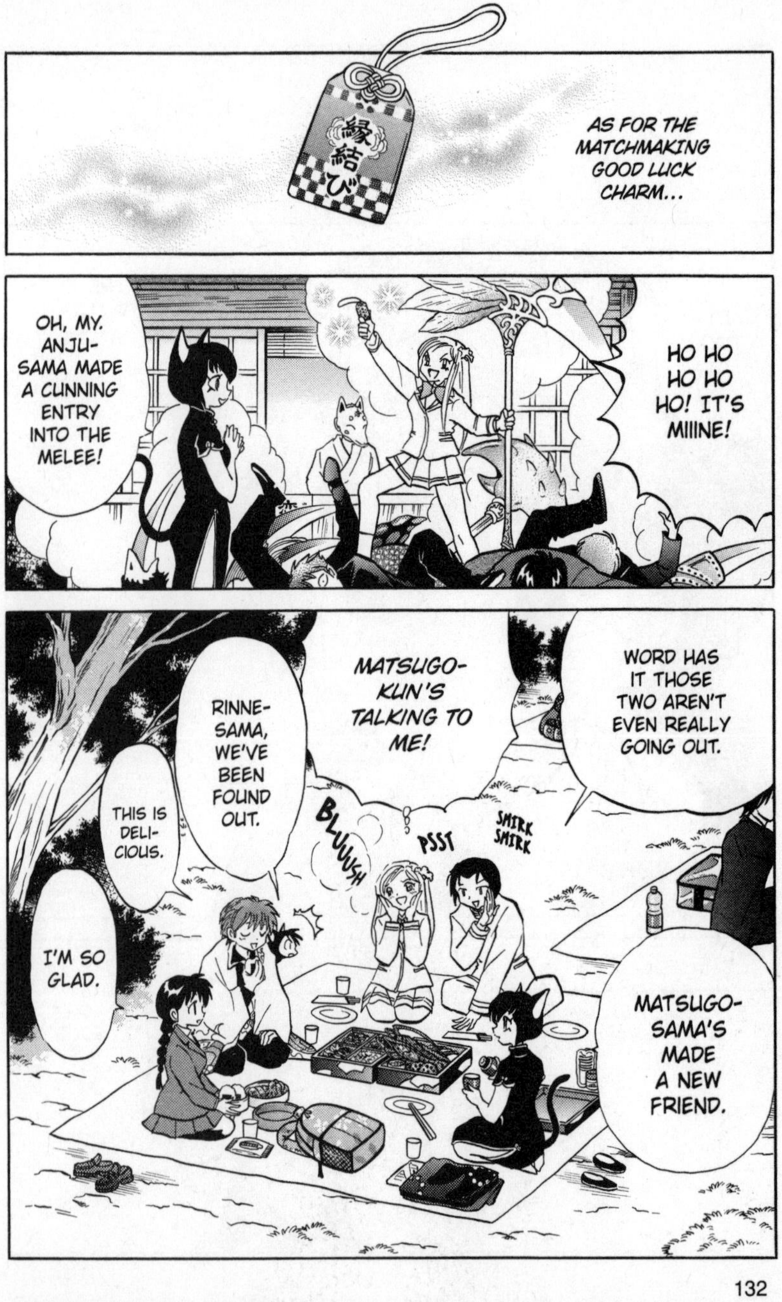
縁結び
AS FOR THE MATCHMAKING GOOD LUCK CHARM...
HO HO HO HO HO! IT'S MIIINE!
OH, MY. ANJU-SAMA MADE A CUNNING ENTRY INTO THE MELEE!
WORD HAS IT THOSE TWO AREN'T EVEN REALLY GOING OUT.
MATSUGO-KUN'S TALKING TO ME!
SMIRK SMIRK
PSST
BLUUUSH
RINNE-SAMA, WE'VE BEEN FOUND OUT.
THIS IS DELICIOUS.
MATSUGO-SAMA'S MADE A NEW FRIEND.
I'M SO GLAD.

CHAPTER 196: THE LEGENDARY SACRED ASHES

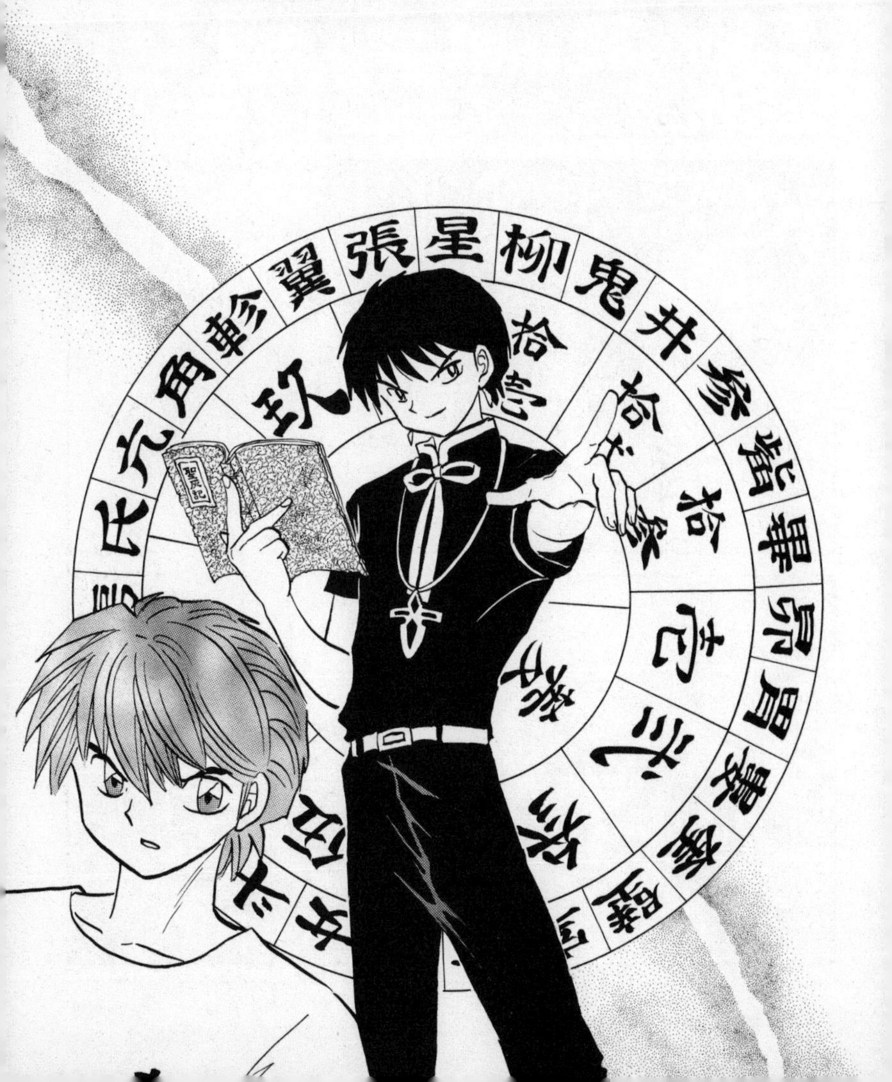

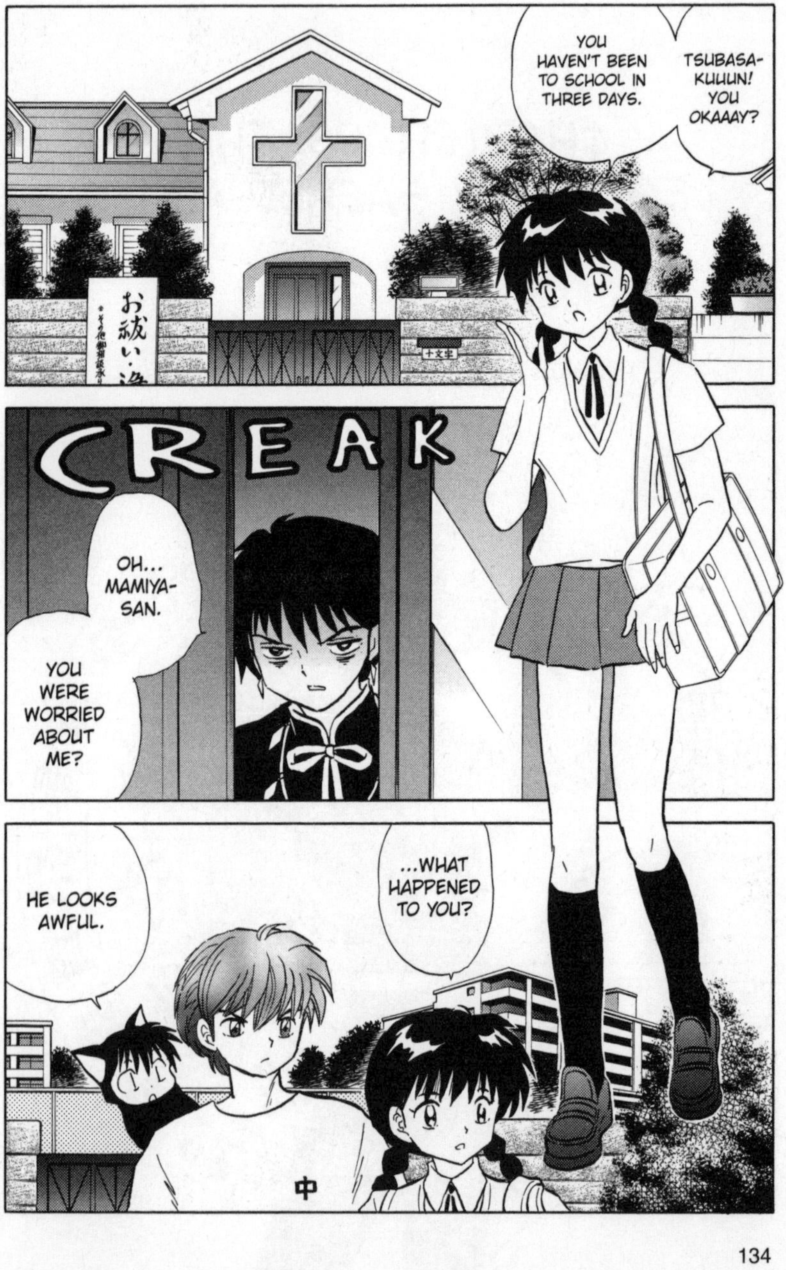
TSUBASA-KUUUN! YOU OKAAAY?
YOU HAVEN'T BEEN TO SCHOOL IN THREE DAYS.
CREAK
OH... MAMIYA-SAN.
YOU WERE WORRIED ABOUT ME?
...WHAT HAPPENED TO YOU?
HE LOOKS AWFUL.

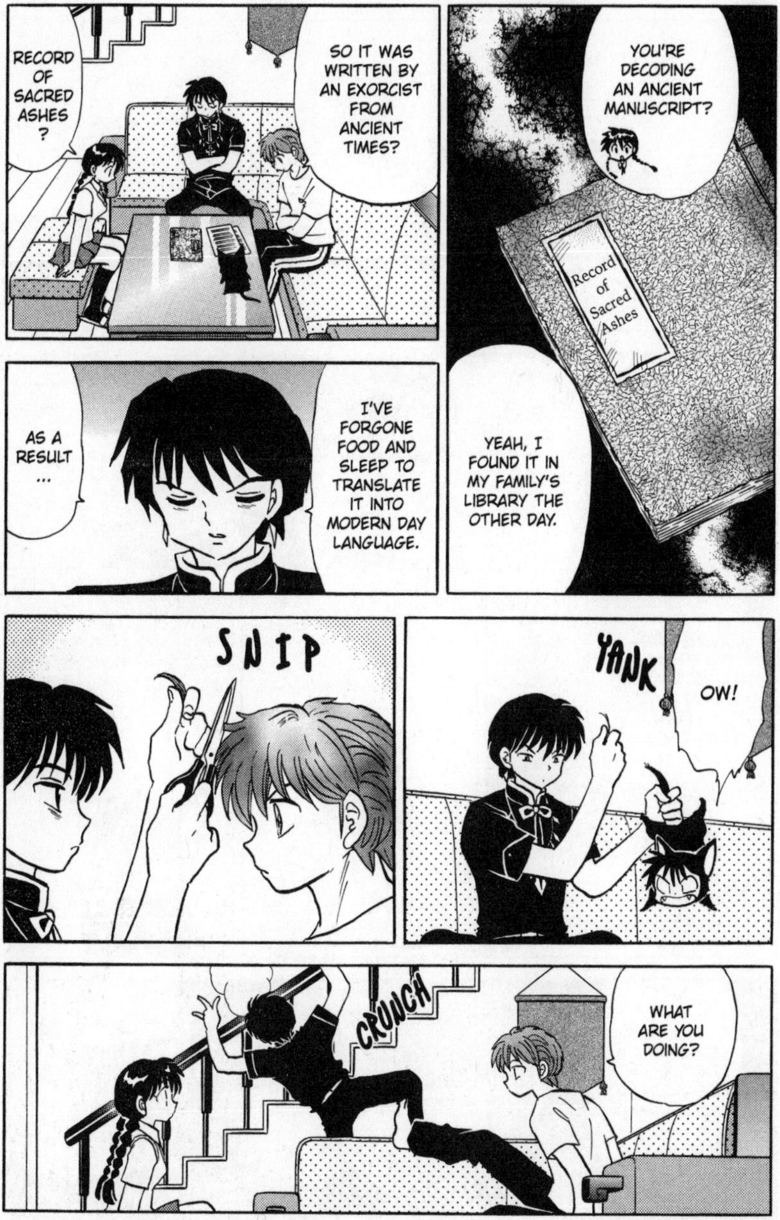
YOU'RE DECODING AN ANCIENT MANUSCRIPT?
Record of Sacred Ashes
YEAH, I FOUND IT IN MY FAMILY'S LIBRARY THE OTHER DAY.
SO IT WAS WRITTEN BY AN EXORCIST FROM ANCIENT TIMES?
RECORD OF SACRED ASHES ?
I'VE FORGONE FOOD AND SLEEP TO TRANSLATE IT INTO MODERN DAY LANGUAGE.
AS A RESULT ...
YANK
OW!
SNIP
WHAT ARE YOU DOING?
CRUNCH

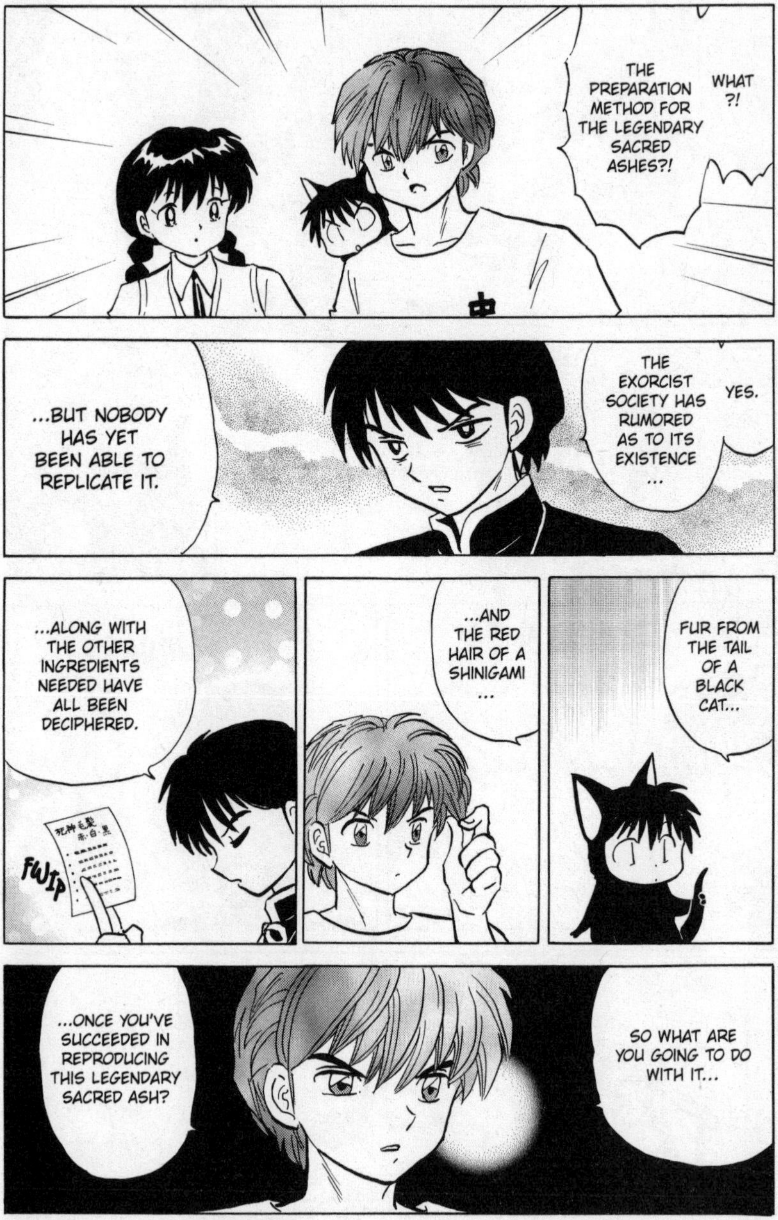
WHAT ?!
THE PREPARATION METHOD FOR THE LEGENDARY SACRED ASHES?!
YES.
THE EXORCIST SOCIETY HAS RUMORED AS TO ITS EXISTENCE ...
...BUT NOBODY HAS YET BEEN ABLE TO REPLICATE IT.
FUR FROM THE TAIL OF A BLACK CAT...
...AND THE RED HAIR OF A SHINIGAMI ...
...ALONG WITH THE OTHER INGREDIENTS NEEDED HAVE ALL BEEN DECIPHERED.
FWIP
SO WHAT ARE YOU GOING TO DO WITH IT...
...ONCE YOU'VE SUCCEEDED IN REPRODUCING THIS LEGENDARY SACRED ASH?

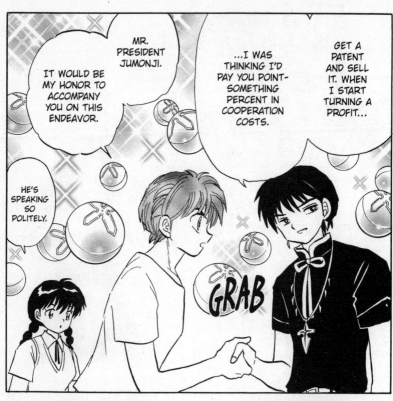

GET A PATENT AND SELL IT. WHEN I START TURNING A PROFIT...
...I WAS THINKING I'D PAY YOU POINT-SOMETHING PERCENT IN COOPERATION COSTS.
MR. PRESIDENT JUMONJI.
IT WOULD BE MY HONOR TO ACCOMPANY YOU ON THIS ENDEAVOR.
GRAB
HE'S SPEAKING SO POLITELY.
WHAT A WINDFALL!
WHOOSH
ALL WE HAVE TO DO IS GET THE INGREDIENTS ON THIS LIST.
THE NEXT INGREDI-ENT IS...
WHIP

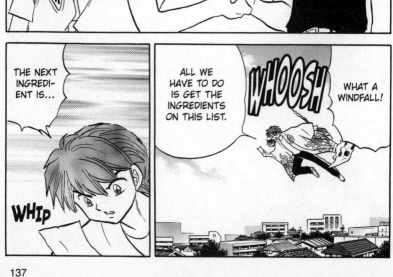

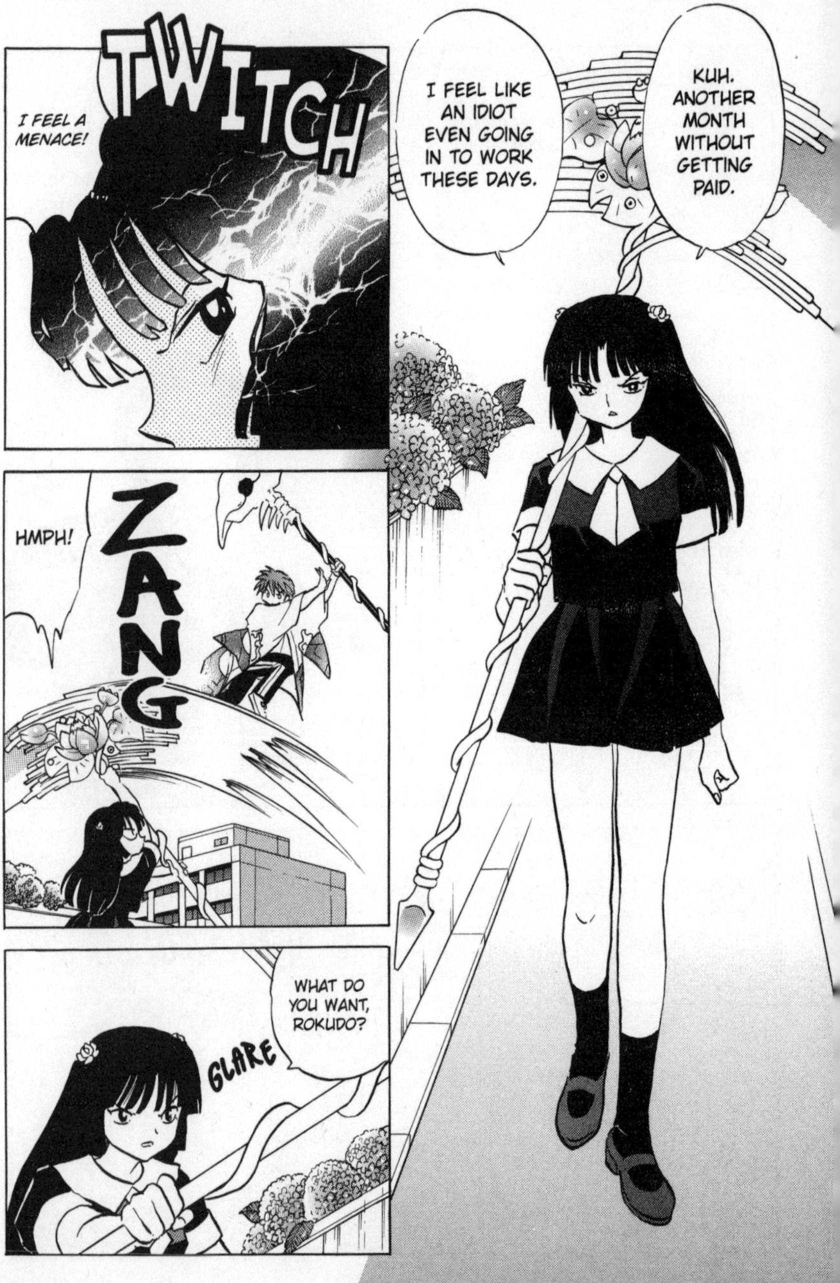
KUH. ANOTHER MONTH WITHOUT GETTING PAID.
I FEEL LIKE AN IDIOT EVEN GOING IN TO WORK THESE DAYS.
TWITCH
I FEEL A MENACE!
ZANG
HMPH!
WHAT DO YOU WANT, ROKUDO?
GLARE

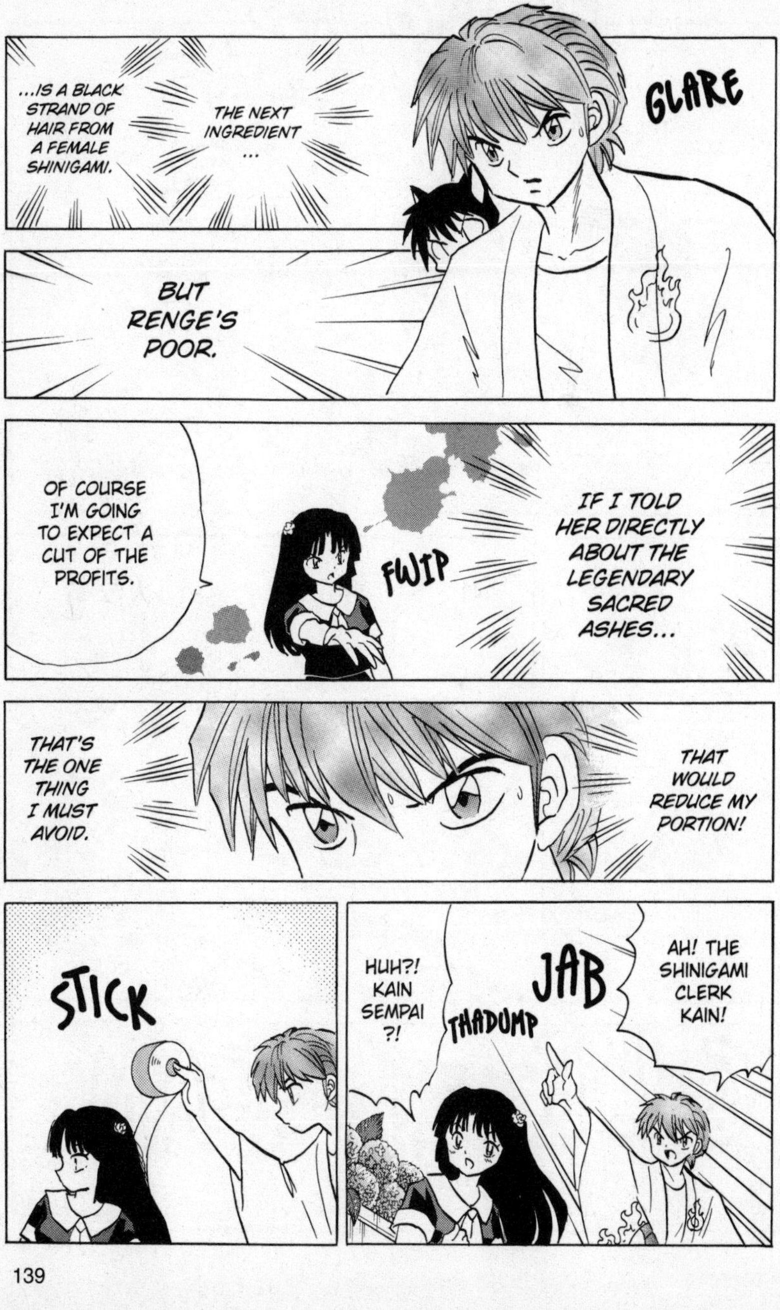
GLARE
THE NEXT INGREDIENT ...
...IS A BLACK STRAND OF HAIR FROM A FEMALE SHINIGAMI.
BUT RENGE'S POOR.
IF I TOLD HER DIRECTLY ABOUT THE LEGENDARY SACRED ASHES...
FWIP
OF COURSE I'M GOING TO EXPECT A CUT OF THE PROFITS.
THAT WOULD REDUCE MY PORTION!
THAT'S THE ONE THING I MUST AVOID.
AH! THE SHINIGAMI CLERK KAIN!
JAB
THADUMP
HUH?! KAIN SEMPAI ?!
STICK

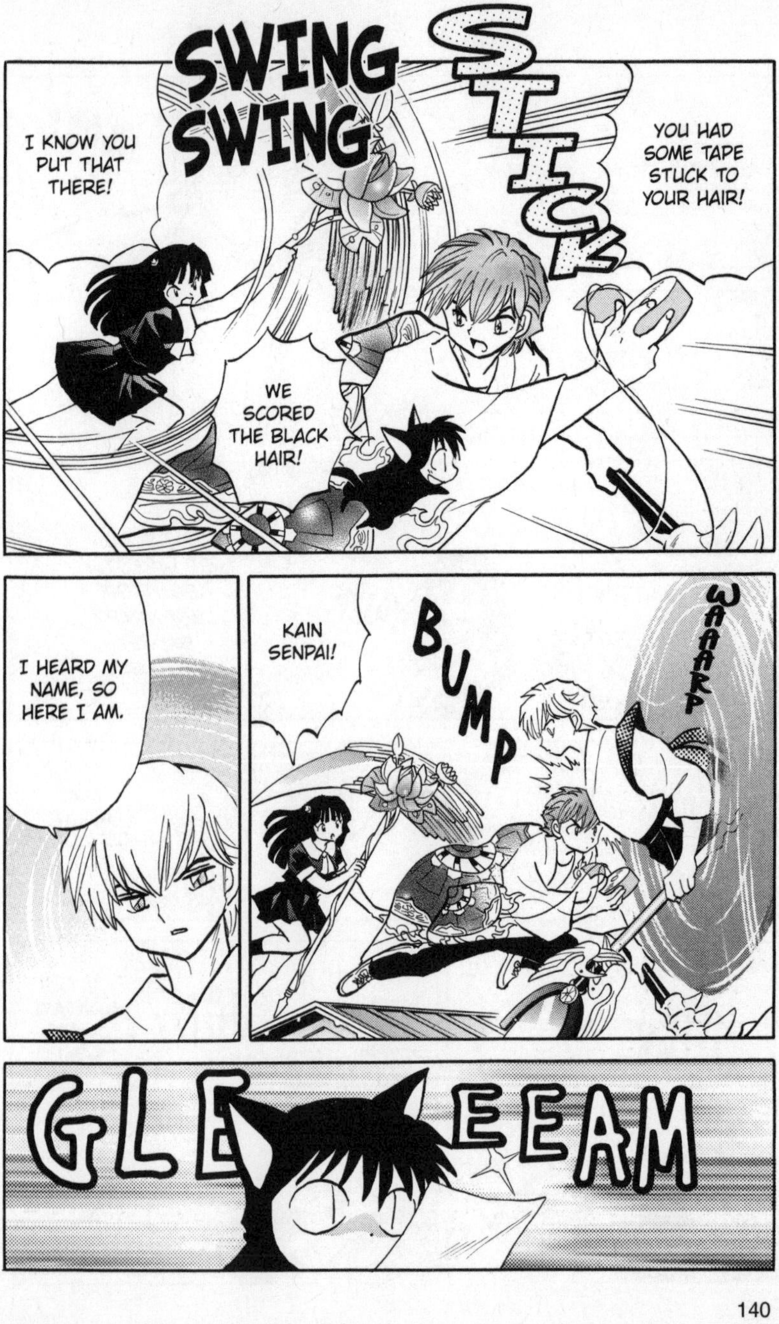
SWING SWING
STICK
YOU HAD SOME TAPE STUCK TO YOUR HAIR!
I KNOW YOU PUT THAT THERE!
WE SCORED THE BLACK HAIR!
WAAAARP
BUMP
KAIN SENPAI!
I HEARD MY NAME, SO HERE I AM.
GLE EEAM

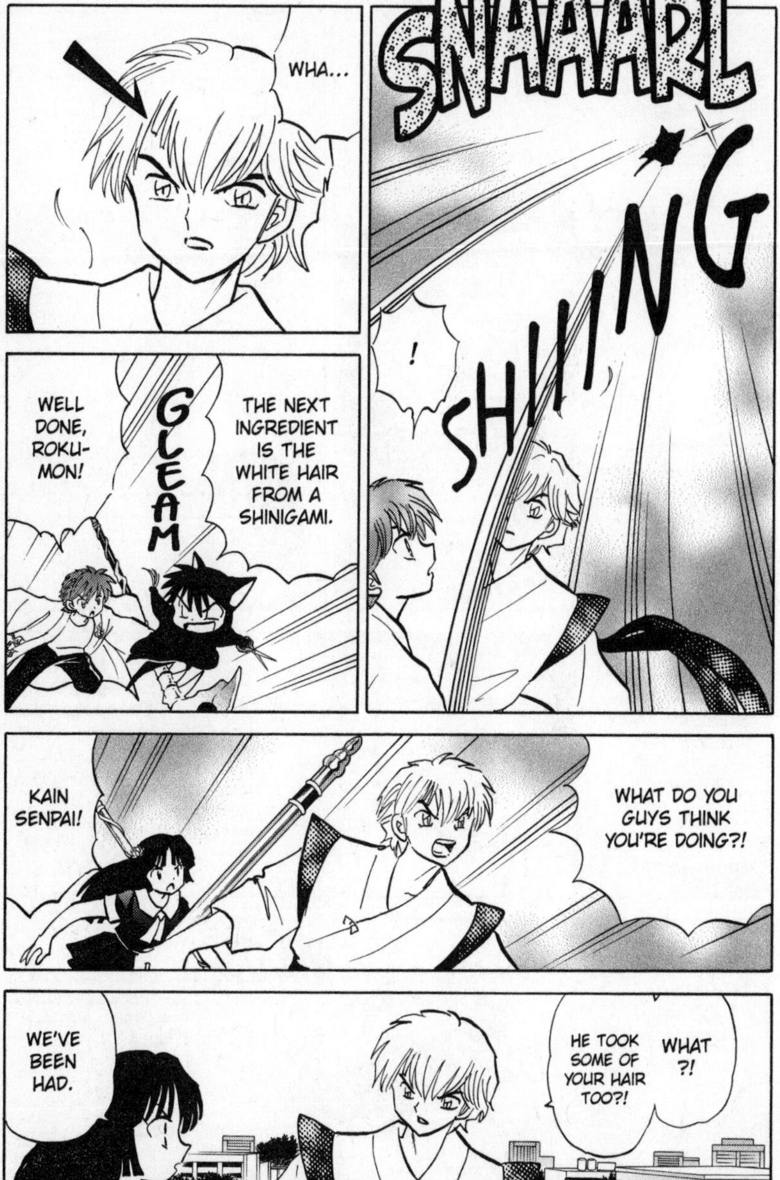
SNAAARL
SHIIING
!
WHA...
THE NEXT INGREDIENT IS THE WHITE HAIR FROM A SHINIGAMI.
GLEAM
WELL DONE, ROKU-MON!
WHAT DO YOU GUYS THINK YOU'RE DOING?!
KAIN SENPAI!
WHAT ?!
HE TOOK SOME OF YOUR HAIR TOO?!
WE'VE BEEN HAD.

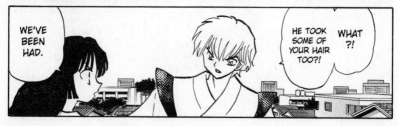

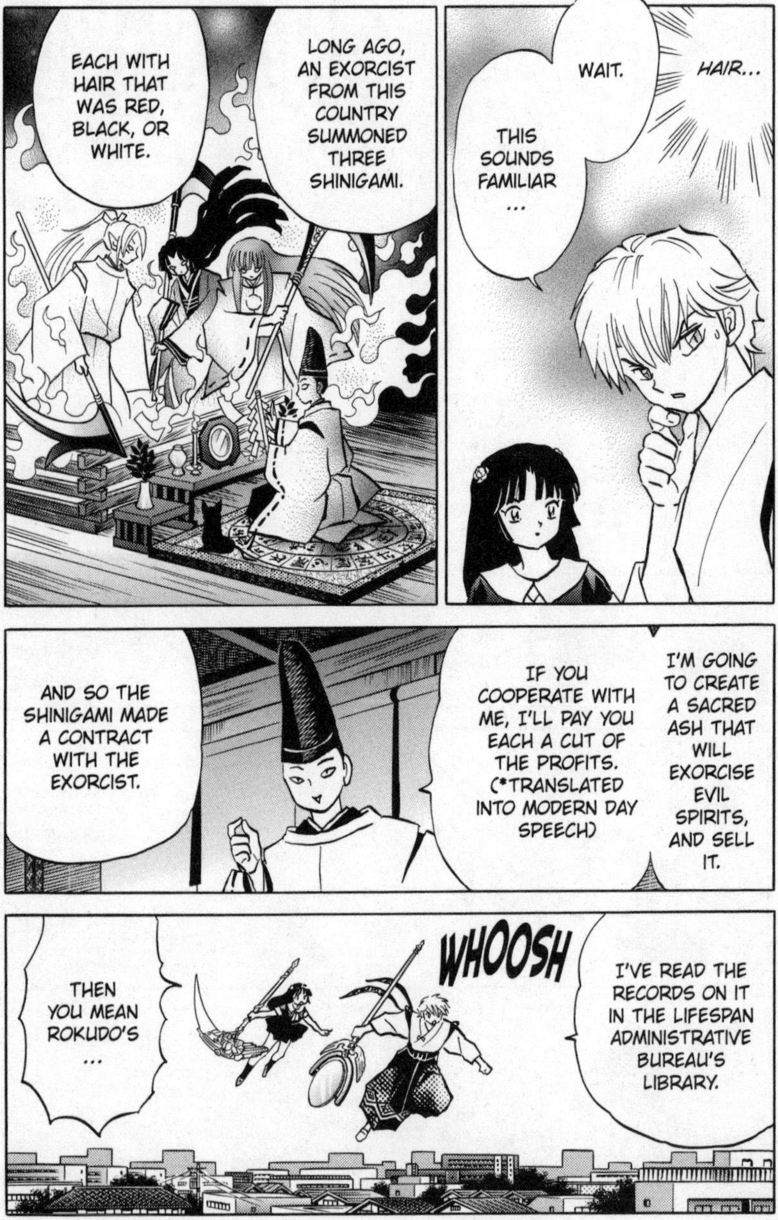
HAIR...
WAIT.
THIS SOUNDS FAMILIAR ...
LONG AGO, AN EXORCIST FROM THIS COUNTRY SUMMONED THREE SHINIGAMI.
EACH WITH HAIR THAT WAS RED, BLACK, OR WHITE.
I'M GOING TO CREATE A SACRED ASH THAT WILL EXORCISE EVIL SPIRITS, AND SELL IT.
IF YOU COOPERATE WITH ME, I'LL PAY YOU EACH A CUT OF THE PROFITS. (*TRANSLATED INTO MODERN DAY SPEECH)
AND SO THE SHINIGAMI MADE A CONTRACT WITH THE EXORCIST.
I'VE READ THE RECORDS ON IT IN THE LIFESPAN ADMINISTRATIVE BUREAU'S LIBRARY.
WHOOSH
THEN YOU MEAN ROKUDO'S ...

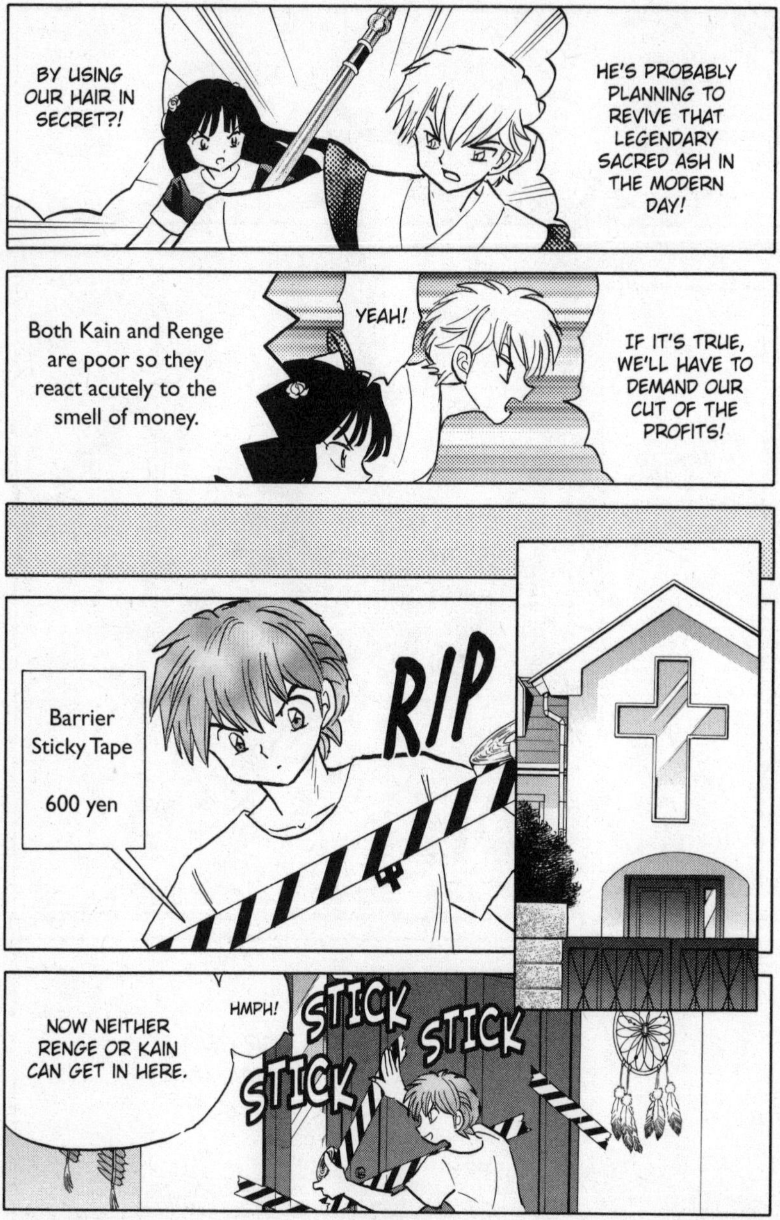
HE'S PROBABLY PLANNING TO REVIVE THAT LEGENDARY SACRED ASH IN THE MODERN DAY!
BY USING OUR HAIR IN SECRET?!
IF IT'S TRUE, WE'LL HAVE TO DEMAND OUR CUT OF THE PROFITS!
YEAH!
Both Kain and Renge are poor so they react acutely to the smell of money.
RIP
Barrier Sticky Tape
600 yen
STICK
STICK
STICK
HMPH!
NOW NEITHER RENGE OR KAIN CAN GET IN HERE.

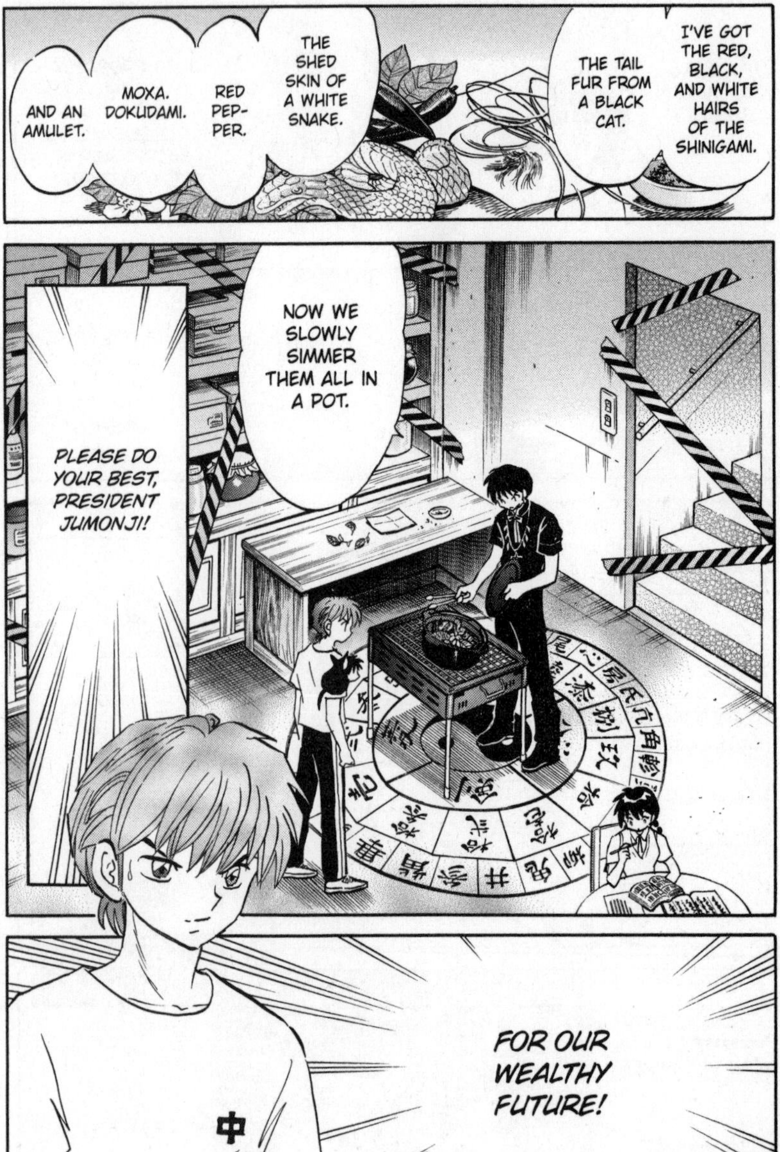
I'VE GOT THE RED, BLACK, AND WHITE HAIRS OF THE SHINIGAMI.
THE TAIL FUR FROM A BLACK CAT.
THE SHED SKIN OF A WHITE SNAKE.
RED PEP-PER.
MOXA. DOKUDAMI.
AND AN AMULET.
NOW WE SLOWLY SIMMER THEM ALL IN A POT.
PLEASE DO YOUR BEST, PRESIDENT JUMONJI!
FOR OUR WEALTHY FUTURE!

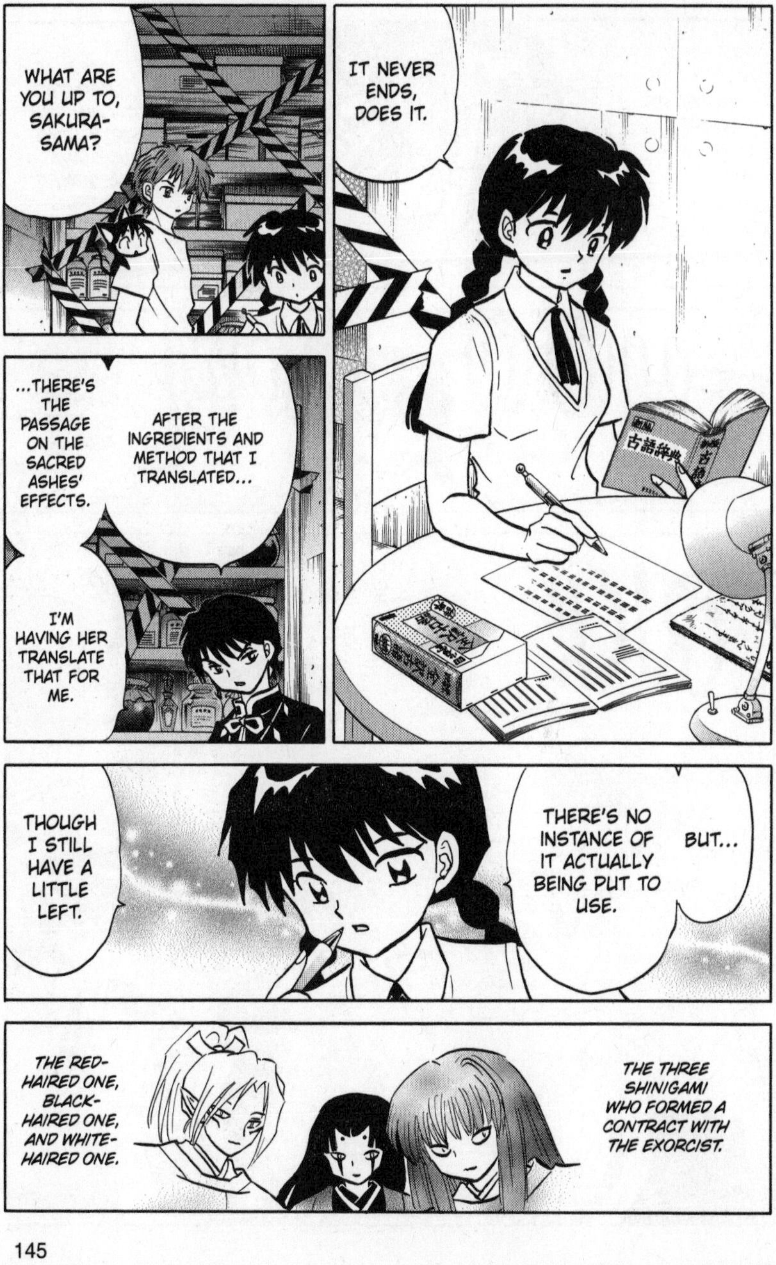
IT NEVER ENDS, DOES IT.
WHAT ARE YOU UP TO, SAKURA-SAMA?
AFTER THE INGREDIENTS AND METHOD THAT I TRANSLATED...
...THERE'S THE PASSAGE ON THE SACRED ASHES' EFFECTS.
I'M HAVING HER TRANSLATE THAT FOR ME.
BUT...
THERE'S NO INSTANCE OF IT ACTUALLY BEING PUT TO USE.
THOUGH I STILL HAVE A LITTLE LEFT.
THE THREE SHINIGAMI WHO FORMED A CONTRACT WITH THE EXORCIST.
THE RED-HAIRED ONE, BLACK-HAIRED ONE, AND WHITE-HAIRED ONE.

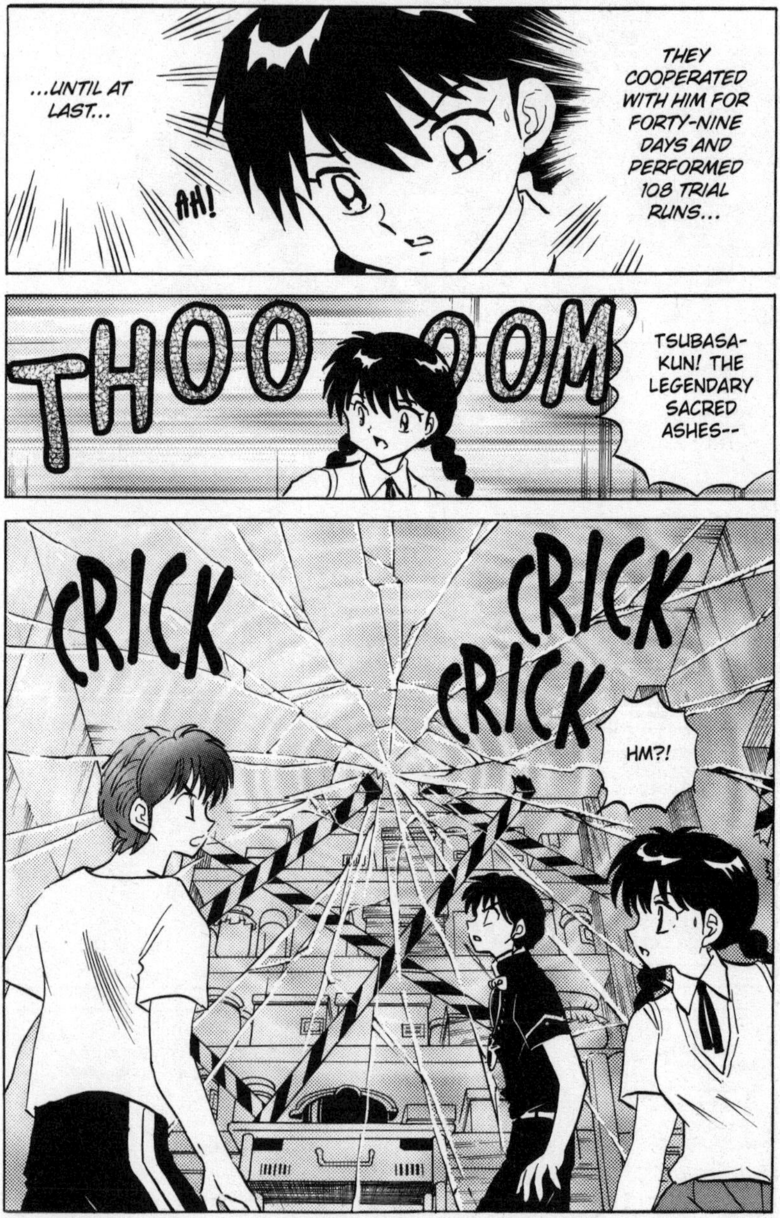
THEY COOPERATED WITH HIM FOR FORTY-NINE DAYS AND PERFORMED 108 TRIAL RUNS...
...UNTIL AT LAST...
AH!
TSUBASA-KUN! THE LEGENDARY SACRED ASHES--
THOO OOM
CRICK
CRICK
HM?!
CRICK

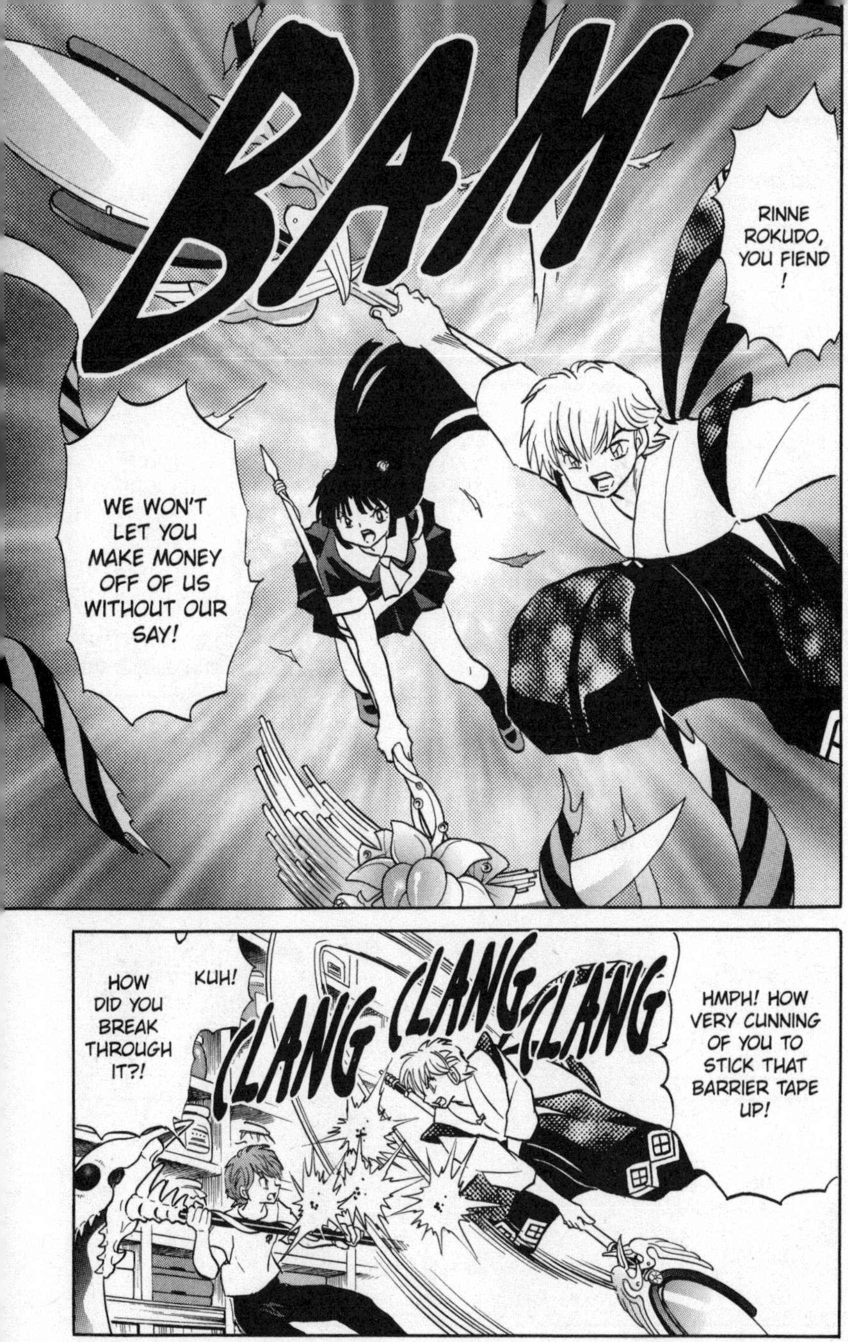
BAM
RINNE ROKUDO, YOU FIEND!
WE WON'T LET YOU MAKE MONEY OFF OF US WITHOUT OUR SAY!
HMPH! HOW VERY CUNNING OF YOU TO STICK THAT BARRIER TAPE UP!
CLANG CLANG CLANG CLANG
KUH!
HOW DID YOU BREAK THROUGH IT?!

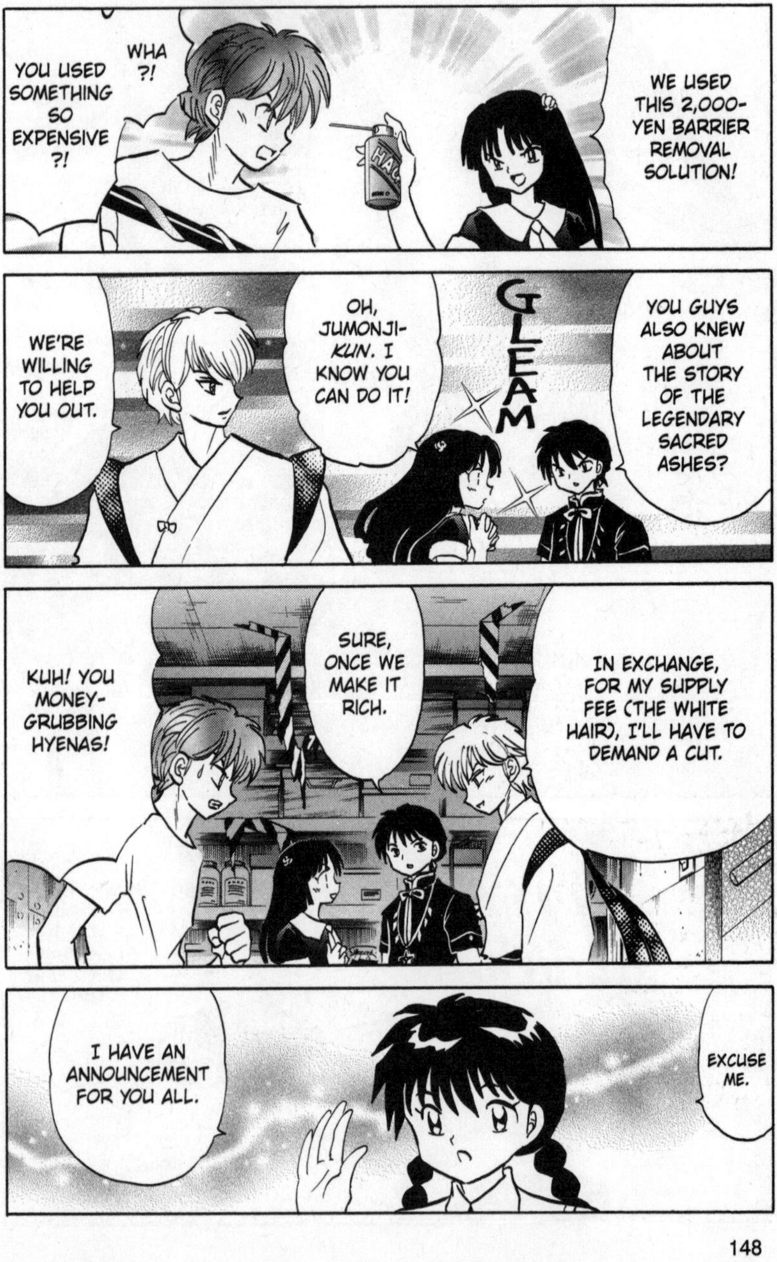

WE USED THIS 2,000-YEN BARRIER REMOVAL SOLUTION!
WHA ?!
YOU USED SOMETHING SO EXPENSIVE ?!
YOU GUYS ALSO KNEW ABOUT THE STORY OF THE LEGENDARY SACRED ASHES?
GLEAM
OH, JUMONJI-*KUN*. I KNOW YOU CAN DO IT!
WE'RE WILLING TO HELP YOU OUT.
IN EXCHANGE, FOR MY SUPPLY FEE (THE WHITE HAIR), I'LL HAVE TO DEMAND A CUT.
SURE, ONCE WE MAKE IT RICH.
KUH! YOU MONEY-GRUBBING HYENAS!
EXCUSE ME.
I HAVE AN ANNOUNCEMENT FOR YOU ALL.

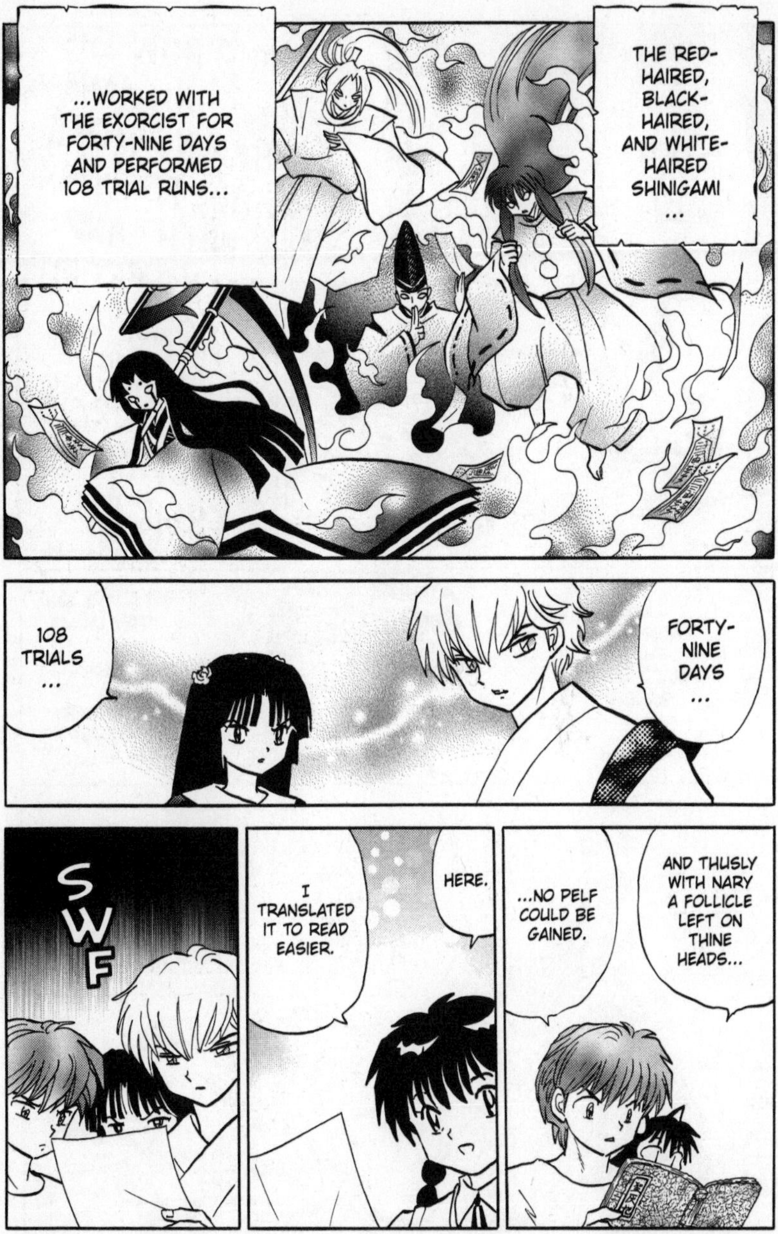
THE RED-HAIRED, BLACK-HAIRED, AND WHITE-HAIRED SHINIGAMI...
...WORKED WITH THE EXORCIST FOR FORTY-NINE DAYS AND PERFORMED 108 TRIAL RUNS...
FORTY-NINE DAYS...
108 TRIALS...
AND THUSLY WITH NARY A FOLLICLE LEFT ON THINE HEADS...
...NO PELF COULD BE GAINED.
HERE.
I TRANSLATED IT TO READ EASIER.
SWF

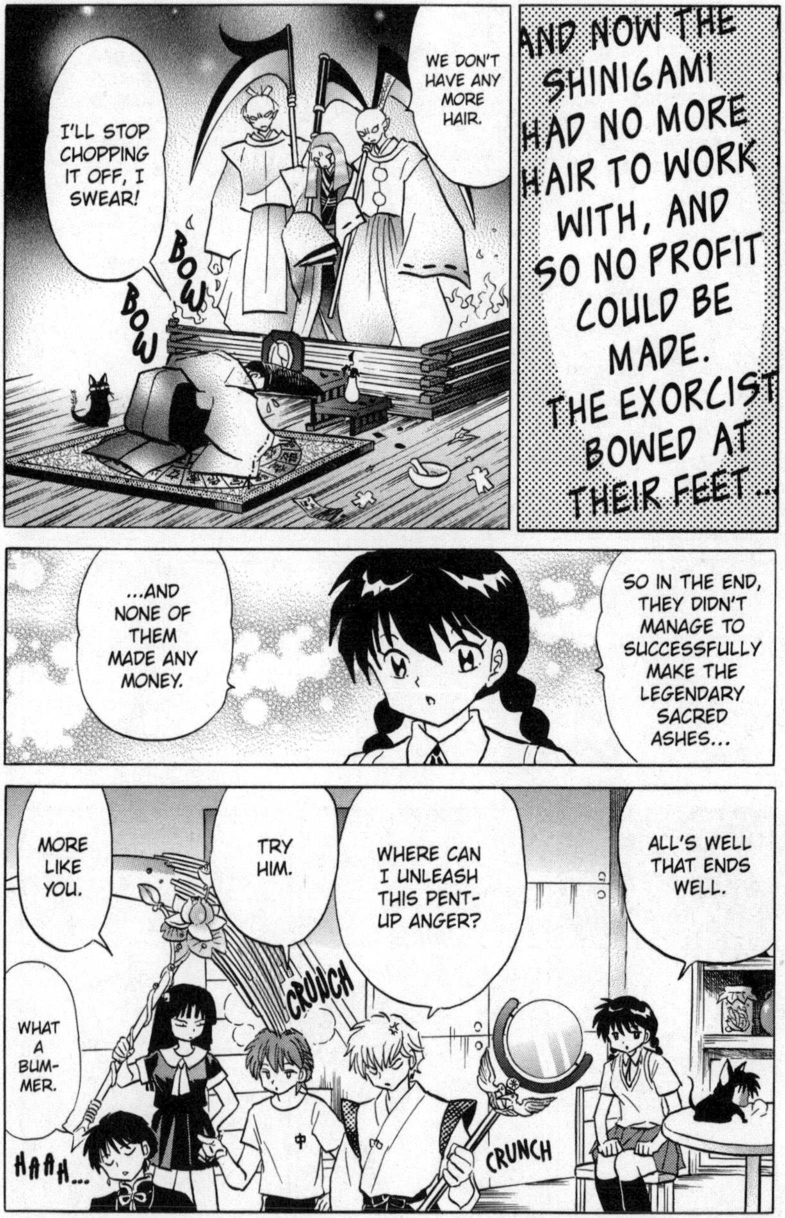
AND NOW THE SHINIGAMI HAD NO MORE HAIR TO WORK WITH, AND SO NO PROFIT COULD BE MADE. THE EXORCIST BOWED AT THEIR FEET...
WE DON'T HAVE ANY MORE HAIR.
I'LL STOP CHOPPING IT OFF, I SWEAR!
BOW
BOW
SO IN THE END, THEY DIDN'T MANAGE TO SUCCESSFULLY MAKE THE LEGENDARY SACRED ASHES...
...AND NONE OF THEM MADE ANY MONEY.
ALL'S WELL THAT ENDS WELL.
WHERE CAN I UNLEASH THIS PENT-UP ANGER?
TRY HIM.
MORE LIKE YOU.
CRUNCH
CRUNCH
WHAT A BUM-MER.
HAAH...

CHAPTER 197: FROM WITHIN THE WALL

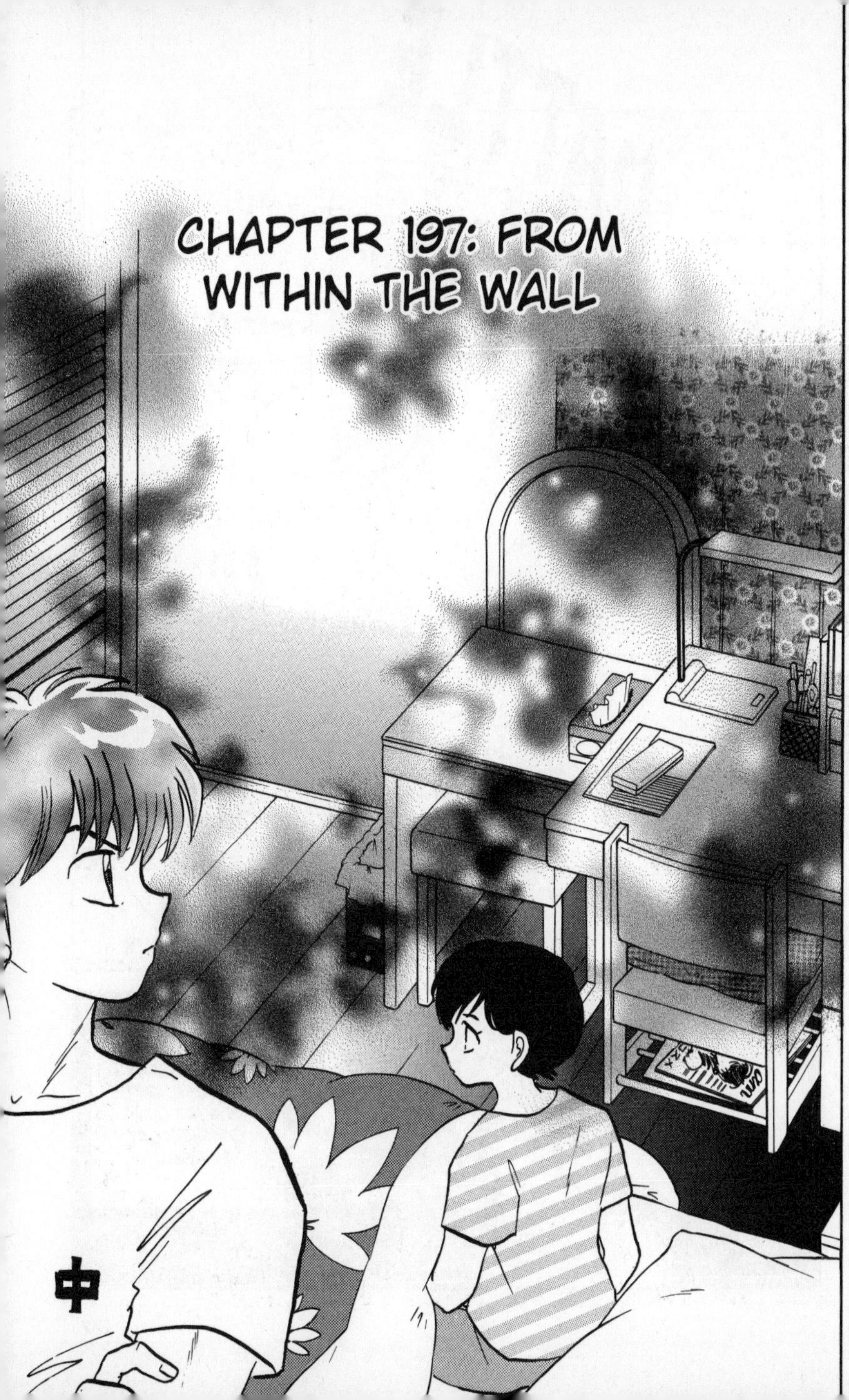
中

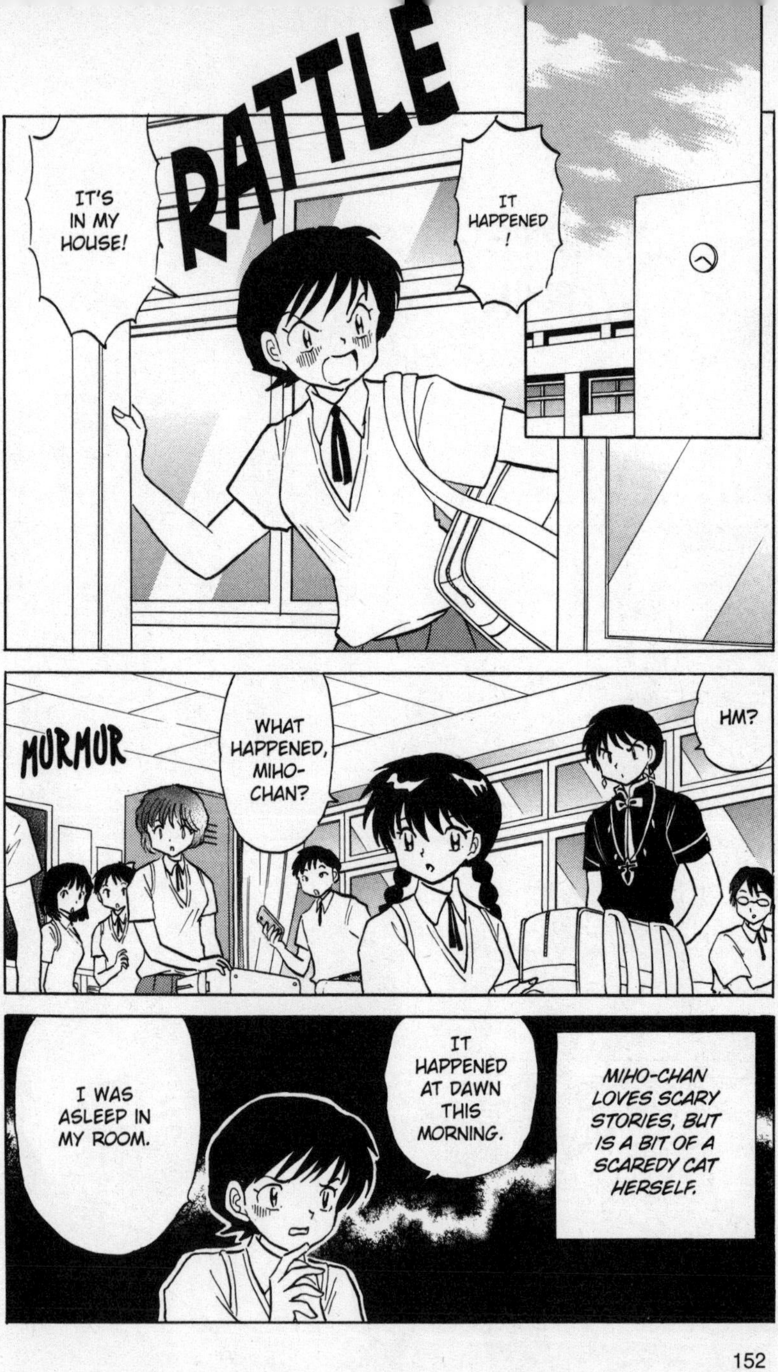
RATTLE
IT HAPPENED!
IT'S IN MY HOUSE!
HM?
WHAT HAPPENED, MIHO-CHAN?
MURMUR
MIHO-CHAN LOVES SCARY STORIES, BUT IS A BIT OF A SCAREDY CAT HERSELF.
IT HAPPENED AT DAWN THIS MORNING.
I WAS ASLEEP IN MY ROOM.

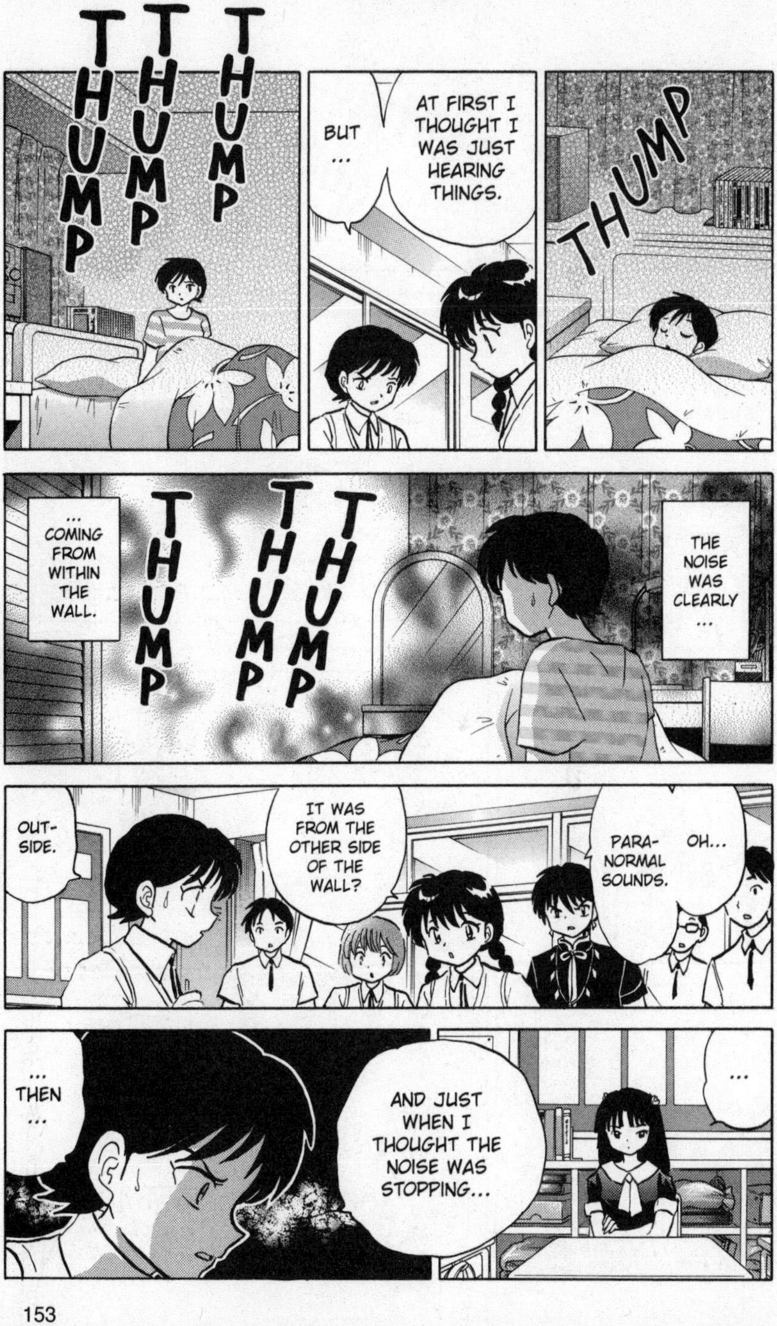
THUMP
AT FIRST I THOUGHT I WAS JUST HEARING THINGS.
BUT ...
THUMP
THUMP
THUMP
THE NOISE WAS CLEARLY ...
THUMP
THUMP
THUMP
... COMING FROM WITHIN THE WALL.
OH...
PARA-NORMAL SOUNDS.
IT WAS FROM THE OTHER SIDE OF THE WALL?
OUT-SIDE.
...
AND JUST WHEN I THOUGHT THE NOISE WAS STOPPING...
... THEN ...

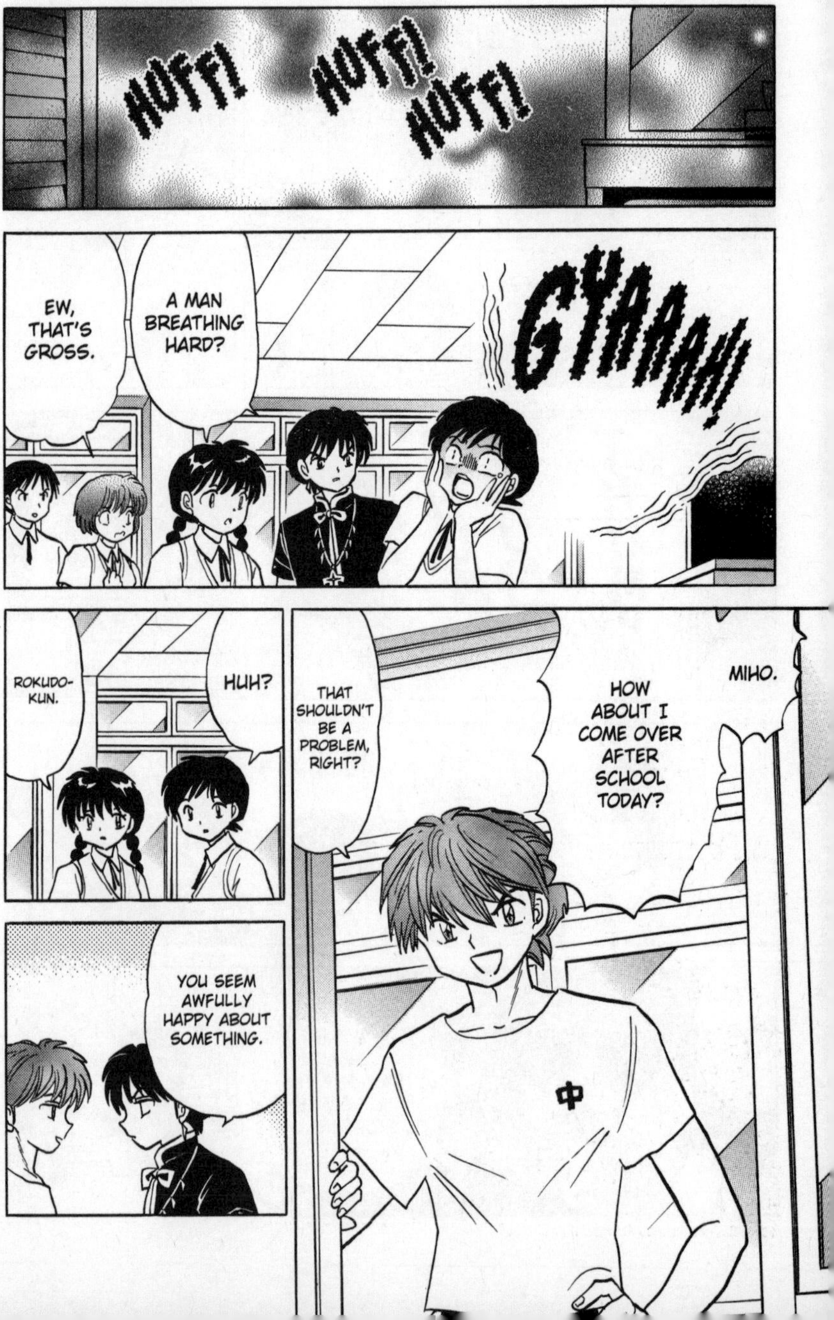
HUFF! HUFF! HUFF!
GYAAAH!
A MAN BREATHING HARD?
EW, THAT'S GROSS.
MIHO.
HOW ABOUT I COME OVER AFTER SCHOOL TODAY?
THAT SHOULDN'T BE A PROBLEM, RIGHT?
HUH?
ROKUDO-KUN.
YOU SEEM AWFULLY HAPPY ABOUT SOMETHING.

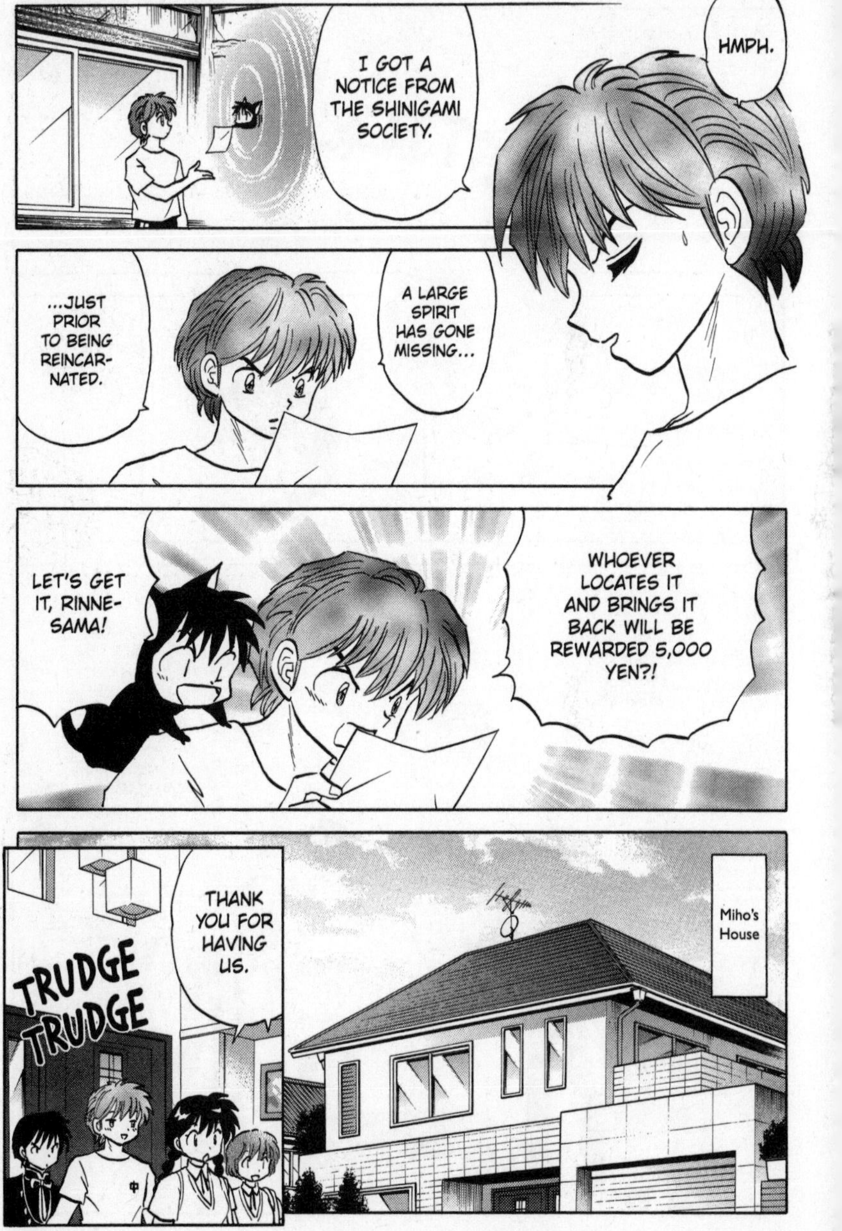
HMPH.
I GOT A NOTICE FROM THE SHINIGAMI SOCIETY.
A LARGE SPIRIT HAS GONE MISSING...
...JUST PRIOR TO BEING REINCAR-NATED.
WHOEVER LOCATES IT AND BRINGS IT BACK WILL BE REWARDED 5,000 YEN?!
LET'S GET IT, RINNE-SAMA!
Miho's House
THANK YOU FOR HAVING US.
TRUDGE TRUDGE

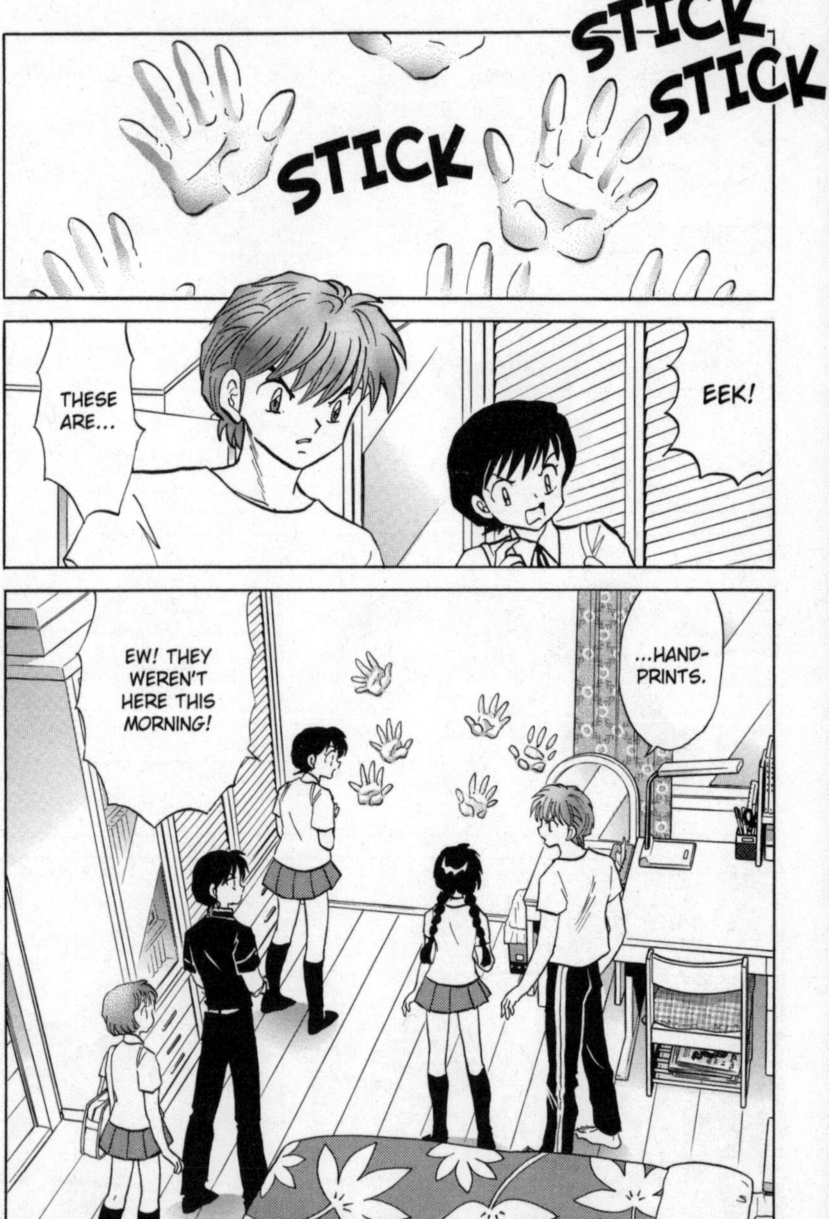
STICK
STICK
STICK
EEK!
THESE ARE...
...HAND-PRINTS.
EW! THEY WEREN'T HERE THIS MORNING!

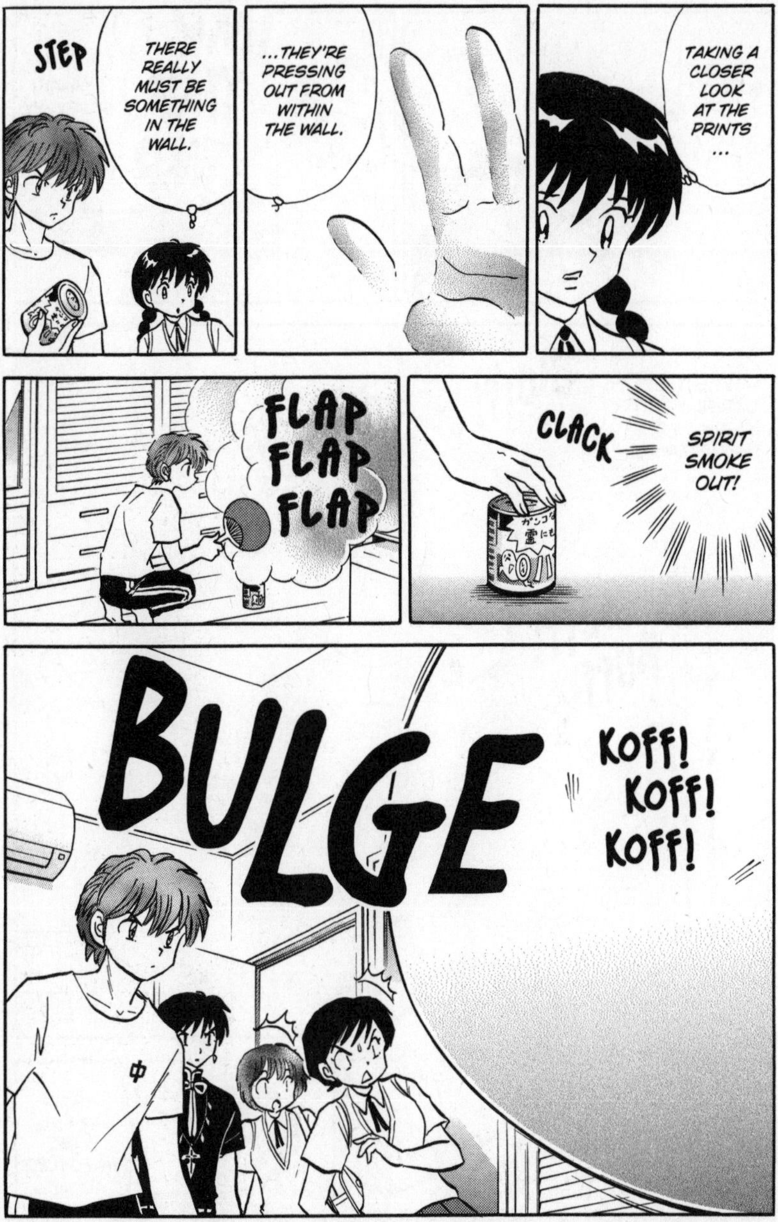
TAKING A CLOSER LOOK AT THE PRINTS ...
...THEY'RE PRESSING OUT FROM WITHIN THE WALL.
THERE REALLY MUST BE SOMETHING IN THE WALL.
STEP
SPIRIT SMOKE OUT!
CLACK
FLAP FLAP FLAP
KOFF! KOFF! KOFF!
BULGE

TMP TMP TMP
GYAAAH! SCARYYYY!
ROKUDO, I KNOW WHAT THIS IS.
NO MISTAKE ABOUT IT.
HUFF!
IT'S THE LARGE SPIRIT MISSING FROM THE AFTERLIFE.
HUFF! HUFF!
LOOKS LIKE A SUMO WRESTLER TO ME.
SANZUNO KAWAZEKI.

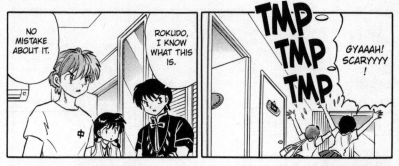

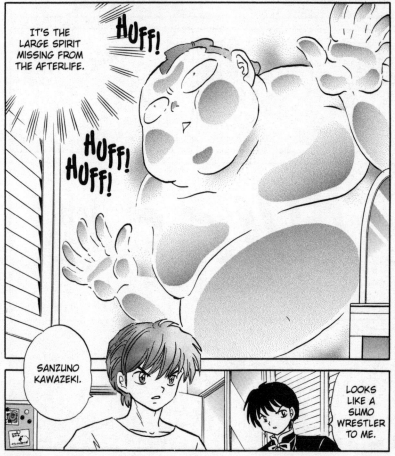

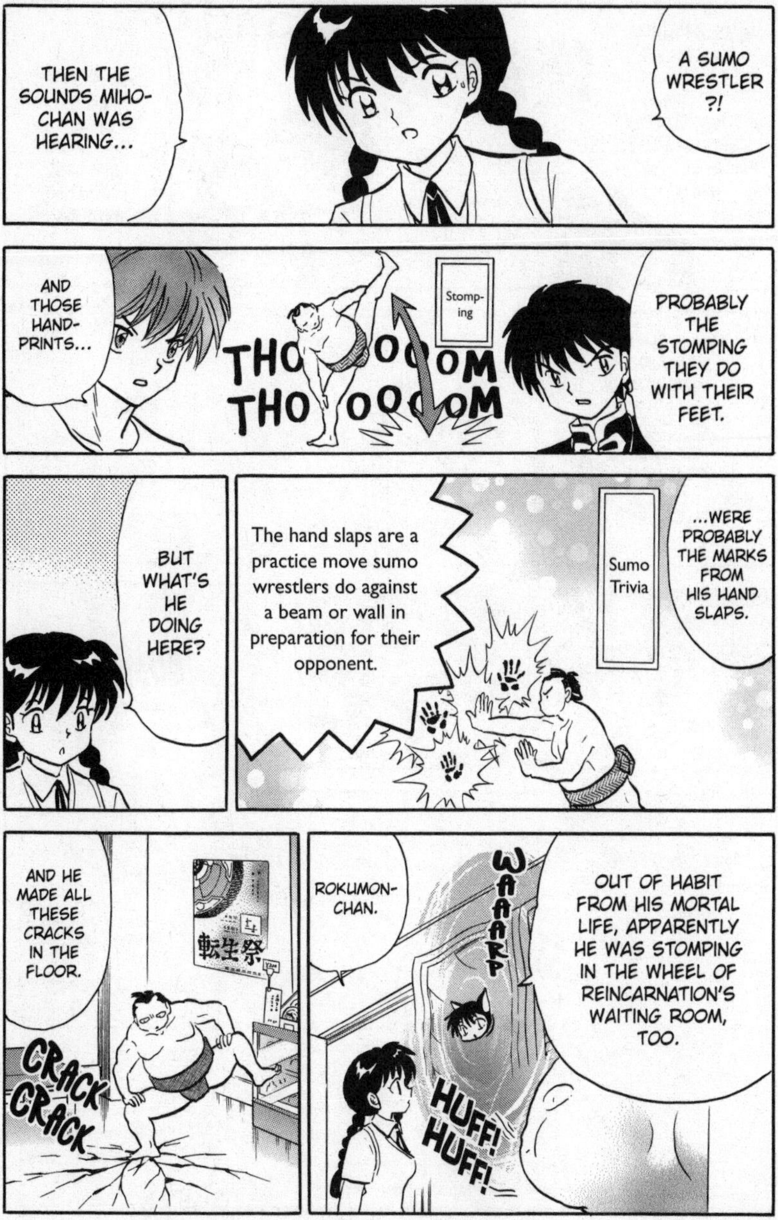
A SUMO WRESTLER ?!
THEN THE SOUNDS MIHO-CHAN WAS HEARING...
PROBABLY THE STOMPING THEY DO WITH THEIR FEET.
Stomping
THOOOOM THOOOOM
AND THOSE HAND-PRINTS...
...WERE PROBABLY THE MARKS FROM HIS HAND SLAPS.
Sumo Trivia
The hand slaps are a practice move sumo wrestlers do against a beam or wall in preparation for their opponent.
BUT WHAT'S HE DOING HERE?
OUT OF HABIT FROM HIS MORTAL LIFE, APPARENTLY HE WAS STOMPING IN THE WHEEL OF REINCARNATION'S WAITING ROOM, TOO.
WAAARP
HUFF! HUFF!
ROKUMON-CHAN.
AND HE MADE ALL THESE CRACKS IN THE FLOOR.
転生祭
CRACK CRACK

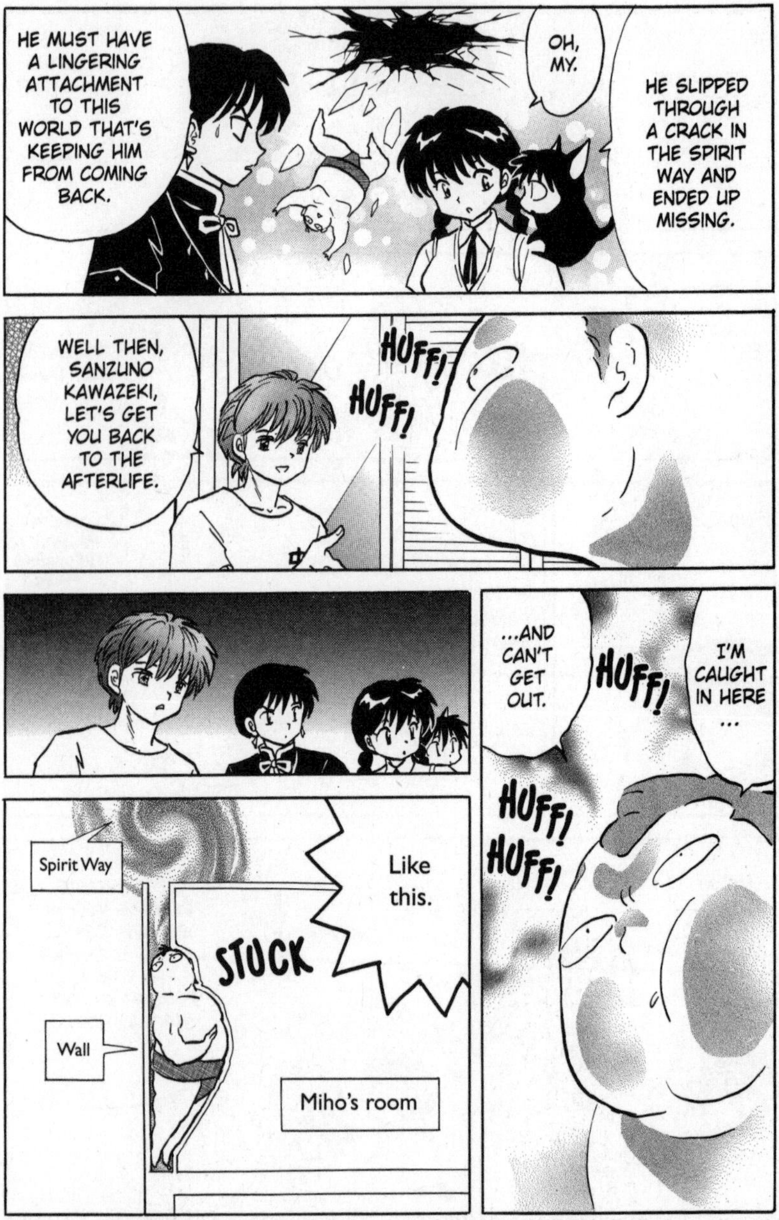
HE SLIPPED THROUGH A CRACK IN THE SPIRIT WAY AND ENDED UP MISSING.
OH, MY.
HE MUST HAVE A LINGERING ATTACHMENT TO THIS WORLD THAT'S KEEPING HIM FROM COMING BACK.
HUFF!
HUFF!
WELL THEN, SANZUNO KAWAZEKI, LET'S GET YOU BACK TO THE AFTERLIFE.
I'M CAUGHT IN HERE ...
HUFF!
...AND CAN'T GET OUT.
HUFF!
HUFF!
Like this.
STUCK
Spirit Way
Wall
Miho's room

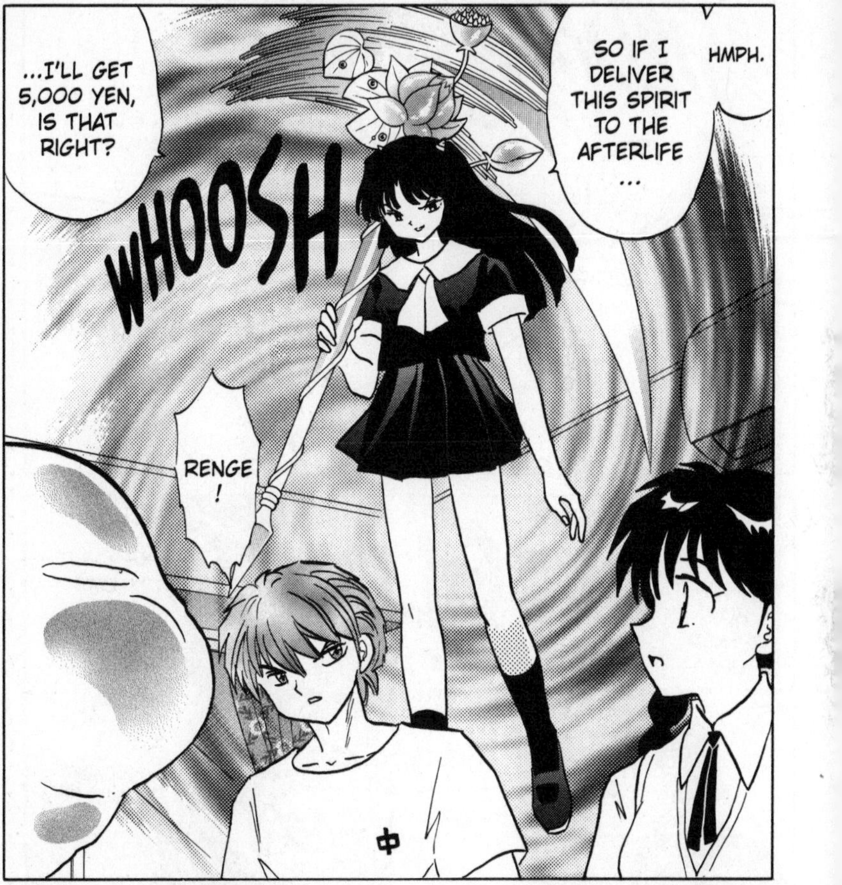
HMPH.
SO IF I DELIVER THIS SPIRIT TO THE AFTERLIFE ...
...I'LL GET 5,000 YEN, IS THAT RIGHT?
WHOOSH
RENGE!

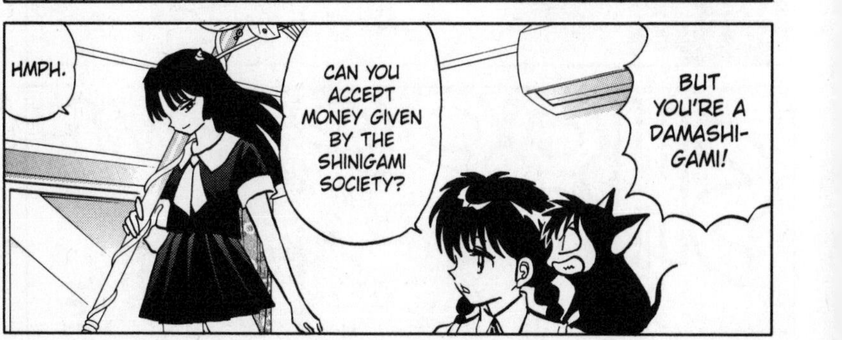
BUT YOU'RE A DAMASHI-GAMI!
CAN YOU ACCEPT MONEY GIVEN BY THE SHINIGAMI SOCIETY?
HMPH.

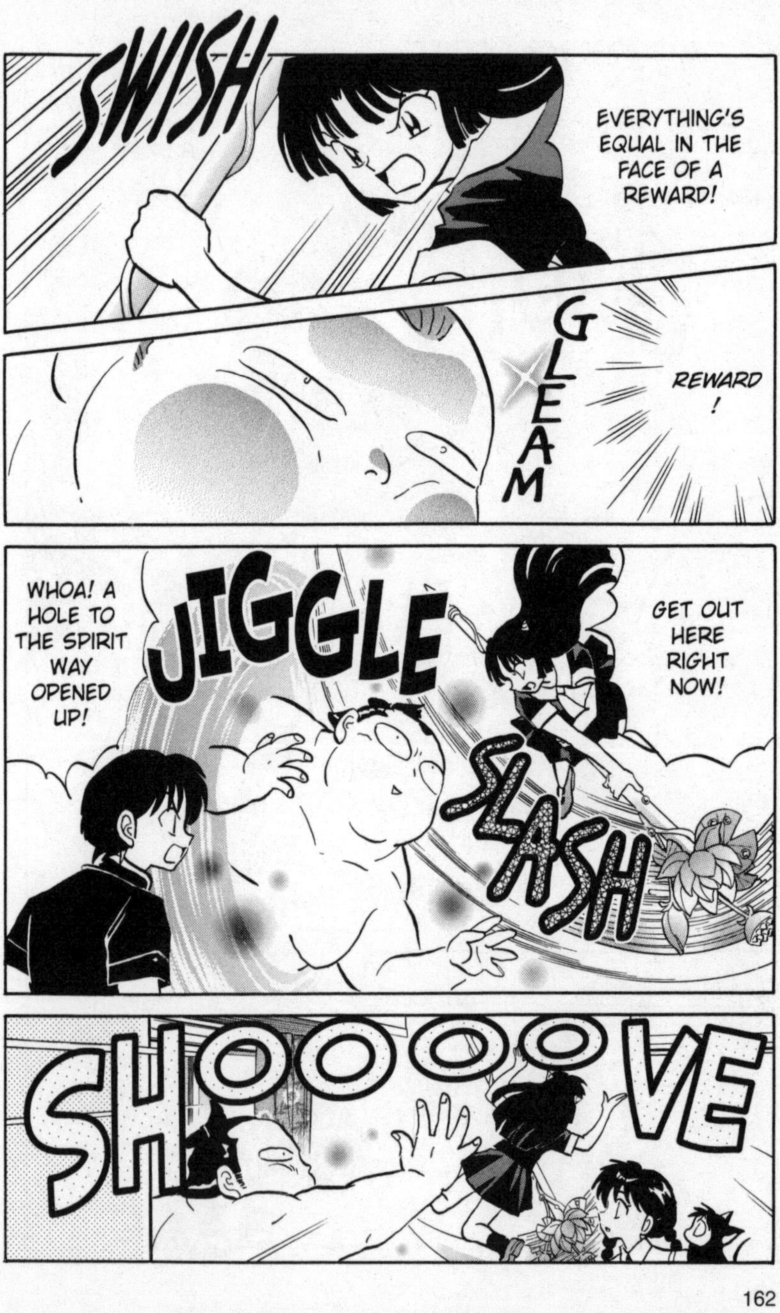
EVERYTHING'S EQUAL IN THE FACE OF A REWARD!
SWISH
REWARD!
GLEAM
GET OUT HERE RIGHT NOW!
JIGGLE
WHOA! A HOLE TO THE SPIRIT WAY OPENED UP!
SLASH
SHOOOOVE

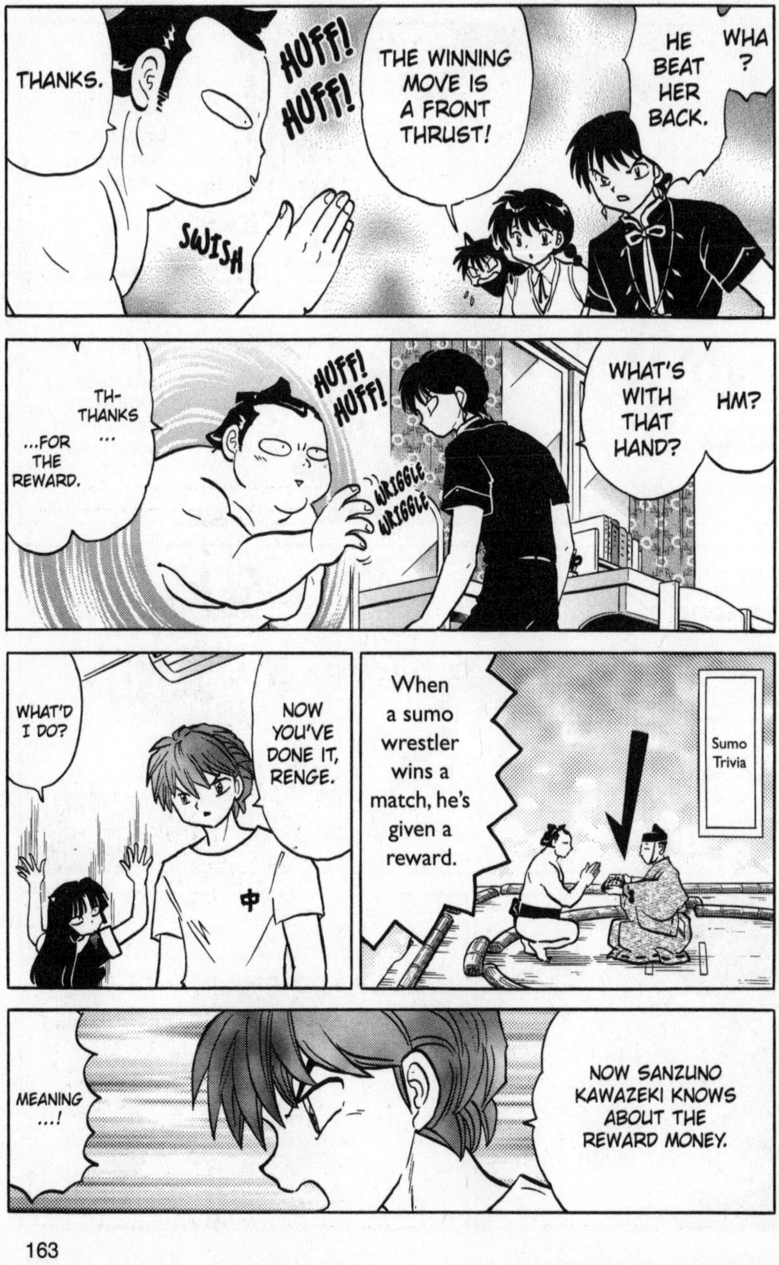
WHA ?
HE BEAT HER BACK.
THE WINNING MOVE IS A FRONT THRUST!
HUFF! HUFF!
THANKS.
SWISH
HM?
WHAT'S WITH THAT HAND?
HUFF! HUFF!
TH- THANKS ...
...FOR THE REWARD.
WRIGGLE WRIGGLE
Sumo Trivia
When a sumo wrestler wins a match, he's given a reward.
NOW YOU'VE DONE IT, RENGE.
WHAT'D I DO?
NOW SANZUNO KAWAZEKI KNOWS ABOUT THE REWARD MONEY.
MEANING ...!

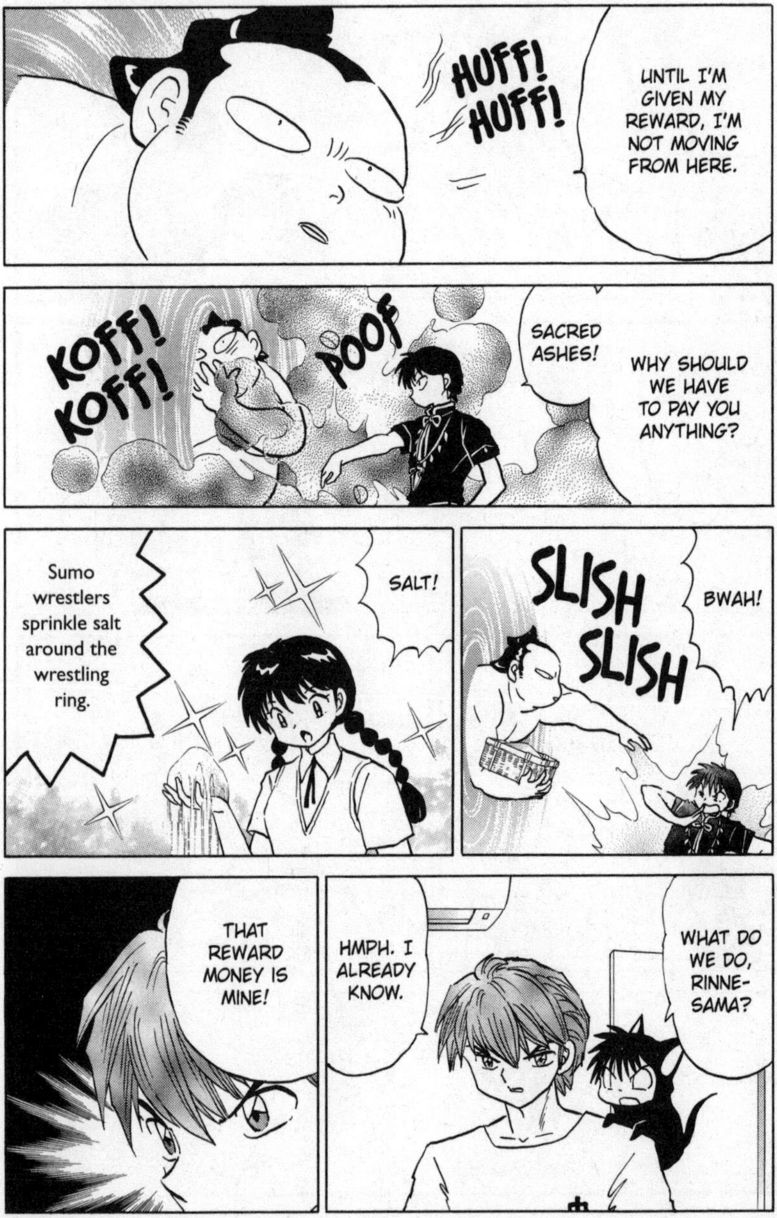
UNTIL I'M GIVEN MY REWARD, I'M NOT MOVING FROM HERE.
HUFF! HUFF!
SACRED ASHES!
WHY SHOULD WE HAVE TO PAY YOU ANYTHING?
POOF
KOFF! KOFF!
BWAH!
SLISH SLISH
SALT!
Sumo wrestlers sprinkle salt around the wrestling ring.
WHAT DO WE DO, RINNE-SAMA?
HMPH. I ALREADY KNOW.
THAT REWARD MONEY IS MINE!

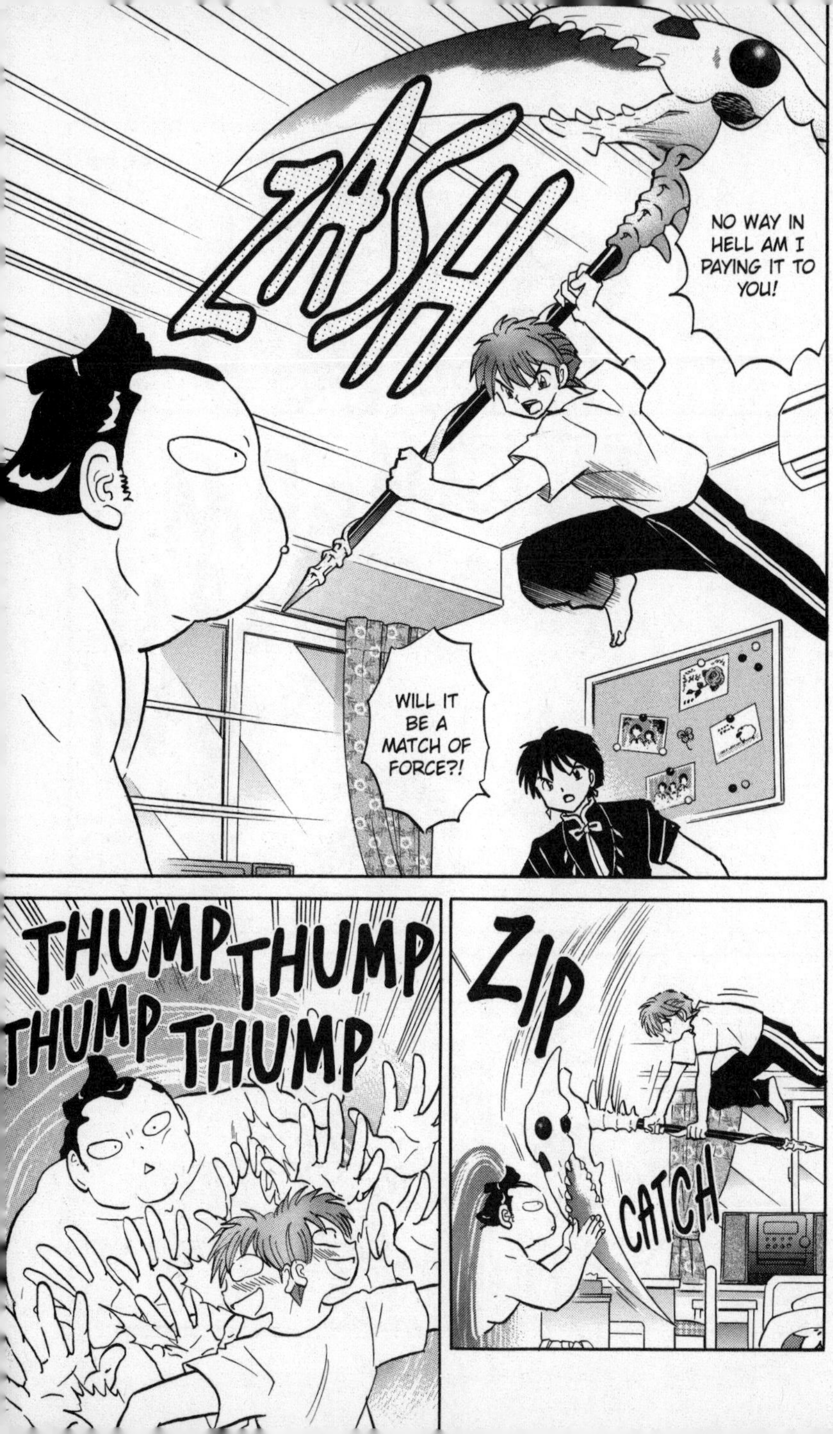
NO WAY IN HELL AM I PAYING IT TO YOU!
ZASH
WILL IT BE A MATCH OF FORCE?!
ZIP
CATCH
THUMP THUMP THUMP THUMP

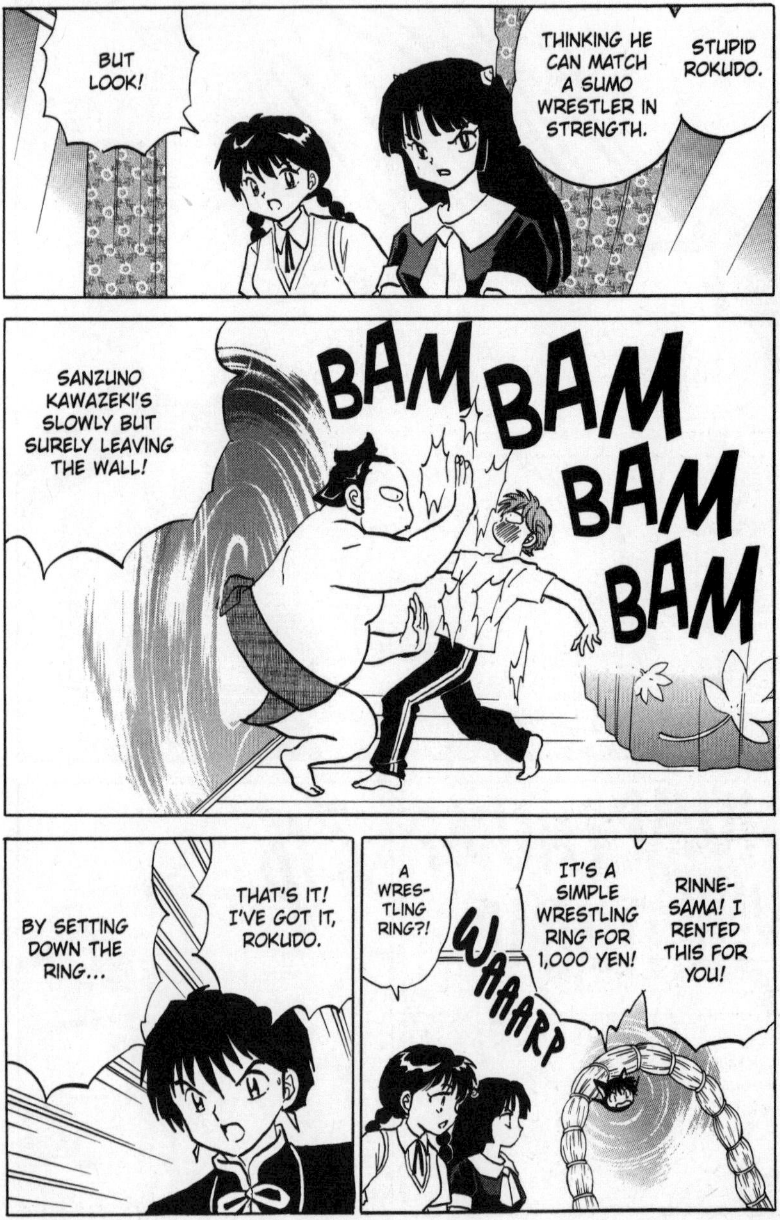
STUPID ROKUDO.
THINKING HE CAN MATCH A SUMO WRESTLER IN STRENGTH.
BUT LOOK!
BAM BAM BAM BAM
SANZUNO KAWAZEKI'S SLOWLY BUT SURELY LEAVING THE WALL!
RINNE-SAMA! I RENTED THIS FOR YOU!
IT'S A SIMPLE WRESTLING RING FOR 1,000 YEN!
WAAARP
A WRES-TLING RING?!
THAT'S IT! I'VE GOT IT, ROKUDO.
BY SETTING DOWN THE RING...

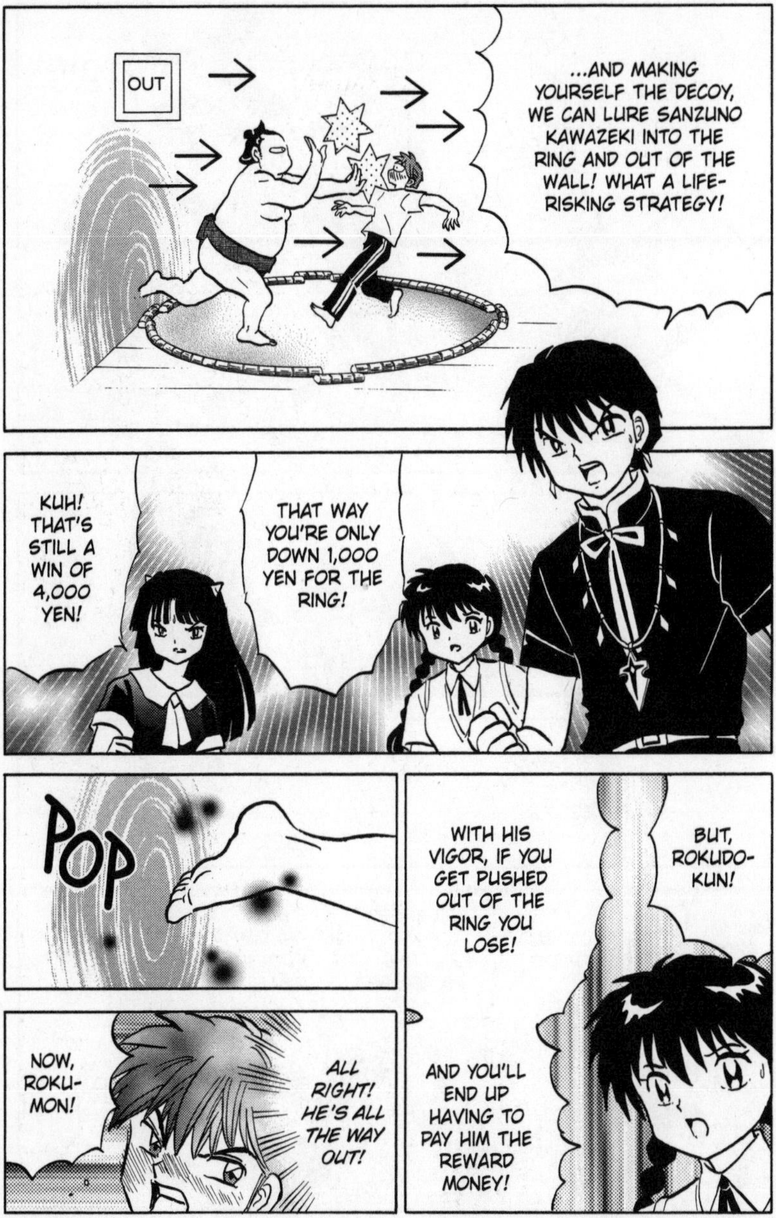
...AND MAKING YOURSELF THE DECOY, WE CAN LURE SANZUNO KAWAZEKI INTO THE RING AND OUT OF THE WALL! WHAT A LIFE-RISKING STRATEGY!
OUT
THAT WAY YOU'RE ONLY DOWN 1,000 YEN FOR THE RING!
KUH! THAT'S STILL A WIN OF 4,000 YEN!
BUT, ROKUDO-KUN!
WITH HIS VIGOR, IF YOU GET PUSHED OUT OF THE RING YOU LOSE!
AND YOU'LL END UP HAVING TO PAY HIM THE REWARD MONEY!
POP
ALL RIGHT! HE'S ALL THE WAY OUT!
NOW, ROKUMON!

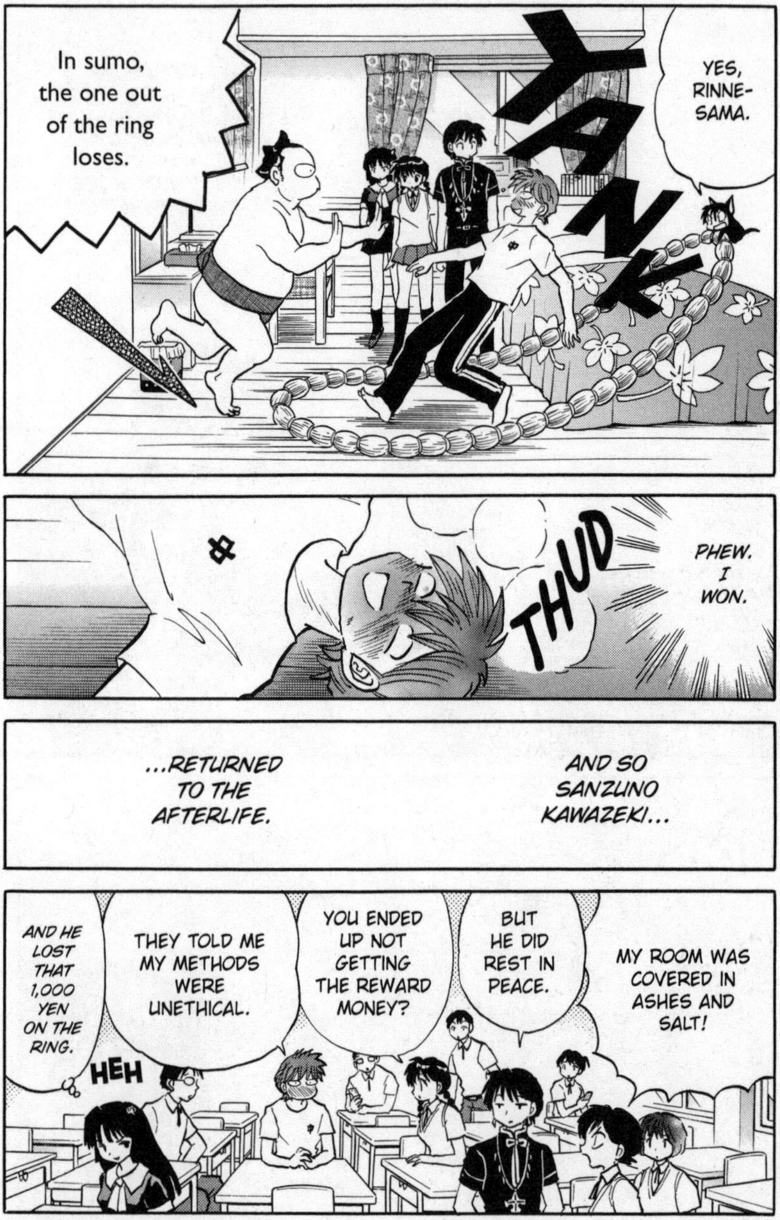
YES, RINNE-SAMA.
YANK
In sumo, the one out of the ring loses.
PHEW. I WON.
THUD
AND SO SANZUNO KAWAZEKI...
...RETURNED TO THE AFTERLIFE.
MY ROOM WAS COVERED IN ASHES AND SALT!
BUT HE DID REST IN PEACE.
YOU ENDED UP NOT GETTING THE REWARD MONEY?
THEY TOLD ME MY METHODS WERE UNETHICAL.
AND HE LOST THAT 1,000 YEN ON THE RING.
HEH

CHAPTER 198: ALL-YOU-CAN-EAT CHERRY TOMATOES

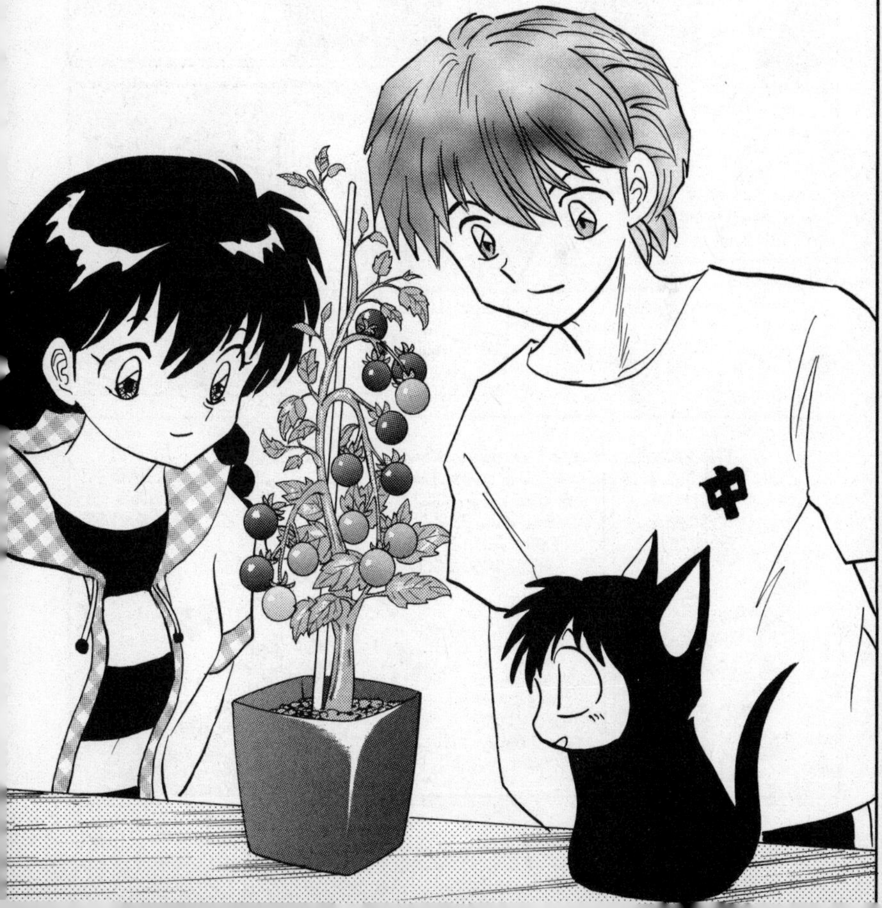
中

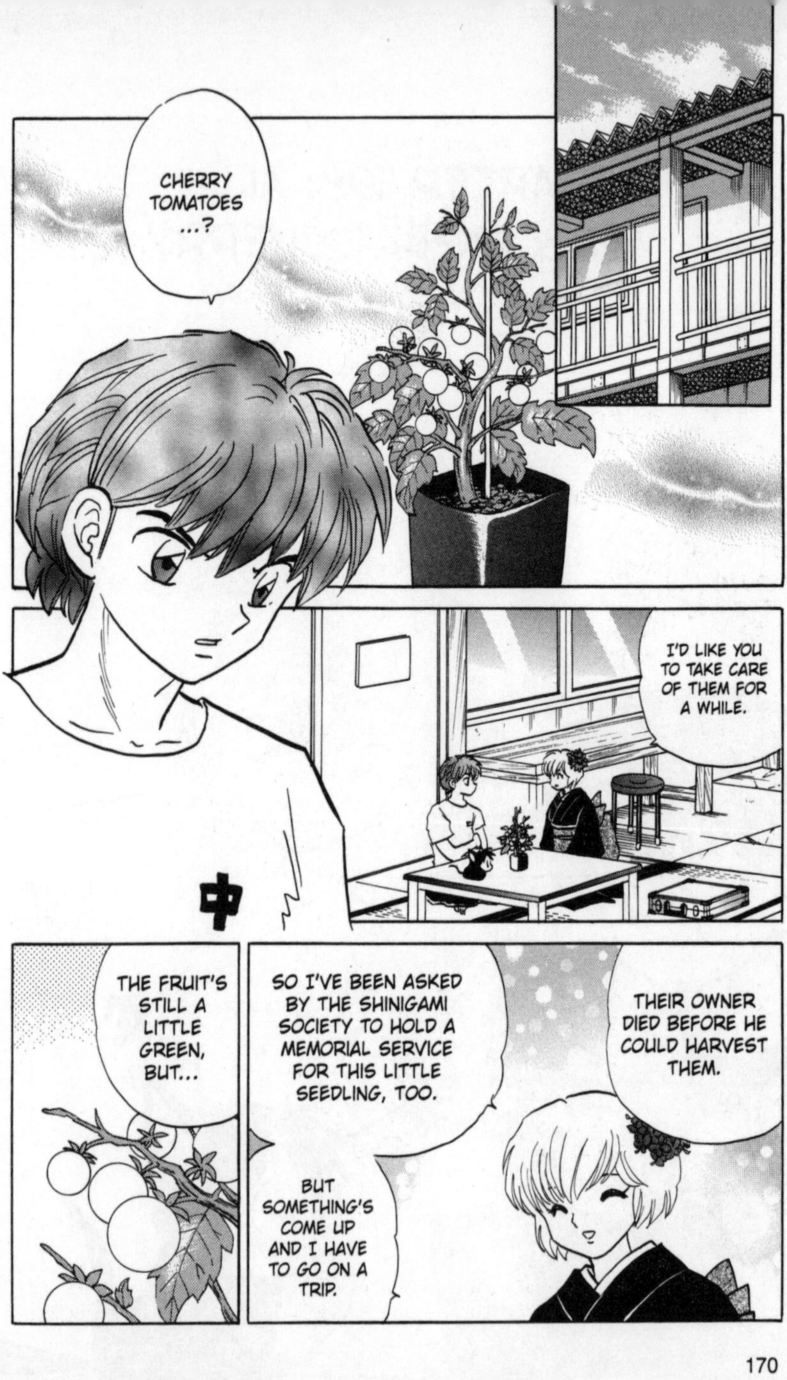
CHERRY TOMATOES ...?
I'D LIKE YOU TO TAKE CARE OF THEM FOR A WHILE.
THEIR OWNER DIED BEFORE HE COULD HARVEST THEM.
SO I'VE BEEN ASKED BY THE SHINIGAMI SOCIETY TO HOLD A MEMORIAL SERVICE FOR THIS LITTLE SEEDLING, TOO.
BUT SOMETHING'S COME UP AND I HAVE TO GO ON A TRIP.
THE FRUIT'S STILL A LITTLE GREEN, BUT...

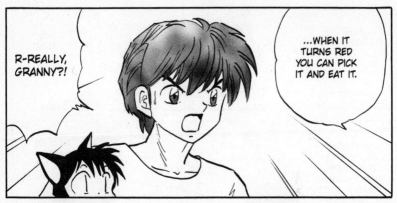

...WHEN IT TURNS RED YOU CAN PICK IT AND EAT IT.
R-REALLY, GRANNY?!
DO. NOT. CALL. ME. GRANNY.
NOOGIE NOOGIE NOOGIE
EITHER WAY, I'LL TAKE GOOD CARE OF THEM.
POP
ALSO, HERE ARE SOME AM-POULES.
FEED IT ONE WHOLE BOTTLE EVERY DAY.
PLIP
NO MATTER WHAT, YOU MUST NOT FORGET TO DO THIS.

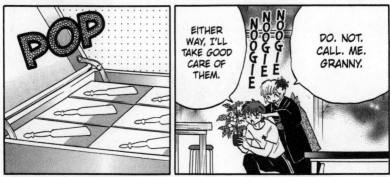

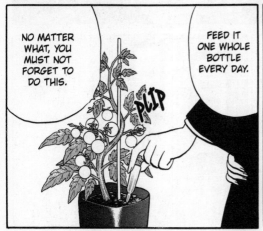

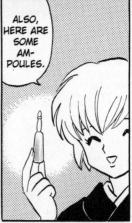

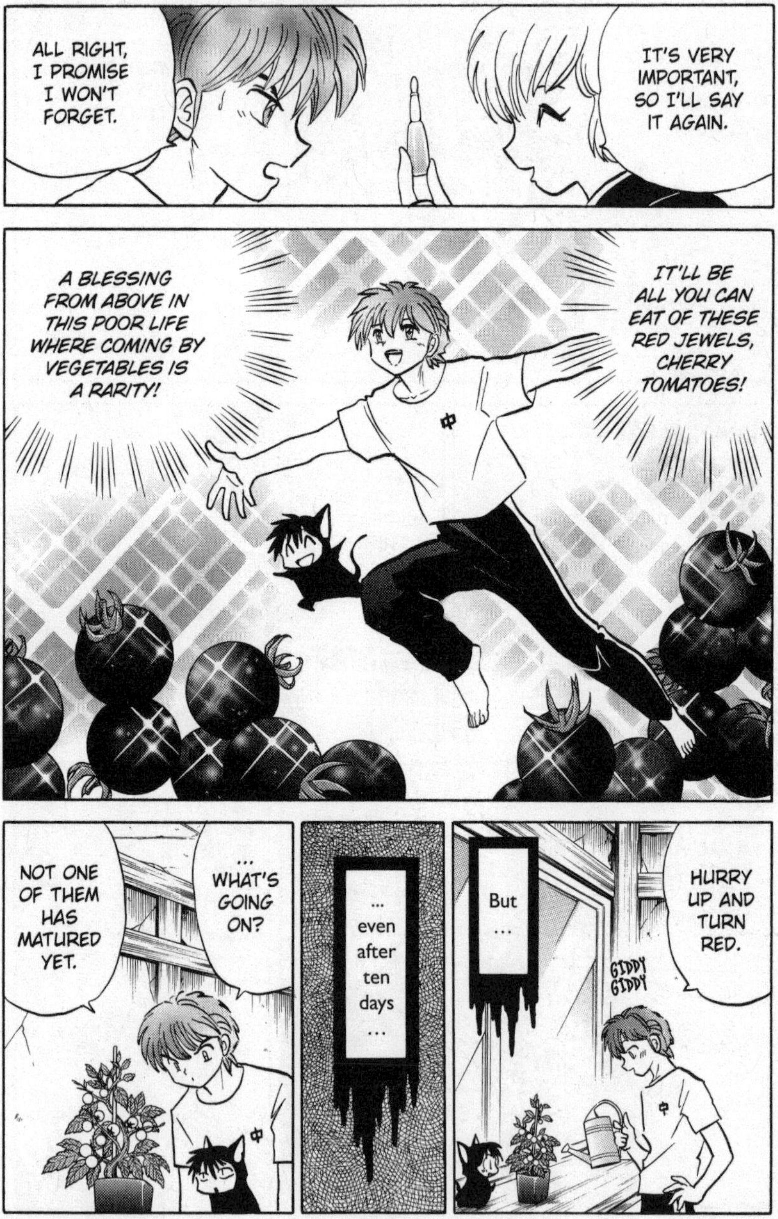
IT'S VERY IMPORTANT, SO I'LL SAY IT AGAIN.
ALL RIGHT, I PROMISE I WON'T FORGET.
IT'LL BE ALL YOU CAN EAT OF THESE RED JEWELS, CHERRY TOMATOES!
A BLESSING FROM ABOVE IN THIS POOR LIFE WHERE COMING BY VEGETABLES IS A RARITY!
HURRY UP AND TURN RED.
GIDDY GIDDY
But ...
... even after ten days ...
... WHAT'S GOING ON?
NOT ONE OF THEM HAS MATURED YET.

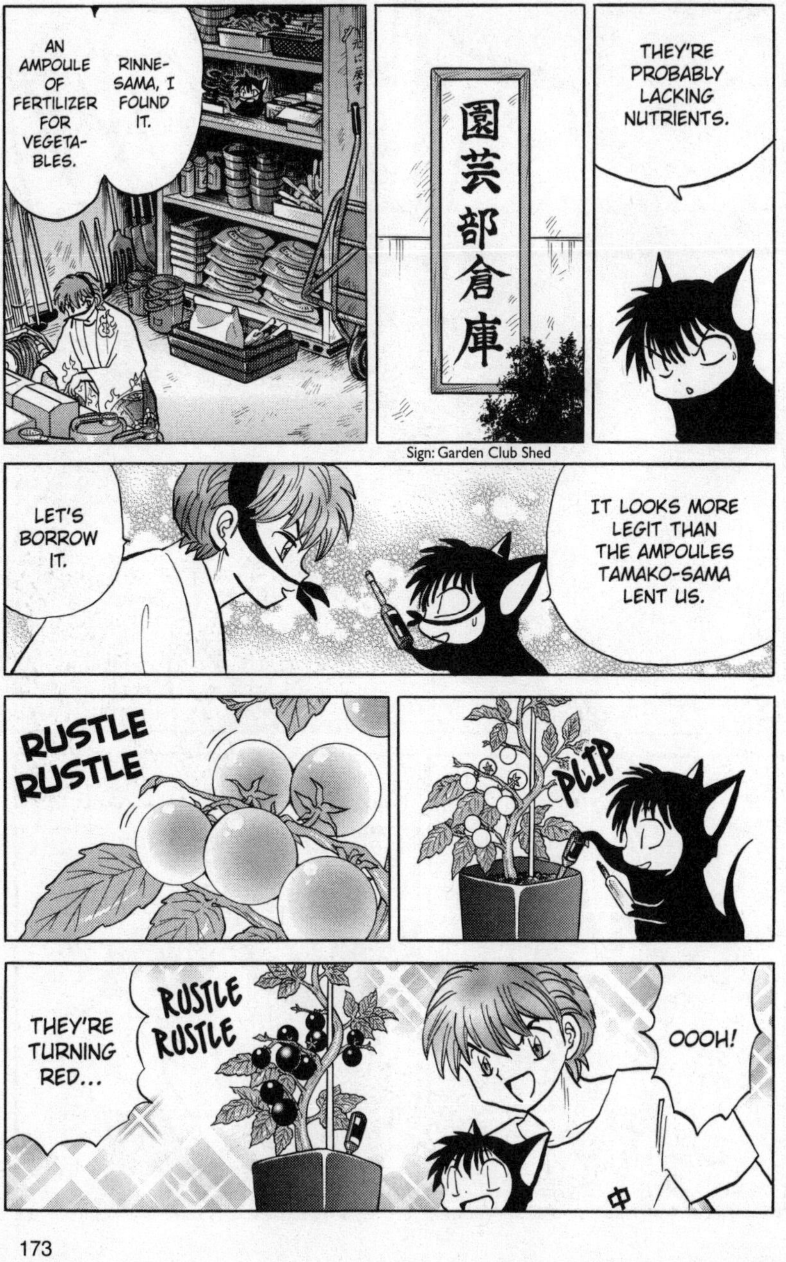
THEY'RE PROBABLY LACKING NUTRIENTS.
園芸部倉庫
RINNE-SAMA, I FOUND IT.
AN AMPOULE OF FERTILIZER FOR VEGETABLES.
Sign: Garden Club Shed
IT LOOKS MORE LEGIT THAN THE AMPOULES TAMAKO-SAMA LENT US.
LET'S BORROW IT.
PLIP
RUSTLE RUSTLE
OOOH!
中
RUSTLE RUSTLE
THEY'RE TURNING RED...

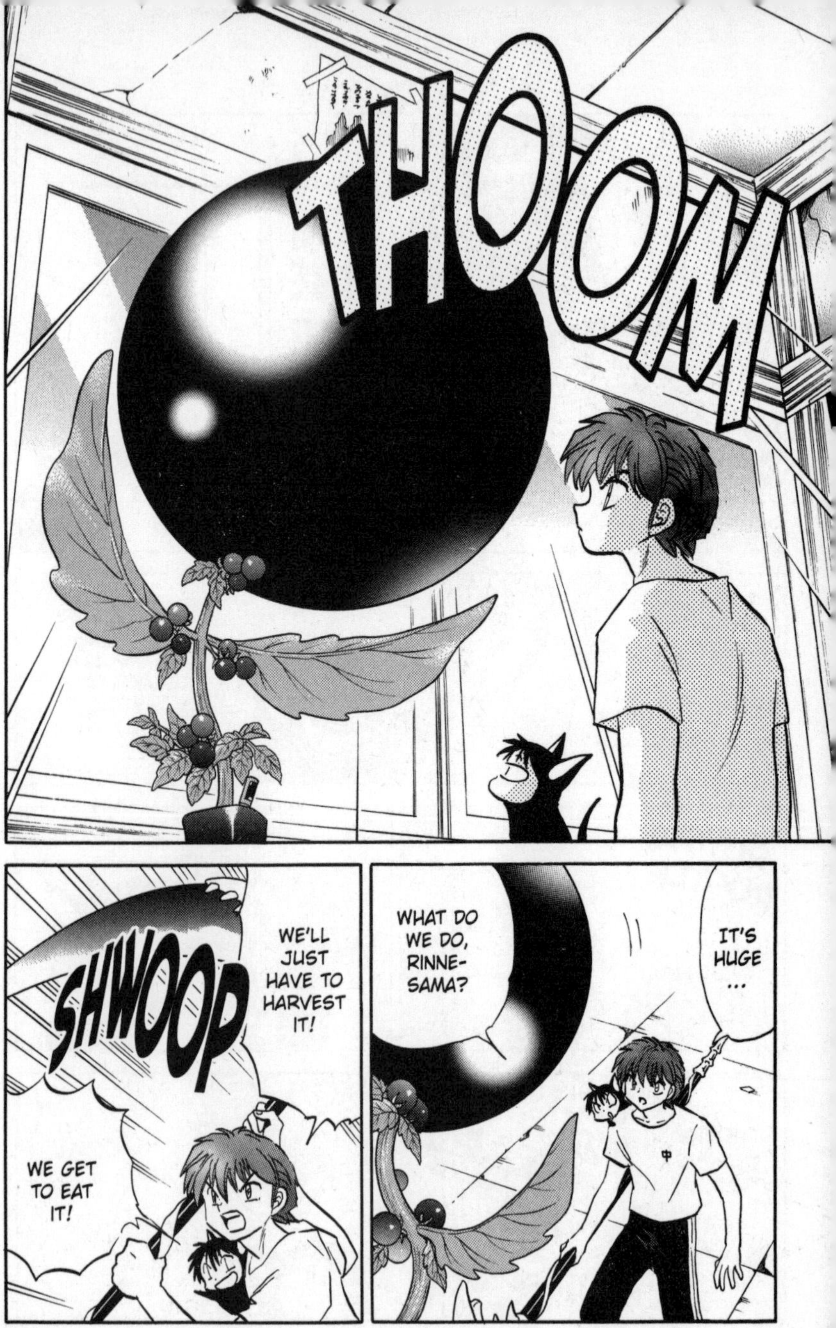
THOOM
IT'S HUGE ...
WHAT DO WE DO, RINNE-SAMA?
WE'LL JUST HAVE TO HARVEST IT!
SHWOOP
WE GET TO EAT IT!

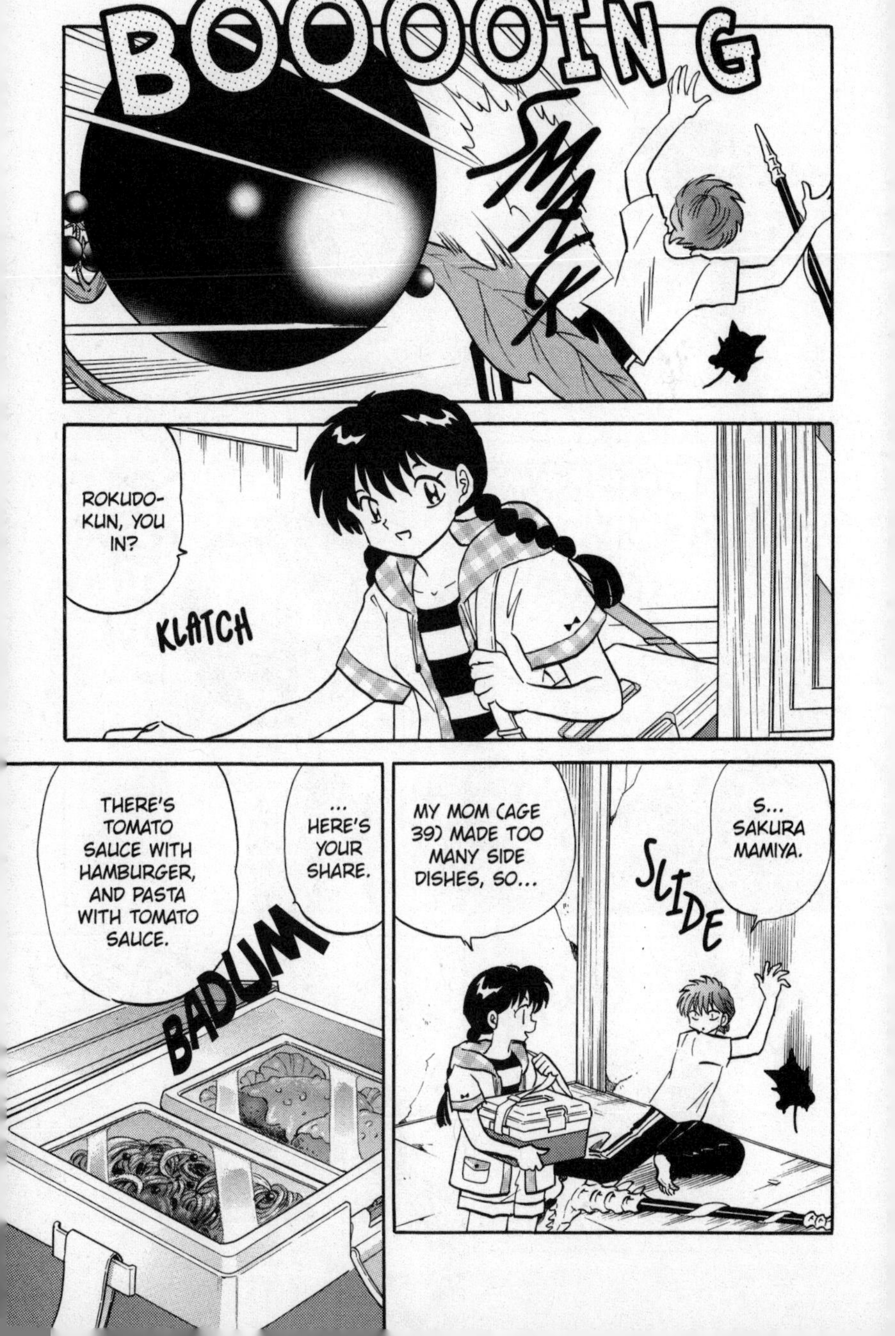
BOOOOING
SMACK
ROKUDO-KUN, YOU IN?
KLATCH
S... SAKURA MAMIYA.
SLIDE
MY MOM (AGE 39) MADE TOO MANY SIDE DISHES, SO...
... HERE'S YOUR SHARE.
THERE'S TOMATO SAUCE WITH HAMBURGER, AND PASTA WITH TOMATO SAUCE.
BADUM

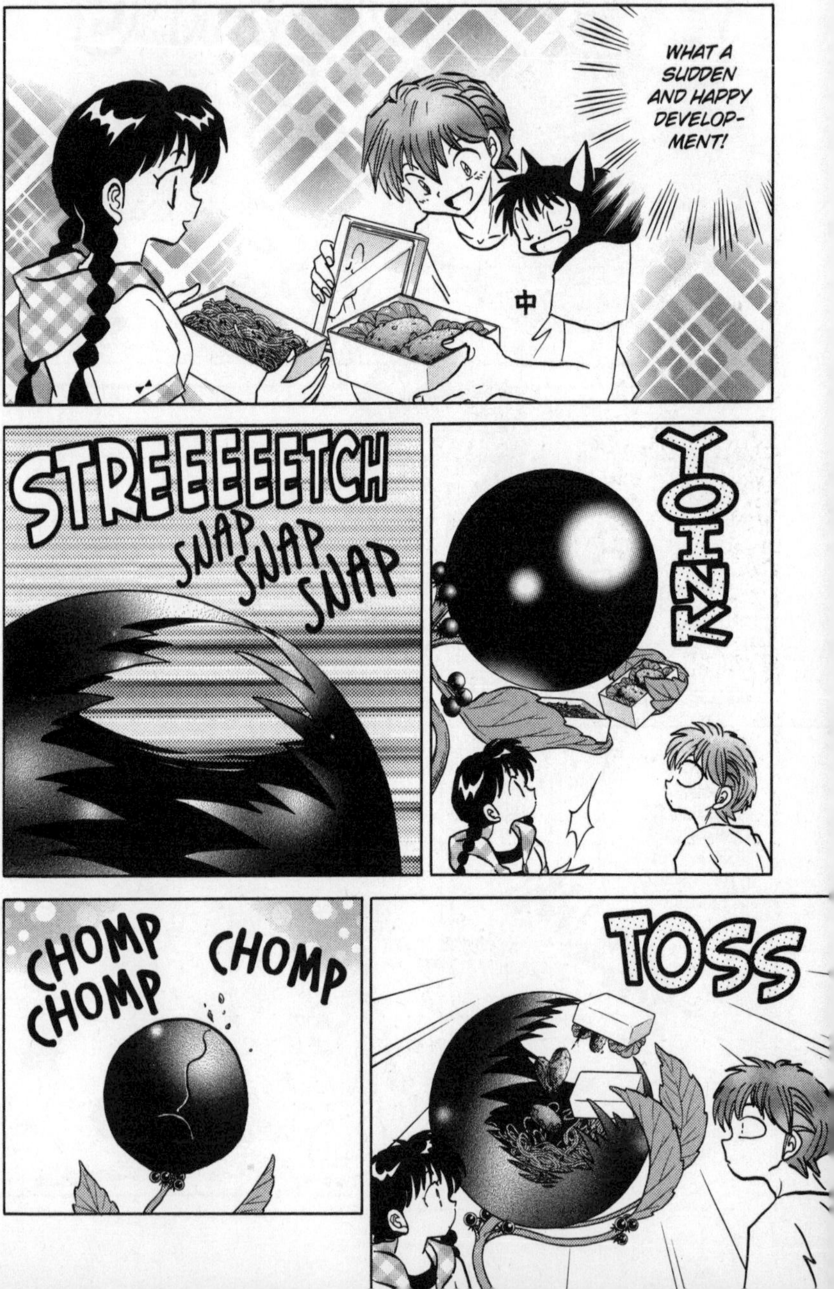
WHAT A SUDDEN AND HAPPY DEVELOP-MENT!
YOINK
STREEEEETCH
SNAP SNAP SNAP
TOSS
CHOMP CHOMP
CHOMP

DAAAZE

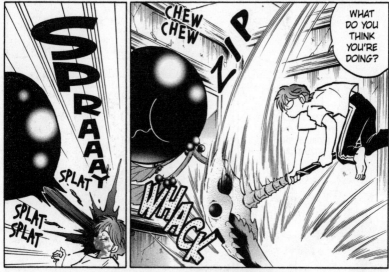

CHEW CHEW

ZIP

SPRAAAY
SPLAT
SPLAT
SPLAT

WHACK

WHAT DO YOU THINK YOU'RE DOING?

HE VOMITED BLOOD ?!

HUUUUH ?!

THIS IS...

NO, THAT'S NOT IT.

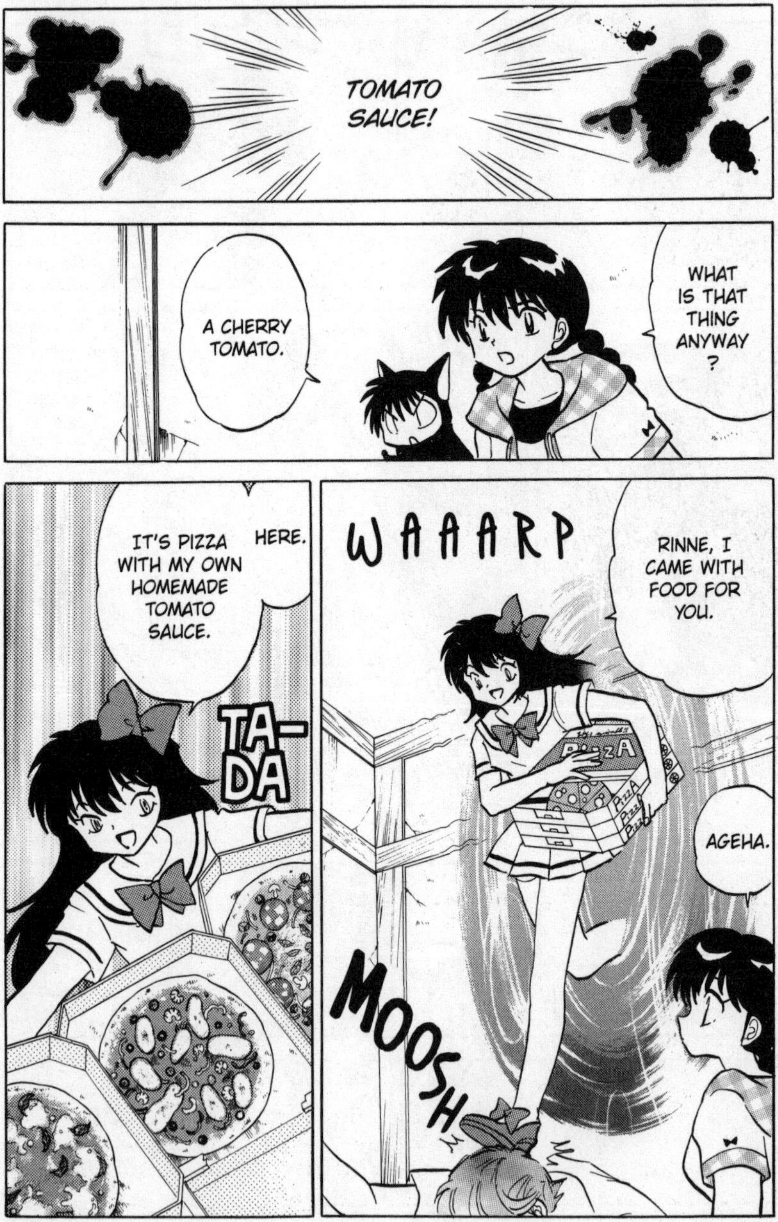
TOMATO SAUCE!
WHAT IS THAT THING ANYWAY?
A CHERRY TOMATO.
RINNE, I CAME WITH FOOD FOR YOU.
WAAARP
AGEHA.
MOOSH
HERE.
IT'S PIZZA WITH MY OWN HOMEMADE TOMATO SAUCE.
TA-DA

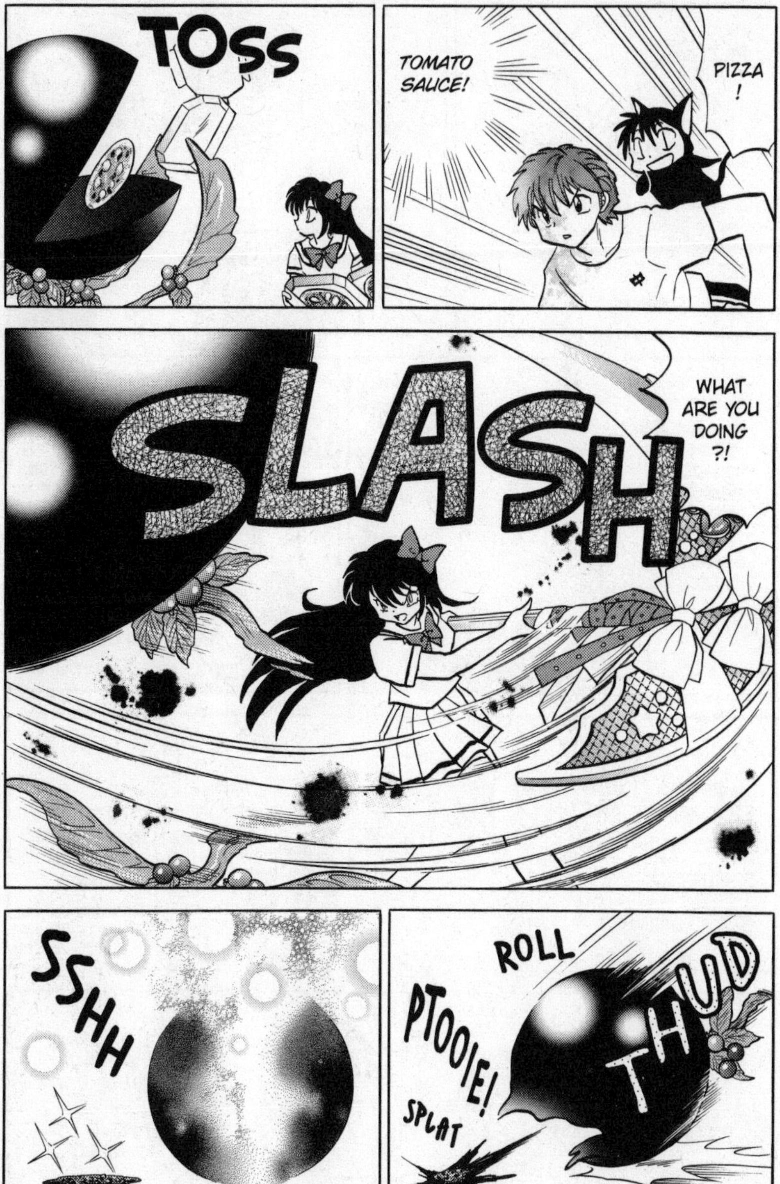
PIZZA!
TOMATO SAUCE!
TOSS
WHAT ARE YOU DOING?!
SLASH
THUD
ROLL
PTOOIE!
SPLAT
SSHH

AAH! IT WAS PURIFIED ?!
I BROUGHT THOSE FOR RINNE, YOU MEANIE.
I KNEW IT.
HE ONLY ATE THE PIZZA.
AND THEN LEFT THE SAUCE.
THAT'S RIGHT.
THEIR OWNER DIED BEFORE HE COULD HARVEST THEM.
SO I'VE BEEN ASKED BY THE SHINIGAMI SOCIETY TO HOLD A MEMORIAL SERVICE FOR THIS LITTLE SEEDLING, TOO.
SO IT EATS THE MAIN INGREDIENTS AND SPITS OUT THE TOMATO SAUCE.
BECAUSE IT WAS NEVER HARVESTED ITSELF.
IT'S PROBABLY JEALOUS OF THE OTHER TOMATOES.
I'M SORRY, SAKURA MAMIYA. YOUR GENEROUS OFFERING WENT TO WASTE...
KUHI
IT'S OKAY.
AT LEAST WE STILL HAVE AGEHA'S PIZZA.

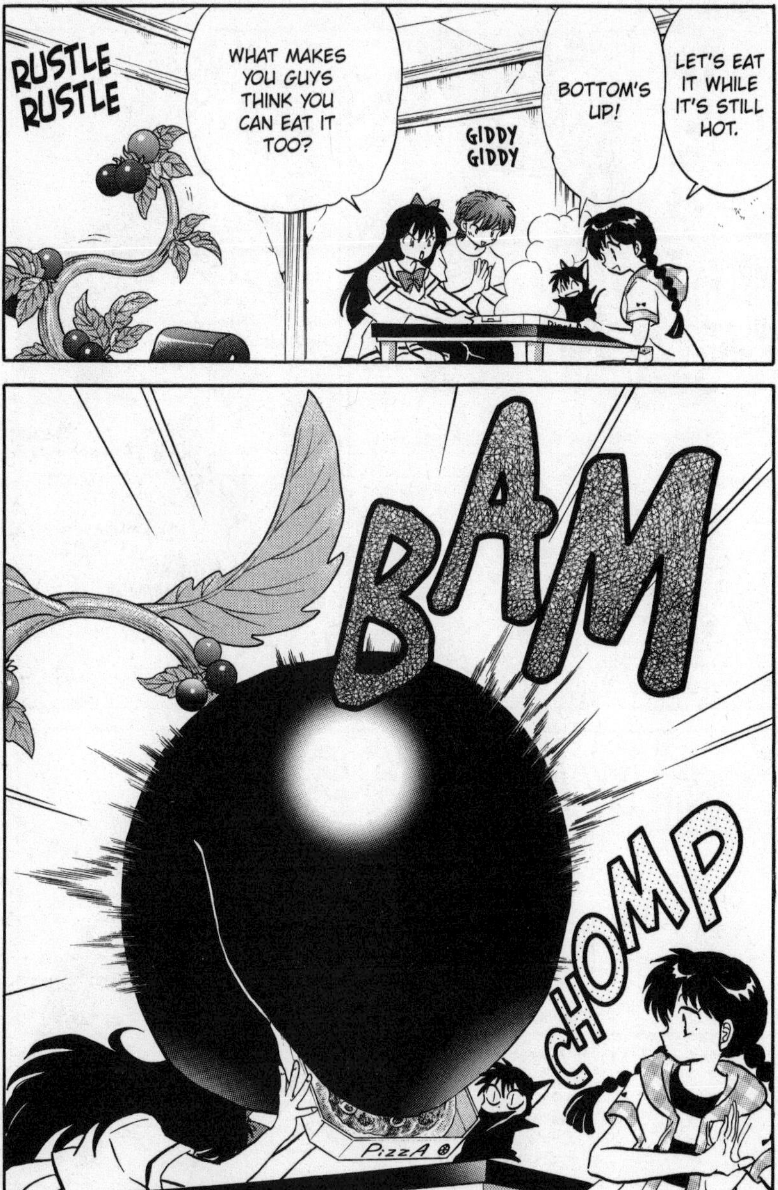
LET'S EAT IT WHILE IT'S STILL HOT.
BOTTOM'S UP!
GIDDY GIDDY
WHAT MAKES YOU GUYS THINK YOU CAN EAT IT TOO?
RUSTLE RUSTLE
PizzA
BAM
CHOMP
PizzA

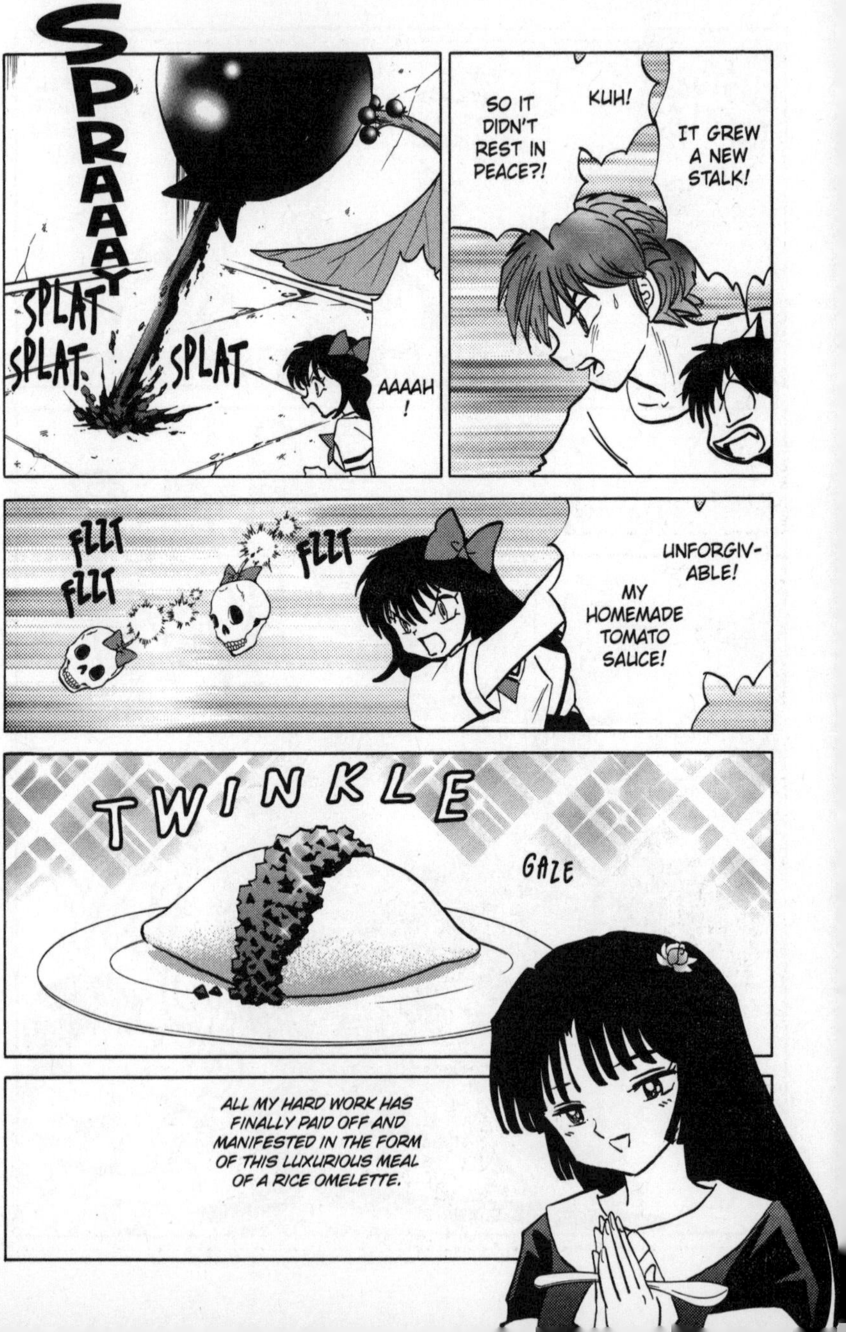
IT GREW A NEW STALK!
KUH!
SO IT DIDN'T REST IN PEACE?!
SPRAAAAY
SPLAT
SPLAT
SPLAT
AAAAH!
UNFORGIV-ABLE!
MY HOMEMADE TOMATO SAUCE!
FZZT
FZZT
FZZT
GAZE
TWINKLE
ALL MY HARD WORK HAS FINALLY PAID OFF AND MANIFESTED IN THE FORM OF THIS LUXURIOUS MEAL OF A RICE OMELETTE.

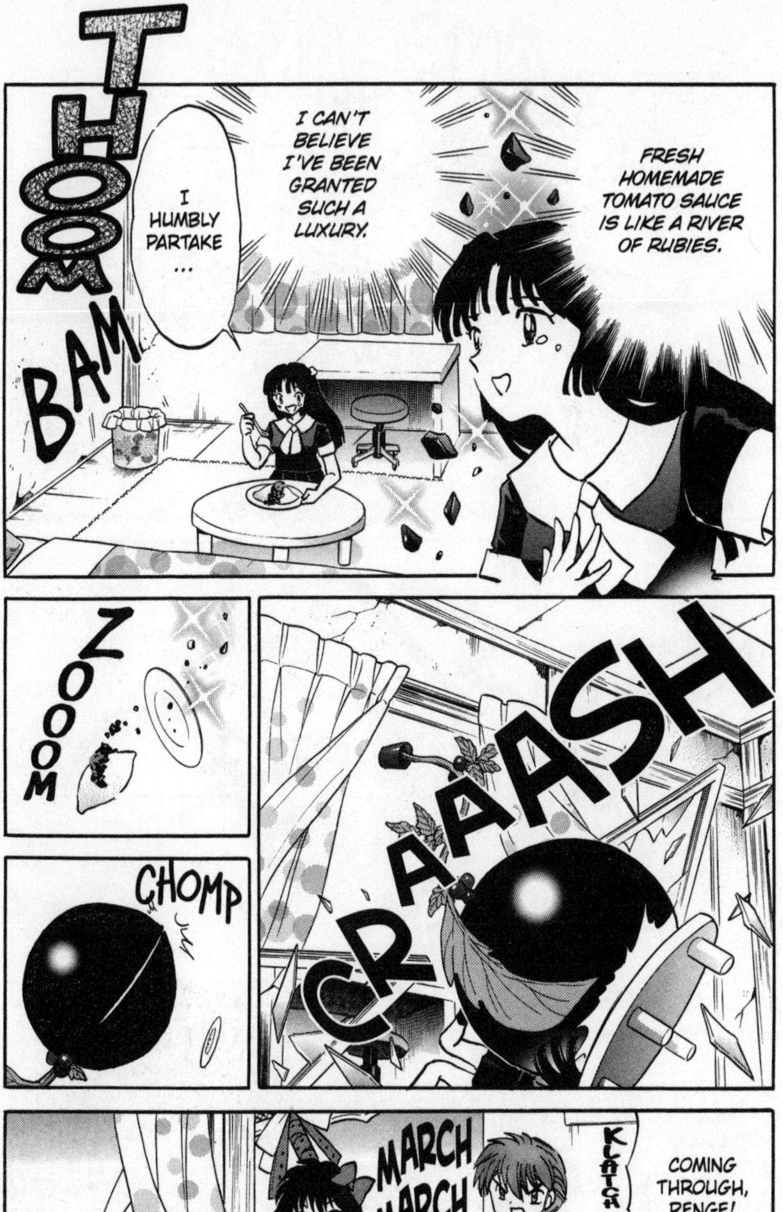
FRESH HOMEMADE TOMATO SAUCE IS LIKE A RIVER OF RUBIES.
I CAN'T BELIEVE I'VE BEEN GRANTED SUCH A LUXURY.
I HUMBLY PARTAKE ...
BAM
THOOOM
CRAAASH
ZOOOOM
CHOMP
COMING THROUGH, RENGE!
KLATCH
MARCH MARCH

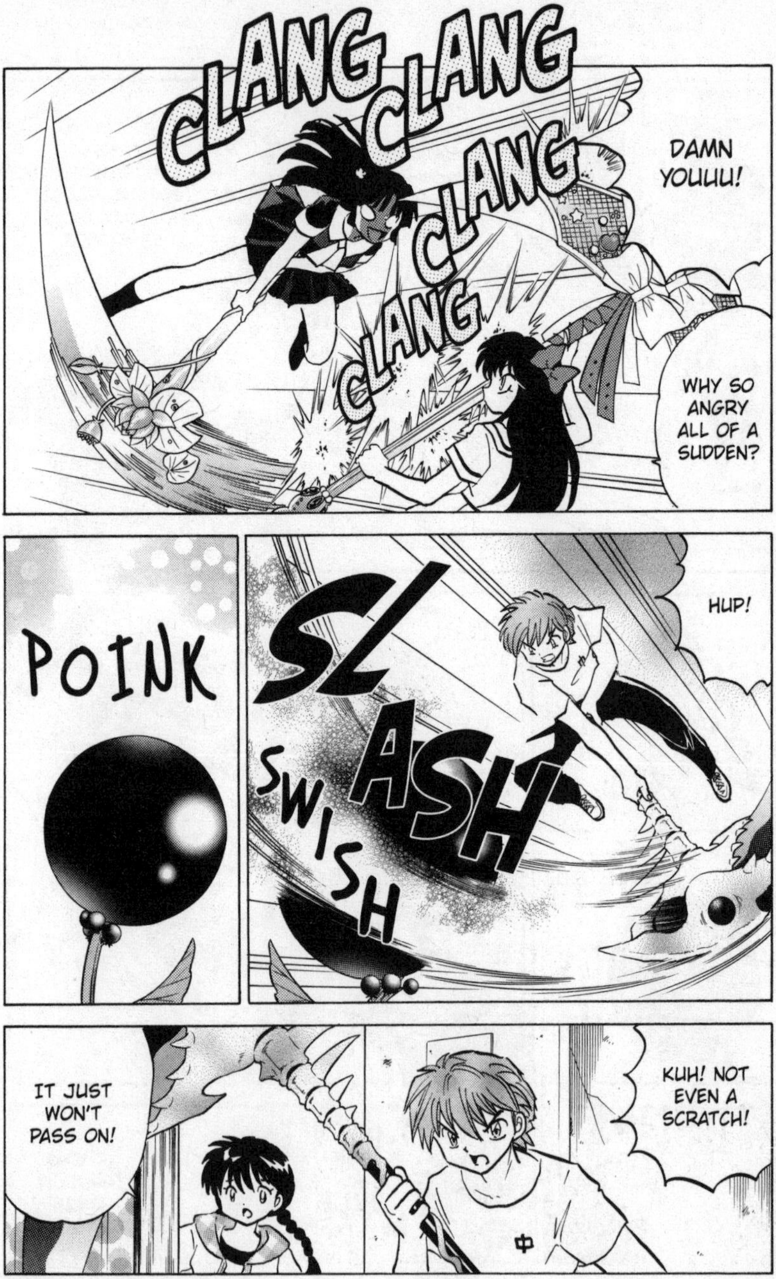
CLANG CLANG
CLANG CLANG
DAMN YOUUU!
WHY SO ANGRY ALL OF A SUDDEN?
HUP!
SLASH
SWISH
POINK
KUH! NOT EVEN A SCRATCH!
IT JUST WON'T PASS ON!

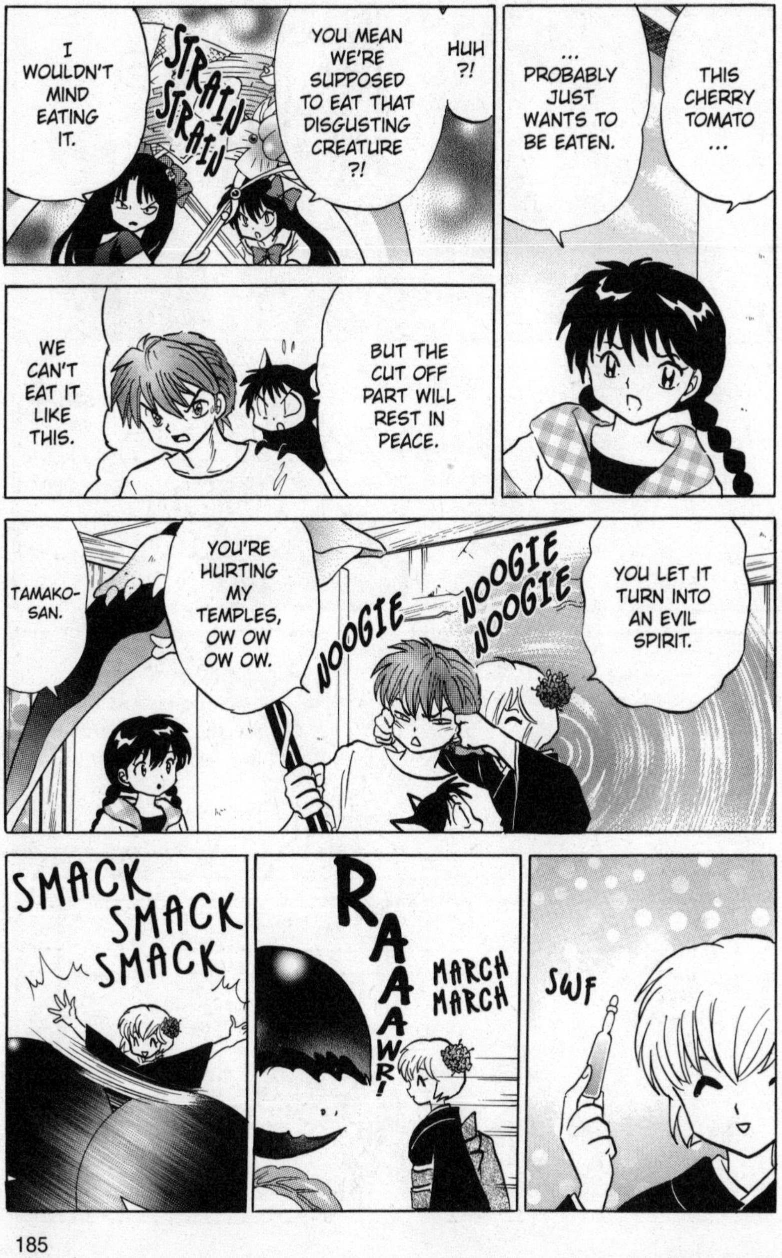
THIS CHERRY TOMATO ...
... PROBABLY JUST WANTS TO BE EATEN.
HUH ?!
YOU MEAN WE'RE SUPPOSED TO EAT THAT DISGUSTING CREATURE ?!
STRAIN STRAIN
I WOULDN'T MIND EATING IT.
BUT THE CUT OFF PART WILL REST IN PEACE.
WE CAN'T EAT IT LIKE THIS.
YOU LET IT TURN INTO AN EVIL SPIRIT.
NOOGIE NOOGIE
NOOGIE
YOU'RE HURTING MY TEMPLES, OW OW OW OW.
TAMAKO-SAN.
SWF
MARCH MARCH
RAAAAWR!
SMACK SMACK SMACK

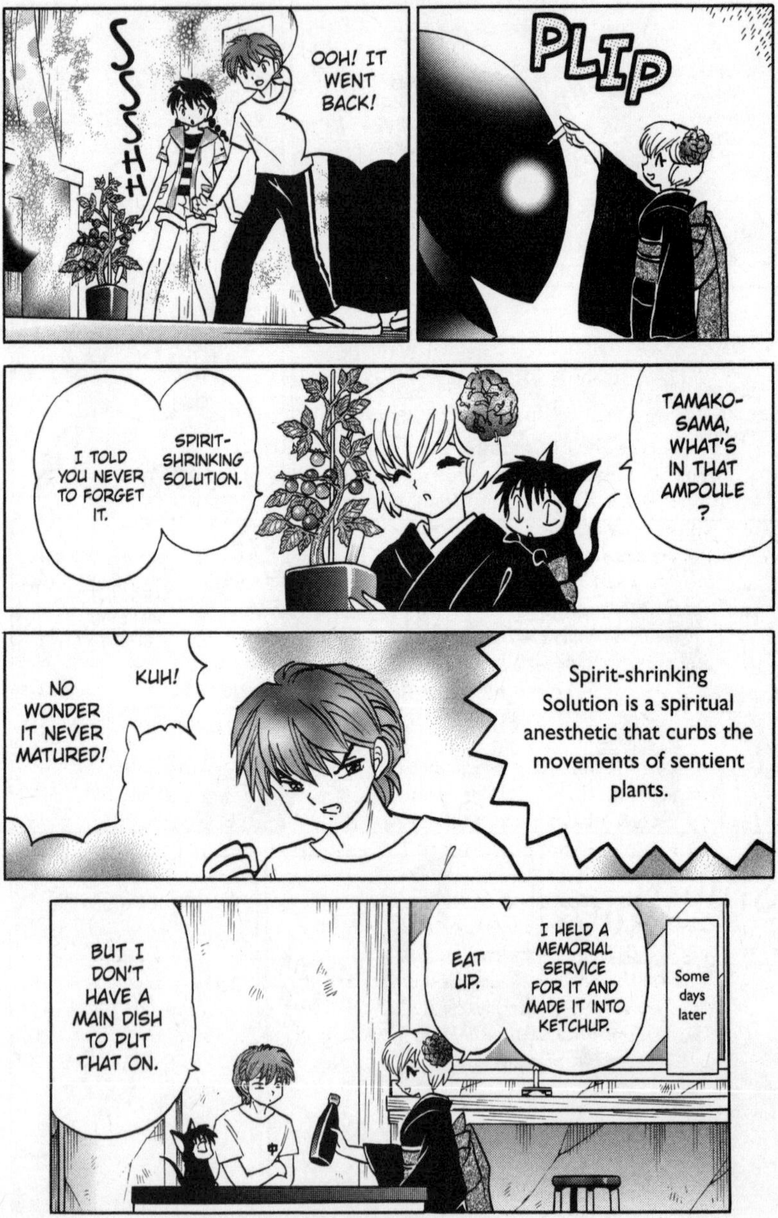
PLIP
SSSHH
OOH! IT WENT BACK!
TAMAKO-SAMA, WHAT'S IN THAT AMPOULE?
SPIRIT-SHRINKING SOLUTION.
I TOLD YOU NEVER TO FORGET IT.
Spirit-shrinking Solution is a spiritual anesthetic that curbs the movements of sentient plants.
KUH!
NO WONDER IT NEVER MATURED!
Some days later
I HELD A MEMORIAL SERVICE FOR IT AND MADE IT INTO KETCHUP.
EAT UP.
BUT I DON'T HAVE A MAIN DISH TO PUT THAT ON.

RIN-NE VOLUME 20 - END -

Rumiko Takahashi

The spotlight on Rumiko Takahashi's career began in 1978 when she won an honorable mention in Shogakukan's annual New Comic Artist Contest for *Those Selfish Aliens*. Later that same year, her boy-meets-alien comedy series, *Urusei Yatsura*, was serialized in *Weekly Shonen Sunday*. This phenomenally successful manga series was adapted into anime format and spawned a TV series and half a dozen theatrical-release movies, all incredibly popular in their own right. Takahashi followed up the success of her debut series with one blockbuster hit after another—*Maison Ikkoku* ran from 1980 to 1987, *Ranma ½* from 1987 to 1996, and *Inuyasha* from 1996 to 2008. Other notable works include *Mermaid Saga*, *Rumic Theater*, and *One-Pound Gospel*.

Takahashi won the prestigious Shogakukan Manga Award twice in her career, once for *Urusei Yatsura* in 1981 and the second time for *Inuyasha* in 2002. A majority of the Takahashi canon has been adapted into other media such as anime, live-action TV series, and film. Takahashi's manga, as well as the other formats her work has been adapted into, have continued to delight generations of her fans around the world. Distinguished by her wonderfully endearing characters, Takahashi's work adeptly incorporates a wide variety of elements such as comedy, romance, fantasy, and martial arts. While her series are difficult to pin down into one simple genre, the signature style she has created has come to be known as the "Rumic World." Rumiko Takahashi is an artist who truly represents the very best from the world of manga.

RIN-NE
VOLUME 20
Shonen Sunday Edition

STORY AND ART BY
RUMIKO TAKAHASHI

KYOKAI NO RINNE Vol. 20
by Rumiko TAKAHASHI
© 2009 Rumiko TAKAHASHI
All rights reserved.
Original Japanese edition published by SHOGAKUKAN.
English translation rights in the United States of America,
Canada, the United Kingdom and Ireland arranged with
SHOGAKUKAN.

Translation/Christine Dashiell
Touch-up Art & Lettering/Evan Waldinger
Design/Yukiko Whitley
Editor/Megan Bates

Printed in the U.S.A.

Published by VIZ Media, LLC
P.O. Box 77010
San Francisco, CA 94107

10 9 8 7 6 5 4 3 2 1
First printing, March 2016

www.viz.com   WWW.SHONENSUNDAY.COM

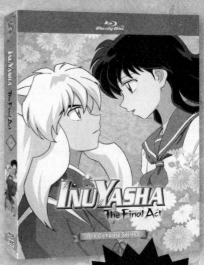
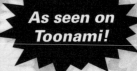